The Course of Remembrance
and Other Essays on Hölderlin

STUDIES IN KANT AND GERMAN IDEALISM

Eckart Förster, Editor

THE COURSE OF REMEMBRANCE AND OTHER ESSAYS ON HÖLDERLIN

Dieter Henrich

Edited, with a Foreword, by Eckart Förster

Stanford University Press, Stanford, California   1997

"The Course of Remembrance" was originally published in German in 1986 as *Der Gang des Andenkens: Beobachtungen und Gedanken zu Hölderlins Gedicht*, © 1986 Klett-Cotta Verlag.

Stanford University Press
Stanford, California
© 1997 by the Board of Trustees of the Leland Stanford Junior University
Printed in the United States of America

CIP data are at the end of the book

Stanford University Press publications are distributed exclusively by Stanford University Press within the United States, Canada, Mexico, and Central America; they are distributed exclusively by Cambridge University Press throughout the rest of the world.

Contents

A Note on Prior Publication

Six of the essays by Dieter Henrich that are assembled here were originally published in German in the following places:

"Der Weg des spekulativen Idealismus. Ein Résumé und eine Aufgabe." In D. Henrich and C. Jamme, *Jacob Zwillings Nachlaß. Eine Rekonstruktion* (*Hegel-Studien*, suppl. 28), pp. 78–96. Bonn: Bouvier, 1986.

"Philosophisch-theologische Problemlagen im Tübinger Stift zur Studienzeit Hegels, Hölderlins und Schellings." *Hölderlin-Jahrbuch* 25 (1986–87), pp. 60–92.

"Über Hölderlins philosophische Anfänge. Im Anschluß an die Publikation eines Blattes von Hölderlin in Niethammers Stammbuch." *Hölderlin-Jahrbuch* 24 (1984–85), pp. 1–28.

"Hölderlin über Urteil und Sein. Eine Studie zur Entstehungsgeschichte des Idealismus." *Hölderlin-Jahrbuch* 14 (1965–66), pp. 73–96.

"Hegel und Hölderlin." In Dieter Henrich, *Hegel im Kontext*, pp. 9–40. Frankfurt am Main: Suhrkamp, 1971.

Der Gang des Andenkens. Beobachtungen und Gedanken zu Hölderlins Gedicht. Stuttgart: Klett-Cotta, 1986.

"Hölderlin in Jena" was written for this volume.

Abbreviations

StA Friedrich Hölderlin, *Sämtliche Werke*. Große Stuttgarter Ausgabe. Friedrich Beißner and Adolf Beck, eds. Stuttgart: W. Kohlhammer, 1946–85.

GA Martin Heidegger, *Gesamtausgabe*. Frankfurt am Main: Vittorio Klostermann, 1976–.

The Course of Remembrance
and Other Essays on Hölderlin

Foreword

Eckart Förster

FRIEDRICH HÖLDERLIN has long been recognized as one of the greatest poets of the German language. His philosophical importance, by contrast, has only surfaced more recently. Although Schelling and Hegel acknowledged him early as their equal, for a long time Hölderlin's philosophical position remained unknown outside the small circle of his friends. Indeed, his theoretical fragments were first published in the twentieth century—the last one as recently as 1961. Since then, Hölderlin's role in the formation of German Idealism, especially his impact on Hegel's philosophical development, has been the subject of numerous studies. Today Hölderlin's standing as a key figure in the transition from Kant to Hegel is beyond question.

I

Little recognition of his achievements dignified Hölderlin's lifetime. Only his epistolary novel, *Hyperion*, and a handful of his poems received recognition during his life. Years after he had been diagnosed to be incurably mad and his life had been reduced to a solitary existence at the house of the Tübingen carpenter Zimmer, the Swabian Romantics, attracted no less by the spectacle of a life destroyed by madness than by the power of the poet's language, were drawn to their *Landsmann* and collected a number of scattered poems into a first edition of Hölderlin's works (1826). Although a second, much enlarged edition followed twenty years later, its impact on the literary world was marginal: during the second half of the nineteenth century, Hölderlin was almost entirely forgotten. With the dawn of the twentieth century, however, this situation changed: his words suddenly spoke to a new generation of readers and seemed to articulate their particular predicament and inner turmoil. Before long philosophers, literary scholars, utopians, and ideologues alike claimed Hölderlin as their own. In what follows, I shall indicate some of the highlights of his subsequent reception.

It was a philosopher who set the stage for the Hölderlin renaissance in our century. When Friedrich Nietzsche, in his *Untimely Meditations*, launched a scathing attack on German philistine culture, he presented the "glorious Hölderlin" as an antidote to the prevalent bourgeois values. Hölderlin had felt deeply the modern crisis of values and had been filled with longing for a cultural and religious renewal. Nietzsche saw Hölderlin as a kindred spirit who had, however, been crushed by the adversity of his own time and who "in the strongest sense of the word had been destroyed by the Philistines."[1]

Nietzsche's message eventually fell on fertile ground, and he became the voice for a number of movements that emerged in this rapidly changing intellectual climate (Expressionism, *Lebensphilosophie*, German Youth Movements, and others); he also provided a context for a new evaluation of Hölderlin. Hölderlinean themes reverberated in Nietzsche's writings and seemed to point to deep affinities between their thoughts and lives that found a resonance with his readers: "Hölderlin's work was more understandable after being illustrated by Nietzsche."[2] Within two decades, no fewer than four editions of Hölderlin's works appeared: by Berthold Litzmann (1896), by Wilhelm Böhm (1905), by Norbert von Hellingrath (1913–23), and by Franz Zinkernagel (1914–26). All of them provided previously unpublished material, Böhm's edition making available for the first time many of Hölderlin's theoretical essays and fragments.

Another philosopher drawn to Hölderlin was Wilhelm Dilthey. It was Dilthey's lifelong intention to develop a methodology for the human sciences (*Geisteswissenschaften*) that would establish them in their own right and place them on a par with the natural sciences. He attempted to elucidate our ability to recognize ourselves in society and in the history we create, and grounded this attempt in a hermeneutics that gave priority of place to the category of "life." Against the positivistic climate of his time, Dilthey insisted on the irreducibility of life to scientific explanations and on the need for an intuitive or *erlebnishaft* way to comprehend life: "Nature we explain, psychic life [*das Seelenleben*] we understand."[3] Dilthey assigned to art and especially to poetry a key function in the achievement of such understanding: art tries to express what life truly is, and does so more fundamentally than any scientific or historical explanations. It is the prime organ for the comprehension of "life," whose reality it grasps and communicates through the artistic rendition of a lived experience or *Erlebnis*. For Dilthey, Hölderlin commanded special importance as the poet who gave exemplary expression to life under modern conditions.[4]

One of the merits of Dilthey's interpretation was that he took seriously for the first time the philosophical dimension of Hölderlin's poetry. In 1905, in a famous treatise for the Berlin Academy, *Die Jugendgeschichte Hegels*, Dilthey had presented a detailed history of Hegel's early philosophical development. Rather than drawing on the complete system of the mature philosopher as had been the common practice in the nineteenth century, Dilthey made the early formation of Hegel's thought the object of his study. In this context, he drew attention to the friendship between Hegel and Hölderlin and to the latter's role in Hegel's development. In the following year, Dilthey dedicated an entire study to Hölderlin.[5] In addition to illuminating affinities between Hölderlin and Nietzsche, between *Hyperion* and *Thus Spoke Zarathustra*, Dilthey pointed out for the first time structural analogies between Hölderlin's Empedocles fragments and Hegel's essay "The Spirit of Christianity." Ernst Cassirer soon followed Dilthey's lead and argued for the distinctiveness and independence of Hölderlin's thought with relation to Goethe, Fichte, Schelling, and Hegel.[6]

In contrast to this philosophical orientation was the appropriation of Hölderlin by the poet Stefan George and his circle of followers: inspired by Nietzsche's diagnosis of European culture, the George circle aimed at cultural renewal through the formation of a "new league" of spiritual aristocracy that would function as the germ cell of a new mythologic-aesthetic culture. Through an aesthetics modeled on French Symbolism, George intended to elevate art once again to a sacred level. After the turn of the century, Hölderlin rapidly became the exemplary prophet of George's aesthetic utopianism. In his circle's journal, George wrote about Hölderlin: "Through rupture and contraction [*aufbrechung und zusammenballung*] he is the rejuvenator of language and thus the rejuvenator of the soul . . . with his uniquely irreducible prophecies [he is] the cornerstone of the next German future and the voice of the New God."[7]

Norbert von Hellingrath, a student of classical philology who was comparing the various German translations of Sophocles, was greatly influenced by George and his circle. Sensitized by George's symbolism, Hellingrath came to see Hölderlin's translations, which previous interpreters had regarded as the fruits of madness, as an unparalleled achievement, indeed, as the only German renditions of Sophocles that re-created the art form of the original and equaled its rhythmic and expressive powers. Hellingrath's research soon led him to the discovery of Hölderlin's previously unknown Pindar translations, which he published in George's *Blätter für die Kunst* in 1910. Inspired by these events, Hellingrath turned his attention to the hymns and fragments of the poet's late period, which had been disregarded for a century as the products of insanity. Soon Hellingrath became convinced that he had discovered the greatest poet of the German language, a discovery he described as a religious experience. He began to prepare a new, historico-critical edition that gave pride of place to Hölderlin's mature work. Its fourth volume (1916) made available late hymns and fragments that had never been published before. Especially in these late hymns Hellingrath saw the "heart, core and summit of Hölderlin's work, the essential legacy"[8]—a view that set the stage for all subsequent Hölderlin interpretations. Although soon to be superseded by Friedrich Beißner's Große Stuttgarter Ausgabe of Hölderlin's works, Hellingrath's edition laid the foundation for recognition of Hölderlin's unparalleled poetic mastery. Decades later, Martin Heidegger recalled the experience of first encountering Hölderlin's mature work in Hellingrath's edition and likened the impact it had on him to that of "an earthquake."[9]

Heidegger's reception of Hölderlin is perhaps unique. Beginning in the winter semester 1934–1935 with his lecture course on the hymns "Germania" ("Germanien") and "The Rhine" ("Der Rhein"), Heidegger entered into a dialogue with the poet that continued throughout his life: "My thinking stands in an unavoidable relationship to the poetry of Hölderlin."[10] More specifically, after the attempt in *Being and Time* (1927) to elucidate the meaning of "being" through recourse to the implicit understanding of being that characterizes human existence, Heidegger turned away from the language of philosophy and assigned to art, and to poetry in particular, the role of bringing us into proximity with being. In his subsequent writings, Heidegger interpreted the history of metaphysics from Plato to Hegel as the history of the forgetting of being and saw Hölderlin's late hymns as marking the advent of another history. He interpreted Hölderlin's lament of the absence of the gods in the light of this forgetfulness and Hölderlin's call for the gods' return as a readiness for a new thinking in the nearness of being. Thus, for Heidegger, to understand Hölderlin within the context of the debates of German Idealism is to misunderstand him; instead, Hölderlin represents the alternative to the entire metaphysical tradition that reaches its peak in Hegel's system: "The historical destination [*Bestimmung*] of philosophy culminates in the recognition of the necessity of gaining a hearing for Hölderlin's word."[11]

Not surprisingly, Heidegger's interpretations draw on Hölderlin's late hymns at almost the complete expense of his philosophical fragments. Especially in the last few decades, this approach has met with increasing skepticism. In 1961, in volume 4 of the Große Stuttgarter Ausgabe of Hölderlin's works, Beißner published for the first time a fragment that Hölderlin had composed in 1795 in Jena, to which Beißner gave the title "Judgment and Being" ("Urtheil und Seyn"). Its importance was soon emphasized by Dieter Henrich in "Hölderlin on Judgment and Being." As Henrich pointed out, "it throws an entirely new light on the history of the origins of idealist philosophy."[12] The fragment showed for the first time that, while still in the proximity of Fichte, Hölderlin launched a critique of Fichte's *Wissenschaftslehre* and outlined an alternative position with regard to the foundation of philosophy, a position that had no parallel at the time. This fragment cast new light on the formation of post-Kantian philosophy in the last decade of the eighteenth century—a period that previously had been regarded as well understood. In addition, Henrich argued, it explains how Hegel, when he joined his friend in Frankfurt two years later, so quickly abandoned his own Kantianism and aligned himself with the new way of thinking.

In the wake of Henrich's publication, a rapidly growing number of studies have attempted to illuminate the formation and context of Hölderlin's philosophy and its impact on his contemporaries, as well as its importance for Hölderlin's own poetry and poetology. In addition, there has emerged a new interest in the intellectual constellations at key stages of Hölderlin's biography, most notably his student years at the theological seminary in Tübingen with, among others, Hegel and Schelling; his time in Jena when his philosophy matured in the immediate proximity of Fichte, Schiller, and Goethe; and the years in Frankfurt and Homburg near Hegel.[13]

II

Hölderlin was born in Swabia, southern Germany, on March 20, 1770, the same year as Hegel, Beethoven, and Wordsworth. He was two years old when he lost his father; his stepfather died seven years later. The atmosphere of grief and sorrow that overshadowed his upbringing scarred him for life. "When my second father died," he later recalled in a letter to his mother, "when I felt, with an incomprehensible pain, my orphaned state and saw, each day, your grief and tears, it was then that my soul took on, for the first time, this heaviness that has never left me and that could only grow more severe with the years."[14] This emotional burden was compounded by his mother's withholding his paternal inheritance, thereby insuring his lifelong dependence on her.

In 1788, after completing the local monastery schools, Hölderlin entered the *Stift* in Tübingen, a Lutheran theological seminary to which the most talented students of the state were sent to be trained for the priesthood. Hegel matriculated at the same time as Hölderlin; two years later they were joined by Schelling, a brilliantly talented prodigy five years their junior. The three eventually formed a close friendship, and for a while they shared the same room.

The *Stift*, which was directly responsible to and rigidly supervised by Duke Karl Eugen of Württemberg, granted few liberties to its students. "It is good and salutary for one whose future occupation will be the care of souls that his will should be broken whilst he is young"[15] was the motto of the chancellor of the institution, and its rules and regulations were designed accordingly. When the French Revolution broke out in 1789, it was greeted with excitement and enthusiasm by the students of the *Stift*. For Hölderlin, as for many of his friends, it was one of the most important intellectual events of their lives. "Pray for the French," he wrote to his sister, "the champions of the rights of man" (*StA* VI, 71). Decades later, Hegel recalled this period with the following words: "All thinking beings have joined into celebrating this epoch. A sublime feeling ruled the time, an enthusiasm of spirit thrilled the world, as though a genuine resolution of the divine with the world had finally come about."[16]

Another event that shook the foundations of the *Stift* during Hölderlin's time was the philosophical revolution initiated by Kant. Kant's critique of transcendent metaphysics and its consequences for the orthodox theological dogmatics taught at the *Stift* were the subject of heated debates among the students. In August 1790, Hölderlin wrote to his mother that the continuous study of philosophy had now become a necessity for him. A few months later he reported his skepticism about rational proofs for God's existence, and of his encounter with Spinoza, whom the students at the *Stift* absorbed through Friedrich Heinrich Jacobi's *On the Doctrine of Spinoza, in Letters to Moses Mendelssohn*. This book, first published in 1785 and reprinted four years later with important additions, addressed Lessing's alleged Spinozism, at the time widely equated with atheism, and gave rise to the important "pantheism debate" in Germany. With revolutionary zeal, the students also read and discussed Rousseau, Leibniz, Herder, Franz Hemsterhuis, and especially Plato. With similar enthusiasm, Hölderlin and some of his friends devoted themselves to writing poetry, which they read to each other at regular meetings of their poetry club. While still in Tübingen, Hölderlin had his first poems published and conceived the plan for an epistolary novel, *Hyperion*.

In 1793, Hölderlin and Hegel graduated from the *Stift* and took positions as tutors in private households—Hegel in Switzerland, Hölderlin, as a result of Schiller's recommendation, at the house of Charlotte von Kalb, a close friend of both Schiller and Goethe. The house was located on the remote estate of Waltershausen in Franconia, and Hölderlin's duties left him enough free time for intensive studies of Kant and Greek philosophy, as well as for work on his novel. Here he encountered the first installment of Fichte's *Wissenschaftslehre*, which he read immediately. At Charlotte's instigation, Hölderlin sent a fragment of *Hyperion* to Schiller, which the latter published in his journal *Thalia*. In November 1794, Hölderlin and his pupil traveled to Jena, where they spent the following two months. Hölderlin met Goethe, frequented Schiller's house, and regularly attended Fichte's lectures: "Fichte is now the soul of Jena," he wrote to his friend Christian Ludwig Neuffer. "And thank God that he is! I have never met a man of such depth and mental energy" (*StA* VI, 139). From Jena they traveled to Weimar, but Hölderlin's increasing difficulties with his pupil finally made a termination of his employment mutually desirable. Supplied with money for three months by Charlotte, Hölderlin returned to Jena to resume his studies and work on his novel.

What followed was intellectually the richest period in Hölderlin's life. During the five months he was in Jena, Fichte worked out the practical part of the *Wissenschaftslehre*. Schiller rewrote his *Letters on the Aesthetic Education of Man*, which appeared in installments in *Die Horen*. Schiller invited Hölderlin's contributions to his journals, commissioned him to translate Ovid, and recommended *Hyperion* to his own publisher, Cotta. Friedrich Immanuel Niethammer, formerly a fellow student at the *Stift* and now professor at Jena, requested articles by Hölderlin for his newly founded *Philosophical Journal* and introduced him to the philosophical counterculture. At Niethammer's house, they discussed questions of religion with Novalis and Fichte. Goethe spent several months in Jena, and Hölderlin met him frequently at Schiller's house. Hölderlin formed a close friendship with Isaak von Sinclair, a law student whom he knew from Tübingen. He even entertained a plan to lecture in philosophy at the university.

Then, in late May or early June of 1795, for reasons not entirely clear, Hölderlin left Jena abruptly—a flight, in his own words, "from people and books" (*StA* II, p. 408). Before long, he regretted his decision. At his mother's home in Nürtingen he felt depressed and lonely. "I am frozen and numb in the winter that is around me," he wrote to Schiller in an attempt to justify his departure. "The heavens are as iron, and I am as stone" (*StA* VI, p. 181). He met with Schelling for philosophical discussions but otherwise remained intellectually isolated. The Ovid translation and a number of poems sent to Schiller for publication were rejected by his former mentor.

In January 1796, Hölderlin moved to Frankfurt, where he took up a new position as tutor in the prosperous household of the banker Jacob Gontard. He soon fell deeply in love with his employer's young wife, Susette. Before long, their mutual attraction grew into a clandestine love affair. Susette became the inspiration for the Diotima of Hölderlin's poems and his novel. In her proximity, away from Schiller's dominating influence, Hölderlin finally found his own unique poetic voice.

One year after Hölderlin's arrival, Hegel joined his friend in Frankfurt, where Hölderlin had secured for him a post as tutor. In anticipation of their reunion, Hegel composed the poem "Eleusis," which he dedicated to Hölderlin. Together with Sinclair, who had become an influential officer at the nearby court of the Landgraf of Hessen-Homburg, and with Jacob Zwilling, also a former student at Jena, they resumed their philosophical discussions. Yet social tensions in the Frankfurt society, the humiliations Hölderlin felt as a "servant" of the affluent bourgeoisie, and defamatory remarks by Susette's maid to Gontard made Hölderlin's life increasingly miserable. In September 1798, after a confrontation with his employer, Hölderlin left the house and moved to Homburg, in Sinclair's vicinity.

During the next years, while Hölderlin's conception of his own vocation became progressively clearer to him, his efforts to support himself as a writer became increasingly ineffectual. He completed *Hyperion* and began work on a tragedy about Empedocles. He wrote his major poetological essays and developed his theory of the modulations of poetic tones. Yet plans for a journal that he hoped to edit and for which he counted on the collaboration of Schiller, Goethe, and Schelling failed for lack of support. In the middle of 1800 he returned to Swabia. After a brief visit in Nürtingen, he tried to settle in Stuttgart. Over the next two years, Hölderlin wrote some of the elegies, odes, and hymns for which he is best known. During this period, he accepted two more positions as household tutor, one in Switzerland, the other in Bordeaux. Both were short-lived and ended abruptly. He returned from France in mental disarray, having learned in the meantime of Susette's death. He continued to work amid growing depression, writing several major poems—"Remembrance" ("Andenken"), "Patmos," "Celebration of Peace" ("Friedensfeier")—and completing his translations of Sophocles.

In 1804, Sinclair made it possible for Hölderlin to return to Homburg once again, by arranging a sinecure as court librarian to the Landgraf. But when the state of Hessen-Homburg was dissolved two years later, Sinclair could no longer support him. At the instruction of Hölderlin's mother, in September 1806, at the age of 36, Hölderlin was forcibly removed from his rooms in Homburg and committed to a mental asylum in Tübingen. Diagnosed as incurably mad and as having at most three years to live, he was eventually taken into the home of the Tübingen carpenter Zimmer, a fervent admirer of his novel *Hyperion*. In Zimmer's house Hölderlin spent the remaining 36 years of his life, largely ignored or forgotten by his own family and former friends but warmly cared for by his host family. A number of poems of chilling beauty and deceptive simplicity survived from this period of Hölderlin's life. He died in 1843.

III

The present volume contains Dieter Henrich's most important essays on Hölderlin's philosophy, together with his study of Hölderlin's poem "Remembrance" ("Andenken").

The first essay, "The Path of Speculative Idealism," was originally written for a volume documenting the search for the unpublished writings of Hölderlin's friend Jacob Zwilling. Here, Henrich describes the philosophical motivation and methodological orientation of his own work on German Idealism and gives a survey of the constellations of thinkers and problems most crucial to the reconstruction of the history of the period. Although written later than most of the essays that follow, this piece can serve as an introduction to the subsequent chapters.

"Dominant Philosophical-Theological Problems in the Tübingen *Stift* During the Student Years of Hegel, Hölderlin, and Schelling" reconstructs the debates that dominated intellectual life in the seminary during the last decade of the eighteenth century. It focuses in particular on the attempts by theological orthodoxy to absorb the threat to its teaching posed by Kant's critical philosophy, and explains the importance of Kant's writings and of Jacobi's *Spinoza* for the students in their rebellion against the official doctrine.

The emergence and early development of Hölderlin's philosophical studies while still a student in the Tübingen *Stift* is traced in "Hölderlin's Philosophical Beginnings." Using Hölderlin's entry into Niethammer's *Stammbuch* on the occasion of Niethammer's departure for the

University of Jena as a foil, Henrich discusses the philosophical problems that occupied Hölderlin during his student years and that laid the ground for his own unique position.

"Hölderlin on Judgment and Being" is Henrich's by now classical study of Hölderlin's most important philosophical fragment. As Henrich shows, this fragment, which Hölderlin wrote in Jena in the immediate vicinity of Fichte, formulates a critique of Fichte with regard to the foundations of philosophy that had no parallel at the time and that secures for Hölderlin a key role in the formation of post-Kantian thought.

"Hölderlin in Jena," written for the present volume, gives an account of the research of the "Jena Program" as it nears completion. It describes among other things new insights into the metaphilosophical discussions to which Hölderlin was introduced in Jena through Niethammer, especially the skepticism toward any first-principle philosophy of the type Reinhold and Fichte were advancing.

The influence Hölderlin had on Hegel's philosophical development when they were reunited in Frankfurt in 1797 is examined in "Hegel and Hölderlin." Henrich argues that Hölderlin provided his friend with his most important and final formative impetus. He also gives an explanation why Hegel, in the end, parted philosophical company with Hölderlin regarding the proper characterization of the absolute.

The last essay is devoted to the interpretation of one of Hölderlin's greatest poems, "Remembrance." Henrich here tries to elucidate its lyric composition and structure and at the same time seeks to show how the hymn incorporates and develops Hölderlin's philosophical thought. In addition, "The Course of Remembrance" contains perhaps the most detailed account of Henrich's multifaceted and complex critique of Heidegger, who himself had devoted a lecture course and an influential essay to the interpretation of this poem.[17] As Henrich wrote in another context: "Heidegger's explanation of the process of modern thought as the history of an increasing dissimulation [*Verstellung*] of truth would require a separate examination. At least it seems to have been gained from the study of original sources. Moreover, after the end of classical philosophy of history, his is the only account to offer a genuinely new pattern for the explanation of this process. And yet, it too came about without any real contact with those thoughts and experiences that determined this process."[18]

Thus Henrich's essays on Hölderlin, in addition to illuminating a key period in the history of post-Kantian thought, may also be an occasion for a renewed confrontation with Heidegger.

PHILOSOPHICAL ESSAYS

ONE

The Path of Speculative Idealism: Retrospect and Prospect

Philosophical and Methodological Premises

Those portions of Hegel's unpublished writings that his sons felt obliged to preserve were handed over to the Königliche Bibliothek in Berlin in 1889. Among them were many of the religious-theoretical manuscripts dating from Hegel's youth. Dilthey was quick to recognize their significance, for they opened up the prospect of a new understanding of the inner development of Hegel's system on the basis of the motives and conceptual steps that were woven into the course of his development, and so into the problematics of the age. The foundation stone thus fell into place for a new understanding of classical German philosophy—an understanding of the path leading from the transcendental philosophy of Kant and Fichte to the construction of an idealism that must be deemed "speculative," in the technical sense of the word. In it the theoretical elements of transcendental philosophy were combined with, or carried over into, other elements so as to yield a new kind of metaphysical knowledge, as well as an ontology that would ultimately support the metaphysics.

It was already of great interest to Hegel himself, and to the historiography of philosophy influenced by him, to shed light on the very possibility of these developments. A number of works appeared in the second third of the nineteenth century that undertook either, on the one hand, to make the path from Kant to Hegel clear and intelligible in terms of considerations internal to it, or else to present it as inevitable. These works were written from the point of view of Hegel's younger contemporaries. Consequently, they included analyses of many authors who were soon forgotten but who played a considerable role in teaching and in the philosophical publications of the day. It was, however, Karl Rosenkranz's biography of Hegel that first introduced a developmental-historical approach to the historiography dealing with the classical German philosophers. Even in the more closely developmental-historical study of Hegel's early writings that was initiated by Dilthey, the emphasis is still on the formation of the work of a single thinker. And in our own century as well, philosophical understanding of the road from Kant to Hegel has proceeded chiefly by way of analyzing the theories generated by the system builders representative of classical German philosophy, and by way of considering the consequences for the future development of the systematic form as such—consequences that could be drawn from these works themselves. Richard Kroner's *From Kant to Hegel* marks the high point—and indeed the end point—of this brand of comprehensive understanding inspired by Hegel. Even at the time of its publication it seemed to have gone too far, both in its systematic construction and in its assimilation of the critique that Hegel himself had applied to his predecessors. Today it strikes us as a rather negative, if impressive, foil to the sort of understanding of the course of classical German philosophy that might shed light on the actual development of its positions. But no work has appeared since that could meet its standards, match its scope, or philosophically illuminate that course of development with genuine historical insight—indeed, no one has yet been able to write such a work.

Today, however, the prospect has begun to emerge for just such a new general understanding of the path from Kant to Hegel. This prospect has arisen, on the one hand, from the extension of Dilthey's developmental-historical analysis of the genesis of the theories of classical German philosophy, in general and in relation to one another. It has also arisen, on the other hand, from a mode of interpretation, which was established only in the second half of this century and which concerns the inner enabling conditions of these theories themselves. It may not be immediately obvious, and so must be spelled out, why all historical explanation is predicated on this mode of interpretation.

The dominant tendency of the traditional form of interpretation was to take the architectonic of the great theories, and with it often their own self-interpretation, as an obligatory point of departure. The aim of interpretation was consequently to make the theories that were found in the great works, along with their ramifications, more transparent than the authors themselves had managed to make them. But, although this method rightly emphasized the systematic intentions of those works, it had the disadvantage of subordinating itself to just

those theoretical possibilities that were available to the authors themselves, indeed to the ones they had explicitly in mind. For precisely this
reason, however, the conceptual connections, problem areas, and lines
of argument that were most crucial for and characteristic of the structure of the works—such as, for example, the method of transcendental
inquiry, or of speculative-dialectical synthesis—were taken up and
elaborated only if they had already been dealt with and elucidated by
the authors themselves. The philosophy of our century, unlike that of
the past, has brought with it a heightened sensitivity to the difficulties
and intricacies of conceptual analysis and philosophical argumentation. This sensitivity has led first and foremost to a particularism in
the treatment of problems, which is incapable of doing justice to the
intentions of classical German philosophy. But this particularism has
had to prove itself useful in interpreting theories that for their part
rested on thoroughly systematic intentions, and so in fact helped to
shape the method of theoretical analysis specifically appropriate to
them. In virtue of this increased sensitivity, however, it has also become possible to understand the situation of thinkers on their own
terms—on the way toward their theories and in the process of constructing them—in light of the alternatives that were open to them, or
in which they became immersed. And because those thinkers could
draw conclusions only by the limited means at their disposal, they
often did so with some difficulty, and for reasons that were not particularly well formulated. The doctrines and texts of the classic theories can
be better construed and more vividly evoked in terms of the dynamic
of their inner formation than through any conformity to their own self-
interpretation.

Gaining some distance from that self-interpretation leads one to a
closer approximation of the actual evolution of classical German philosophy, provided it does not engender an indifference to the ultimate intentions of the thinkers, and so favor the dubious method of "rational
reconstruction." Such a distance is of great importance in many respects for an interpretation guided by developmental-historical interests. I shall note only two of the ways in which this is so. First, it facili-
tates a recognition of the theoretical possibilities that were either not
understood or, if they were taken into account, not fully worked out,
but which nonetheless determined the profile and dynamic of a theory
in the process of its final formulation. Second, it allows one to determine what sort of relation obtained among successive theories, and
among their various elements, in cases where the definitive formulations of those theories diverged in such a way that the later ones could
not properly be said to have followed from the earlier ones in the man-

ner of an inference. It had been Hegel's own thesis, and Kroner's too, that the foundations of Kant's theory ultimately had to lead to Hegel's *Logic* in just that way. Kantians always quite rightly denied this, but they were never able to view the subsequent reception of Kant's philosophy as anything other than a history of misunderstandings.

The new interpretive procedures, by contrast, allow one to recognize the discontinuity between Kant and the movement that drew on his work, and yet still bring philosophically significant information to bear on the internal relation between the two. The new procedures also allow one to recognize the autonomy and tenability of Fichte's later thought vis-à-vis Hegel's system, which was founded on speculative logic, and to regard that thought as the second high point in the development of classical German philosophy—at the same time uncovering the structural parallels between the enabling conditions of each. An example of this is found in their respective treatments of the various senses of negation.

If one is able to recognize and elaborate theoretical possibilities independently of the systematic context in which they were finally put to use, then more will fall into place than just one's interpretation of the various systems, or the stages leading up to them. One can also discern more clearly the consequences of the systematic intentions that took shape from some other purely theoretical interest, without having to move entirely from the realm of philosophy to the history of ideas, the social history, or the *Geistesgeschichte* of the age. If one can trace the inner enabling conditions of a theory, one is then also able to see the relationship between the basic systematic intentions arising from a certain life situation and its philosophical needs on the one hand, and the inner structure of the ideas that lent theoretical force to the systems themselves on the other. For the true motivation behind those systems, their sounding board as it were, lay precisely in those particular needs and intentions.

Thus, while the new history of the classical German philosophy of Kant and Hegel pursues a knowledge of the historical conditions that affected its founders as they were in the process of developing their theories, it is at the same time shaped and made possible by a more sophisticated insight into the enabling conditions and the potential of those theories themselves. In only a few decades those theories effected a cumulative theoretical achievement that will, by all accounts, continue to command the attention of any thinking committed to some understanding of cognition itself, and to an understanding of the constitution of, and the possibilities for, conscious life as a whole.

A new complete account of the history of classical German philoso-

phy would have to present its course in such a way as to distance it
from the mere succession of great system builders. If it acknowledges
the gulf separating the theories of Kant, Fichte, and Hegel in their mutual independence, such an account must also place great emphasis on
the contexts from which the theories emerged in each case. And it
would have to show which forces were at work within those contexts,
which theoretical motives were dominant in them, and which theoretical possibilities could emerge from them.

This deviation from the mere succession of important theories will
be especially marked for the second stage of development leading up
to speculative idealism proper. By Hegel's account, the transition from
Fichte to Schelling was almost purely the result of a logic already at
work in Fichte's thought. The new account, by contrast, must see the
position first adopted jointly by Schelling and Hegel in 1801 as the late
consequence of a series of steps leading away from Fichte and bringing
with it the independent development of one of the motives that was in
conflict with transcendental reflection. This motive sprang up outside
the universities from the unification philosophy (*Vereinigungsphilosophie*) of the eighteenth century, which had gained some attention in the
1780s by way of the similarly quasi-popular reception of Spinoza, and
surrounding the work of Jacobi. It was the renewed acclaim of unification philosophy as a grand theory that made it possible to recognize
conceptual elements even in Fichte's thinking that were deserving of
attention and that could be turned to new ends. This attracted attention
to Fichte's theory, though his thinking in fact had a different orientation
altogether. What had at one point been a vital interest was thus transformed into a theoretical exercise. In moments critical and productive
both for self-understanding at large and for the development of theories, it was thus possible to bring the potential for and the impulse toward speculative-idealistic thinking to a real and in its own way decisive realization. Schelling's philosophy of nature was only one of the
stages along the way, and not one that fundamentally guided the
path itself.

The patterns underlying these moments will necessarily remain in-
visible to anyone undertaking to record the evolution of classical German philosophy purely in terms of the rich works of its most important
representatives. For these patterns are documented only in the texts of
those authors who stood at the very beginning of the whole course of
development, or who were seen by their contemporaries as only minor
figures in literary life. Since such texts were not really guided by theoretical interests, and since they were almost entirely unmotivated by
academic ambitions, they even remained hidden from the sort of histo-

riography that at that time, as in the mid–nineteenth century, took notice of philosophers even of secondary stature. Only under the influence of Dilthey, and in the history of life and ideas that he initiated,
have some of the general contours surfaced for the first time and moreover been deemed important for philosophical understanding.

Since there have been very few prominent works relating directly to
this subject, this first step has been possible only in conjunction with
historical-philological research, and often in connection with local interests of a somewhat antiquarian nature. In the meantime, however,
a certain amount of historical-philological enthusiasm and competi-
tiveness has figured into the job of clearing the ground for the new history of Kant and Hegel. Significant contributions can be made in this
field only by one who possesses philosophical acumen as well as a talent for historical fieldwork. It must not be forgotten, of course, that
these efforts too are justified only with a view to comprehending, with
a new certainty and genuineness, both the intentions and the enabling
conditions of inspired thinking.

The attempt to clarify the situation surrounding Hölderlin around
1795 has drawn to a close, along with the search for Zwilling's unpublished writings, since there is at present no definite prospect either of
discovering new source materials or of coming across any new information concerning the contents of the sources that have been made available since the publication of "The Oldest System Program of German
Idealism." In order to assess this stopping point, and with the aim of
indicating a further exercise that must now be undertaken by means of
historical fieldwork, I shall in what follows offer a survey both of the
constellations crucial to the reconstruction of the history of classical
German philosophy in its second, properly speculative phase, and of
some matters involved in investigating them. The survey shall be
based not on the mere temporal sequence of the constellations themselves but on the considerations from which the prospect of a new history of the second stage of classical German philosophy has in fact
emerged.

Constellations Along the Way

Tübingen, 1790–1795

Carl Immanuel Diez's Radical Kantianism.   It cannot be considered a
mere historical accident that the three men who most visibly and effectively shaped the thinking of speculative idealism all came from the
halls of the Tübingen *Stift*. This common beginning can be accounted

for readily enough in terms of their country's deep roots in pietistic speculation. What does demand an explanation, however, is not just the direction of their path of thought but above all the force, the resoluteness, and the self-confidence with which they embarked on that path and reached its highly conspicuous terminus, and all this while still in their youth and under the influence of the powerful theoretical developments taking shape far away, in the middle of Germany. This must be understood not just in terms of their personal friendship but also in terms of the setting of their education. Their friendship indeed drew its substance from that setting, which accounts for the common direction of their paths—paths that were nonetheless ultimately independent and soon to diverge.

One initial task incumbent upon a history from Kant to Hegel is to account for the dynamics of the first steps taken in the direction of speculative idealism. For that it was necessary to shed some light on the historical darkness surrounding the problematics in which the Tübingen students found themselves around 1790. The sources that had to be uncovered to this end were the works and the influence of the generation of students immediately preceding that of the three friends, a generation that had taken up a radical-critical stance with regard to the theological teachings of the university. The *Repetenten** at the *Stift* who occupied a unique doctrinal mission in German university life exerted influence in various ways on the paths taken by the three friends: thus Karl Philipp Conz on Hölderlin's Greek studies, and Gottlob Christian Rapp on Hegel's treatment of the problem of motivation in the analysis of *Sittlichkeit*—whence the original idea in Hegel's Tübingen manuscripts to the effect that subjective religion, motivating toward freedom, is not private but public religion. The decisive influence exerted on the general structure of the climate and the style of criticism must nonetheless be attributed to Carl Immanuel Diez.[1] He worked out a radical critique of religion on a Kantian basis. It was greeted with only moderate enthusiasm, but impelled a Professor Gottlob Christian Storr, who had been informed and supported by Diez's intimate friend Friedrich Gottlieb Süsskind, to a counterattack, which in turn became the target of the critiques found in the early works of Hegel and, above all, Schelling. Since Storr opposed Diez's critique of religion with resources themselves drawn from Kant's work, it seemed necessary to ground this second critique of Storr not directly in Kant, but in a new philosophical groundwork that sought to attain both the consciousness of freedom and the transcendental dimension of the life predicated on

---

* *Repetenten* is an outdated term for the persons, usually advanced students, who "repeated" professors' lectures and prepared students for examinations. —Ed.

freedom. Schelling undertook this task in his first philosophical publications.[2] The countercritique against Storr is also the dominant theme in Hegel's Bern manuscripts, except that Hegel at that time still thought it possible to carry out the critique through a more sound rendering of Kant's work itself.

Diez's writings and letters will now soon be published, after a regrettable delay.[3] They will show that Diez's position must have taken shape in the years 1790–92—that is, before the appearance of the religious writings of Fichte and Kant—and that it was this position of Diez's to which Storr's religious writings were a reaction, which in turn gave rise to the fundamental philosophical countercritique by Hegel and Schelling. Diez himself studied medicine in Jena from 1792 onward. It has recently come to light that Reinhold credited him with exerting considerable influence on the development of his own philosophical theory, also from 1792 onward.[4]

Schelling's Kantian Reading of Plato.   It may be gathered from Schelling's letters to Hegel, in Bern, that Storr's countercritique occasioned his decision to turn away from criticism in the field of archeology toward criticism grounded in philosophy. Schelling's first essay and both of his dissertations, as well as the fragments to be found in the introduction to Gustav Leopold Plitt's edition of Schelling's letters, provide some quite extensive source material regarding the extent to which Schelling's previous historical critique had been guided by philosophical considerations. But only now that Schelling's dissertations have been edited and translated have these sources attracted attention on account of their philosophical implications.

The source materials having to do with Schelling's philosophical work prior to his turn toward speculative theory on the other hand are even more abundant. And they have been readily accessible in the unpublished writings kept in Berlin. Before anyone had posed the actual task of sketching out a history from Kant to Hegel, however, they were ignored.

Schelling's unpublished writings contain, along with his commentaries on Paul's letters to the Romans and to the Galatians, a commentary on Plato—and, along with some notes relating to his second dissertation, preliminary elaborations of a treatise on the spirit of Platonic philosophy.[5]

The Plato commentary must be understood as a working manuscript only, not as the draft of a potential publication. It deals with the text of the *Timaeus*, although in trying to understand it Schelling appeals to the doctrine of the modes of being developed in *Philebus* (23c ff.). The interpretation of that doctrine forms the core of Schelling's commentary. The interpretation is guided entirely by Kantian theory. Reinhold's theory of the faculty of representation is incorporated only superficially at this point, on a merely terminological level. Schelling's aim is to show that Plato is developing, in the guise of a dialogue concerning eternal ideas and the origin of the world, the Kantian notion of the concepts under which every existent thing in the world is to be subsumed and which have their proper place and origin in the unity of the understanding, or the faculty of representation. Plato's mode of presentation, which always carries the subjective over into the objective, could be extended to some degree beyond the bounds of the particular historical situation in which he expressed truths available to all human beings—in the same way Schelling himself had sought to explain the mythic language of Scripture. For his part, Plato speaks "in the very tone that must even now be assumed by the oppressed lover of truth."

Inasmuch as Schelling sees the Kantian categories in the γένη of the *Philebus*, however, he at the same time introduces a modification into the organization of Kant's doctrine of the categories. Πέρας is the general form of unity corresponding to the ἄπειρον as the indeterminate manifold, but the former is now to be associated with the category of quality. Departing entirely from Kant, then, and perhaps inspired by Reinhold, Schelling interprets the role of the categories to be the mediation of a fundamental opposition conceived in terms of the antithetical relation between the two basic categories. The κοινόν then proves to be the first category, through which a mediation of unity and the qualitative manifold comes about. It is identified as the category of quantity. Αἰτία is then the next category, which points up the fact that this mediation is not given but must be brought about in relation to every unified manifold. It is, in this sense, the category of causality.

This reconstruction of the Kantian doctrine of the categories on the basis of Plato's text is of use to Schelling only inasmuch as it shows the emergence in Plato's thought, in a form appropriate to its age, of what he takes to be the true and timeless philosophy of Kant. One must also see in this reconstruction, however, a foreshadowing of the fact that when Fichte's *Wissenschaftslehre* appeared shortly thereafter, Schelling saw in it the very model of the doctrine of categories that he had introduced in his own Plato interpretation, advanced now on entirely new foundations.

One must also assume that Schelling himself gained further theoretical input from the dimension of Plato's work that treats of the unity of the soul, and thus of subjectivity in terms of a prior "objective" ideality—the dimension, that is, that Schelling's interpretation initially sought to reduce to the Kantian unity of the subject. For Schelling later deemed it necessary to expose transcendental philosophy itself to the influence of the ideas of Jacobi's *Spinoza* in order to counter Storr's conception of the grounds of rational belief, which he had annexed to Kant's philosophy of religion. Schelling would make it clear at once, by reference to that conception, that the thinking at work in Storr's annexation was plainly fallacious.

Knowledge of Schelling's interpretation of Plato sheds new light on the role of Platonic thought in the development of speculative-idealistic philosophy in general. It was with reference to Plato that Hölderlin too first attempted to free himself from the Kantian position, also in the framework established by Schelling. Even Hegel's *Logic* can be described as a form of dynamized Platonism. And Schelling later settled on a conceptual form derived from Plato for his own presentation of the monism of the absolute. All of this, including Schelling's early interpretation, presupposed an extensive literature on Plato that had, for its part, already attempted to transform the appeal to Plato's theory of forms—conspicuous in Kant himself—into a detailed exegesis that would call upon Plato to bear witness to the truth of Kantian philosophy. It is of some significance that Wilhelm Gottlieb Tennemann, the author of central portions of this literature on Plato, worked at the University of Jena.

Frankfurt-Homburg, 1795–1797

Schelling's essay "Of the I as Principle of Philosophy" is the first published work whose ideas entered into the domain of speculative-idealistic thought. This essay, however, pales somewhat in comparison with the documents we have come to know from Hölderlin's circle of friends, in terms of a clear departure from the Kantian orientation of Fichte's *Wissenschaftslehre*, and in terms of a clear and penetrating critique of its general line of thought. Until the end of the century, and until he was reunited with Hegel in Jena, Schelling was at pains to preserve some common ground with Fichte. One notices in this respect that his arguments and theoretical strategies, in comparison with those of the Homburg circle, lack a certain decisiveness. His drive toward speculative idealism proper seems weak in comparison. This can be accounted for in terms of the theoretical reservations that he quite rightly had, as well as by his theoretical gifts, which, though at the mercy of public criticism, surpassed those of the Homburgers. On the other hand, there were good reasons for the peculiar decisiveness of the breakthrough, carried out in Hölderlin's circle, beyond the transcendental boundaries set by Fichte. This breakthrough was so powerful that it drew Hegel, when he arrived in Frankfurt, almost immediately into the Homburg circle. It also has the effect that, when Hegel read Schelling's works intensively, he was not attracted to their characteristic indirection and ambivalence in the construction of speculative idealism.

None of the philosophical texts that have been preserved from the Hölderlin circle was composed with publication specifically in mind, nor even as a preliminary study for eventual publication. They were all texts communicated from one person to another, and this in various ways. Hölderlin's "Judgment and Being" sketches out a philosophical idea, downplaying the intended application to Hölderlin's anthropology. "The Oldest System Program of German Idealism," on the other hand, is a report on a text that concerns a kind of enlightenment grounded in philosophy but whose actual philosophical foundations remain obscure. Only Sinclair's and Zwilling's reflections proceed in such a manner as to acknowledge openly all of the motives that influenced them. Sinclair is thus entirely dependent on Hölderlin's ideas, while Zwilling, still young and embarking on a career as an officer, sketches out a highly original notion that was to solve the very problems that stood before Hölderlin's eyes in "Judgment and Being." The various drafts of *Hyperion* provide us with a more intimate understanding of the sort of problems these were.

This singular point of departure and the range of reactions to it, including not only Hölderlin's and Zwilling's texts but also Hegel's early Frankfurt manuscripts, allow us to think our way into the theoretical dynamics that were at work in the thoughts and conversations of these friends. We can recognize the lack of clarity that remains in Hölderlin's distinction between absolute being and counterposing reflection. And we can recognize the distinctive development of Hegel's and Hölderlin's ideas, up until their final separation.[6] Hegel arrived at the outline of a system more closely related to Zwilling and to a Platonic ontology of logical form, albeit the form of antithesis, than to Hölderlin's thinking, which for its part remained bound up with the conceptual structure of Fichte's theory. Hölderlin and Hegel were, however, still in agreement with regard to the new fundamental thesis that not only must the unity of the origin be secured and recollected from within separation, but moreover the separation itself belongs to that unity, qua unity. Hegel's later philosophy of spirit is predicated on this important conceptual step, and Hölderlin's theory of tragedy and historical downfall is rooted in it directly. But it has not yet been shown how the detailed thoughts in Hölderlin's hymnal poetry preserve and develop the motives of the Homburg ideas—the unity of nature in the manifold of the divine, the self-refusal of the god, the gathering recollection of the rivers, and the poet of the people, whose song is, in a single giving of thanks, an evocation and unification of the vital tendencies toward "inwardness" (*Innigkeit*).

Speculative Thought in Its Final Forms

The new understanding of the path of speculative thought centers, as philosophical analysis, on unfolding the potentials of a theoretical structure, and as a historical analysis, on elucidating historical constellations. A fundamental and important methodological consequence follows from this immediately, namely, that it becomes impossible to keep in view the intellectual path of each figure in the various constellations, in addition to the particular motives that were decisive for each of them in turn. The progressive evolution of speculative thought cannot be captured in a series of individual intentions and their results. One can certainly find a personal profile of talents and problems, and so a series of insights, in each figure who contributed to the evolution of this thinking. But they are all so interconnected in a common process of understanding from the outset that the ideas they developed can only be understood in terms of the entire range of problems and philosophical possibilities peculiar to the theoretical structure of speculative thought itself. The playing field of possible conceptual moves derives from this range of problems. Thus the moves that were actually carried out must be made intelligible in relation to it, and judged in relation to the basic questions they were meant to address. Organizing research around editions of collected works, as is still widely done, can easily bring about a narrowing of perspective by concentrating in each case on a single thinker. Analysis and historical elucidation consequently tend toward distortions. Precisely because the new understanding of the course of speculative thought takes its own point of departure for the most part from the context of problems itself, it must be structured synoptically from the very outset and take that course as a whole as its proper theme.

Barring this approach, the philosophical milieu that formed during the beginning of the nineteenth century in Jena around Schelling and Hegel would be just as inaccessible as the one between Hegel and Hölderlin just before the end of the eighteenth. The conceptual structure of Hegel's *Logic* emerged from within that setting.[7] And as far as Schelling is concerned, it turned out that he could make no further contributions to the actual development of speculative thought since his thinking did not follow in the steps of the theory that Hegel had been refining between 1802 and 1804. Schelling's later philosophy may be said to have retreated in measured steps into the theoretical sphere whose essential features had already been laid down by the circle of friends in Homburg.

The greatest task now facing the new history of speculative thought has to do with understanding and discussing in relation to one another the final forms that speculative thought attained. The conditions of the development of Hegel's *Logic* must be uncovered as well. The emergence of Schelling's work from the context of problems central to speculative thought must be understood in relation to the *Logic*. And both must be placed alongside Hölderlin's poetic work, which, on the basis of a philosophical insight standing at the center of speculative thought, denies that philosophy is itself competent with respect to the very problems it engenders. Finally, we must set Fichte's later *Wissenschaftslehre* alongside the work of the three Tübingen friends in its final forms. Fichte wanted to defend the Kantian boundaries against all ontology. His work is thus fundamentally incompatible with Hegel's *Logic*. But Fichte's work too is defined by certain features of the speculative mode of conceptualization. And in its final synthesis, the theory of the absolute, it relates directly to the agenda of speculative thought and its conceptual form.

It will not be sufficient to assess the situation in Jena after 1800 in this much broader framework without at the same time inquiring into the actual grounds from which speculative thought got under way in the first place and into its ability to acquire legitimacy. Work aiming at a new history from Kant to Hegel leads, then, to an actual attempt to understand the possibility, and even the inevitability, of speculative thought itself. Recent efforts to gain an understanding of its most impressive epoch finds its final and genuine justification in this task.

Jena, 1792–1796

This sketch of the outline and prospectus of a new history of speculative thought has been occasioned by the conclusion of the search for documents from Hölderlin's circle of friends in Homburg. The present sketch shall for its part conclude with the formulation of a further research project. This project arises from questions that can only be posed once we are clear about the philosophical potential of the Homburg circle, which has now been established. In light of this, then, the questions follow inevitably.

The search for Zwilling's unpublished writings has been guided above all by the hope of making available Zwilling's notes in a letter to a Jena professor. Ludwig Strauß made reference to these notes, indeed in the context of outlining Zwilling's worldview. Having laid the foundations for Zwilling's practical philosophy, he used the notes as source material attesting to Zwilling's views on aesthetics. Strauß indicates that the notes begin with a critique of Fichte's theory of the absolute I. Strauß himself had made a presentation of Zwilling's theory on the basis of the fragment "On the All," but the Fichte critique itself was of no special interest to him in connection with this project. One nonetheless has the impression that the letter was quite wide-ranging.

The existence of the letter confirms the fact that there was at least one party in Jena interested in the conversations of the Homburg circle, and also that those conversations in Homburg related to other discussions that were already taking place in Jena. The originality of the thinking in Homburg and the self-confidence with which it was carried on cannot at any rate be understood independently of the notable fact that Hölderlin, Sinclair, and Zwilling all studied together in Jena, the center of philosophical activity in Germany. Zwilling spent about a year and a half there, Sinclair about a year, and Hölderlin about half a year. When the nineteen-year-old Zwilling wrote his letter to Jena, he had in fact just set out from there. One can hardly suppose, then, that he could have worked out an original position against both Fichte and Hölderlin in the less than four weeks since his departure. Hölderlin's "Judgment and Being" had already come to light more than a year earlier in Jena. Hölderlin had long since returned home from there and then gone on to Frankfurt. A year earlier the friendship between Sinclair and Hölderlin in Jena had reached its highpoint, and proved genuine up to the time of Hölderlin's breakdown and subsequently in Sinclair's preservation of essential portions of Hölderlin's works. Zwilling's acquaintance with Sinclair dates back to their youth, which they spent together in Homburg. The draft of the letter seems to imply that the reader also knows Sinclair. It is very probable that Zwilling and Sinclair also interacted somewhat in Jena and so had some knowledge of each other's projects and contacts. If the ideas of Hölderlin's "Judgment and Being" had some influence on Zwilling's notes, this influence must have been felt during Hölderlin's residence in Jena. One may assume that his colleagues and acquaintances throughout his life remained at once important for, as well as attentive to, the further development of his ideas.

Thus, although Zwilling's correspondence is still unavailable to us, the very fact of its existence opens the door to a whole range of conjectures and new intellectual concerns. One would like to know, to begin with, to which Jena professor Zwilling's letter could have been addressed. Zwilling assumes that the reader will be receptive to his arguments and that he will take young students seriously as theorists. He further assumes that it is sensible and even urgent to remain in contact with him. This in turn suggests that, in the second year after his arrival in Jena, a critical discussion of the foundations of the *Wissenschaftslehre* was at least possible in Fichte's presence. And this, for its part, already indicates the decisive move toward speculative thought. And if one could imagine Hölderlin's "Judgment and Being" appearing the year before, in quiet isolation, then Zwilling's letter would have to have been addressed to someone open to its ideas, even among the professors.

But it must be assumed, really, that Hölderlin's ideas regarding Fichte had found their way into wider circles even by the year 1795. Hölderlin had access to all the celebrities in the area. Niethammer had even invited him to contribute to a journal whose announced plan was remarkably ambitious.

But these considerations raise the question whether Hölderlin really hit upon his program in the setting of Jena so wholly independently, and made it so convincing in conversation, that the eighteen-year-old Zwilling could have simply fallen under its spell. One could also imagine that soon after Fichte's arrival in Jena discussions were already under way in which people were putting forward the kind of ideas first documented in Hölderlin's philosophical text. It could be, at any rate, that Hölderlin profited more from such conversations than his text itself reveals. "Judgment and Being" is unique among Hölderlin's theoretical texts—precisely because it deals directly, and in a programmatic form, with fundamental questions of philosophy. If we had never come to know of Sinclair's "Philosophische Raisonnements," the originality of the conception of "Judgment and Being" would perhaps never have seemed so striking. The two texts taken together, more than Hölderlin's single page alone, make clear the scope of the systematic program of "Judgment and Being."

Hölderlin's later theoretical texts are indeed no less original. But they do not show the same thetic certitude in dealing with fundamental questions. This might be explained by the fact that these texts are predominantly drafts of essays on the theory of art, and that Hölderlin's other working philosophical manuscripts, though surely written out, have not been preserved. One also cannot help but wonder about the circumstances, unknown to us now, in virtue of which "Judgment and Being" has come down to us. One should keep in mind that it was only in the setting of Fichte's Jena that Hölderlin was able to arrive at his philosophical conception in the manner distinctive of his one-page text. Still, Hölderlin's philosophical originality is certainly beyond doubt. The draft of "Judgment and Being" takes up with great perspicuity the problems already laid out in Hölderlin's anthropology, as well as in the format of the novel *Hyperion*. We must nevertheless admit that we know nothing of the circumstances in which Hölderlin's originality was brought to its first compelling expression, thoroughly determining his own path and even Hegel's. Consequently we know nothing of the conversations, influences, and provocations in which his originality actually became philosophically fruitful in Jena.

Such considerations and questions reveal the deficit in our knowledge of the conditions of the rise of speculative idealism. It remains to carry out what is now the most pressing, and presumably the final, historical line of research toward the new understanding of the history from Kant to Hegel. Namely, we have on the whole virtually no knowledge of the state of the discussion or of the philosophical situation surrounding Fichte during the years 1794–96. It was precisely there that Hölderlin's independence and originality grew. And it was there too that he must have influenced Zwilling, who developed his original conception according to the guiding principle of the Homburg circle.

The question concerning the exact nature of the conversations of the Jena students and professors associating with Fichte brings with it a further question concerning the general climate into which Fichte entered when he took over Reinhold's professorship. For one cannot assume that the situation awaiting Fichte had no effect on the reception of his *Wissenschaftslehre* or on the sorts of criticism that it immediately drew. The criticisms coming from the strict Kantians cannot have been the only ones. In order to see more clearly the situation to which Hölderlin and his Homburg friends were exposed, we must also try to understand the situation surrounding Reinhold, who was renowned for his theory of representation but who had become increasingly dissatisfied with it before his departure from Jena.

Jena was at that time one of the two centers of intellectual life in Germany, the other being its companion star, Weimar. This explains both Jena's great attraction for students and its central position in philosophy. But information concerning the situation in Jena in which the Homburg philosophy took shape, if it is available in print at all, is scattered throughout numerous publications that are either in part apocryphal or else motivated by extraphilosophical interests. No attempt has ever been made to trace the intellectual profile of the situation in Jena between 1792 and 1796 so as to explain how this step in the direction of speculative thought was possible, in itself or in light of the circumstances. For it was such an essential step that in its absence even Hegel's system would have been without one of its most important historical preconditions.

The philosophy of the Homburg circle, then, has emerged in sufficiently sharp outline, and this has brought to our attention the deficit in our knowledge concerning Jena. For the two decades since the reception of the work of Ludwig Strauß, research has concentrated on the Homburg circle. Now it has become necessary to concentrate on the situation in Jena in which and out of which the Homburg circle emerged—in fact, one should really refer to the group as it was before Hegel joined in as the "Jena circle of Homburgers." Once one is aware of the circle itself, it becomes necessary to bring together from a diverse literature, guided by disparate interests, the scattered documents that concern the focal points of the conversation in Jena and the ideas that dominated that conversation. It is advisable, then—perhaps above all—to commence with the search for as yet unpublished documents in estates and archives. It must at least be possible to present the ideas of the professors around Reinhold and Fichte during those years and to identify the addressee of Zwilling's letter. One should not rule out the possibility that the letter itself may yet come to light in the process.

Just by posing these problems we are able to see otherwise fairly familiar connections in a new light. To conclude, I shall mention only one such connection, namely, the Jena interest in Greek skepticism and in philosophical skepticism in general. This interest became unavoidable with Jacobi's second principal philosophical work and Gottlob Ernst Schulze's and Salomon Maimon's reaction to Reinhold. But Tennemann and Niethammer also worked on skepticism early on. The effort to pinpoint correctly the position of the skeptic in the philosophical system makes up a prominent feature of the texts of Hölderlin and Sinclair. One is also reminded of Hegel's later Jena essay on skepticism, not to mention the work in Jena on Spinoza, which, for reasons likewise yet to be made explicit, can be traced back to the Jena professor, Heinrich Eberhard Gottlob Paulus—who, like Diez, Niethammer, and Hölderlin, also hailed from Swabia. The thinkers who took their point of departure from Kant, Reinhold, and Fichte went on to do original work, constructing the theories of speculative idealism. And it could indeed be said that they did so from within a horizon of problems relating to skepticism, albeit according to the philosophical possibilities opened up by Spinoza.

Indeed, we know much already of the influence of Spinozistic themes on the history of the reception of Kant's critical philosophy.[8] What has not yet been followed up is the specific way in which the figure of Spinoza came to be seen as occasioning the revision and completion of Kant's system of reason, projects called upon to bear witness to the emergence of a final, and ultimately binding, philosophic potential, even for post-Kantian philosophy. It is relatively easy to see how Jacobi and Reinhold foreshadowed the favorable conditions for such an advance. But as to how such conditions were transformed into the actual ideas and inquiries in collaborative philosophizing, resulting finally in the great historical force of the thinking of the Homburgers in Jena— this would need to be spelled out in a fine-tuned investigation into the few years of the first heyday of Jena philosophy.

It remains an open question whether this line of research yet to be taken up will yield results of the same importance and explanatory power as those that have shed light on the Homburg circle. But the task itself is now inevitably set—forming perhaps the final link in the historical-philological discovery of the path of speculative idealism.

Translated by Taylor Carman

Dominant Philosophical-Theological Problems in the Tübingen *Stift* During the Student Years of Hegel, Hölderlin, and Schelling

THE years in which Hegel, Hölderlin, and Schelling were students were not only the years in which the French Revolution ran its course but also the years of the transformation of the entire German intellectual world under the decisive influence of the philosophy that had been founded by Immanuel Kant. When Hegel and Hölderlin arrived at the *Stift*, this philosophy had already gained a dominant influence at several universities. It was established and diffused through one of the most important scholarly reviews: the *Allgemeine Literatur-Zeitung*, whose "pieces" (*Stücke*) were published in Jena six times a week. In these, anonymous but clearly eminent reviewers endeavored to place Kantian methods of argument in the proper light and so far as possible to disarm the resistance of other philosophical schools to Kantian doctrine.

Only from 1789 on, with the appearance of Karl Leonhard Reinhold's Elementary Philosophy, did controversies arise within the Kantian school itself, controversies that, moreover, concerned the foundations of the still novel theory. Very soon it became clear that the changing modes of thought and argumentation that originated with Kant were to lead to an intellectual movement that would more than once reformulate Kantian ideas from the ground up and, with these new formulations, penetrate all domains of life and the understanding of life, especially in faith and in literature. In 1792 Fichte's first work appeared—an investigation of the foundations of any doctrine founded on revelation; in 1793 Schiller published his treatise "On Grace and Dignity," which was Kantian but also a criticism of Kant; in 1794 Fichte came before the public with his *Wissenschaftslehre*.

Although the number of those who came under Kantian influence and who began to use his language continued to increase, and indeed did so rapidly, there were only a few who entered this second movement—a movement that sought to take the Kantian impulse still further. Most made a common front against the rewriting of the Kantian modes of argument—now reinforced by the literary journals that had earlier put themselves at the service of the Kantian program, the *Allgemeine Literatur-Zeitung* among others. In that, at least, the Kantians now found themselves in agreement with their own opponents, who had earlier met the spread of Kant's teaching with a critical voice. Among these opponents, too, was the voice of the *Tübingischen Gelehrten Anzeigen*, whose important reviews of philosophical works had as their author the still youthful professor *extraordinarius* Johann Friedrich Flatt. Since the occupant of the full professor's chair (the Leibnizian logician Gottfried Ploucquet) was prevented from teaching by a stroke, but still alive and therefore without a successor, the whole responsibility for instruction in theoretical philosophy in Tübingen lay in Flatt's hands.

It is therefore all the more astonishing that the new, post-Kantian movement received some of its most important stimuli from the circle of those who had in those years begun their studies in the Tübingen *Stift*—even more astonishing, however, that this happened immediately after their period of study in Tübingen or even from their room in the *Stift*. Little more than a year after his theological examinations, Hölderlin, now at the University of Jena, formulated a philosophical position of his own—both under Fichte's influence and at the same time in opposition to him. Two years later, in Frankfurt, Hegel was able to renew conversation with his friend. Hölderlin's position now enabled Hegel to make a change of intellectual direction that was decisive for his philosophical path. Schelling, who had entered the *Stift* at the age of fifteen in 1790, claimed a place in the post-Kantian movement with two books even before his examination. He was the first author who, as he himself wrote to Hegel, greeted "the new hero, Fichte, in the land of truth."

We cannot explain this solely from the accident of a concentration of talents in one place and in one house. Neither can we attribute it merely to what the Orientalist H. E. G. Paulus, at the time of the reform of the *Stift* in the year 1794, praised as the "most fruitful circumstance" of an institution "whose pupils" educate "themselves through unconstrained interaction with many students of like age, like aims and the most various mental culture."[1] We must rather suspect that the context of problems to which their studies had brought Hölderlin, Hegel, and Schelling enabled this confluence of talent under these circumstances, and the ensuing result. Wherever classical German philosophy attracts attention, it is precisely this result that will secure the memory of the Tübingen *Stift* and encourage contemplation marked by astonishment and admiration.

I

Many attempts have been made to sketch the educational development of the three friends and to grasp it in terms of the intellectual constellations in which it took place. The sources are not scarce, and it is easy to find the publications of the period. The complexity of the intellectual problems to which the friends were exposed, however, is considerable. The intricacies these problems produced through their relations with each other can only become accessible and comprehensible to someone of a later generation with some effort. The conversations during the time they studied together are almost entirely unavailable, and not merely because their content often had to be concealed from those who were responsible for watching over and reporting on the course of their studies. Confidential correspondence, therefore, is among our most important documentation. Letters were first exchanged between Hegel, Hölderlin, and Schelling, however, when they were all separated from each other, with Schelling remaining in the *Stift* for two more years. Much therefore can only be inferred. However, a picture of the intellectual problems that weighed on them in those decisive years of study in the *Stift* can be drawn with the help of supporting correspondence from other students who had left the *Stift* earlier. Through former classmates who were now *Repetenten* at the *Stift*, Hegel, Hölderlin, and later Schelling remained connected to the intellectual life there. By placing the issues discussed in these letters in relation to the intellectual problems that had unfolded in public debate, one obtains a reliable point of reference for what can ultimately be made comprehensible only through a process of reconstruction.

Until now, only a few such collections of letters have come to light. The most important of them have to do with another constellation of three friends deserving attention for its own sake: Niethammer, Süsskind, and Diez. Supported by a private stipend, Friedrich Immanuel Niethammer left Tübingen for Jena in 1790 to seek Reinhold's help in clarifying his doubts concerning the foundations of faith. The result of these efforts was a series of philosophical essays and philosophical-theological books following the teaching of Kant. In 1794 he attempted unsuccessfully to obtain a position as professor *extraordinarius* in Tübingen in order to establish Kantian philosophy "in the fatherland." In

1798, having in the meantime become professor of theology at Jena, Niethammer, along with Fichte, fell under suspicion of atheism. Friedrich Gottlieb Süsskind spent a year at the University of Göttingen in 1790–91, then returned to the *Stift* as *Repetent*. He, unlike Niethammer, had had not a crisis of faith but a crisis in his theological orientation; this led him to reorient his studies from dogmatics and exegetics to church history. From 1798 on he was, however, the occupant of the chair for dogmatics at the University of Tübingen. The third friend, and the correspondent of the other two, was Carl Immanuel Diez, Süsskind's best friend. From 1790 to 1792 he was one of the *Repetenten* at the *Stift*, and as such was partly responsible for the *Loci*, the exercises on the units of study in dogmatics, which took place every Monday and in which Hegel and Hölderlin had to participate. Diez was the son of a professor of medicine who was, at the same time, the private doctor of many of his colleagues in philology and theology. During Diez's experience as a *Repetent* he resolved to abandon theology as well as the Christian faith, and went to Jena to study medicine. Reinhold, however, attested that once there Diez immediately had an important influence on the change in his own philosophical conceptions. Diez first became known to us as a Kantian radical, an *enrage*, in connection with a report on Hegel's student days. The accuracy of that report is attested by a letter from Süsskind to Diez in which Süsskind takes notice of the death of the orthodox consistory councillor, Rieger: "If the blessed man had learned in addition that the *Repetenten* contest the real and perhaps also the logical possibility of revelation—he would, it is true, have died even sooner."[2]

Niethammer, Süsskind, and Diez, like Hölderlin, Hegel, and Schelling, had Gottlob Christian Storr as a theology teacher. Süsskind, who became his successor, was in addition related to Storr and was in continuous contact with him during his studies. To understand the theological-philosophical problems of students at the *Stift* between 1789 and 1793, one must begin from the work of this important scholar of the New Testament and church dogma. Even Kant mentioned him as the "famous Doctor Storr in Tübingen." In 1789, Storr had for the first time made his theological views known to their full extent when he presented them in the second book of his work on the Letter to the Hebrews under the title *On the True Meaning of the Death of Jesus*. In 1793 he published his work on dogma, which later served as the required textbook for many generations of Württemberg pastors.[3] In the same year, he published an attack on Kant's philosophical theory of religion, which had only begun to appear in 1792.[4] Storr's thought had a dominant influence on all the students at the *Stift* who studied under him—

as will be clear even in those cases when they directed all the energy of their thought against him.

Storr was famous for his acuity of mind, his comprehensive learning in the exegesis of the New Testament, and the systematic power with which he had worked out a thoroughly original theology. With it, he opposed the theological innovations of the preceding generation. The characteristic tendency of that generation had been to reduce the proper content of Christian teaching to what was capable of being translated into "subjective religion," that is, to personal ethical experience and the ethical life of the religious community. It drew a distinction between the true and the obsolete doctrines in the heritage of the church on the basis of its advanced historical knowledge. This knowledge made it possible to distinguish what on the one hand arose in the tradition from the ways in which the lives and deeds of Christ and the apostles accommodated the spirit and the circumstances of their time, from what on the other hand was and would always remain part of the true ongoing Christian teaching. Storr opposed this thesis—that the founders of Christianity had "accommodated" themselves to a lost world—with the Protestant principle of scriptural authority, put forward in a new form and with renewed rigor. Insofar as the scriptures in the canon are of divine origin, they also have divine authority; they are to be taken and received only, and wholly, in their literal sense. Exegetical-theological work must find its aim in examining and making sure that the Scriptures have come down to us in their authentic form without textual corruption. The task of dogmatics is accordingly to come to terms with the Gospel in its entirety. And that means that the one saving doctrine, contained in the Bible as the divine Word, is to be presented in a continuous relation to the corresponding passages of the scriptural canon. From this point of view it is forbidden to the exegete to lay claim to the inspiration of the Holy Spirit in his interpretation, just as it is forbidden to the systematic theologian to infer the meaning of God's Word only on the condition that its meaning could also be discovered or even deduced independently of Scripture through rational reflection. The attestation of the truth of the Word cannot, therefore, be obtained from its meaning alone. It is attested rather because we know that it is divine "instruction." This in turn we know from all we know of the life of Jesus and of the miracles that accompanied his work on earth. The meaning of these miracles is the confirmation of Jesus's status as a divine envoy and bringer of salvation and therewith at the same time the confirmation of the truth of his religious teaching, which could never have been gained through reason. At the end of the preface to his *Dogmatics*, Storr warns his Tübingen students with the words of

Philipp Melanchthon: to remember that they are God's seedbed since it is from among them that the Son of God takes the servants of the Gospel, who in accordance with His will are prepared for this vocation in institutions of learning. He concludes with these words: "Let us fulfill this so important vocation with loyalty and conscientiousness toward God, toward the church and toward those who come after us; let us investigate the truth, evaluate it, assert it, and pass it on unfalsified to our heirs."[5]

This single warning both incorporates Storr's whole teaching and gives clear expression to the aim and manner of his influence. No one who rejected his teachings, however, denied respect for this man, whom they regarded as pious, mild in his relations to others, and powerful as a thinker. Niethammer, who held that Storr's *Dogmatics* lacked adequate justification, nevertheless publicly confessed in 1796 in his highly respected *Philosophical Journal* that "never in five years" had he "listened to [Storr's] sermons, which are mostly concerned with dogma, without gaining spiritual edification."[6] For those who considered themselves his followers, however, he was, even many years later, simply "our Storr." When in 1797 Storr was called to Stuttgart as court preacher and left Tübingen, the university seemed to Flatt to have become desolate.

If one does not know the strength of the opponent, one cannot see what was needed by way of inner resolve and independent reasoning for those who did not merely withdraw from his influence but wanted to set their own superior conception against him. The grounds, however, that moved Diez, Niethammer, Hegel, and Schelling to do precisely that are not hard to make out. Storr's teaching "propagated," as Hegel wrote to Schelling on December 24, 1794, "the old system more faithfully than was done anywhere else." It was influenced by the spirit of the times, both in its exegetical means and in its argumentation, seeking soberly to extract the literal meaning from texts and to reconstruct this meaning step by step in every detail. But the content of Storr's *Dogmatics* was meant to preserve for him everything that had become entirely unacceptable to the majority of his contemporaries. It was for that very reason that the neological theologies had appeared and become dominant, theologies whose influence Storr now wanted to end, as he in fact succeeded in doing for decades in the church in Württemberg.

What now appeared unacceptable was everything in Storr's teaching that could be labeled "supernaturalism." Those who refused to accept Storr's views yet remained Christian theologians were considered by him to be "heterodox." Even according to the very meaning of the word, supernaturalism stands opposed to a naturalism. A "naturalist" in the theological sense is one who sees all the truths of Christian doctrine as coinciding with only those truths that reason, at least in principle, would be capable of comprehending even without the guidance of revelation. The supernaturalism proper to Storr, however, is characterized by more than the fact that it entirely rejects such naturalistic teachings. Storr also insists emphatically on those doctrines that seemed to the "heterodox" to stand in a sort of contradiction with reason that could be neither tolerated nor resolved. These doctines contradict what reason must insist on as an indispensable determining principle. Depending on which element of doctrine it is that one realizes stands in such a contradiction, in each case another form of heterodoxy results.

One can easily guess which articles of faith ("symbols") of Christian doctrine could principally drive men into such heterodoxies, for these articles have since the earliest times been occasions of heresy: the doctrine of the Trinity and with it of the divinity of Jesus; the doctrine of original sin; and the redemption of human sins by the death of Jesus before God's justice. Heterodoxy can, however, also arise from the doctrine of the presence of the Son in the Communion and from the assumption of miracles as grounds for the affirmation of the teaching of Jesus. In fact, Storr's thesis of the authority of the whole text of the Bible to the extent that it has come down to us uncorrupted is connected with this view. Other heterodox thinkers might judge that this thesis goes too far, since it is possible to believe in the divinity of the teaching of Jesus without therefore also having to assert that the text of the evangelists and apostles was inspired to thoroughgoing, literal truth by Christ's teaching and the divine spirit, or that their possession of such truth is confirmed by the role of the apostles as the envoys of God and God's Son.

By the second half of the eighteenth century all these heterodoxies had long been widespread. Storr rejected all of them. Because, however, he equally rejected every understanding of the Bible that based itself in the spirit as a source of understanding, and insisted rather on laying out the meaning of Scripture in full clarity, his justifications in the articles on dogma often tended to estrange his readers. Clarity and precision of discourse on the one side, and the content of the divine truth that sought to make itself clear with the help of these qualities on the other, seemed hard to reconcile.

As soon as reason was given the authority, by its own criteria, to make judgments about good and evil and thus about what is morally possible, special difficulties concerning some of the symbols of faith arose—especially given the way that Storr handled them. Thus one understands in what sense the impression made by Kant's moral philosophy necessarily undermined certain symbols that are central both for Christian doctrine and for Storr's teaching. The vicarious redemption of sins through the crucifixion (the symbol of the *satisfactio vicaria*) is a prime example. In 1794, Carl Friedrich Stäudlin, a graduate of the *Stift* and a former pupil of Storr's but now professor in Göttingen, summed up the difficulties in a few concise phrases aimed at Storr: "If one takes literally the teaching of Scripture that Jesus bore the divine punishments for the sins of the human race, insoluble difficulties arise that penetrate deep into our moral consciousness and shake the holiest practical principles."[7] "A divine judge can reward virtue only in its maker, and punish sin only in its maker. Moral obligations cannot be transferred like financial obligations."[8] "It cannot help in the least if one either refers things to an impenetrable decision of God's or proclaims that the doctrine of a vicarious absolution only means forgiveness of sins for men who have truly become better."[9] In the first case, decisions that contradict the clearest principles could not be taken to be God's decisions. In the second case, one does indeed avoid the misuse of the doctrine of the redemption of sins that consists in thinking that one may neglect one's own improvement. The offense of the teaching itself, however, is not avoided but only hidden under the insupportable ambiguity that our attainment of grace is supposed to lie both in our own achievement and in that of another.

Stäudlin drew from this insight a rather involved theory about the purpose and the effects of the death of Jesus. In light of Storr's teaching this theory is heterodoxy, although it permits no doubt of either the divinity of Jesus or the reality of miracles and revelations. Storr, however, advanced his own interpretation of "the true meaning of the death of Jesus" in the treatise of this title in 1789, and then again in his *Dogmatics* (1793). This interpretation lends itself much more to the true spiritual edification in Storr's sermons of which Niethammer had spoken: through obedience unto death, Jesus earned from God the permission and reward to bless men, so beloved by him in spite of their sins, with a grace beyond any they could conceive. However moving this Christological thought may be, it presupposes that it was God's justice that allowed Him to require such obedience unto death from His Son; whereby it is once again presupposed that Christ suffered as a representative for the guilt of all men. And precisely this teaching, in the view of the younger students in the *Stift* as well, challenges, as Stäudlin said, "the holiest practical principles" of moral consciousness.

Storr, however, saw clearly that the surrender of this doctrine of redemption would subvert his whole system. To name only one consequence, surrender would lead directly to a theory of accommodation, for the meaning of Scripture could then no longer be maintained in its clear literal sense. In addition, the reason for such a surrender approaches a naturalism at least of practical reason: its criteria are instituted as the highest conditions of the credibility of a revelation and are thereby accorded primacy. Flatt's younger brother had studied in Göttingen and published there, under Stäudlin's influence, the philosophical-exegetical *Investigations on the Teaching of the Reconciliation of Man with God*, whose conclusions did not agree with Storr but more closely approached Stäudlin.[10] It is reported that Storr made it a condition to this young Carl Christian Flatt, when in 1804 he was invited to join the faculty in Tübingen, that he renounce the fundamental doctrines of this work. Flatt junior, who in the meantime had once again become a follower of Storr, then apparently bought and destroyed as many copies of his book as he could.[11]

Thus, from the striking example of the doctrine of reconciliation it can be seen that the decisiveness of Storr's orthodoxy, taken together with the wide scope and systematic spirit in the construction of his doctrine, inevitably elicited a contrary reaction as resolute as it was systematic. Modifications in the interpretation of particular articles of faith ran the danger of falling behind what Storr had set forth in carefully thought-out unity, a unity impressive in the quality of its systematic form as well as in its motivation. Nevertheless, it was quite clear that the spirit of Storr's teaching conflicted with all the insights of the age and with its philosophy too. It was easy to see, then, why in the end it was possible to counter Storr's wide-ranging views only with an equally wide-ranging naturalism.

Theological naturalism is the religious doctrine that reduces the claims of faith to assertions that reason could ascertain on its own. Every particular form of theological naturalism must therefore be constructed on the basis of rational concepts or theories. Thus it is understandable why the theological problematic informed by the work of Storr became entangled with the problematic set down by Kant in theoretical philosophy as well.

Kant's critical philosophy developed a new conception of reason that is the precondition for the concept of freedom in his moral philosophy: reason generates rules that make possible both knowledge of objects in experience and the formulation of thoughts of an unconditioned. The morally good will itself rests on such a formulation, namely the idea of a maximal agreement of freedom with itself in all possible actions. That freedom, by means of its inherent ideality, actually confronts us with unconditional demands is supported in the first instance by our moral consciousness. Moreover, that the idea and the imperative of freedom are not mere fictions is supported by the fact that theoretical knowledge cannot enter into the domain in which freedom has its place. We know only what we can experience. Reason itself, however, extends further than the knowledge of objects. It is reason that knows and determines the boundaries of possible objectivity. At the same time, however, reason justifies the principles of moral consciousness, which are in no way obtainable from a science of what is but only from the self-consciousness of practical reason. In philosophy, as Kant says following Rousseau, everything must in the end be subordinated to freedom.

This theory was put forward by a thinker who everyone soon realized would be counted among the greatest the world had ever known. As a result, no one could teach philosophy without working out his relation to Kant's teaching. In addition, however, the theory irresistibly attracted the younger generation, who were conscious of being moved and carried by the currents of the age but who were, in the eyes of their elders, swept away by these currents without having sufficiently examined them. As far as Storr and his teaching were concerned, what opposition could be both greater and clearer than the one between Storr's insistence on the divine authority of the Word and Kant's principle of the autonomy of reason?

Johann Friedrich Flatt was Tübingen's only philosopher of importance; in theology, however, he was Storr's devoted pupil.[12] At an early age he had made a reputation for himself in Germany through numerous essays, books, and book reviews, in which for the most part he studied Kantian doctrines—always concluding that they were not adequately grounded. But his writings also demonstrate a broad familiarity with Kant's works. Flatt's acuity as well as his knowledge earned him respect among Kantians and esteem among those who for their part were trying to answer Kant's arguments—for example the Göttingen professor Johann Georg Heinrich Feder, who tried to keep philosophy in Göttingen free from any Kantian influence. In Tübingen, Flatt gave lecture courses that were more accommodating to Kant's theories than were the pointed reviews he dashed off for the *Tübingischen Gelehrten Anzeigen*. In his lectures, he maintained that Kant had denied on insufficient grounds the possibility of knowledge of things in themselves, and consequently knowledge of God's essence and existence. But what really concerned Flatt was to argue further that a minimum of natural theology could and must be salvaged and made to support a doctrine of revelation in the spirit of Storr.

Kant's own doctrine clearly did not issue in the sort of philosophical naturalism in which everything we can know and talk about meaningfully must belong to the realm of things in nature. Kant contested only the possibility of a scientific knowledge of objects that do not belong to that nature to which we are bound through experience. But ideas are also concepts of reason. We have knowledge, grounded in practical self-consciousness, of the reality of at least one idea, namely the idea of freedom. Religion, too, is to be grounded on such practical certainty. However, the articles of faith of this religion do not exceed the rational theology of deism: over and above the thought of its effectiveness in the world—a thought that it cannot surrender—the good will implies the existence of the *être suprême* and the immortality of free beings.

During the first years of Hegel's and Hölderlin's studies none of Kant's writings touching directly on the relation of the critical philosophy to Christianity and to Christian theology had yet appeared. But books by other authors had been published that sought to show that Kantian practical religion was identical with the essential content of a Christian doctrine freed of dogmatic accommodations. A short time later, some began to propose applying the method of the critical philosophy to dogmatics itself. In 1791 Stäudlin published his *Ideas for a Critique of the System of the Christian Religion*.[13] In 1795 Niethammer followed this program with his *Religion as Science*.[14] The Kantian form of argument had found its way into theology itself. Storr and his school could not remain indifferent to this.

Even earlier, however, rumors had circulated to the effect that naturalism was spreading throughout the *Stift*. Ephorus Schnurrer disputed the rumors, though he must have known even more than Storr. As a member of the "Inspectorate," Schnurrer was responsible for overseeing theological studies within the *Stift*, and he often made a point of being present during instructions in the *Loci*. Schnurrer himself was anything but a naturalist, but was confident in his opinion that youthful convictions are unstable and that only a solid education and good will should be considered of any importance. The consequences, however, that could really be drawn from an attempt that dared to oppose Kant's system directly to Storr's became clear from the letters and writings of the *enrage* Diez. Almost never has anyone drawn from Kant's teaching such far-reaching conclusions for his own thought and life. Though among his peers he encountered almost universal opposition, he nevertheless worked out the model of a position radically opposed to Storr's theology on all points. Only a few years later the same model, from a completely different perspective and with far greater philosophical skill, was elaborated by Schelling.

The fundamental modes of argument of the *Critique of Pure Reason* provided Diez with the arsenal for his general offensive, and he applied these more or less directly to the theological problematic. How does he do this? To begin with, Storr attributes authority to a revelation whose contents cannot be captured by reason, and holds that Christian faith must be founded on this authority. Kant, however, shows that all knowledge is bound to the conditions of possible experience, and further, that these conditions include the possibility of deriving any event from other data of experience. Such a derivation is simply excluded by the concept of revelation itself. Because we can have no experience of God's actions, revelation as such is underivable. Even if a manifestation of God in this world can be thought in accordance with the mere concept of God, it is impossible to make room for such a manifestation in the domain of what man, from his own standpoint, can know anything about. Storr's efforts to show the "authenticity" of the biblical sources, however, had the sole aim of subjecting the divine origin of Jesus's teaching to direct proof. But such a proof is ruled out in principle. Revelation is thus impossible for human beings.

Second, on the same grounds it also follows that the texts of the Gospels, which were, after all, written by human beings, cannot in truth have been divinely inspired texts. Since they do treat of supernatural insights and truths, they must have been written by persons misled by those illusions in human thought whose grounds Kant had revealed in his critique of metaphysical theories. Since reason ensnares itself in contradictions when it oversteps the bounds of possible experience, it is to be expected that such contradictions will also affect the text of the Gospels. Diez inferred from this that the texts advanced as proofs for Storr's theology do not admit of a consistent interpretation in their own terms. In his *Loci* he therefore always attempted, assuming the validity of Storr's principle that theology had to be grounded in Scripture, to derive contradictory conclusions from the literal sense of biblical passages. He also planned to publish a collection of exegetical essays that would follow this mode of argument.

Third, if Storr's biblical criticism really allows the conclusion that Jesus taught and led his life the way the evangelists report, he must have been a "visionary" whom the apostles followed as victims of "superstition." For they could not really know any of the things they sought to pass along.

Fourth, if Storr can show that the spirit of Jesus's ethical teaching is based on the principle that man should also orient himself in his actions to revealed truths and their authority, it follows that Kantian and Christian ethical teaching are incompatible—contrary to the opinion of many who wish to combine them.

Diez knew, of course, that Kant himself maintained that a will that is rational and good leads to a belief in God. From that principle, theologians might conclude that God must be thought of as omnipotent, and that it follows that He must be able to find the means for a revelation recognizable as such. Diez countered all conclusions of this sort with the thesis that practical certainty could never be carried over into the domain of theoretical doctrine. What and for how long we assume— for the sake of the consistency of ethical practice—something that also belongs to the content of ecclesiastical dogmatics depends solely on the circumstances that shape our actions. Dogmatic proofs can never be constructed on the basis of such assumptions.[15]

Diez's position was really nothing but the purest naturalism. But it was bound up with a practical attitude in ethics—in such a manner that it excluded all inferences from ethics that would limit naturalism. Diez knew that other Kantians had not reached these conclusions. He also saw that Reinhold allowed himself to reason about all sorts of theological positions that might be derived from Kant. In addition, his own study of Kant was still incomplete. It now had to be developed with an eye to the controversies forming within the Kantian school itself. Thus as early as 1790, Diez wrote an essay on Reinhold's Elementary Philosophy.[16] The essay has not survived, but the thoughts that grew out of it must have lain at the heart of the conversations in Jena in 1792 in which Diez influenced Reinhold himself.[17] In the spring of 1791 Diez had announced to Süsskind the plan for a "theory of the first principles of all philosophy."[18] He spoke of himself as "audacious" for contemplating so ambitious a project. From this work nothing has survived either. But we can ascertain for ourselves the ends for which he thought he had to elaborate such a theory: it would have meant showing that the foundations of knowledge exposed by Kant permitted no such additional superstructure, as Reinhold himself seemed to think. We have reliable evidence that Diez was "often" talked about in a group that discussed Kantian matters—a group that included Schelling.[19] In his magisterial examination in 1792, Schelling for his part presented as the first of his examination papers an essay entitled "On the Possibility of a Philosophy as Such, with Some Remarks on Reinhold's Elementary Philosophy." His second paper concerned the question of the relationship between Kant's critiques of theoretical and of practical reason. These texts have not survived either, but their relation to Diez's philosophical-theological problematic must be assumed. Thus by 1792 the ground had been laid for the emergence from the *Stift* of new attempts at determining the relation between Kantian philosophy on the one hand and religion and Christian theology on the other.

The *Stift* was supposed to prepare future pastors for their duties. Those who obtained a parish, however, had first to pledge their names in writing to uphold the symbolic books of the church. In contrast to other churches in the state, however, the Stuttgart pledge included not just the Confession of Augsburg but also the Formula of Concord. The latter lays out, down to the smallest details, all the religious elements that Storr's theology in turn had undertaken to justify. In his *Dogmatics* Storr had justified the requirement of a pledged signature. He also identified its meaning with the principle that only those who held themselves to the teachings of Christ and were capable of presenting and defending them could be teachers of a congregation.[20] This ruled out the possibility that one might interpret the signature to mean only that a pastor would not preach against the religious elements, so that he could pass over difficult points in silence.

Diez did not merely write a piece against the rightfulness of requiring such a signature. He also agitated against it—not just in the *Stift* but also in exchanges of correspondence that reached far beyond the borders of Württemberg. For Diez and for many other members of the *Stift*, the requirement of one's signature was the chief hindrance to the vocational path set for them. Storr had appealed to the conscience of his students and insisted that no one can be a Protestant who does not assume the "authority" of holy Scripture as the sole reliable guiding principle concerning teachings and teachers:[21]

To misuse the name of a Protestant Christian teacher for the subversion of the name of Christ and of holy Scripture, and in the guise of a Christian teacher, fraudulently to procure payment for the hostile effort to shake the fundamental pillars of Christianity and of Protestantism—a payment that is meant only for the preservation and defense of Christianity—this no upright and conscientious man can allow himself to do.

Diez took to heart this admonition in the only way still open to him after he had convinced himself of the groundlessness of this theology that laid claim to being the true teaching of the Christian church of his fatherland. I quote a shocking and impressive passage from a letter from Diez to Niethammer of December 1791. In it, the consequences of Diez's critique of theology find expression as clearly as Storr's theology did in the admonition to his students, the future pastors:

Friend! A piece of news that will be as unexpected for you as I am filled with joy to give it to you! I, Master Immanuel Carl Diez, *Repetent* at the Tübingen *Stift*, am . . . resolved to leave high-holy theology, insensible of the charms the strumpet has given herself through false makeup, and insensible of the whore's wages that she has promised me with a certainty she otherwise nowhere possesses . . . and will next Easter go to Jena . . . in order there to pay homage to a new goddess, medicine, and to dedicate myself to her service.

Thus did the doctor's son draw the conclusions to which his inner distress and his Kantianism had driven him in equal measure. Diez died of typhus in 1796 in Vienna. Schelling wrote of Diez to this same Niethammer: "Yes, certainly he was an excellent, worthy man! Do you know that he fell victim to his diligence in the hospitals?"

The church chooses her teachers, so said Storr, with the aim that they not merely teach the true Christian doctrine but also defend it. He himself, however, was the teacher of these teachers. The defense of doctrine was therefore his first task when it became clear to what extent conclusions drawn from Kantian arguments called in question and subverted the authority of his Christianity. It was for these reasons that Storr in 1793 wrote his academic polemic, initially intended for use in the University of Tübingen, under the title *Remarks on Kant's Philosophical Theory of Religion*.[22] In the following year it was translated into German by Süsskind—who in the meantime had been won over to Storr again and had become a *Repetent* in the *Stift*—and published with Süsskind's commentary on the "Grounds for Assurance About the Possibility and Actuality of a Revelation." These remarks were composed with reference to Fichte's first publication but in fact relate to the debate with Diez, his friend. Both writings inaugurated a second phase in the Kant reception in Tübingen theology. Compared to the first, it presents a very different profile.

II

This change in profile was made possible and prompted by changes taking place in the Kantian literature itself. Fichte had, in 1792, published his *Attempt at a Critique of All Revelation*, which first appeared anonymously and which was taken for a work of Kant's. Fichte's book aimed to define the bounds of what could be accepted as revelation. He drew the bounds as a naturalist in that he accepted as possible revelation only what was equally acceptable as a postulate of human reason according to Kant's analysis. But he did not exclude the possibility that certain men and periods, in a condition of complete corruption of the will, might need such revelation. In saying this he was compelled to suppose that God can really issue such revelation, and therefore that man can assure himself that a doctrine represented as God's teaching really is revelation. Thus Fichte's work ended with a conclusion far from Diez's thesis, yet readers had been able to take it for a work of Kant's.

Kant himself began in 1792 with the publication of a philosophical theory of religion in a series of essays. In the spring of 1793 it was available as a book (printed in Jena and thus outside the domain of Prussian censorship). In conception and aim it is entirely different from Fichte's critique of revelation. Kant wishes to show in what way a philosophical theory developed on the basis of the *Critique of Practical Reason* can be used to interpret the religious texts of Christianity. He emphasizes from the start that this interpretation will make no claims to authority with regard to biblical theology, and he carefully avoids all assertions about divine revelation communicated in the Bible. Thus his work has more limited implications than Fichte's critique of revelation with regard to the knowability of divine communications or manifestations. By contrast, Kant works out a genuine theory of justification. It is admittedly only the result of a carefully reasoned form of moral interpretation: Jesus is the personified idea of the purest moral disposition. Insofar as we take on such a disposition, insofar, that is, as we have taken Jesus into ourselves, his death can be *understood* as a lifting of the debt of sin from our earlier lives, a debt we would otherwise have had to continue to bear. At the same time, Jesus's death is the assurance of divine grace, an assurance that this sin will no longer be part of the new human being we have become. In Stäudlin's interpretation of *satisfactio vicaria*, Kant's terse and involved remarks are developed into a distinctive theology of justification that now presents itself as biblical theology.[23]

If one keeps in mind the theological problematic in Tübingen as it stood prior to the appearance of these two works, one can easily understand that they might not be unwelcome to Storr. Fichte's theory is indeed naturalism and thus irreconcilable with Storr's doctrinal principle. But with Fichte the possibility of a revelation as such can no longer be contested. At least the beginning of a defense of Christian doctrine, then, is allowed by one of the preeminent Kantians. Kant derives his whole interpretation from practical reason, and in that sense also remains a naturalist. But he does not treat Christian doctrine as altogether untenable. Inasmuch as he does not attack biblical theology as such, his work offers a starting point for reestablishing that theology in its own right, even in relation to the philosophy of pure practical reason.

With considerable skill, Storr and Süsskind make use of the possibilities that the highest authorities of Kantian naturalism seemed to have offered them. To be sure, they criticize Fichte's and Kant's insistence on the exclusiveness of the claims of practical reason. But their critique is now immanent to Kant's own theory: it is directed toward an adoption of the fundamental ideas of critical moral theology with the goal of laying a new foundation for orthodox church doctrine. For what after all were the grounds of Kant's insistence from the outset that belief in God was indispensable for the good will and the self-consciousness of freedom? It is not at all easy to answer this question consistently on the basis of Kant's own writings. Flatt had already accused Kant of contradiction on this point early on. But Kant had certainly insisted on two reasons throughout: (1) Without belief in God man loses the hopes that are indispensably bound up with the idea of a pure moral disposition and its realization in the world. (2) The belief in God strengthens the powers that work toward the development of a moral disposition, insofar as it simultaneously represents the law of reason as the will of the highest being in the world.

Storr and Süsskind now join to these premises the idea that the theology of the church and the acceptance of revelation from God can and must also strengthen the grounds of conviction and the practical force of moral truth. But if this is the case, and if there is no further reason to contest the possibility of divine revelation as such, one who seeks to better his moral outlook is actually subject to a *duty* not to remain stubbornly indifferent to the proofs for the divinity of a given revelation. With this argument, Storr opposed the isolation of the Kantian moral interpretation from biblical theology. Thereby, he also opposed the indifference that the Kantian enthusiasts among his students showed toward the study of his own dogmatics. Basically, though, his argument aims to endow the demand to study the authenticity of the canonical writings, along with Storr's own theology, with a status approximating that of a postulate of pure practical reason.

Süsskind's reasoning makes clear how far this mode of argument can be extended. It is true, he argues, that faith in the contents of revelation as practical postulates can be required only if those contents have practical significance for our acting from a good will: "Christian revelation [contains] not one single exegetically demonstrable doctrine . . . that [is] merely speculative."[24] Moreover, it is "a duty to investigate precisely, with respect to every theory of revelation, if it can be practical for us, because it is a duty to seek out conscientiously every means of facilitating the determination of our will according to the moral law."[25] This duty extends furthermore to doctrines that are only "positive" and that could never be derived from reason as such. Even church rituals, including participation in Communion, can be justified from postulates: church and sacraments are indispensable means toward the preservation and furthering of Christianity, which in turn rests on revelation and whose doctrines are indispensable means for the furthering of morality. "Thus it is the duty of each to contribute to the preservation of these external arrangements."[26]

One observes with astonishment that the principle of the autonomy of reason begins to present itself in complete harmony with the authority of revelation and the church. It is natural enough to suspect that something strange is going on here. One can admittedly best do justice to Storr's and Süsskind's reasoning if one brings its apologetic character into the foreground—that is, if one assumes that they merely wished to show the Kantians that their own principles ought properly to lead them to the same results they themselves had in fact reached following a quite *different* path. But this picture would not adequately characterize the inner situation in which the Tübingen theologians were caught. Kant had shaken their confidence in non-Kantian methods of proof. Only Flatt was still trying to establish the respectability and theological relevance of older philosophical modes of thought and argument. By contrast, Storr and Süsskind, who in their role as teachers of dogma could not avoid involving themselves in philosophical argumentation, were really caught by the Kantian current in the intellectual climate of their time, a force to which their students had long since adapted. It was only much later, when the Kantian movement, and with it the power of Fichte and Schelling, seemed to be extinguished for a while, that Süsskind dared to come forward with a natural theology he had constructed himself.[27] During the height of the Kantian movement, however, not just the apologetics of Storr's school but also Storr's own dogmatics were full of Kantian insertions and were indeed dependent on them for the stability of their own construction. In Storr's case, as in others, Rudolf Bultmann's thesis proves true: that precisely the most important dogmatics of every age is unable to keep its distance from the philosophy of the day. The price for this in Tübingen was to be paid in the peculiar form of an amalgam of autonomy and authority. Those who have come after therefore scarcely have any reason to cast the first stone.

At the same time, however, one understands why contemporaries who were serious thinkers could not come to terms with this amalgam. To most of those in Tübingen it did indeed at first seem to contain the solution to all doubts and scruples of conscience. From Schelling himself we learn what a degree of influence Storr's and Süsskind's efforts toward the theological domestication of Kant initially achieved. As he wrote to Hegel in a letter of January 6, 1795:

Would you like to know how things are with us?—Dear God, an αὐχμός has occurred that will soon spread all the old weeds. Who will uproot them? We expected everything from philosophy and believed that the shock it imparted even to minds in Tübingen would not fade so soon. But unfortunately it is so! . . . It is true that there are now hordes of Kantians . . . but after much trouble our philosophers have now found a spot . . . and have built huts [there], where it is nice to live. . . . And who will drive them out in this century? . . . To put it bluntly, they have extracted some ingredients of the Kantian system (from the surface, it goes without saying) and prepared from it . . . such strong theological concoctions about *quemcumque locum theologicum* that theology, which was already growing frantic, will soon rise up healthier and stronger than ever. Every possible dogma is now stamped a postulate of practical reason.

Schelling, in his "annoyance with the nonsense of the theologians," contemplated "taking refuge in satire and deriving the whole of dogmatics—including appendages from the darkest centuries—from practical grounds of faith" (to Hegel, Feb. 4, 1795). It was not just a lack of time that kept him from executing this plan but also the fear that the satire would be taken literally by most readers.

III

If we did not know a good deal more about Schelling's thoughts during this period, one of the remarks in the passage quoted would quickly jump to our attention: the Tübingen theologians, he says, had only drawn some ingredients of Kant's system "from the surface" for their philosophical concoctions.[28] Schelling is clearly of the opinion that the true content of Kant's practical philosophy is to be distinguished from what Storr's followers adopted in their exegesis of Kant, though they strove to be true to the text. And when Hegel wrote back (at the end of January 1795) that Fichte's critique of revelation had undoubtedly opened the floodgate to the "nonsense" Schelling mentioned, Schelling agrees with him and expresses the suspicion that Fichte himself may have only wished to write a satire "to poke fun at superstition and so laughingly to win the gratitude of the theologians" (Nov. 4, 1795). And yet Fichte's book had been taken by many Kantians for a work of the Königsberg master himself![29] This passage shows that Schelling had ceased to maintain Kantian doctrine true to Kant's own words and arguments against the Tübingen theologians, or to restore it to its rights.

We must even assume that he had *long since* begun to move in the direction of a new and, as it was soon called, "deeper" grounding of the truths that "with Kant" had only just "dawned" (Nov. 4, 1795). Two years earlier he had already been connected with the undertaking Diez tried to begin in response to similar problems: a "theory of the first grounds of all philosophy" by means of which, as Schelling now says, "the last gates of superstition" will be "slammed shut."

We have already seen that it was Schelling's intention to come out publicly with writings that would achieve precisely this, and thus "to be one of the first to greet Fichte in the land of truth"—not the Fichte of the *Critique of All Revelation*, which after all could just as well have been a satire, but rather the author of the *Wissenschaftslehre*, which had just come into circulation as a series of pamphlets. But Schelling was never a mere follower of Fichte. In the letters to Hegel quoted above, Schelling refers to his plan "to set out the highest principles of all philosophy," an "Ethics à la Spinoza" (Jan. 6, 1795). This brings into play a motif both significant and rich in consequences. Schelling explains the sense in which he wishes this expression to be understood by means of the following principle: "*Philosophy must begin from the unconditioned*" (Feb. 4, 1795, emphasis added). It only remains to ask where, for any philosophy, the unconditioned is to be found. As the subtitle of the work Schelling sent to press in March 1795, *Of the I as Principle of Philosophy: The Unconditional in Human Knowledge*, clearly shows, this principle has for him the status of a methodological orientation for philosophy as a whole. It was doubtless also meant to indicate the character of Fichte's mode of argument to a public who cannot yet have been familiar with Fichte's ideas.

Schelling himself, with Fichte, sets the unconditioned commencement of thought in an absolute I that consists in pure activity and to which we as finite wills have to adapt. Why then does Schelling not simply acknowledge himself a Fichtean—why does he say that he has become a Spinozist? Schelling's further explanations are of course familiar to everyone who is acquainted with the philosophy of this period. But their meaning has still not been determined. This meaning is, however, perfectly suited to set us on the track of another problem in the Tübingen *Stift*—a problem that did not begin with Kant but arose only in 1790, and in which therefore the generation of Diez and his friends no longer participated. Without a grasp of this problem, however, it is impossible adequately to understand the philosophical influence the young students at the *Stift* themselves exerted.

Schelling addresses Hegel as a "confidante of Lessing" (Feb. 4, 1795). Taken together with his own avowal that he is now a Spinozist, all his statements point to a single origin: Friedrich Heinrich Jacobi's book *On the Doctrine of Spinoza*. It had first been published in 1785 and had at the time created as great a sensation as Kant's *Critique of Pure Reason*, for it revealed that Lessing had actually been a Spinozist. For Lessing, the thought of a God who stands above the world had remained incomprehensible—primarily because a creation of the world from nothing was inconceivable. The transcendent, infinite God would therefore have to be replaced by an immanent infinity. Consequently, for Lessing the orthodox conceptions of God "are no more." One can easily see that Jacobi's Spinoza book contains weapons that could have been put to good use in the criticism of orthodox theology. It is also reliably reported that Hölderlin, Hegel, "and other friends" read and thoroughly discussed Jacobi's Spinoza book during their time at the *Stift*.[30]

But was it really only Lessing's Spinozist heresy that captured their attention? Jacobi, the author of the book, did not declare himself a follower of Spinozism. His thesis was rather that, according to Lessing, any philosophy seeking to derive truths about the absolute through syllogistic inferences reduced itself to absurdity. It was therefore always necessary to begin from (philosophical) faith. This faith, however, inevitably and irreconcilably conflicts with what can be known from reasons.

Now it was precisely this thesis of Jacobi's that as early as 1790 had helped Hölderlin out of an initial crisis of faith.[31] At that time, Hölderlin also understood Kant's determination of the boundaries of all knowledge, which must establish conditions for its explanations, as the finite counterpart to Jacobi's unmediated certainty of the infinite. Is it then Jacobi's own doctrine and not the Spinozism of Lessing that fostered the growth of such lively interest in the Spinoza book in the *Stift*? In that case Schelling's assertion that he had now become a Spinozist could not be understood as straightforwardly as one might have thought. It would presuppose a more complex background of discussion and shared reception of literary works during his years at the *Stift*. And it is from precisely this prehistory that one would have to understand why Schelling, a full ten years after the declaration that Lessing was a Spinozist had reached an astonished public, and under the impact of Fichte's *Wissenschaftslehre*, himself became a Spinozist.

To all these questions we have received up to the present no firm answer. One can, however, make some headway if one takes a look at the second edition of the Spinoza book, which appeared in the year 1789. Astonishingly enough, it has never since been printed entirely without omissions.[32] We may, however, suppose that the friends discussed this very edition, and that again for reasons thoroughly specific to Tübingen: Johann Friedrich Flatt, contrary to everything one would suspect, was filled with a deep admiration for Jacobi.[33] In one of his reviews of Jacobi in the *Tübingischen Gelehrten Anzeigen* he assigns to Jacobi's second book, *David Hume on Faith*, "a truly outstanding place among all the philosophical works of our age." He further says it is impossible to read this book through "without feeling admiration and respect for the truly great man it has as its author."[34] His review of the second edition of the Spinoza book[35] begins in a very similar tone: "The more the reviewer reveres the profundity and acuity of this famous author," and so on. Jacobi in turn esteemed Flatt highly. In an appendix to the second edition he names him "an acute and learned investigator whom I admire greatly."[36]

Jacobi himself refers us to this appendix, and so does Flatt, the teacher of the *Stiftler*, who in his review refers to it as one of the two most important essays in this work. But what is the content of this text, to which the friends in the *Stift* were drawn with such force in 1790? In it Jacobi had sought to fulfill the obligation to base his own doctrine of belief not just on the reduction of Spinozism to fatalism and absurdity but also in a fundamental theory of his own. The outline of this theory is as follows: human consciousness forms itself under the aegis of two fundamental representations: a context of what is conditioned, and the absolute or unconditioned. All explanations occur in this context of what is conditioned, and therefore none of them can disclose an unconditioned. We need not even look for the unconditioned, for we have the same certainty of its existence as of our own conditioned existence—indeed an even greater certainty. Thus, philosophy can and must always begin from the unconditioned. But since this unconditioned lies outside the sphere of distinct knowledge, we can only assume it as it is given to us: "it [simply] is," and in this sense it corresponds, according to Jacobi, to what had been, for Spinoza, "being" (*das Seyn*) or substance.[37]

These thoughts also provide grounds for resisting Storr's orthodoxy—and indeed such resistance does not directly entail philosophical naturalism. Storr wanted to demonstrate the certainty of revelation by means of carefully considered arguments and thus, from Jacobi's point of view, to capture the infinite for us in what is properly speaking a merely finite mode of knowledge. Jacobi's line of thought can moreover be brought into relation with Kant.[38] Critical philosophy wished to subordinate everything to the immediate consciousness of the moral vocation of man. It can therefore be brought together with conceptions of the absolute that differ from those affirmed by Jacobi: Jacobi put in the place of the unconditioned the personal God of deism. However, he lacked convincing grounds for precisely that move.

With the appearance of Fichte's *Wissenschaftslehre* Jacobi's theory of the necessity of beginning from the unconditioned that cannot be mediated by acts of reasoning necessarily appeared in a new light—a light that might well have given occasion to study the historical Spinoza. And immediately, still in 1794, Schelling put Fichte's absolute I in the place of the unconditioned, which he defined in the manner of Jacobi and whose origin he traced back to Spinoza's *Ethics*. He explained this to Hegel by reminding him of Jacobi's fundamental principle: "Philosophy must begin from the unconditioned." Schelling is a Spinozist, however, in several senses—first of all in the sense that he refuses the status of the unconditioned to the orthodox conceptions. He is also a Spinozist in a subsidiary sense: he recognizes that the place of the unconditioned could be filled differently, and even with the consciousness of the absolute I, in a way that leads to Spinoza's philosophical conclusions rather than Fichte's. Finally, and no doubt above all, Schelling is a Spinozist in that he interprets Spinoza's departure from the definition of infinite substance in the same sense that Jacobi had. Jacobi, an adversary of Spinoza but nevertheless influenced by the thought of his greatest opponent, had appropriated this departure for his own and for all thought that organizes itself according to the founding truth of the unconditioned.

In this way Schelling, allying himself with both Jacobi and Kant, moves to the terrain of a foundational philosophy that from the outset goes beyond Fichte's own arguments yet understands and applauds Fichte in a context that Fichte had not initiated. This explains the swiftness, the ease, and also the independent character of Schelling's reception of Fichte. Thus we can grasp the contours of the intellectual context that leads from Jacobi and Kant through the problematic of the young students of the *Stift* to the formation of their mature achievements.

This gives us the means to consider and investigate other trends in the domain in which Schelling took his bearings. It also allows us to interpret them in light of the evidence known to us from the later course of development of the three friends from the *Stift*. In particular, it is now possible to make intelligible what enabled Hölderlin, as early as 1795, to oppose his own conception of the absolute to Fichte's *Wissenschaftslehre*—probably the first of Fichte's disciples to do so. And we can further begin to understand what ideas Hölderlin and Schelling may have exchanged when they met in the summer and winter of 1795 for long discussions in the *Stift* and in Nürtingen, where, as Hölderlin reports, they spoke "without always agreeing" (*StA* VI, p. 203). The few available sources can, if followed persistently, cast more than a glimmer of light on the movement that began in the *Stift* and was to change the intellectual world.

With it, theology was also transformed, along with the language it used. Those who came out of the *Stift* eventually developed ideas that made it possible to begin from God without thereby forcing freedom to submit to conditions external and foreign to it. They also shed light on the movements of consciousness that begin within consciousness yet bring it into conflicts corresponding to those they themselves experienced at the *Stift*. These conflicts are resolved, however, if the path of consciousness reaches an understanding of the unconditioned and absolute—the absolute that is internal to consciousness yet precedes it as its own ultimate ground.

The transformation of theology was indeed effected above all by Friedrich Schleiermacher. His thoughts developed later, but from motivations and sources closely related to those of the students of the *Stift*. In his thought, however, one does not find the same unremitting intensity with which Hölderlin, from the Tübingen context, worked by means of his "speculative pro and con" (*StA* VI, p. 183) toward insights of his own, and with which Hegel elevated the shared ideal of their youth to the form of reflection, that is, to his system.[39] To be sure, Schelling thought and wrote with greater fluency. But he was drawn throughout his life into a long series of intellectual projects, none of which satisfied him. And none of these reached the depth and density that makes Hölderlin's and Hegel's work so unforgettable.

Anything from the pens of such figures must have struck Storr and Flatt as naturalism and as confirmation of their worst fears. They put their hopes in better times, when the spirit of the age would dissipate and God would lead his church back on the proper path. Any understanding of why this path could not simply retrace their own was denied to them. The intellectual climate in which they had to orient themselves eluded their command, although they asserted their convictions with all the strength of their conscience and intellect. But precisely in doing so they unleashed in large part the movement whose further course in Germany they could only watch with resignation. If their own university today proudly memorializes the very movement that began at their *Stift*, it also has every reason to remember Storr and Flatt and to hold them in high esteem.

Translated by Abraham Anderson

Hölderlin's Philosophical Beginnings: On the Occasion of the Publication of a Page by Hölderlin in Niethammer's *Stammbuch*

Oft erfüllet uns Gott, was das erzitternde
Volle Herz kaum zu wünschen wagt.
Wie von Träumen erwacht, sehn wir dann unser Glük
Sehn's mit Augen, und glauben's kaum.

Often God grants us what the full
Trembling heart hardly dares to wish for.
As if wakened from dreams, we then see our happiness
See it with our eyes, and scarcely believe it.

Klopstock

Tüb. 20 March
1790

Written in fond memory
Your friend
C. Hölderlin

THE lines Hölderlin wrote in Niethammer's *Stammbuch** he took from Friedrich Gottlieb Klopstock's ode "To Bodmer."[1] In his inscription, however, he changed the first of the lines in such a way that the verses can stand by themselves. One must nevertheless keep in mind the structure and the argument of the entire ode if one is to grasp clearly the meaning of the entry from Hölderlin's own point of view.

Klopstock's ode interprets and makes vivid the depth of the happiness the poet experienced when he "for the first time met Bodmer's embrace," and it does so in contrast to all the renunciations God's order imposes on the lives of mortals: God separates through insuperable distances of time and space many who seem destined for each other.

---

* A *Stammbuch* is a personal album of memorabilia in which friends and relatives would enter poems, quotations, and drawings. The *Stammbuch* became obsolete in the nineteenth century. —Ed.

For Him they are eternally and infinitely present in their relations with one another. Nevertheless, and precisely because of His intuition of this, He separates them—forever. For this reason, the happiness He reveals to those His insight nonetheless brings together is so much the greater. The longer part of the ode, then, which treats of those divisions that cannot be overcome before God, ends with the lines:

> Also ordnet es Gott, der in die Fernen sieht,
>   Tiefer hin ins Unendliche!

> Thus God orders it, who sees far off,
>   deeper into the infinite!

These are then immediately followed by the lines expressing the inconceivable happiness of those allowed to find each other, which Hölderlin chose for Niethammer:

> Oft erfüllet er auch, was das erzitternde
>   Volle Herz kaum zu wünschen wagt.

> Often He also grants what the full
>   Trembling heart hardly dares to wish for.

Hölderlin, preserving the sense of the lines, replaced the two words *er auch* ("He also") with the words *uns Gott* ("God . . . us") and so fashioned an independently meaningful text for his inscription.

In every other respect the inscription is faithful to the wording and punctuation of the original; moreover, it gives the precise arrangement of Klopstock's lines, so that one can assume that Hölderlin wrote the page in the *Stammbuch* with a printed copy of Klopstock's ode open before him.[2]

For Hölderlin, the idea behind Klopstock's lines remained present and important long after the inscription in Niethammer's *Stammbuch*. It underlies the final turn of thought in the concluding stanza of "The Migration" ("Die Wanderung"). Here everything divinely born, like the servant maidens of heaven, eludes anyone who would win it by "stealth"; indeed it becomes a (confusing, disturbing) dream to the one who loses hold of it. But

> Oft überraschet es einen,
> Der eben kaum es gedacht hat.

> Often it takes by surprise the one
> who has hardly given it a thought.

Hölderlin has crossed out the word *gehofft* ("hoped") and replaced it with *gedacht* ("thought").[3] One can follow the history of the motif, then, from Klopstock's lines to Hölderlin's thoughts on the possible presence of the divine as these are found in his hymns. To do so, however, is not the task of what follows.

It can be assumed that Hölderlin, as he inscribed the lines on the page of Niethammer's *Stammbuch* from an edition of Klopstock, referred to the original only in order to be able to cite the text accurately. They must already have been known to him and had meaning for him—with their precise and comprehensive relevance, it can hardly be supposed that he stumbled upon them in the course of merely browsing through Klopstock's work.

The inscription, unknown until now,[4] makes possible a number of observations and reflections. We must begin with Hölderlin's relation to Niethammer and then consider the relation between the entry and the circumstances of Niethammer's life at the time in order to arrive at an account of the situation in which Hölderlin wrote the inscription in Niethammer's *Stammbuch*.[5] These reflections lead to conclusions about Hölderlin's path to philosophy.

Hölderlin and Niethammer in the Year 1789

Friedrich Philipp Immanuel Niethammer was born on March 24, 1766.[6] He attended the same monastery schools as Hölderlin, subsequently entered the Tübingen *Stift*, and concluded his university studies by passing the theological examination in the fall of 1789. Hölderlin, who was his fourth cousin, was related to him in a number of ways.[7] It may be that the informal *Du* in Hölderlin's inscription, which would otherwise be quite unexpected given their difference in age and status, can be explained by this fact. Hölderlin also calls himself *Dein Freund*. The title *Freund* (often together with the formal *Ihr*) has admittedly always been the rule in *Stammbüchern*, and the request for an inscription, when not addressed to celebrities, was really equivalent to the assumption of a relation of friendship. Such a relationship need not have been very deep, especially if it had been established in youth. The conjunction of *Dein* with *Freund* in Hölderlin's inscription, then, could also be explained by the use of *Du* between cousins and by their fairly casual friendship during their time at the seminary. We have, however, grounds for suspecting a deeper intimacy between Hölderlin and Niethammer during the year 1789. And the existence and contents of the page in the *Stammbuch* strengthens this supposition considerably, as shall become clear.

On September 29, 1789, Hölderlin's friend and classmate from Maulbronn, Christian Ludwig Bilfinger, wrote Niethammer a letter in which he alludes to a special relationship between Niethammer and Hölderlin. The allusion cannot be interpreted with any certainty. But the letter also tells of Hölderlin's current whereabouts and comments on his relation to Christian Ludwig Neuffer in a way that presumes Niethammer's special interest in Hölderlin.[8] Bilfinger moreover seems to imply that Niethammer is less interested in him, Bilfinger, than in Hölderlin, although at the same time Bilfinger professes his "rather considerable devotion" to Niethammer.

Bilfinger had broken off his studies at the seminary in the fall of 1789 in order to begin studying for a law degree (*StA* VI, p. 495). Apparently before his departure he had made an entry in Niethammer's *Stammbuch* on August 16, 1789, signing without the intimate *Du* as *Ihr Freund*, as he also signed a letter one month later. One can already see from this that we cannot rule out the possibility that the *Du* between Niethammer and Hölderlin derived from an especially close relationship in 1789. Moreover, very few of Hölderlin's classmates are represented in Niethammer's *Stammbuch* at all.

Somewhat more light can be shed on the relationship between Niethammer and Hölderlin if one is clear about the reasons that led Hölderlin to choose the verses from Klopstock. In general, sentences quoted in *Stammbuch* inscriptions can be understood in terms of the convictions, the preferences, and the experiences that two people shared. Klopstock's ode and the lines chosen by Hölderlin have, however, an even more personal meaning. They speak of a longing that is so great, that so entirely fills the heart, and that knows its hopes to be so imperiled that it cannot even crystallize into a wish, but that nevertheless finds fulfillment. Anyone who chooses to write these lines in a friend's *Stammbuch* must be referring to such a wish in his friend's heart—either to give him hope or to share his joy in the fulfillment of the wish—and thus puts these sentiments, by means of the quoted verses, in a concrete context.

If one recalls the train of thought of Klopstock's ode, that what we scarcely dare to hope it entrusts to the inscrutable judgment of God, one will have to assume that anyone who quotes Klopstock's ode with an awareness of its whole meaning must also have in mind an experience in the life of the friend, an experience that, like Klopstock's encounter with Bodmer, was more important than all earthly desires. It can be shown that this was in fact the way things stood.

The Relation Between the *Stammbuch* Inscription and Niethammer's Path to Philosophy

Niethammer had to present a dissertation accompanied by a detailed autobiography in the course of assuming his position in the faculty of theology at Jena in 1797.[9] From this Latin text we learn the circumstances Hölderlin is referring to in his entry from Klopstock's ode: after noting his success at the examination in theology, Niethammer mentions that up to that time he scarcely even knew the critical philosophy by name.[10] Immediately, however, as the result of mere chance, he had begun to sense that he would have to attend to it seriously. After the examination he went back to the *Stift* in order to continue his studies until suitable employment should arise.[11] He was then asked by a *Magister* (and hence neither Bilfinger nor Hölderlin), whom he had already tutored in logic, to give lessons in theological moral theory (*doctrina moralis theologica*). And since Niethammer judged that he himself still had much to learn in this domain, he undertook the task and began to study the philosophical and theological textbooks. The best way to continue the story is to cite the following passage from Niethammer's text, translated from the Latin:[12]

And yet the more I investigated and the deeper I penetrated, the more quickly and utterly the foundations of this science seemed to collapse. And my doubts grew so much that it soon became necessary to give up this task of tutoring. In this state of doubt I had open ears for what was reported about the usefulness and the significance of the critical philosophy and about the advantages by which it surpassed other kinds of theory, and which increased continually; and I have never wished for anything more than that I might find in this way of philosophizing the conviction I had fruitlessly sought in others, and that it would be permitted to me to trace out its whole circumference. I was deterred, however, partly by the difficulties of this study, which at that time were greater than they are now, and partly by the overwhelming anxiety caused by received opinion concerning the extent of the difficulties, and did not believe I could make any progress studying on my own. A hope that survived this fear, and my only wish, was that it might be allowed to me to direct my work on this philosophy under the guidance of a man who, because he was himself initiated into its secrets, could easily make it accessible to others. To whom better than Reinhold, who already enjoyed such high esteem throughout Germany, could such a hope and such a wish turn?

My wish was granted to me by a lucky chance. A certain man, to whom I would joyfully give public thanks were it not most ungrateful to deprive him of the only fitting reward to one who does good and acts justly—that awareness of remaining hidden—offered me on his own impulse the means that permitted me to visit Jena for a semester.

Niethammer left for Jena during the Easter vacation of 1790. It has never been established with certainty who it was that made his visit possible, but he was later able to extend it to a whole year through a scholarship from the church fund.[13] He had been fully informed about living and study conditions in Jena by a friend, Karl Fischer.[14] Shortly before Niethammer's departure for Jena several of his friends besides Hölderlin made inscriptions in his *Stammbuch*, in particular Carl Immanuel Diez (on March 23), who wrote on the back of an older page of the *Stammbuch* inscribed by Diez's friend Klett—possibly for lack of time to prepare his own page to insert in the *Stammbuch*. Diez played an important part in Niethammer's decision to go to Jena;[15] this was the basis of the friendship between the two, which lasted through the years from Diez's medical studies in Jena (1792–94) to the abrupt end of Diez's life.

Before we delve into the history of the period prior to Niethammer's departure for Jena, we ought to note separately how precisely Hölderlin's Klopstock inscription is related to the state of mind Niethammer found himself in before his departure, sure that he would now be able to go to Jena. Seven years later, in his autobiography, Niethammer described his state of mind in words that could scarcely come any closer to those in Hölderlin's Klopstock quotation: never had he desired anything more than to arrive at a secure sense of conviction by means of the critical philosophy. Because he did not have faith in his own ability to study it successfully by himself, there remained only the hope and the "sole" desire to study under Reinhold. And it was a "lucky chance" that granted him this wish in the form of the generous patron (probably Krais). No doubt these statements were written with hindsight and for a self-confident Jena faculty that must have felt confirmed in its view of itself by Niethammer's high estimation of the situation in Jena. Yet Niethammer's subsequent declaration that he is indebted to Jena for the "palingenesis" of his spirit, and that he would congratulate himself as long as he lived[16] on his decision to go to Jena, sounds like something other than flattery tendered with an eye to academic success, especially since he had already won general recognition in the philosophical faculty. His look back at the half year after his theological examination in Tübingen, in which he connected his hope to study with Reinhold with the greatest desire of his life, the desire for lasting conviction, is therefore entirely credible.

Hölderlin, when he selected the verses from Klopstock for Niethammer, must have known that Niethammer's hope to study in Jena was rooted in his life's quest for firm conviction and that this hope was therefore uniquely important to him. He must also have known that Niethammer regarded the offer of his sponsor as an incomparably lucky twist of fate. These are the experiences Hölderlin is referring to with the verses from Klopstock—the poet who had assured him of the possibility of giving voice in the German language to the crucially significant experiences in our lives, in lines expressing at once thanks and celebration.

In an important sense, Hölderlin also wrote the lines so that he himself would be remembered. While writing them, the whole movement of thought in Klopstock's ode stood before his eyes. Behind his inscription, then, there is a reference to himself and to his own life in all the lines he does *not* quote:

> Der die Schickungen lenkt, heißet den frömsten Wunsch,
>   Mancher Seligkeit goldnes Bild
> Oft verwehen, und ruft da Labyrinth hervor,
>   Wo ein Sterblicher gehen will.
>
> He who directs our fate
>   Often commands the most pious wish
> And golden images of blessedness
>   To fade away, calling forth labyrinths
> Where a mortal desires to go.

Renunciation is our *usual* lot. But in its light we experience our happiness, if it is granted us, in the whole depth of our hearts—"and scarcely believe it." The dreams from which it wakes us are those of a full heart, trembling precisely because it knows that a too deeply cherished wish, if forever denied, will cast a shadow on our lives and leave us sighing. It is not just wishful dreams, but also burdensome dreams between anxious hope and the need for renunciation, from which divine dispensation awakens us when it is suddenly granted. Niethammer experienced such happiness; Hölderlin did not. It is in this sense, too, that he wrote Klopstock's lines for Niethammer with reference to his own past.

In the fall of 1789 Hölderlin flirted with the idea of leaving the *Stift* and studying law. He argued with himself and with his mother about this plan, which would have freed him from a situation he found oppressive.[17] Hegel too had wanted to study law rather than theology.[18] This would have suited his particular talents and inclinations, which ultimately led him to become the author of the most important theory of right and history of the nineteenth century. For Hölderlin, however, whose poetic gift was already unfolding and who cultivated it with an ambition he often professed even then, the study of law would have been nothing but an escape. Nevertheless he submitted with a heavy heart to circumstances, and to the will of his mother: "Parental counsel comforts after all. Whatever happens, I at least have this consolation, at all events!" (*StA* VI, pp. 15–16, letter 29).

Hölderlin's resignation to life at the *Stift* must also be seen in relation to the decision of Bilfinger, who had left the *Stift* in the fall of 1789 to study law. And Niethammer's friend Fischer was already in Jena to study law and wrote him from there, where Schiller had just assumed his professorship. In the summer Bilfinger had sought Niethammer's counsel and company—at a time when he and Hölderlin must already have been close. Even if Niethammer's crisis of faith arose only in the fall of that year, one must nonetheless suspect that his inclination to the pastoral vocation had already weakened before then. He returned to the *Stift* to study, without seeking a position as a vicar, until he could find employment "suitable to him."[19] Between Niethammer, Bilfinger, and Hölderlin there must have been either direct or indirect discussion of all the prospects theological study might either open up or close off. And Diez, Niethammer's friend, soon saw his Kantian studies and his own influence on the direction of Niethammer's philosophical ambitions in connection with his own "long-contemplated apostasy"[20]—an apostasy Diez would carry out in 1792 by transferring to medical studies at Jena.

Hölderlin's inscription, then, is at once an entry into his friend's sense of a happiness scarcely to be hoped for and a memento of his own situation in life, which, with regard to his study plans, was marked by a sense of resignation in the face of something inevitable.

Hölderlin's Letters to Niethammer in Light of the *Stammbuch* Inscription

The page in the *Stammbuch* taken together with Bilfinger's letter to Niethammer provides us with an insight into the relation between Hölderlin and Niethammer that would not have been possible on the basis of the three letters to Niethammer from 1795 to 1801 taken by themselves. These letters were written after Hölderlin's months in Jena. One might have thought that the closer acquaintance between the two derived from Hölderlin's stay in Jena. It now seems clear, however, that the warm reception Hölderlin found with Niethammer, who had in the meantime advanced to a professorship, had its basis not just in their distant blood relationship or in their common Swabian fatherland and place of study. While at the *Stift*, Hölderlin and Niethammer must have been even closer than when they were in Jena.

In the letters to Niethammer it is easy to find traces of this early intimacy. Thus the first letter begins with the two sentences: "I had always
wanted to say so much to you [*Dir*] and have never said anything to
you. I had hoped to write so many things to you, and have not yet written you anything."[21] The first of the two sentences must refer to Hölderlin's shyness in Jena. Both sound as if Hölderlin had wanted to resume
the intimacy of the Tübingen period in the years 1789 and 1790. For
clearly after this time, and also later in Jena, he had more to say than
the "so much" he later still hoped to write, though in neither case did
he manage to say it. The second letter acknowledges Niethammer's
gentle admonition and his warm interest in Hölderlin's situation, not
just in the promised manuscript.[22] Would Niethammer have come to
trust Hölderlin enough to ask him to contribute to his highly acclaimed
journal just on the basis of a public acquaintance with him, one conditioned by the milieu and the social life of Jena? Maybe, for we now
know that during his Jena months Hölderlin had conceived ideas with
profound implications.[23] Yet it will be more illuminating if we can trace
the lively discussions of Jena back to an earlier friendship at the *Stift*, a
friendship that convinced Niethammer of Hölderlin's talent and at once
led him to care for his well-being.

In the third letter too, which is suffused with Hölderlin's disappoint-
ment at Niethammer's silence, Hölderlin speaks of the "concern with
which you followed my life in days past" and of the "friendship, in
which I could once rejoice." And he recalls Niethammer's "counsel,"
"which previously you did not refuse me, when I asked you for it."[24] It
is likely that this all refers to matters in the year before Niethammer's
departure for Jena. Niethammer's friendliness during those months,
which Hölderlin mentions warmly a number of times in his letters,
would more likely have been the consequence of an earlier friendship
than the cause of a new one, for the relationship, on Hölderlin's side,
was now cloaked in diffidence. This attitude can be explained by Hölderlin's knowledge that he had not yet been able to show any evidence
of his labor, while Niethammer's work had been recognized by the
world early on, and was so increasingly.[25]

In the summer of 1789, Niethammer, Bilfinger, and Hölderlin must
already have been caught up in discussions about a vocation other than
the priesthood. That autumn Niethammer fell into his crisis of faith,
which Hölderlin must have known all about, and known it moreover
from Niethammer's confidences as a friend, so that he could make use
of it in an inscription in the *Stammbuch* that at the same time expressed
his own concerns. This could also be why he was one of the few who
made any inscription in Niethammer's *Stammbuch* at all at the time of

his departure. He was in fact the only one who did so with any clear reference to Niethammer's own experience. In contrast to the discussions of the previous summer, Niethammer's crisis was defined by theoretical doubts of a kind that led him to place his hope in philosophy. And so, in the end, Hölderlin's inscription also raises the question how Niethammer's course of study, which brought on his doubt, is to be cast in relation to Hölderlin's academic experience and so to the question concerning Hölderlin's own philosophical beginnings.

Two Stages on Hölderlin's Way to Philosophy

Niethammer's task was to teach moral theology, a subject in which the truths of religion must be represented in their practical efficacy in the cultivation of a Christian life.[26] In this discipline, which had first assumed doctrinal form a century before, the grounds for belief in doctrinal teachings and instruction concerning the grounds for moral conduct are blended together, so that in it every change in the theory of metaphysical knowledge and of the foundations of moral theory has immediate and direct effect. One could write a long essay on the way in which the new Kantian theory of the impossibility of a proof for the existence of God and of the foundation of morality in the autonomy of the will necessarily affected these concerns in moral theology.[27] Kantian philosophy, which had been gaining popularity in Tübingen since 1785 partly through Flatt's teaching and partly through increasing knowledge of the literature, by the later 1780s began to spread like wildfire. Many of the advanced students there began to write qualifying essays (*specimina*) on Kantian themes.[28]

The Kantian circle around Diez, which drew radical conclusions from Kant's theory for the critique of religion, attained the high point of its influence during Diez's period as *Repetent*. Diez is certainly justified in ascribing to himself an influence on Niethammer's course of studies in the fall of 1789. Considering the state of Diez's studies at the time, this influence can have stemmed only from an examination of the consequences of Kant's critique of metaphysics for the philosophy of religion and from a view of the importance of the study of Reinhold for clarifying and securing the truth of criticism. The critique of metaphysics must also account for the fact that Niethammer saw "the foundation" of moral theology "collapse."[29] The hope for instruction from Reinhold became the basis for Niethammer's desire to go to Jena and was thus the occasion for Hölderlin's inscription.

Since Hölderlin was caught up in this web of issues, it must be assumed that his own studies were not unaffected by them. Indeed, there are clear indications of this in the letter to his mother accompanying the text of his second sermon. Hölderlin reports to his mother with all due clarity concerning his philosophical studies of the previous year (*StA* VI, pp. 63 ff., letter 41). Since the letter was written in February 1791, the beginning of his studies, which is what Hölderlin is talking about, can be dated to the beginning of the year 1790. Hölderlin writes:

> I studied that part of philosophy that treats of the rational proofs for the existence of God and of His attributes that we can know from nature, and with an interest of which I am not ashamed, although it led me for a time to thoughts that would perhaps have made you uneasy had you known of them. For I quickly sensed that these rational proofs for the existence of God and also for immortality were so imperfect that they could be overthrown altogether by clever opponents, at least in their principal parts.

It is these themes and conclusions that must have had a central significance for the rise of Niethammer's doubts as well. One may well suspect that the parts of metaphysics that could not hold firm are here called "principal parts" since it is on them that the system of theological doctrine in matters of dogma and morals rests.

Hölderlin continues by saying that "writings by and about Spinoza"[30] fell into his hands while he found himself in this condition, and he reports on Jacobi's conclusions concerning the implications of Spinoza's theory. But those thoughts, which he said might well have made his mother uneasy, are still different from those drawn from Spinoza. Hölderlin in fact clearly says that his doubts arose *before* the encounter with Jacobi and Spinoza, and that they were in some measure calmed through this encounter. Hölderlin's doubts early in the year seemed primarily concerned with reason's power to yield knowledge. But the way he talks about these ideas and the anxiety they might awaken shows clearly enough that they must have involved doubts concerning even the tenability of the truths of religion, doubts that could then be suspended provisionally through the separation of Spinozistic reason and Christian revelation in the manner of Jacobi.

Such doubts were also surely familiar to Niethammer, since they are precisely the ones laid at his door by Diez. The hope Niethammer placed in the critical philosophy, then, is for that very reason not merely a hope for philosophical clarity. It is the hope for a conviction that would allow him to be clear about the relation between reason and doctrine in matters of faith. When in the following year Hölderlin writes to his mother that he has achieved such clarity, he says that it was made possible by Jacobi's distinction between theory and truth. Niethammer dedicated all his philosophical effort to a clarification of the relation between the critique of reason and the truth of revelation, which soon turned him into an advocate of Fichte's theory in the *Attempt at a Critique of All Revelation*.[31]

The earliest philosophical manuscript from Hölderlin's hand that has come down to us is his notes on Jacobi's Spinoza book. These notes cannot be characterized as mere excerpts. They must be understood instead as an attempt to make intelligible the discussion between the position of Spinoza, as Lessing had presented it to Jacobi, and Jacobi's own position, by examining the text of the Spinoza book. A thorough analysis of the manuscript from this point of view, with an eye to the philosophical studies that preceded it and the purpose of its composition, remains to be done. A great deal could be learned concerning the state of Hölderlin's philosophical orientation at the time he wrote these notes by an attempt to interpret Hölderlin's view of Jacobi's text.

We should make note of just two other findings that shed some light on Hölderlin's ideas concerning the either/or represented by Spinoza and Jacobi. First, the notes imply that Hölderlin had already studied Kant. For they import Kantian elements into the development of the doctrine of Spinoza that Jacobi puts into Lessing's mouth. This becomes clear in the selection of the passages from the Jacobi book and from the emphases in the selection. It becomes clear above all from the fact that Hölderlin sets forth some of Spinoza's theorems in terms of Kantian concepts that cannot be found in Jacobi's text. Thus Hölderlin interprets Lessing/Spinoza's predicate "infinite" as "indeterminabilis" (*StA* IV, p. 207, l. 28). And he takes the appearance of the term "the manifold" as an occasion for relating it, with respect to succession and duration, to the specifically Kantian terms "form" and "appearance" (ibid. p. 208, ll. 1–2). Already in Hölderlin's notes, then, we see at work what was to be the characteristic procedure of the texts Hegel and Schelling wrote in Tübingen, and of a good portion of the literature taking its point of departure from Kant, namely the reformulation of historical positions in Kantian language.

Second, it is no less significant that these Kantian reformulations are to be found only in the summary of Spinoza's position as maintained by Lessing. One can conclude from this that in writing the notes Hölderlin was already inclined to regard the implications of the Kantian critique as bound up with the foundations of Spinoza's theory precisely where the conclusions of the theory as such had to be drawn. Jacobi's own position would then appear at once as a counterpoint to both Spinoza and Kant—a counterpoint that would be in a unique position to defend freedom and an active and omniscient God against all philosophy. In the philosophical position Hölderlin himself developed more than four years later in Jena, Kant and Spinoza have once again become separated. However, this Spinoza can now admit the freedom of a consciousness related to objects in Kant's sense (cf. already *StA* IV, p. 207, ll. 12–24). Moreover, he is given a theoretical position that now corresponds to the position Jacobi had earlier constructed in favor of the reality of freedom and the existence of God—a position Jacobi himself maintained was irreconcilable with Spinoza's doctrines. Hölderlin's Jena position therefore transported Spinoza into the position that had earlier characterized Jacobi—but now surrendering Jacobi's personal God while preserving the freedom in finitude that emerges from "being" through original division (*Urteilung*). Traces of this position can already be recognized in the early notes on the Spinoza book—at least in retrospect, and as long as we avoid the view that those initial movements would necessarily lead to the Jena position.

If one follows these reflections one sees that this renewed assurance of the truths of Christian faith won through Jacobi's own theory, which Hölderlin reports to his mother in 1791, can hardly have lasted long. In his way of appropriating the train of thought of the Spinoza book one recognizes the factors that soon made it unstable again. The notes on the Spinoza book lead too easily toward a new position in which Kant's analysis of the correlates of knowledge are inwardly and systematically bound up with another truth, presupposed in it and surpassing it, which can no longer be reconciled with the truth of Christianity. This truth too, it must be acknowledged, can no more be arrived at by the method of argument proper to the classical theological doctrines of metaphysics than could Jacobi's. Nevertheless, it differs from a truth of faith. Because of its content it also differs from any assurance in the personal God of Christian revelation, and even from Jacobi's deistic certainty concerning God.

Aside from all this, Hölderlin's notes on the Spinoza book at any rate confirm that his appropriation of Jacobi and Spinoza occurred on the basis of a previous study of Kant's philosophy that was at once fairly thorough and rooted in issues having to do with Hölderlin's orientation in life. The relative chronology of Hölderlin's studies, first of Kant and then of Jacobi/Spinoza, is therefore confirmed by the earliest surviving text. This relative chronology of the second phase of study, it is true, cannot be immediately converted into any definite determination of the beginning point of the second phase. It is quite possible that Hölderlin became familiar with the writings "by and about Spinoza" (*StA* VI, p. 64, letter 41; the order is also worth noticing) before the summer semester of 1790—this is possible in particular for Hölderlin's initial study of Jacobi's Spinoza book. Only the beginning of his philosophical studies in general with a study of Kant's critique of metaphysics can be placed with great certainty in the early months of the year 1790.

Neuffer's ode "To Hölderlin" of 1790 provides a further clue to Hölderlin's philosophical studies in that year:

> Endlos quälest nur du dich mit Erforschungen,
> Die kein endlicher Geist irgend ergründen kann,
> Steigst in's leere Gebiet täuschender Träume.

> Endlessly you torture yourself with researches
> Which no finite spirit can ever fathom,
> And climb into the empty region of deceptive dreams.

> (StA VII, pp. 195 f.)

Neuffer's summons to *carpe diem* culminates in the poet's call to song: "Take the lyre, which you have long left untouched!" Granted, it is impossible to determine with certainty when Neuffer's poem was composed and to what part of the year it refers. But one can assume that his summons can scarcely have been needed in the early months of the Alderman's Days that the alliance of friends celebrated,[32] for in this period Hölderlin wrote the first Tübingen hymns for the book of the alliance. The weeks after "To Silence" ("An die Stille") was entered on Hölderlin's third Alderman's Day were no doubt occupied with preparations for the master's examination, and so at any rate scarcely free for the lyre, wine, and dance as opposed to the writing desk.[33] In that case, Neuffer must have been referring either to the end of the year or to the beginning. In any event, we can date to the first months of the year Hölderlin's "Tübingen Castle" ("Burg Tübingen," StA I, pp. 101 ff.), a poem whose underlying tone still places it closer to the elegically colored odes of the second half of 1789 than to the early hymns of the following spring. Hölderlin does not seem to have written any poetry in the winter months of the beginning of the year, and these are the months during which the studies that he was talking about in the letter to his mother must have gotten under way. By the end of August Hölderlin says, with emphasis: "There is still a great deal more I intend to do. I may say to you as your son, without the appearance of immodesty, that an ongoing, continuous study, in particular of philosophy, quickly became a necessity for me."[34] Here for the first time, Hölderlin makes it known that his philosophical studies have acquired a new significance for him, over and beyond preparing him for theology and a pastoral vocation. Such a state of mind already presupposes a period of continual preoccupation with philosophy. One would suspect that Hölderlin's self-confidence, which even leads him to hint in the letter to his mother that something original might be expected from him in philosophy, itself presupposes his already having begun to come to terms with Jacobi and Spinoza.

The Inception and the Form of Hölderlin's Thought

There is sufficient reason to believe that the first signs of Hölderlin's independence in philosophy date from the period when Niethammer became convinced that all his hopes lay in Jena. Niethammer's lack of confidence in his ability to survey the critical philosophy on his own gave Hölderlin, who knew that the way to Jena was closed to him, the best reason for concentrated study of this material. The same held for Diez.[35] He reports to his mother that during this period of concentration he was soon led from Kant to Jacobi/Spinoza.

Five years later Hölderlin, now in Jena himself, placed Fichte's new *Wissenschaftslehre* in the context of his studies and was thus able to cultivate a productive and critical relation to it that would have far-reaching consequences for the whole course of speculative idealism. In the conception of "Judgment and Being," with which he answers Fichte's philosophy of the subject, the limitation of our cognitive capacities is systematically preceded by a thought that both encompasses Jacobi's position and at the same time links it to the fundamental theory of Spinoza, rejected by Jacobi, of a "being" that in its undifferentiation precedes all the separations on which the theoretical possibility of knowledge itself rests. Critique of knowledge and highest certainty stand here in a determinate order corresponding to Hölderlin's earlier encounter first with Kantian critique and then with Jacobi's doctrine of faith. It was in his early studies, then, from which Neuffer calls him back, that Hölderlin achieved the beginnings of an independent path in philosophy and prefigured the position he would take up within it.[36]

During the entire period of his productivity Hölderlin saw the place of philosophy in the movement of his life and its meaning for his state of mind in essentially constant terms: philosophy was crucial for him, indispensable, but did not hold out the promise of fulfilling his own nature, which was bound up with the vocation of the poet. Philosophy also brought with it a threat to his inner equilibrium, although he always had to return to it precisely during periods of dejection.

It is interesting to know that even the initial stages of Hölderlin's philosophical studies were already marked by this ensemble of motives and consequences: experiences of dejection and a futile rebellion against the circumstances of his life; rising doubts about the truth of the teaching on which his pastoral vocation would be based; the end of his first love.[37] The consolation of friendship does not change such a condition, nor can poetry raise itself immediately to the heights of one's own inner ideal. At such times work itself can be a means to outer stability. And yet there is another more important reason such work might be dedicated to philosophy: philosophy alone, as Niethammer also recognized, is able to secure conviction, even though it cannot articulate that at which Hölderlin's poetry was already aiming. Neither can it remedy, but only repress, worry and dejection. Thus the circumstances in which Hölderlin first took up philosophy accord fully with his view of the status and the value of philosophy. If one considers Hölderlin's inscription in Niethammer's *Stammbuch* in the context of all the other documents from the time it was made, it does more than just fit in well with the picture these documents paint of Hölderlin's philosophical beginnings. It adds previously unknown features to this picture and thus makes it significantly more vivid.[38] At the same time it makes clear how much of Hölderlin's life and the dynamics in which his work developed becomes known to us, in spite of Adolf Beck's admirable lifelong search, only because of accidents in the preservation of documents—and how much consequently will always escape us. The fabric of associations and friendships in the Tübingen *Stift* was doubtless unique in its time—through the simultaneous effects of long familiarity and the friendships that it made possible and of a way of life experienced in common and a course of study that inspired great achievements. In the life and thought of those who studied there, interwoven as they were with the lives of so many others in similar circumstances, there began a period of intellectual and political ascendancy and transformation, a deepening of the claims and drives toward self-understanding that could hardly have arisen in any other—or for those concerned pleasanter—way. With the early intimacy between Hölderlin and Niethammer we have come to know only a small segment of this fabric and force field. Yet this already sheds new light both on documents that have been known for a long time from Hölderlin's later period and on the genesis of the greatest poetry in the German language. For Hölderlin's philosophical effort went into that poetry as one of the enabling conditions of its form and one of the moments of its voice.

Translated by Abraham Anderson

FOUR

Hölderlin on Judgment and Being:
A Study in the History of the Origins
of Idealism

Problems for a History of the Origins of Idealism

Chronologically speaking, the two decades at the end of the eighteenth century are a vanishingly small span of time—shorter than that which has elapsed since the end of the last World War. Yet the consciousness of mankind and the thoughts of philosophers made more progress in those decades than it had during many centuries of stagnation. The certainty that they were overcoming traditional boundaries in the understanding of truth and freedom inspired productive minds to engage in bold projects and resulted in a concentration of achievements that is rivaled only by the classical periods of Athens and Florence. Anyone at the present time seeking to contribute to the understanding of the foundations of modernity can find the best orientation by beginning here. Interest in the thought of this period has a universal character— it is not merely scholarly or limited to our cultural inheritance. Nor is it primarily directed to individual figures and theories. The richness of the meaning of our subject obliges us to try to uncover the essence and to seek to grasp the motivations of the time from one or another of its results. It looks as if there are good reasons for proceeding this way. The qualities that distinguish the period include the scope and the pace of communication in literary life. Every new idea engendered itself with an eye to all the others, which themselves had just been born. Thus each idea and the path it took reflected all the ideas of contemporary thinkers.

It is of course not possible to grasp these reflections if one cannot recognize in them the images of their originals. That is why an overview of the whole development of these decades is a precondition for a convincing interpretation of any one of its thinkers and his ideas. One thus falls into the circle of having to grasp the whole before grasping its parts. The circle can be avoided only by many preliminary investigations of various details in diverse fields. It explains the inadequate state of our knowledge of precisely this age, which scholars have tried their hardest to understand. Whole fields of specialized research have evolved that examine the conditions and the environment of individual great men of the age. But this specialization leads to the situation that researchers have insufficient contact with general trends or with specific details of the thinkers outside their immediate focus. On the basis of their own investigations they use the results of other areas of research without having sufficient command of the subject. Thus it happens almost inevitably that premises and context are seen only from the point of view of the thinker being interpreted at the moment. The character of the age as a whole can thus be addressed only in a derivative and therefore unproductive manner. In the end the question actually disappears from view: the knowledge of the whole development of the age becomes a merely implicit and no longer even expressible presupposition.

The history of the age of Kant and Goethe finds itself in this condition. One looks in vain to find useful studies that have freed themselves from the perspective of a given thinker of the period. Thus we do not really know what happened during the period. We don't even know what we ought to ask.

As a result even the best of the specialized studies suffer obvious defects. Even in these we often find an uncertainty about the appropriate context of interpretation. The dependence of the texts under interpretation, some of which have the status of "classics," is not grasped with real concreteness and facility. Their sources and motives are sought only in the limited region of neighboring classics, whose interpretation in turn is in the hands of still other groups of specialists working in isolation from each other. Important contributions by one figure to several of these areas are an exception to the rule. In philosophy, serious philological work on Hegel has developed at some remove from philological work on Fichte. The Schelling specialists have followed their own path. We also find the beginnings of an interpretation of the early philosophy of the Romantics. The latter has in turn up to now steered clear of the monopoly on Hölderlin interpretation, which moves at dizzying heights and sets an example—for the time being an inimitable one—for all the other specialties.

Yet it is obvious that problems of interpretation of these works converge with problems of the knowledge of their genesis. Thus, for example, the question regarding a possible connection between Kantian philosophy and the ideas of Spinoza was of equal urgency to Fichte, Schelling, Novalis, Hölderlin, Hegel, and many lesser figures. The fact that this question acquired such general relevance must have historical as well as philosophical grounds. One cannot derive it from just one of the thinkers who posed the question. Only an interpretation that discovers the inner unity of the ideas of the age along a single interpretive path, and that at the same time knows and can interpret the work and concerns of each individual author, can uncover it. Insofar as this period belongs to the self-understanding of modernity, the problem of the relation between pantheism and enlightenment is also of more than merely historical interest.

The following study[1] belongs in the broader context of such an undertaking. It therefore strives to bring into focus the constellation in which idealist philosophy arose and in which the conviction grew that the path of freedom could be completed only in the form of pantheism.

The rise of this philosophy is one of the most astonishing events in the history of abstract thought.[2] Kant had needed ten years to complete the *Critique of Pure Reason*. It took as much time again for his work to gain wide recognition in Germany. But even in his lifetime his work gave rise to a multitude of new attempts to design systems. In the new self-confidence of German theory deriving from Kant, and in the eschatological unrest that emerged from France and affected the thinkers of Germany, there arose a variety of conceptions that to date have hardly been surveyed. The most important of these outbid each other in rapid succession, until this style of intellectual production finally became a mannerism and came to rest under the rule of Hegel's world philosophy. In the few years between 1790 and 1798 all the insights were developed that provided the groundwork for the later systems. This period holds the secrets of the true meaning of idealist speculation.

Yet only with difficulty can one trace even its external development. Despite unusual publicity, owing to special circumstances this development unfolded to a large degree in the obscurity of private relationships. It has been known for a long time that the situation in the Tübingen *Stift* and at the University of Jena fostered such relationships and made them fruitful. But the motives and circumstances from which idealist speculation emerged in these two places are still unclear. That uncertainty still prevails on this score can be seen, for example, in the fact that the authorship of a text as important as the so-called "Oldest System Program of German Idealism" has variously been attributed to Schelling, to Hölderlin, and to Hegel. In addition, Hölderlin's importance for the birth of idealism has remained a subject of debate even within the highly developed field of Hölderlin research.

The standard assessment of Hölderlin's place in philosophy has changed three times. After Ernst Cassirer's[3] early, important attempt to separate what was distinctive to Hölderlin's thought from the dialectical mediation of his friends, Wilhelm Böhm[4] and Kurt Hildebrandt[5] advanced the thesis that Hölderlin was premier among his friends also as a thinker; the turn against Fichte's idealism to the philosophy of nature, they proposed, originated with him. Johannes Hoffmeister[6] and Ernst Müller[7] contradicted them. They replied rightly that Hölderlin was never a philosopher in the same sense as his friends and that Fichte's importance for him had been much underestimated by Böhm and Hildebrandt. The difference between these two judgments concerns the Hölderlin of the period of *Hyperion*. His later essays on poetology have received the attention they deserve only in the last few years.[8] Though these essays have yet to be fully interpreted, that there is a considerable power of abstraction at work and that the thought expressed in them is entirely original can no longer be doubted. This realization has not yet led, however, to a revision of the history of Hölderlin's philosophical development. Since readers have become aware of the unique value of his late hymns, these poems, and with them the late period of his career, have taken center stage in Hölderlin studies—and for good reason, as far as Hölderlin the poet is concerned, but to the detriment of all questions having to do with the common philosophical development of the three young friends in Tübingen.

Hölderlin's Fragment "Judgment and Being"

Only by reference to this increased interest in Hölderlin's later period can we explain how a publication that thirty years ago would have become a sensation has failed to evoke any response. This is the philosophical fragment to which Friedrich Beißner has given the title "Judgment and Being."[9] It turned up in 1930 at an auction at Liepmannssohn, and at present is in the possession of the Schocken Library in Jerusalem. It was first published in the fourth volume of the Stuttgart Edition of Hölderlin's works, which appeared in 1961. If its dating is correct, and if the ideas it contains are Hölderlin's own, it throws an entirely new light on the history of the origins of idealist philosophy.

Beißner has hypothesized that the sheet of paper dates from the early months of 1795, when Hölderlin was in Jena, near Fichte (*StA* IV, p. 402, l. 18). A compelling case for this dating can be made only on the basis of objective evidence. The sheet was probably torn from the flyleaf of a book. The location of the text gives no indication of its date, or none that is helpful at present. Aside from the reference to Fichte and Kant, its content gives no clues concerning when it was written. But a statistical examination of Hölderlin's spelling makes it possible to confirm Beißner's hypothesis. Hölderlin's writing style changed in Jena, and did so before the letter to his mother of April 20, 1795, in which the new spelling prevails completely.[10] In "Judgment and Being" it is already largely present, though in some compounds Hölderlin still uses the older spelling.[11] One can see from what follows that his hand is unsteady when he writes words that are affected by the change.[12] We must therefore assume that he wrote the page before April 20, probably around the beginning of the month. This date is astonishingly early in the history of speculative idealism. On May 23, 1794, Fichte had held his first lecture in Jena. His prospectus *Concerning the Concept of the Wissenschaftslehre* appeared not long thereafter, and the first sheets of his main work in the middle of June. Hölderlin's text, then, was produced less than a year later, after Fichte's new theory had become known. It was produced at the same time as, and therefore independently of, Schelling's work *Of the I as Principle of Philosophy*. Schelling gave the latter to the publisher in March 1795, and it came on the market at the Easter book fair.[13] At this time Hegel was still occupied in applying Kant's moral system to the religious orthodoxy and the politics of the day. He had not yet begun a careful study of Fichte. Hölderlin therefore arrived at the thoughts on judgment and being, which he wrote on the sheet now in the possession of the Schocken Library, without the help of his friends.

The following thoughts elaborate the course of reflection on that page: the traditional concepts basic to knowledge, namely judgment and being, are set in an entirely new and unconventional relation of opposition, judgment constituting the separation, being the unity, of subject and object. This interpretation makes it possible to understand the meaning of the word "judgment" (*Urteil*) as "original division" (*ursprüngliche Teilung*) into the elements of subject and object. It compels us to distinguish between the object of knowledge and what can be called "being." "Being" is what precedes every relation of the subject to an object, and can therefore never become an object of knowledge. Insofar as it is an original unity between subject and object, one can designate being through a boundary concept of knowledge as intellectual intuition. Such intuition, however, is entirely different from the form of knowledge that characterizes self-consciousness. For there subject and object can perfectly well be distinguished, even though it is the same thing that appears as subject and as object. If it is object, it is so insofar as it is separated from itself. It is also important not to differentiate self-consciousness from some more fundamental I and hold that the latter is what constitutes intellectual intuition and being. For it is meaningless to talk about an I where this I does not grasp itself as an I and is not self-conscious. The principle of identity is derived from self-consciousness. For that reason it does not signify any absolute unification of subject and object. Thus being is also not definable as identity.

Hölderlin's page develops these thoughts in a different order. It first gives the etymology of "judgment" (*Urteil*) from the original division (*Urteilung*) of intellectual intuition and then designates the consciousness "I am I" as the paradigmatic case of such original separation (*StA* IV, p. 216, ll. 1–11). There then follows a reflection about modal concepts, the meaning of which is not immediately obvious in this context (ibid., ll. 12–21). In the second part of the text[14] Hölderlin then observes that what precedes all original division cannot be appropriately regarded either as identity or as I. It must be deemed "being" and can only be conceived as intellectual intuition.

This text shows its reverence for the authority of three philosophers—Fichte, Spinoza, and Kant—and attempts to combine their fundamental ideas. The presence of Fichte is the most conspicuous. With Fichte, I and not-I are distinguished from each other, and the principle of identity is derived from the proposition "I am I." The text was clearly written with reference to him—though at the same time with critical intent. Spinoza is responsible for the thought that the ground of all oppositions is to be sought in an "absolute being" (*Sein schlechthin*), of which there is neither creation nor emanation. Any movement in this being can only be conceived as the separation and unification of its modes. "Separation" and "unification" are, however, Platonic concepts that had been applied to the interpretation of Spinoza's doctrine by Hemsterhuis. The third decisive thinker for Hölderlin's text is Kant. It will become clear as we proceed that the connection between Spinoza's being and Kant's critique is what allows us to understand Hölderlin's turn against Fichte.

Grounds for Doubt Concerning the Dating of the Text

The first thing to take note of, however, is the astonishing fact that Hölderlin, while still in Jena, had already become critical of Fichte. This could never have been inferred on the basis of the texts known previously. It might even seem plausible to claim that these texts compel an interpretation that rules out the assumption that the text on judgment and being could have been written during the Jena months. On April 16, 1795, Hegel was still reporting to Schelling about Hölderlin's letters: "Hölderlin writes to me often from Jena; he is filled with enthusiasm for Fichte, from whom he expects great things."[15] All other texts that can be dated with certainty from the winter of 1795 seem to confirm that Hölderlin's relation to Fichte was one of a not terribly advanced pupil filled with admiration. This is why Lawrence Ryan asserted that the Jena versions of *Hyperion* document a continuous approximation to Fichte.[16]

The sketch "Of the Law of Freedom" ("Über das Gesetz der Freiheit") seems to have been composed in late autumn of 1794 (*StA* IV, p. 401, l. 2). In it Hölderlin is entirely occupied with problems in Kant's philosophy that had been raised by Schiller. He attempts to round out Schiller's distinction between the beautiful soul and natural moral talent, which belongs to the study of the faculty of desire, with an analogous distinction between two forms of imagination (*Phantasie*). Hölderlin obviously hoped thereby to find both a philosophical concept of the subjectivity of the artist and the origin of art in moral virtue become second nature. Schiller's letters *On the Aesthetic Education of Man* had at that time not yet been written.[17] Thus Hölderlin had attacked a still unsolved problem posed by the work of Schiller, although not in a way that suited the latter's own subsequent approach. The preface to the *Thalia* fragment of *Hyperion* (*StA* III, p. 163), which appeared in November 1794, shows Schiller's thoughts about moral culture similarly extended to cover the whole life history of man.

From the letter to Neuffer of October 10, 1794, we know that Hölderlin was at that time already unwilling to limit himself to modifying and expanding on Schiller's theme at the periphery of Kantian theory. Over and beyond Schiller's insistence that duty could be fulfilled from inclination, he wanted to dare a further advance beyond the Kantian frontier.[18] With this step Hölderlin wanted at the same time to make an assertion about the origin of unity in man. In so doing he put himself under the guidance of Plato. Old Platonic wisdom should provide new support for the thesis of the *Critique of Judgment*, that beauty is to be taken as a symbol of morality: beauty is an intimation of the supersensible origin of man, not as the moral law, valid for reason, but as the archetype of that unity already binding together reason and sensibility in a beautiful moral life in this world.

This project entered into the three versions of the introductory section of *Hyperion* that were written in Jena.[19] It is also set forth in the poem "The God of Youth" ("Der Gott der Jugend"), on the new version of which Hölderlin began working at the end of his Waltershausen period.[20] It does not fall within the scope of this study to lay out *in extenso* the difficulties and the contradictions Hölderlin inevitably ran into when he tried to complete his project. They are not essentially different from those involved in Schiller's position in "On Grace and Dignity." It would thus make sense to interpret simultaneously the problem that occupied both Hölderlin and Schiller.[21] Hölderlin faced the peculiar aporia of trying to bind together elements of two theories that by their nature necessarily confounded any such effort—Schiller's version of Kant's ethics and Plato's theory of forms. With Schiller, Hölderlin sees love as the power that unifies the two fundamental human drives. At the same time, however, in the domain of one of these drives the archetype of all unity is supposed to appear as beautiful nature. But if unity properly means the unification of the two drives with each other, one can hardly understand why an image of unity should appear solely in the "realm of the senses," given that this unity can be understood only when both powers of man interact with each other. This problem forces the teaching of the "wise man" in the metrical version, the "stranger" in "Hyperion's Youth" ("Hyperions Jugend"), into a circular movement that, by means of several parenthetical reflections, conceals a defect of the original project. It could well be the case that Hölderlin noticed the problem inherent in his effort without being able to resolve it.

In any case he seems initially to have dropped the idea of publishing an essay on the aesthetic ideas he had already written about to Neuffer from Waltershausen (*StA* VI, p. 137, letter 88). From the Jena period two fragments have come down to us that, unlike "Judgment and Being," are preliminary drafts of manuscripts meant to be published. One of them treats the concept of punishment (*StA* IV, pp. 214–15); it is plainly quite independent of the Waltershausen sketch. The other is part of a dialogue (ibid., p. 213); one cannot find here either any indication that the Waltershausen project was its theme.

In all these texts Hölderlin relies heavily on the thoughts of others, in particular Kant and Schiller. It is true that he poses questions in his own way and indeed that he follows his declared program of going further than Schiller beyond the Kantian frontier. But the means he deploys to these ends are largely taken over from the texts before him. His aim is original, but his method is not. Because he is not yet capable of developing by his own means what he wants to say, the introduction to *Hyperion* fails too, though one ought not to confuse the introduction with the principle underlying its design.

All these observations could support the view that Hölderlin could not conceivably have written the text "Judgment and Being" at the same time. Its line of thought is free of the uncertainty that dominates the speeches of *Hyperion* and that causes the philosophical fragments to break off. It represents a self-confident assault on Fichte's fundamental idea. How can it have been written by a poet who up to now had worked entirely within Kant's conceptual framework and only a little beyond his formulated doctrine, and who had scarcely made his way into the widely admired teaching of Fichte?

If in posing these questions one does not wish to cast doubt on the statistical study of Hölderlin's spelling, one can still suppose that Hölderlin did indeed write this text down but did not compose it. One might suppose that it is an extract from the work of another. It is true, however, that we know of no publication of even comparable content from so early a time. One might also suppose that Hölderlin had noted down a conversation or that he had developed the ideas of someone else. Reconsidering the text from the point of view of these suggestions, however, also makes this supposition look highly unlikely. Dittographies and other mistakes characteristic of copies do indeed occur. But there is at least one instance that can be understood only on the assumption that the hand of the author was at work.[22] This view is also supported by the division of the sheet of paper, for one side is intended for the discussion of "judgment" and the other side for "being." It is most likely that Hölderlin first wrote down the discussion of "being" and only then used the front side of the flyleaf for the discussion of "judgment."[23] When one writes notes in a book it is natural first to use the page across from the title. In this way the reflection on the modal concepts would be an addition to the whole sequence of thought and would no longer stand in its middle, which would be less natural. If we assume such an order, it is also possible to suppose that Hölderlin did not write his text in a single sitting. Lines 9 through 11 seem to be a later addition inserted between the remark on "judgment" and the already completed reflection on the modal concepts.[24] No copy and no transcription from memory can exhibit such features. The features of the text themselves therefore remove any grounds for doubt about Hölderlin's authorship.

Sinclair's Outline of a System and Hölderlin's Philosophical Path

One need not assume that Hölderlin's text is a product of solitary reflection. After the year in Waltershausen, during which he was in contact with his friends almost solely by correspondence, he was in Jena, free of burdensome obligations, engaged in free exchange with others who, like him, were studying in close proximity to Fichte. Although he reports a fair amount concerning his reclusiveness and nothing about philosophizing with others, we know that his Tübingen friend Johann Caspar Camerer lived nearby.[25] We also know that Hölderlin shared living quarters with the young Sinclair (*StA* VI, p. 741, ll. 21–22). In such an environment conversations about Fichte, about what was right and what was wrong with his theory, were inevitable.

It is from his friendship with Sinclair that we can derive the most compelling evidence concerning the early origins of the text on judgment and being. The dates of this friendship must therefore be called to mind: on March 26, 1795, Sinclair wrote to his mentor Franz Wilhelm Jung about Hölderlin, the friend of his heart *instar omnium*, who had become his shining, lovable role-model (ibid., l. 18). The days they spent together ended with Hölderlin's departure. Sinclair left Jena only because of the student unrest of that summer; indeed, he subsequently received an order of expulsion.[26] The two friends saw each other again soon after Hölderlin's arrival in Frankfurt. Hölderlin had arrived there shortly before the beginning of 1796. On January 11 he was already back from what was probably a stay of several days in Homburg.[27] From June to December 1795 they must have exchanged many letters. In a letter to Johann Gottfried Ebel, Hölderlin asked in a postscript that Ebel give his greetings to Sinclair. His own letter to Sinclair, he says, is at "this time" only half-finished.[28] It can be inferred from this that Hölderlin regularly sent Sinclair letters of considerable length, and naturally received such letters from him as well. Little time seems to have elapsed between these letters. For it is unlikely that Hölderlin would not have sent the letter he had already half-finished on November 9 until his letter to Ebel of December 7. He must have written another letter in the meantime.[29] During the first half year in Frankfurt Hölderlin visited Sinclair regularly[30] and no doubt also received visits from him, for it was Sinclair who was more interested in their relationship: "I have just been in Homburg yet again, at Sinclair's urgent request," Hölderlin writes on February 11, 1796, to his brother.[31] There must have been some connection between the content of their letters, their conversations, and the continuous discussion they had enjoyed in Jena. Although all their letters have been lost and no reports from third parties have survived, we can still conclude that philosophical themes connected with the problems of "Judgment and Being" held sway.

The conclusion finds support in a document of great significance, namely, Sinclair's early philosophical remains, which were unaccountably neglected by Hölderlin scholars when they were generally available in the original. Varnhagen von Ense tried with great persistence to gain possession of these fragments.[32] Later efforts were inspired above all by the hope of finding texts by Hölderlin among them. Because this turned out not to be the case, these Sinclair fragments, which are of the utmost value for the history of the origins of idealist philosophy, seemed worthless. Varnhagen, how we do not know, got hold of one fascicle; the Prussian State Library later kept it with his collection as "Philosophical Reasonings and Lists of Propositions" ("Philosophische Raisonnements und zusammengereihte Sätze").[33] During the war it was stored along with the entire collection of autographs in Silesia. Since then it has been missing. Probably it was not destroyed but rather has been retained to this day by Polish officials.[34]

The Sinclair scholar Werner Kirchner, who unfortunately died young,[35] had been able before the war to prepare copies of the manuscript. He did it initially because he thought that the "Philosophical Reasonings" were transcripts of Fichte's lectures. Otherwise he would not have devoted so much effort to transcribing precisely this text. This supposition cannot be sustained and was abandoned by Kirchner himself. Hannelore Hegel is currently engaged in editing his transcriptions as part of a work on Sinclair's philosophy; she is thereby making generally accessible one of the most crucial documents of the early history of idealism.[36] An older Swiss dissertation has proved unequal to the task,[37] yet Hölderlin studies could have picked up valuable clues from it as well.

It is very difficult to date a text whose original is not available. In the present case, however, on the basis of reliable criteria it is possible to confirm the guess of Lotz and Kirchner that the fascicle dates from the year 1796. Kirchner copied a short text Sinclair had jotted on the announcement of a concert. The announcement reads: "On popular demand today the 6th of December 1795, the young Herr Pixis from Mannheim, 9 years old, will have the honor of giving a second instrumental concert at the Alleehaus at Homburg." Sinclair's text on this sheet of paper contains *in nuce* the idea that lies at the basis of the fully elaborated manuscript.[38] This therefore provides a *terminus a quo*. The *terminus ad quem* is also discoverable, so that one can rule out the hypothesis that Sinclair had only much later made use of an old concert program because he happened not to have any notepaper handy. Ludwig Strauß has noted, from the few items in the literary remains of Sinclair's Homburg friend, Zwilling, extracts from a draft of a letter Zwilling wanted to write to a Jena professor on April 26, 1796.[39] The draft says: "As often as I examine the *Wissenschaftslehre*, I rejoice over the sublime conception of the imagination. Sinclair, who has excellent command of the Greek language, said to me that Prometheus meant nothing other than reflection. To this Prometheus, who tore us loose from Olympus, I oppose the imagination, which has borne us up again." This interpretation of Prometheus can be made sense of only in relation to the ideas elaborated in Sinclair's "Philosophical Reasonings."

Here it is possible neither to offer an account of these ideas nor to give them the evaluation they merit. It must therefore suffice to sketch them in outline and to quote a few sentences. This will make it clear enough that Sinclair depends intellectually on Hölderlin and that he had been familiar with the ideas Hölderlin set down in his text on judgment and being.

According to Sinclair, the original unity is without all positing; it is *athesis* and can as such also be called peace. In this unity there emerges a division through reflection. All knowledge has its being within the space of this division. It can be called original division (*Urteilung*) partly because it is the first division, partly because we cannot get beyond it with knowledge. That this knowledge does not spring from itself is manifest from the fact that its highest proposition has the character of a demand. In the medium of reflection the original unity expresses itself in this demand, namely, as what wants to be restored. It thus grounds our consciousness of limitation and of the possibility of feeling. As soon as one wishes to posit this unity, it becomes an object of reflection, a *theos*. The Greek word for *god* points to the origin of the concept of God in positing reflection and its distinction from the truly original athetic unity of peace. The true concept of origin is not, however, to be attained through positing. We can present to ourselves the omnipresent God, who is Spinoza's God, only if we realize that no reflection occurs simply through itself and that it presupposes a unity— a being utterly independent of it. The thought of this being is possible only as the thought of the overcoming of all reflection and division. Fichte made the mistake of wanting to grasp it through positing. But in that way it becomes an absolute I, an absolute thesis. It is the truth of skepticism not to content itself with acts of positing and to point out their finitude, their insufficiency in the face of the demand for unity. What skepticism accomplishes is more than the idealists' insistence on the right of reflection and the dogmatic denial of all division. It also achieves more than those who have fruitlessly demanded a return to the athetic origin. But it does not yet achieve the highest. The points of view of all philosophy can be united in an entirely new form of positing. "That the I reflects on its positing, that it wants to know what exists independently of its positing, proves that it has a striving to overcome the division made by reflection and to transform being-for-the-I into an absolute being." Fichte did not think about the relativity of the fundamental concepts of positing. Had he done so, "he would have arrived at a higher positing than the positing for an I, at an Ἀεὶ ἑαυτὸν Θέσιν, at an aesthetics." That positing happens with an eye to the being that always is, to Spinoza's being, is the meaning of aesthetics and at the same time explains the word we use to name it. Sinclair assigns it three tasks: (1) to ascertain the being that precedes all reflection; (2) to restore the peace that surpasses all divisions—an end that leads to the infinite and that can never fully be realized within the sphere of reflection, and so must remain a demand; (3) to work out the meaning of everything that shows itself and is not what it is through reflection. To this belongs above all nature in its beauty. "Peace has never left nature; nature has no purpose, it is." Only reflection in the form of teleology brings forth a purpose in nature.

The last sentence in particular makes clear that Sinclair was concerned to bring Hölderlin's central term "peace" (*Friede*) into speculative relation with his experience of nature. It is unimaginable that it was written without his friend in mind. The distinction between the original division and being is the same as in Hölderlin's text. The thought, too, that this being is the necessary presupposition of a whole, of which subject and object are the parts, reemerges in Sinclair's more definite claim that reflection must presuppose a being that it cannot reach through positing. This thought, however, also incorporates the ideas Hölderlin first mentioned after his departure from Jena.

For these ideas we have primarily four sources: the letters to Schiller of September 4, 1795, and to Niethammer of February 24, 1796; the preface to the penultimate version of *Hyperion*; and the poem "To the Unknown One" ("An die Unerkannte").[40] In the context of Sinclair's manuscript they fit so easily together that one is tempted to overlook the differences among them. Hölderlin wrote to Schiller that he was seeking to develop the idea of an infinite progress of philosophy—of philosophy itself, not only an infinite progress of the moral ordering of the world within philosophy. To this end, he says, one must begin from an incessant demand addressed to every system: subject and object must be united in an absolute that cannot appropriately be called an "I."[41] In the text on judgment and being this demand corresponds to the "necessary presupposition" of a whole. Here it also means the postulate of a restoration of unity in infinite progress, as formulated by Sinclair, as well as his belief in the aesthetic realization of unity in the intuition of beauty. Hölderlin concludes his remarks with the sentence "I believe that I can thereby prove in what measure the skeptics are right, and in what measure not." Therewith he claims as his own an idea that plays an important role in the composition of Sinclair's manuscript and even in his later system.

The preface to *Hyperion*, which the publisher, Cotta, sent back to Hölderlin for revision, rests on the same foundations. "The blessed unity, being, in the unique sense of the word, is lost to us." We have torn ourselves loose from it in order to reach it. But "neither our knowledge nor our action reaches, at any period of our existence, a point where all strife ceases." The peace of all peace is irretrievably lost. Yet we would not even seek after it if that infinite unification, that being in the only sense of the word, were not present to us. It is present—as beauty. The outline Hölderlin sent to Niethammer of the ideas for a series of philosophical letters agrees entirely with the premise of the preface—apart from a few peculiarities that can be explained in terms of Hyperion's development. It leads from the starting point, the lost peace, through many shifts between intimacy and estrangement, to nature, which preserves a reflection of the original unity. This nature, pervaded by the unity of peace, the ground that cannot be captured by thought, is, however, the subject of the verses to which Hölderlin gave the title and dedication "To the Unknown One." It is wrongly thought that this poem expresses Hölderlin's return to the nature he had disregarded, and in this sense had not known, in Jena (*StA* I, p. 496, ll. 3 ff). It signifies only that nature cannot be captured in any knowledge because it is grounded in what precedes all division and thus also precedes consciousness. Nature preserves the One, and for that reason no one can know it. One can only entrust oneself to it, so that it eases the pain of separation. It is nature

> Die das Eine, das im Raum der Sterne,
> Das du suchst in aller Zeiten Ferne
> Unter Stürmen, auf verwegner Fahrt,
> Das kein sterblicher Verstand ersonnen,
> Keine, keine Tugend noch gewonnen,
> Die des Friedens goldne Frucht bewahrt.
>
> That preserves the one you seek,
> In starry skies, in distant times,
> Through violent storms, on daring journeys,
> That no mortal understanding ever claimed,
> And not a single virtue has yet gained,
> That preserves the golden fruit of peace.[42]

Sinclair and Hölderlin were at one in this thought. But it was Hölderlin's experience that gave birth to it. It was also Hölderlin who first formulated it and who must first have communicated it to his friend. The latter had at his command only the talent and the persistence required for systematic elaboration, and the free time to put these to use, while Hölderlin used the energy of his best hours for the completion of *Hyperion*.

Only three months passed between Hölderlin's departure from Jena and his letter to Schiller, which already presupposes the mature theory. The very brevity of that span of time leads one to suspect that the groundwork had already been laid in Jena. Independent of this, the similarity of thought between Hölderlin and Sinclair leads to the same conclusion. It never could have become so complete through the exchange of letters alone. Considering the subsequent effect of the text, then, one cannot doubt the results of the statistical study of Hölderlin's spelling.

The Prehistory of the Fragment

The question still remains how this early date can be reconciled with the style and the content of the Jena fragments. If it cannot be answered, the dating and the attribution of the text to Hölderlin may be unchallenged. The existence of the text in the corpus of Hölderlin's work would, however, remain an unsolved riddle and thus a source of frustration for any renewed attempt at understanding. We must therefore turn once again to the text itself and its prehistory.

On January 25, 1795, Hölderlin wrote to Hegel concerning Fichte's philosophy (*StA* VI, pp. 154–56, letter 94). He speaks in this letter like any one of the many Kantians who suspected Fichte of bringing dogmatism back to life. "He wishes to go beyond the fact of consciousness within *theory* itself." Hölderlin has reservations about this theoretical expansion. They are the same reservations that motivate him in the text on judgment and being, in Kantian fashion, to call the whole that precedes judgment a "necessary presupposition." In Fichte's absolute I he recognizes the structure of the old *omnitudo realitatis* but sees at the same time that it fulfills the same function as Spinoza's substance, within which everything and outside of which nothing exists.[43] At first he is unwilling to acknowledge any justification for such an assumption. He attempts to use Kant to catch Fichte in a contradiction: the absolute I is without an object if there is nothing outside it. But then it is also without consciousness. If the absolute I were in me, I could have no consciousness of it. If, however, it is simply impossible to become conscious of it, it is for me, the conscious being, nothing at all, an empty assumption.

This observation is certainly not the same as the criticism of Fichte in "Judgment and Being." But it can be made into it by a single modulation of the thought: if philosophical reasons should arise for assuming an absolute prior to all consciousness, one must then distinguish it from all consciousness. One would therefore do well not to call it misleadingly "I" and to give it unequivocally the function of Spinoza's substance—albeit outside theoretical knowledge. For Hölderlin, whose theme, along with Plato and Schiller, was the possibility of unification, the reason he gives in "Judgment and Being" could easily become compelling: one must conceive, prior to the distinction between subject and object that constitutes all consciousness, a whole that always remains unknowable.

Hölderlin wrote to Hegel that his earlier, Kantian criticism of Fichte had already been written in Waltershausen.[44] Just after this sentence a few lines of the letter are torn off. Yet we can still determine that even in January in Jena Hölderlin regarded the agreement between Fichte and Jacobi / Spinoza as highly suggestive. It had clearly become even more important to him than it had been in Waltershausen. Nonetheless he continued to consider his original criticism worth communicating. The two together, the critique and the broadening of the projection of Spinoza onto Fichte's *Wissenschaftslehre*, can already lead to the position taken in the text on judgment and being. Between the letter to Schiller in September and the letter to Hegel in January, then, this text belongs more to the period of the latter, and thus to the later Jena period.

The close connection with the Kantianism of Hölderlin's early critique underlines a peculiarity of "Judgment and Being" that might easily be overlooked: this text, too, remains in some essential respects within the domain of certain Kantian notions: absolute being is only a presupposition; the I is always self-consciousness; modal concepts belong to different cognitive faculties; the being that is inconceivable for us is intellectual intuition. Hölderlin does not subject Fichte to a line-by-line criticism of the *Wissenschaftslehre*. He sees it through eyes trained by Kant and Jacobi, finds its conformity with Spinoza striking, and judges it according to criteria drawn from the critical philosophy. It could almost be said that Fichte's text merely serves to combine ideas that Hölderlin could not unite in any other way: it wrests from Kant the admission of an original unity and at the same time frees Jacobi / Spinoza from the taint of an uncritical dogmatism.[45] It can do this because it conceives of an undivided unity of subject and object prior to knowledge itself. Its error is only that it names this unity *I*. Hölderlin could not see that Fichte's unique problem was posed precisely by this identification and would be lost without it.[46]

There is no contradiction, then, in the fact that Hölderlin's Jena drafts are by and large Kantian and that at the same time he conceived the idea of "Judgment and Being." Till the end he stayed closer to Kant than his friends, and for that very reason he also remained loyal to the claims of an unknowable ground of knowledge and of infinite progress.[47] It is remarkable, yet perfectly understandable, that precisely because of his Kantianism he was able to free himself from Fichte before the others and to bring into play against him the principle of Jacobi/Spinoza. Schelling, in his essay *Of the I as Principle of Philosophy,* is moving in the same direction—yet he has a greater share of problems and is not as advanced philosophically.

Only one question remains unanswered. In the drafts of *Hyperion,* Hölderlin is still laboring under difficulties that can be solved with the help of "Judgment and Being" and that he actually solved in this way in Nürtingen. Why then did Hölderlin not make use of this new resource, if it was indeed already available to him? One must admit that no compelling explanation suggests itself. However, *Hyperion* is not a philosophical text, just as "Judgment and Being" is not a completed system. In the latter Hölderlin intended above all to expose an error of Fichte's and to diagnose what had led to it. This becomes clearer if one takes the more probable outlook and reads the text as beginning with the section on being. One need not assume that Hölderlin was immediately in a position to develop a theory of the course of human life from the newly recovered Spinoza. Even the preface of the penultimate version of *Hyperion* did not solve this problem satisfactorily. The speech of "the stranger" was supposed to give a theory of the eccentric path. But we can only note that Hölderlin initially carried on with the attempt to develop the theory from Kant, Plato, and Schiller alone—with some glances at Fichte, but without appropriating his position and without criticizing his fundamental idea. After all, *Hyperion* had already been sold to a publisher, while the thesis on judgment and being, by contrast, was a private note. Nor must one assume that Hölderlin had already realized that with the old order of problems he would never succeed in producing a speech that was even poetically compelling. It must have been very encouraging for him to work the new ideas into a system when he noticed that everything that had become essential to his life could be incorporated into it. We do not know when he finally gave up on the speech of the stranger, on which he had spent so much effort. The community of philosophical activity that he shared with Sinclair, however, and that led to the latter's Homburg outline of a system must at any rate have been established in Jena.

Prospect and Program

It is quite possible that Hölderlin was moved to enlist Jacobi / Spinoza against Fichte by voices from within his circle of friends.[48] If Schelling did not do so himself, Hegel certainly would have reported to Hölderlin that their friend had identified himself as a Spinozist.[49] Already in Jena, Fichte was being assailed by Friedrich August Weißhuhn, his boyhood companion, with the charge that his system was "subjective Spinozism."[50] Spinoza's position was also being defended there by the Swabian theology professor Paulus, whose house Hölderlin frequented.[51] Only a little while later other Jena students of Fichte's, among them Schlegel,[52] sided with Spinozism quickly and independently. Their move, too, had been predetermined by the consciousness of their generation.

Yet Hölderlin was the first one who was able, as a result of his thought process and the seriousness of his poetic vocation, to make the critical turn against Fichte and to establish his own philosophical system. Sinclair tried to develop this system, in the same way that he later made Hölderlin's theory of poetry known to the public under his own name.[53] For Hölderlin himself, the system fulfilled its function inasmuch as it allowed him better to understand the meaning of his poetic activity and helped him to complete the work that had occupied him for four years. The poetology of the Homburg years arose from the same need, but it could build on the foundation that had first been laid in Jena and that Hölderlin never again abandoned.

Sinclair too made use of this foundation. He owed it all to Hölderlin, even if his contribution to its solidification must have been considerable. One could show how Sinclair constructed his later systematics on this foundation by treating certain of its features as particularly important. He himself believed that on this account he could compare himself with Hegel.[54] And yet, along with his friend Hölderlin, he lost the power of conviction that had distinguished his early "Philosophical Reasonings." However, he did not lose his gift for systematic elaboration and integration.

If we have correctly interpreted Hölderlin's text on judgment and being, it must also be possible to reconstruct the history of the origins of idealism much more precisely than ever before. Hölderlin thought he could claim to have influenced Schelling.[55] We are now in a better position to judge whether he in fact did. On the whole, Schelling went his own way. But Hegel did not! He arrived in Frankfurt with a philosophy that remained entirely within the Kantian paradigm, although he knew

Schelling's doctrine and had tried to read Fichte. Among the circle of Hölderlin and his friends, Hegel soon changed his mind and moved onto the terrain that in a few years would lead him to the Jena system. Here he appropriated a Fichte who had already been interpreted by his friends and developed a terminology that could much more easily be derived from Sinclair's system than from Schelling.

Still, Hegel came to an understanding of himself with their help. This kind of accord can be understood only because beyond all the idiosyncrasies in their thought he was bound to Hölderlin from the beginning by the fundamental presuppositions they shared. One of these was the experience of their time at the Tübingen *Stift*, which also had a decisive effect on Hölderlin's philosophical development. That it was Hölderlin himself who led the path of freedom in the direction of pantheism, however, still stands in need of a deeper explanation. Such an account can only be given along with an answer to the question concerning the nature of speculative idealism as a whole.

Translated by Abraham Anderson

FIVE

Hölderlin in Jena

The Rapid Development of Thought After Kant

Classical German philosophy took its point of departure from the work of Kant. Up until Hegel, any thinking that wished to make a claim to currency and truth had to be predicated on a study of this work, an original contribution to it, and a preservation of its most essential results. Nonetheless, the current in which philosophy moved following Kant did not entirely accord with the expectations that must have seemed justified at its outset. And yet the achievements flowing from the unforeseen directions of that current are precisely what warrant our speaking of a philosophical era that can and must itself be described as "classical."

Seven years after the appearance of the *Critique of Pure Reason*, Kant prepared the *Critique of Practical Reason* for publication. With it, the foundations of his system had been fully worked out. He now expected that those foundations would be put to the test. From his followers he anticipated new presentations that would prove more perspicuous and elegant than his own principal works, marked as they were by the strenuous effort that went into laying the foundations. But above all he saw before him the extensive task of applying the critical principles to mathematics and to the sciences of nature, of right, and of morals. And he wanted to dedicate the next decade of his own inquiries to this task. Kant could expect three different groups of adversaries to initiate public disputes, although he could rely on his students for support. These adversaries included the last remaining representatives of the Leibniz school; the empiricists, who had in the meantime taken up a kind of popular-philosophical mode of presentation; and finally orthodox theological and theosophical teachers, who in Kant's view merely sought to thwart the justified claims of reason and the progress of scientific knowledge.

These expectations rested on everything Kant himself knew about the consequences of earlier attempts to lay new foundations for philosophical theory. The Cartesians had been embroiled in controversies for nearly half a century. During that time Spinoza constructed a new philosophical system, albeit still under the confining influence of Cartesian assumptions. In Germany the soundness and the implications of Leibniz's new foundational work had been debated vigorously for another 50 years. In England new positions were developing out of the theories of John Locke, without however departing from Locke's mode of inquiry and while tending to accept his basic assumptions along with the questions he posed. Only perhaps in Plato's Athens could one have previously witnessed such a rapid emergence of a whole spectrum of new theories from an intellectual achievement of the stature soon generally credited to Kant's *Critique*.

We refer to that early period as the classical age of Greek philosophy, and some allusion to it is always implied by referring to the period beginning with Kant as the age of classical *German* philosophy. It may not be wholly comparable to ancient Greek philosophy in terms of its world-historical significance, still the comparison is supported by the sheer diversity, the originality, and the resoluteness of thought that emerged and held sway between 1786 and 1830. And the question of its influence is precisely to the point. For with Kant and the movement that he initiated, philosophy was, if only for a short time, a dominating force in German culture and soon throughout Europe. For the first time, philosophy did more than provide new directions for the sciences and develop new foundations for political change: the new philosophical reflection also established and transformed the poetry of the period.

To be sure, there is no longer any continuity between that time and the philosophy and art of *our* age. Two ruptures, one occurring toward the middle of the last century, another ushering in our own, have distanced us from it. That distance has not, however, caused the period simply to sink into prehistory. It has remained current, indeed in three ways. In the first place, the themes and the forms of thought that it brought with it have not been exhausted but have remained productive. Second, the images of a universal, theoretically grounded world-orientation that were envisioned in this period have yet to be superseded. Finally, and because of this, no thinking today can understand itself without coming to grips with the period. There is no consensus, however, concerning how to go about doing so. And only a few scholars, such as Heidegger, have made deep and comprehensive enough efforts to think about it, and with it, in this way.

But none of this concerns us in what follows. To be sure, an inquiry into the course of classical German philosophy may be of the utmost interest to the historian of ideas. And if the historian is a philosopher too, he will want to bring together the many threads woven into that course, but only when, after painstaking effort, he might expect them to point the way toward new conceptual possibilities that had not yet been expressed theoretically at the time. Yet tracing out the path of classical German philosophy after Kant still poses a task of particular significance and fascination, even apart from that, its true motive.

As we have seen, Kant expected, and with good reason, that the appropriation and application of the first *Critique* would be a task to occupy the generation that followed him. Yet just one year after the publication of the *Critique of Practical Reason* events took a turn in precisely the opposite direction. These events had to do with controversies concerning how to understand the critique of reason generally and with attempts by some to ground it in ways that could find only negligible support in Kant's writings. Before long, arguments were being advanced that no longer accorded in any way with the substance of Kantian doctrine. Kant's theory of the spontaneity of the subject and the freedom of the will were combined with ideas about the monistic constitution of the universe, in an apparent desire to make Spinoza's metaphysics compatible with the Kantian framework. Just as it had begun to take shape, then, Kant's school dissolved into a multitude of positions to which even the common vocabulary of the first *Critique* was soon lost. And although Kant supported his literal followers in the opinion that everything that deviated from that vocabulary was simply misguided, the talented ones among them, while still taking their point of departure from Kant, steered the course of thought in what seemed to Kant an altogether undesirable direction. For this reason, then, the age of classical German philosophy cannot properly be described as the age of the influence of Kant.

This entire process simply erupted like a volcano. And this is precisely what is most astonishing and what most cries out for an explanation. Kant had spent over a decade and a half putting together his *Critique of Pure Reason*. It then took only half that time for the entire spectrum of positions, themselves deriving from the work of Kant, to unfold. To be sure, important works were yet to be published, significant controversies yet to arise. Hegel, for example, conceived the formative notion for his mature work only after the turn of the century.

But between 1789 and 1797, all the fundamental decisions crucial to ensuing developments had already been made: styles of thought that
would subsequently evolve into systems were conceived during precisely this time. By this time, too, the line had already been drawn between the two basic positions whose opposition dominated the decades to come: on the one hand Fichte's approach, which works out of
the dynamics of the being-for-itself of the subject in its exemplary
unity, and on the other hand the denial that such a subjective unity is
capable of providing philosophy with an ultimate foundation. A number of young intellectuals were drawn into the current of philosophical
theory; new forms of literature and literary criticism emerged; and Ro-
manticism, drawing inspiration from Fichte, came into its own. The
whole process discharged such immense intellectual energies that it
might well be compared with a sun going supernova.

But our place in the tradition is not so far removed from these events
as to force us simply to register them from some insurmountable historical distance and make them intelligible to ourselves only through mere
speculation. It ought to be possible, and one should at least attempt, to
penetrate to the heart of the process itself, not only keeping in mind
those of its manifestations that have been handed down at each stage
in published form but also, on the basis of those sources, reconstructing what seemed evident to, and what influenced, those figures
who would eventually acquire central significance. Any other form of
interpretation, after all, could only argue *ex eventu* and would have to
take for granted the theories of the day. Its explanations would necessarily be confined to the kinds of reasoning advanced in those theories
themselves. And while we can in no way simply neglect those theories,
we can nonetheless assume that they do not exhaust the unique character of the writings, or even the publications, themselves. The rapid
emergence of an entire spectrum of new theories speaks against it.
Such a possibility is belied, too, by the extraordinary influence and significance of a particular cluster of personalities all acquainted with one
another and of the conversation among them.

An investigation of this sort must forgo a number of approaches that
may have merit in their own right. Thus, for example, Hegel accounted
for the developments leading from Kant to his own system in terms of
the consequences of theoretical inferences, each of which had to take
shape in the form of a theory before the next conceptual step could be
seen to be evident and inevitable. This construct of Hegel's, however,
cannot explain the initial break away from Kant's thought. Nor can it
acknowledge the fact that the Kantian *Critique* and Fichte's later doctrine and Hegel's *Logic* all remain viable theoretical alternatives, and

that nothing concerning their truth is decided by the historical course of events as such.

If the process cannot be understood in terms of theoretical consequences, then perhaps it can be understood as something embedded in a change in the consciousness of the age, which is in turn connected with social and political upheavals. Such an explanation suggests itself especially for the evolution of theory after Kant since it coincides exactly with the revolutionary activity in France. This coincidence was surely apparent to Kant's contemporaries and gave them occasion to offer some account for those events in which they felt themselves to be involved. Some impetus in the growth of modern reflection was indeed a necessary condition for the development of classical German philosophy. And all of its founders followed the events in France with passionate concern, if nonetheless recounting them in widely different ways. But certainly none of this was enough to determine the course of thought itself. A movement in thought can never be directly understood in terms that lack a motivating force for thought itself, that is, in the form of reasons. When thought takes such a fruitful turn, it must have been preceded by a novel arrangement of conceptual problems and possibilities, an arrangement that had come to seem inescapable. One could say a *conceptual space* (*Denkraum*) opens up that provides a basic orientation for the development of particular conceptual styles and achievements, and whose coordinate system can then be filled in by theories in definite ways. It is this basic orientation that pulls together and unifies a philosophical era, over and above the controversies within it. And for this reason one must bear in mind the constitution of this conceptual space and the shifts that occur within it, if one would make intelligible the philosophy of an age and its inner dynamics without begging the question from the outset.

Hegel's Early Development in Context

This is the general framework in which to situate the present, ongoing investigation. Its task is to shed light on the origins of the mode of thought that deviated not only from Kant but also from Fichte's new theory of the structure of subjectivity and knowledge. We are familiar with Hegel's system as the most significant development in thinking of this kind. Hegel himself, in accord with the historical method peculiar to his own thought, referred to Schelling's philosophy of nature as the point of departure, and the point of contention, on the path toward his own speculative *Logic*. And this is valid inasmuch as the logical form of the fundamental concepts of Hegel's system sprang from an immanent critique of the conceptual framework developed by Schelling around the turn of the century. And yet we have known for a long time that this sort of account does not get at the historical origins of Hegel's thought.

Soon after Hegel's death his biographer, Karl Rosenkranz, published excerpts from manuscripts written by Hegel during his days as a tutor in Bern and Frankfurt. In 1889 Hegel's two sons deposited many of those manuscripts in the Königliche Bibliothek in Berlin, together with the unpublished works they had sorted through. Wilhelm Dilthey, to whom we owe many illuminating ideas concerning the history of classical German philosophy, then assigned them as the subject for a prize question of the Berlin Academy, namely, to present the history of the young Hegel on the basis of these manuscripts. Since the essays that were submitted in the competition did not live up to his expectations, Dilthey wrote such a work himself, and moreover saw to the publication of a first edition of the manuscripts with the help of his student Hermann Nohl. The literature dedicated to the interpretation of Hegel's early writings has subsequently surpassed even the scholarship dealing with his mature system.

Dilthey described Hegel's path as one embedded in the set of problems posed by the worldview of his age—but in such a way that, for Dilthey, the mature system is explicable in terms of the internal consequences of the efforts of Hegel's youth. On the one hand, there is no denying that this sort of account is more tenable than Hegel's own. On the other hand, it is shaped thoroughly by Dilthey's interest in the typology and genesis of worldviews. Reading it today, mindful of the task of making intelligible the course of classical German philosophy, one can see that it sidesteps the problem by taking precisely the opposite tack. For while Hegel accounts for the developments leading up to him in terms of the structure of his own system, the question concerning the conceptual constellations and coordinates into which a theory had to fit remains for Dilthey a matter of merely secondary importance. That this approach thereby shunts aside an essential question is shown by the fact that Dilthey's mode of explanation is as ineffectual as Hegel's in solving the riddle of the rapid succession of new positions developing out of Kant's *Critique*, positions it was as impossible for Kant to have foreseen as it was necessary for him to reject. Those philosophical views cannot have just blossomed spontaneously in the nourishing light of a cultural awakening. If the self-understanding of those who proposed them was not wholly idiosyncratic but sought instead to present itself publicly, and so theoretically, then it must have corresponded to a context of problems that was itself publicly available and that would provide a theory with the support of evidence and argument. But since the positions changed with such energy and swiftness, a corresponding shift in the context of problems must have preceded them. And so we have reason to suppose that such a shift did occur, though it may not be evident on the basis of sources already available to us.

Clearly, then, the desire to retrace a path in the history of thought and the turns of events within it, moreover to do so thoughtfully, can lead to a search for new source materials. Once the task became clear to me 25 years ago I embarked on this search, and it seems that it may well soon be drawing to a close. It has since become clear that the history of the rise of Hegel's thought can only be told in conjunction with a reconstruction of Hölderlin's role in the development of classical German philosophy.

The procedure involved in such a search also gives occasion for the following observation with regard to the methodology of the historical sciences: even though the event one sets out to explain is unrepeatable, and even though no general rules within any special theory may be presupposed for the purpose, one can nonetheless formulate and test hypotheses rigorously—indeed, with nothing short of the rigor attainable in the social sciences, with their experiments and their attempts to approximate the theoretical concepts of the experimental natural sciences as closely as possible. There is probably a need for this sort of procedure in many historical disciplines, and it would be of some interest to gather together some conspicuous examples that seem to call for it.

The search that began with Hegel's early development was guided by the following hypothesis: whenever in the midst of a certain mode of thought there emerges a swift turn of events that cannot adequately be explained on the basis of the texts before us, it must have been preceded by a shift in the general array of problems. One must therefore trace the context in which that shift occurred. And if the shift sprang from conversations that can no longer be documented, one must uncover the contents and consequences of those conversations from sources that approximate them as closely as possible. If one applies this hypothesis in three particular cases, more than just the development of the young Hegel in the course of classical German philosophy becomes intelligible. In particular, Hölderlin's status and significance within that course take on clear and distinct contours.

The results of the first two steps in the search can be stated succinctly. First, it has always been thought remarkable that three friends who shared a room at the Tübingen *Stift* all ended up producing works of the highest order. If, however, one inquires into the intellectual climate in which their youthful productivity flourished, especially Schelling's, one winds up having to reconstruct from correspondence and other obscure sources a debate then taking place at the Tübingen theological seminary. It was a debate among the professors and their assistants, but it involved the active participation of the philosophically inclined students as well. Those involved came to view Kant's theory of religion, to which both parties appealed, along with Fichte's contributions to that theory, as inadequate and in need of radical reform. The discussion also yielded a special interest in the theory of Friedrich Heinrich Jacobi. This theory was made available in its entirety for the first time in the second edition of Jacobi's work *On the Doctrine of Spinoza*, which appeared in 1789. Schelling makes frequent references to this edition in his early writings. And Hölderlin too forges his own path in philosophy by way of an appropriation of Jacobi's theory.

Second, at the beginning of 1797, with Hölderlin acting as an intermediary, Hegel assumed a position as private tutor in Frankfurt. The manuscripts dating from the time soon after his arrival and reunion with Hölderlin show a clear change in Hegel's thought. He now rather abruptly takes up a position formulated in direct opposition to Kant and even to Fichte's theory. On this new view, freedom is no longer the overcoming of dependency but rather the unification of opposites. And the principle behind it is not the being-for-itself of the subject but the unity that encompasses those opposites. Dilthey had already seen that the key words "love" and, later, "life" with which Hegel dubbed this principle are in accord with Hölderlin's *Hyperion*. Early on, then, Dilthey drew attention to Hölderlin's role in the development of post-Kantian thought. Moreover, his importance for the development of Hegel's philosophy has been much discussed ever since Norbert von Hellingrath discovered and drew attention to his later poems and his reputation as the greatest lyric poet of the German language began to grow.

But how are we to conceive of a poet exerting such an immediate and lasting influence on the direction of a philosophy that was to ascend to become, as Marx put it, the world philosophy of the age? Could his thoughts, expressed so directly and written in an elegiac poem in the form of letters, have had such an impact just in virtue of their content, along with the conviction lent to them by the personality of the poet? Given such origins, how could they hold their own in the face of the most important theoretical achievements of the day, against which Hegel immediately brought them to bear? With the question framed in this way, it was a foregone conclusion that the answer would be negative. This posed the task, then, of reconstructing the arguments by means of which Hölderlin had been able to set Hegel so swiftly on a course of his own, and at just the time when Hegel himself was in search of secure foundations for a philosophical position.

An explicitly philosophical text by Hölderlin was published for the first time in 1961. It has remained the only one published to date, and I shall return to it in what follows. It was offered up by Christoph Theodor Schwab, Hölderlin's first biographer, to a collector of manuscripts, and was then acquired at an auction at Liepmannssohns by the Schocken Library in Jerusalem. Fortunately, someone took notice when the text appeared again in the catalogue of another auction house in 1970. Thus it was able to find its way into the Württembergische Landesbibliothek with the help of funds from Stuttgart industry and through an agreement with another financially powerful collection.

This text, entitled by Beißner "Judgment and Being," is written on the flyleaf of a book. It seems at first glance to stand out in such singular fashion among Hölderlin's manuscripts that one must wonder whether it is in fact a note on someone else's ideas. It can readily be shown, however, that the ideas are Hölderlin's own and that they shed light not only on the theoretical passages of *Hyperion* but on parts of some of Hölderlin's letters as well. Questions then remained concerning its exact dating and whether the outline in fact corresponds to any highly developed philosophical conception. The answers to both questions are to be found in the far more extensive manuscripts of Isaak von Sinclair. Until recently these were known only in the transcriptions made by the Hölderlin scholar Werner Kirchner, who had mistaken Sinclair's writings for lecture notes. In truth, they are nothing other than Sinclair's own independent elaborations of Hölderlin's ideas—the essentials of which must have been worked out by May 1795, when the page "Judgment and Being" was originally written. Some progress had now been made in discovering the arguments with which Hölderlin won Hegel over in 1797. The unique style of thought and philosophical critique by means of which Hölderlin was able to emerge as the leading figure in an "alliance of friends" in Frankfurt, and later in Homburg, now became clearer. A second step had been taken, then, in tracing out those branches in the course of classical German philosophy from which Hegel's system would ultimately emerge.

And yet this immediately presented an additional problem. The second step of the investigation had raised the question of how it was possible for Hölderlin to exert such influence on Hegel. Now Hölderlin's independent status in philosophy had to be accounted for as well. What kind of intellectual context had enabled Hölderlin to gain the confidence required to make his own contribution to philosophical theory, still in Kant's shadow? Once again, like the two that preceded it, this was a question that had no evidential basis in any previously known facts or texts. It was apparent from the start, however, where an answer would have to be found. For Hölderlin wrote "Judgment and Being" near the end of his stay in Jena.

Hölderlin's Habilitation Plans and the Philosophical Discussion in Jena

Hölderlin was the only one of the three Tübingen friends who had the honor, considered a blessing at that time for a young philosopher, of studying at Jena. His residence there, of course, lasted a mere six months. He arrived, still employed as a private tutor, early in November 1794. After a few weeks in Weimar he returned to Jena in January—"allowed, for the first time since my earliest youth, to apply my talents, undisturbed" (*StA* VI, p. 149). During this time he worked on two versions of *Hyperion*. One might therefore doubt whether he was able to concern himself deeply with philosophical questions at all.

This doubt is put to rest, however, by the notable, though scarcely noted, fact that Hölderlin intended to pursue a lectureship as a philosopher in Jena. The habilitation procedure at what was then the most prestigious university in Germany required the defense of a published dissertation as a prerequisite to holding lectures. But the rather generous and indeed confused practice of applying these requirements confirmed Hölderlin in the hope that he might at least temporarily be allowed to lecture just on the basis of an exam. And he mentions precisely this possibility repeatedly in letters dating from the spring of 1795. Around the turn of the century Hölderlin once again made plans to habilitate, this time in Greek literature. There is no evidence, however, that he had any extensive background in this field by 1795. At that time, apart from the poetry to which he had already decided to dedicate his life, philosophy occupied him entirely.

Hölderlin's remarks on philosophical subjects are often framed by expressions of modesty and caution, as are many of his comments concerning his poetic work: "I . . . must ask that you consider this as good as left unwritten" (*StA* VI, p. 156). Such remarks, however, were counterbalanced by his occasional expressions of self-confidence, and above all by the respect he earned as a philosopher among his philosophical friends. As early as 1790 he wrote to his mother of wide-ranging plans in connection with his philosophical studies. In autumn of 1795 he said to his friend, the poet Neuffer, that he believed he was coming ever closer to his goal by means of the speculative pro and con. Schelling, who in the summer of 1795 had just written his third published work, debated with Hölderlin during this time concerning his own philosophical ideas. All evidence indicates that Schelling unquestioningly acknowledged Hölderlin as at least his equal. When Hegel came to Frankfurt in 1797 he seems to have immediately solicited Hölderlin's philosophical guidance. We can see, then, that by 1795 Hölderlin's intellectual strength and originality were readily apparent and generally recognized. The complete silence that his philosophical friends later maintained in this regard must be understood in light of the poet's fate and the illness to which he later succumbed.

Of course, planning to habilitate in philosophy at Jena, especially, in 1795, required a fair amount of self-confidence. For one thing, it meant being confident enough to take one's place alongside Fichte and some of the most distinguished Kantians of the day. And whoever had an interest in philosophical aesthetics, as Hölderlin apparently did, also had to consider his own lectures worthy of the likes of Friedrich Schiller, who taught aesthetics there until frequent illness forced him to give up teaching. In the past, some of the most promising lecturers in Jena had resigned and given up their lectureships in the face of such competition. It need not be taken as an early symptom of his illness, then, that Hölderlin left Jena suddenly at the beginning of June 1795 and returned to Swabia. Later, in a draft of the ode "Heidelberg," he described his departure as a flight from people and books. He admitted, in a letter to himself, that the flight from people was above all a flight from such close proximity to Schiller—specifically, from the kind of paralysis that can result from excessive admiration. The flight from books was presumably a flight from Fichte, whose very being—unlike Schiller's—we can conceive of as condensed in his *Wissenschaftslehre*. It was in no way a flight from philosophy itself, however. For Hölderlin carried on his philosophical reflections for at least another year, with the intention of completing them and putting them in publishable form. Indeed, he hoped to let his ideas mature in a quieter setting, giving up what was in fact the overly ambitious plan to lecture in the company of such figures while at the same time maintaining his vocation as a poet.

What Hölderlin had in mind was nothing less than a philosophical conception of his own design. The page on judgment and being attests to this, if one considers it in connection with the writings of others obviously inspired by Hölderlin's ideas. One must also see this conception in conjunction with the letters in which, following his departure,

Hölderlin sent word back to Jena concerning the progress of his philosophical work. Finally, it is in this light that one must try to understand the philosophical differences that arose between Schelling and Hölderlin in their conversations of the summer and winter of 1795. Unfortunately, Hölderlin's letters report only the fact of the dispute between the two friends, none of its substance.

If we wish to understand Hölderlin's place in classical German philosophy, we need to clarify the essential features of the ideas that would provide the basis of his lectures in Jena. In addition to this, though, it must be shown how this conception was relevant to the philosophical discussions of the day, and how Hölderlin thought he could both demonstrate his philosophical originality and at the same time defend his ideas. We can assume, then, that his relation to the philosophical problems of the day involved a specific relation to the problems recognized and discussed in Jena. For in Jena Hölderlin achieved more than just intellectual originality. It was at this center of philosophical activity that he sought to shape his ideas in the form of an academic teaching.

Now this poses a problem whose solution would require bringing together in a coherent whole the few surviving texts by Hölderlin, the often vague information concerning his philosophical connections, and finally some picture of the philosophical situation at the University of Jena. One can even formulate a criterion by which to gauge the suitability of any particular attempt to do this. On the one hand, such efforts must be able to situate the manuscript "Judgment and Being" in the context of a broader philosophical discussion. On the other hand, in light of that context, it must be able to account for the disagreements that arose between Schelling and Hölderlin in the second half of 1795. The fundamental ideas behind Hölderlin's conception will remain obscure until these two elements can be brought together coherently.

Even before 1790 the University of Jena was heavily attended principally because of its reputation in philosophy. Karl Leonhard Reinhold, Fichte's predecessor, was known for his impressive ability to explain Kant's philosophy. Carl Christian Erhard Schmid, who had published a widely read commentary on Kant's main works, also taught there with only brief interruption. Two other Kantians there edited and published the *Jenaer Allgemeine Literaturzeitung*, the first noteworthy journal whose express purpose was to promote the Kantian critique in German philosophy. It was felt that this critique could be discussed more profitably in Jena than in Königsberg itself. For Kant held only routine lectures, which hardly offered the opportunity for a discussion of his critical doctrines. Also, a short time later, some of the Kantian-minded professors from Jena came to the fore with philosophical theories of their own—above all Reinhold, but also Schmid and Schiller in the field of aesthetics. Fichte's arrival in Jena in the spring of 1794 provided even more impressive credentials to the university's reputation as the capital of German philosophy.

Hölderlin was but one of the many young men who had been drawn to Jena. We know that he was an influence on those younger than himself who had come to Jena from Homburg and who later belonged to the "alliance of friends" in Frankfurt (and Homburg). It could well be, then, that he had stimulating conversations with other students whom we now know only by their names. For this reason, a collaborative investigation is under way that will yield a profile of the state of the discussion at the University of Jena from 1790 to 1796 and of all the figures who took part in the philosophical exchange. Of course, there have been thousands of publications dealing with the personalities and events during this period. This is hardly surprising, since the concerns of the university can in no way be separated from what was going on at the court in Weimar and in the circles around Goethe, Herder, and Wieland. What is surprising, however, is that until now no inquiry into the details of the philosophical discussion in Jena has even been proposed. Research still too often centers around the biographies of individual figures and is more often than not bound up with the task of editing their works. Consequently, it almost inevitably falls short of what should in fact be of the greatest interest today, namely gaining some understanding of the intellectual climate in which those figures came to fashion their ideas and their works.

The present investigation is now well enough along that this much can be said: we should no longer entertain the possibility of some unknown third party coming to light whose presence might better account for Hölderlin's apparent originality, or even the derivative character of his thought, than is now possible on the basis of the relationships we know about already. In this connection the study of the situation in Jena distinguishes itself from the results of previous investigations dealing only with Tübingen and Frankfurt-Homburg. On the other hand, this study has depended entirely on the possibility of relying on hitherto inaccessible and unknown sources concerning already wellknown figures.

The half year that Hölderlin spent in Jena, during which time he arrived at his philosophical conception, is the same period of time in which three other philosophical projects, some of considerable importance, were also brought to a close: Fichte sent his *Wissenschaftslehre* to the press as a complete work for the first time; Schiller wrote the last two parts of his *Letters on the Aesthetic Education of Man*; and Niethammer brought out the first issues of his *Philosophical Journal*. Hölderlin was in frequent contact with precisely these three men, and he made regular remarks to this effect in his letters home. Letters to Schiller and to Niethammer from the period following his return home have also survived. The nature of Hölderlin's relations to Fichte and Schiller can therefore be inferred from a careful interpretation of his writings. The personal significance that his encounters with Niethammer had for him, however, cannot be explained in the same way.

And yet this relationship must have meant a lot to Hölderlin. Niethammer was by no means a thinker on a par with Schiller or Fichte. He was a Swabian, was in fact related to Hölderlin, and in spite of their difference in age they were already close at the Tübingen *Stift*. In 1790 he had come to Jena, for reasons scarcely different from Hölderlin's own, and had in the meantime been promoted to professor of philosophy. One might suppose that he merely acted as something like Hölderlin's patron. But Hölderlin counted him among his teachers and kept him informed concerning the progress of his philosophical project. And the reason he did so itself suggests that Hölderlin's habilitation plans amounted to more than an unrealistic dream, for Niethammer invited Hölderlin to contribute articles to his *Philosophical Journal*, which he had begun to edit on behalf of a group of scholars (mostly from Jena). The aim of the journal, according to its first announcement in December 1794, was to promote the completion of scientific philosophy. The "Preliminary Report" of May 1795 adds that in virtue of its broad applicability this philosophy should also enjoy a popularity not incompatible with its scientific nature. Moreover, Niethammer intended the *Journal* to live up to the philosophical standards set by the first issues of Schiller's *Die Horen*. He could therefore turn only to authors from whom he could expect something significant. He asked Hölderlin for several contributions, and sent him reminders concerning their delivery after the latter's return to Swabia and again when Hölderlin was in Frankfurt. Eventually it became apparent that Hölderlin would not be able to complete the articles he had promised. Yet their conversations in Jena had convinced Niethammer that Hölderlin's ideas, which had already won his confidence in their days at the *Stift*, were worthy of appearing as the philosophical premiere in a publication with a premise and an agenda of the sort described. Such an invitation from a Jena professor must have bolstered Hölderlin's habilitation plans; indeed Niethammer may well have been the first with whom Hölderlin broached the subject.

The Metaphilosophy of "Judgment and Being"

These, then, are the landmarks by which we have to orient ourselves
if we want to understand Hölderlin's thought in terms of the context
in which it came to fruition. We must now turn to the key text itself,
"Judgment and Being." And since our aim is only to characterize the
broad features of the philosophical position expressed in the text, we
will not need to discuss a number of textual details that require interpretation and that would otherwise have to be included.

It is obvious that the text relates to Fichte's *Wissenschaftslehre* and that
its systematic reflections are meant to lead to a critique of Fichte's
thought. The critique takes issue with Fichte's fundamental principle of the inner constitution of the "I" of consciousness. This critique denies the possibility of detaching the thought "I" from self-
consciousness. Fichte himself had in fact assumed that in the thought
"I" there lies a kind of unity and spontaneity that makes self-
consciousness intelligible. One of the elements involved in self-
consciousness is the knowledge of something quasi-objective, something not conceived of as distinct from that which has the knowledge.
For Fichte, however, a distance of this sort is ruled out in the case of the
consciousness "I." Hölderlin maintains, on the contrary, that there can
be no such theoretical distinction between the consciousness "I" and
self-consciousness. And from this he draws the methodological conclusion that that consciousness "I," or "I am I," is inappropriate as a conceptual starting point for a philosophical system, as it had been for
Fichte's *Wissenschaftslehre*. At the same time, Hölderlin claims that self-
consciousness cannot be made intelligible on the basis of any of its own
constitutive elements. Understanding it requires thinking beyond it, in
terms other than Fichte's. One must think not of the supposedly pure
consciousness "I" but of something radically prior to all consciousness,
something that makes intelligible, even conceivable, the thought "I"
and with it the fact of self-consciousness.

Hölderlin uses the term "being" (*Seyn*) to refer to that which underlies both the fact of, and our understanding of, the I and self-
consciousness, and in so doing brings into play a whole host of other
philosophical intentions. The most important of these is a rejection of
the view that philosophical foundations must restrict themselves to
concepts whose content is derived from the forms of consciousness and
knowledge alone. The fundamental idea is one that would traditionally
belong to the philosophical discipline of ontology. Of course, it could
neither be introduced nor analyzed within such an ontology. It must

instead be conceived as the very precondition of consciousness, and in terms of its content must be defined as that from which the subject emerges directly in relation to the object.

Further important associations are then bound up with the singular term "being." Hölderlin also speaks of "absolute being," alluding to Spinoza, for whom substance is the only thing that is and is conceivable. Hölderlin nonetheless avoids Spinozistic terminology completely. And he introduces the notion of "being" in a way that departs entirely from Spinoza's deductive method. This can be explained in terms of Jacobi's appropriation of Spinoza's ideas, in the course of which he found crucial support in one of Kant's precritical works.[1] In it Kant had claimed that existence underlies any determinate thought of something merely possible, from which it follows that the basis of anything possible must itself be assigned the modal status of necessity. Jacobi appropriated this argument too in his own way, to claim that in all justified knowledge we must proceed from a *certainty* in which *reality as such* is disclosed. For the thought of being immediately discloses a world —and is thus never a *mere* thought. It is no more possible to derive it from other thoughts than to confirm the existence of something real without presupposing the existence of something else. The certainty contained in the notion of being is in this sense the first certain ground for any knowledge. It seemed to Jacobi, then, that the error of Spinoza's method was not that he wished to establish a principle that would somehow include everything real. His mistake lay rather in thinking that he had to arrive at that principle by means of rational argumentation. With the adoption of such a program, he transformed the notion of the certainty of existence, which is always our starting point, into the concept of substance, in relation to which everything real is to be conceived as an attribute or as a mode of one of the attributes.

Jacobi had already applied these ideas to our knowledge of ourselves in one of the supplements to his *On the Doctrine of Spinoza*, included in the second edition of 1789 (Jacobi referred to this as his most important philosophical work). He inquired into this knowledge without ascribing to it the structure of self-consciousness. Yet he himself comes very close to suggesting just such an extension of his own idea. What he does explicitly claim is that knowledge of our own existence is the representation of something conditioned, and that the representation of something unconditioned must therefore precede it internally. In this respect, then, we need not "first search for the unconditioned, rather we have . . . a greater certainty of its existence than we have of our own determined existence."[2]

Hölderlin combines these ideas of Jacobi's with Fichte's principles concerning the nature of self-consciousness in the following way. While Fichte rightly recognizes the opposition inherent in self-consciousness, he fails to see that neither of its elements may be taken as unconditioned. The relation is rather one of total division and is therefore reciprocal—and in this sense, in Jacobi's terms, conditioned. Something unconditioned must therefore precede it, and since conditioning relations amount to divisions, the unconditioned must be conceived in terms of a "being-unified" free of all division. By referring metaphorically to the situation in which division first emerges as *Urteil* ("judgment"), Hölderlin also wants to show that being cannot be disclosed in the form of judgment, which is constitutive of knowledge, and that it is rather what all judgment presupposes.

If one attends to the connotations of Hölderlin's talk of being, shades of meaning not made explicit in the text itself begin to emerge in his conception as a whole. These should be pursued further. For neither his text nor his general conception would find a place in the course of classical German philosophy if it amounted to no more than an effort to force Fichte back into Jacobi's position.

Paying no attention at all to the connections between Hölderlin's text and Jacobi's views of 1789, one would be tempted to read the former as an attempt to outdo Fichte on his own methodological terrain. Fichte's first presentation of the *Wissenschaftslehre* is motivated by a project that Reinhold first introduced into philosophy after Kant; that is, both aim to place Kant's philosophy on reliable foundations by proceeding from a single *principle* and deriving from it the entire scope of philosophical knowledge. This derivation is to acquire scientific form by making use of just one single material principle (apart from the rules of inference). And it can be the one true principle only if it points out something in itself complex and yet evidently unified in the diversity of its elements, something that can be taken to be strictly foundational, prior to and constituting all the various domains of philosophical knowledge. In a work appearing in 1789, Reinhold sought to show that this fundamental something could be nothing other than our form of representation. In 1794 Fichte countered this with the claim that one can and must go even further back. Fichte thus grounded philosophy on a principle of the intrinsic unity of the consciousness "I am," from which he sought to derive the form of mere representation itself.

One might read Hölderlin's text as a continuation of this one-upmanship, now directed against Fichte's theory. He says, in fact, that the consciousness "I am" is neither basic nor self-sufficient and that one must revert to an even deeper foundation. He says moreover that proceeding from the notion of "being," all consciousness containing the thought "I" must be conceived as a "separation," hence that Fichte's "I am I" is a prime case of separation and thus "the most fitting example" of *Urteilung*.

But understanding and classifying Hölderlin's text in this way misses the most essential aspect of the conception underlying it, however correctly it describes one dominant thread in the literal meaning of the text. This becomes apparent when one recognizes that Hölderlin's conception can in no way be included within the methodology of first principles. For if one begins by defining being as self-sufficient and hence absolutely primary, one could never go on to derive the elements that are supposed to be separated out in judgment. On the contrary, those elements are even presupposed when Hölderlin defines being as the undivided unity of what emerges from the division in the form of subject and object. Anyone could have seen that it would be circular to derive subject and object from being, so conceived. Hölderlin could hardly have had such a derivation in mind. None of the concepts or ideas in the text in any way suggests that his conception would be developed in the form of a first-principle philosophy (*Grundsatzphiloso-phie*. His conception does indeed articulate a principle that must be conceived as underlying all consciousness. But it does not seek to construct a chain of theoretical inferences on the basis of that principle. One could say, then, that Hölderlin attempts to base a form of monism on the principle without at the same time falling into a methodological monism by deriving propositions from it. In other words, Hölderlin's conception agrees with the aims of first-principle philosophy inasmuch as it indicates an ultimate ground from which all forms of consciousness and knowledge emerge. Yet it does so through a form of argument that is, from a metaphilosophical and methodological point of view, utterly alien to first-principle philosophy.

It becomes apparent, then, that in identifying the ultimate ground of consciousness and knowledge Hölderlin was able to draw an immediate connection with Jacobi's thought. Indeed, Jacobi had taught that all mediated knowledge presupposes the unconditioned certainty of being. Although his thoughts concerning the nature of this presupposition remained obscure, he was clearly of the opinion that the relation between what is original and what is dependent does not correspond to the relation between a principle and the inferences that can be drawn from it. The content of the certainty that makes up the presupposition cannot properly be captured in a self-evident and hence indubitable proposition, and certainly not in such a way that the concepts contained in the proposition could themselves be defined on the basis of the evidence to which the proposition refers. Such a proposition would belong, according to Jacobi, to the realm of mediation, and the unconditionality of a real, absolute presupposition would have to remain incommensurable with it. Thus while "Judgment and Being" parallels the approach of Reinhold and Fichte in conceiving of diversity—Ur-teil, and with it judgment—as something made possible by the unity of a first principle—being—still the philosophical approach assumed in this text remains fundamentally different from theirs.

Niethammer's Assessment of the Situation

The text of "Judgment and Being" never deals explicitly with the metaphilosophy underlying Hölderlin's conception, and proceeds only in broad outline. For present purposes it has been necessary to point out just how different that metaphilosophy is from Fichte's method. One might object that this approach fails to consider the possibility that the young Hölderlin was wholly unaware of any such distinction and that metaphilosophical reflections may have been the farthest thing from his mind. But one can meet this objection by examining other texts by Hölderlin and by looking more closely at the discussion as it stood during Hölderlin's residence in Jena. The writings of Niethammer not only bear witness to the fact that Hölderlin was intimately familiar with that discussion, and what that familiarity amounted to, but also allow us to draw some conclusions regarding the philosophical dialogue he had with Niethammer himself. Knowing something about that context of discussion is a necessary precondition for properly determining the place of "Judgment and Being" in the development of classical German philosophy.

The discussion Hölderlin entered into through Niethammer took place among Reinhold's students and was essentially limited to Jena and to then past and present Jena philosophers. They had all studied and defended Reinhold's *Theory of the Faculty of Representation*,[3] the first philosophy that sought to ground itself in a single, highest principle. They had then seen not only that this theory had been dismissed in a number of reviews but also that Reinhold himself had begun to recognize that it involved some fundamental errors. Not that he said so publicly. In fact, he was still planning to present his Elementary Philosophy anew, free of defects and errors. But before he left Jena, being replaced by Fichte in the spring of 1794, he was able to publish one more essay from which those in the know could, with a little effort, gather that he now sought not only to reinterpret but to reconstruct his theory completely on the basis of a first, universal principle.

Reinhold drew a distinction between the arguments that induced him to undertake such a thoroughgoing revision on the one hand and the criticisms that had been advanced publicly on the other. He took the latter to be on the whole inconclusive, misunderstandings for the most part, or at best occasions for minor revisions. The arguments that he did acknowledge arose only in personal exchanges. These seemed significant to Reinhold inasmuch as that they did not merely reproach him with isolated deductive errors but also explained *why* his inferences had to go awry, namely because he had included the concept of representation in the very definition of his highest principle. One could then object that from that concept he was trying to derive properties of representation that could in truth be got only from an entirely different concept. One could then claim, for example, that the form of representation had been "produced" only if one had already defined a principle of production with respect to representation, and that definition could only be a definition of the subject and its spontaneity. However, Reinhold found that, conversely, one could in turn arrive at such a concept of the subject only on the basis of a definition of representation. And this raised doubts about whether the method of philosophy could be understood as derivation from a first, unique principle at all.

These doubts did not, however, lead him to give up all attempts to extend the Kantian doctrine and return once again to the ranks of the literalist Kantian commentators. Reinhold himself had in fact been the most outspoken among them prior to publishing his *Theory of the Faculty of Representation*. But that option was no longer open to anyone who had studied all the ramifications of Reinhold's *Theory*. For that work contained within it a number of partial theories that could no longer be written out of the course of philosophical reflection itself. One of these partial theories happened to be a theory of the inner constitution of self-consciousness, and it is reasonable to assume that Hölderlin's critique of Fichte presupposes some knowledge of it. Reinhold's *Theory*, then, had uncovered a domain of problems and propositions from which those who entered into it could not simply turn away.

Far away from Jena, however, one could scarcely see that Reinhold had lost faith in the idea that was central to the methodological constitution of his theory. Thus, in Zurich, in the first drafts of his *Wissenschaftslehre*, Fichte applied and defended the methodology of first-principle philosophy. And although in his reflections Fichte moved away from the concept of representation, which had been the most elemental concept in Reinhold's Elementary Philosophy, toward the concept of a pure I, he nonetheless subscribed to what had long since been regarded in Jena, even by Reinhold himself, as the most problematic feature of Reinhold's metaphilosophy. Fichte arrived in Jena unaware of any of this. One can imagine, then, that his *Wissenschaftslehre* must have met with reservations that were especially difficult for Fichte himself to understand.

Niethammer had come to Jena in 1790 to study Kant with Reinhold. A theological crisis had made philosophy his main concern, and for this reason his true interest lay in the philosophy of religion. He was not particularly gifted theoretically. Ephorus Schnurrer of Tübingen, however, credited him with extraordinary intelligence ("like scarcely one in a thousand"). And this would indeed help him in making his way through the theoretical maze with greater assurance than others.

By the time Reinhold left Jena, Niethammer must have long since become convinced that a theory based on a single principle could never solve the basic problems concerning the foundations of philosophy. Yet he thought it ill-advised to hold forth on this matter in the midst of Fichte's meteoric rise to fame. He left it to the mental prowess of Fichte and Reinhold to discover, or invent, some way out of the situation, which he himself considered to be on the whole a dead end for the methods of critical philosophy. At the same time, he was just as convinced as Reinhold's other students that Kant had not already done everything there was to be done in the area of metaphilosophy. It must have been in these terms, then, that the new philosophical impulse that had begun with Reinhold was received and pursued. It was impossible to foresee where this impulse would lead philosophical speculation. Niethammer inclined to the view that such speculation would never manage to reach completely conclusive results and that one should assume the possibility of unending theoretical progress, as Kant had claimed with respect to the moral perfection of human beings. Yet one could maintain that Kant had determined a secure *direction* for this theoretical progress, for he had attempted to shed light on the laws inherent in the constitution of the rational subject.

With this well-balanced program in mind, then, Niethammer launched his *Philosophical Journal*. His diagnosis of the situation allowed him to offer to collaborate with defenders as well as critics of first-principle philosophy while still remaining true to his own convictions. He did not have to explain publicly that he personally held out no prospects for first-principle philosophy. He limited himself to a clear characterization of the situation, namely, that even in the wake of Reinhold and Fichte the foundations of critical philosophy remained obscure. And in addition he presented contrary arguments to the effect that a first principle could provide critical philosophy with secure foundations after all.

We know from a letter of June 1794, written to a Carinthian industri-
alist who had himself been a student of Reinhold's, that Niethammer
went further in his personal correspondence. The letter was confiscated
shortly thereafter in a police operation against a group of Austrian
Kantians, and consequently to this day it has remained in the archives
of the Imperial-Royal Ministry of the Interior. Niethammer presumably
expressed himself in much the same way to Hölderlin, too:

> Convinced that there is no need whatsoever for a single, highest principle of
> all knowledge, I stand back and look on in silence at the circles spun by philo-
> sophical judgment and its representatives. But although I doubt that a proposi-
> tion—whatever it may be—will ever be able to support the entire structure, it
> cannot be denied that philosophy has advanced considerably because of these
> efforts to find a foundation stone for the structure as a whole.[4]

The reason that a highest principle struck Niethammer as unnecessary
was that the essential task of philosophy, to bring harmony to mankind
in life and in faith, can only be fulfilled by continuing the course set
by Kant. The search for such a principle seemed hopeless to him on
theoretical grounds. Still, he wanted to put in his "two cents" concerning the philosophical movement that had formed around the search.
And this he did first in the introductory essay to the *Philosophical Journal*
under the title "Of the Claims of Common Understanding on Philosophy," which Hölderlin might well have read before its publication in
May 1795.

In this text Niethammer takes up a point Reinhold made once his
elementary philosophy had fallen into crisis, namely, that philosophy
may have to begin by identifying fundamental convictions of general
human understanding and then follow them back to their origins, of
which that understanding can never be conscious. Niethammer goes
on to claim in addition that no philosophy can be true if it comes into
conflict with the convictions of sound understanding that cannot be
shown to be mere received prejudices. For the principle of the "subject"
must be the basis of the formation of those convictions, since it is the
ground on which all truths must be understood. The task of philosophy, according to Kant, is none other than to understand the laws governing all our convictions according to the spontaneity of the subject.
Niethammer then concludes that neither materialism, which denies
freedom, nor Fichte's theory, according to which our involuntary feeling of dependency is a mere illusion, can be considered a plausible
theory. For they contradict two real convictions of general human
understanding, which nonetheless stand mutually opposed. And, in
Niethammer's view, this opposition is what poses the true task for

philosophy. He formulates this in a proposition that bears some of the hallmarks of the thought of Hölderlin and others like him: "The difficult task that philosophy must undertake consists in unifying the different conflicting forms of consciousness in a single system of knowledge . . . without either sacrificing the one to the other, or, which would amount to the same thing, forsaking [*aufheben*] the unity of the subject."[5]

In Niethammer's mind, this proposition served only to indicate the task of philosophical theory as such. Still, Hölderlin could read it as confirmation of an approach that had become decisive for his own thinking even before he arrived in Jena, that is, that conscious life is at once shaped and unbalanced by the basic conflicting tendencies orienting it. And the formative process of life aims at finding a balance and a harmony amid this strife, in which no one tendency is entirely suppressed or denied in its own right. The preface to the fragment of *Hyperion* already identifies the highest and most beautiful state humanly attainable as the ability to withstand what is greatest, and yet to be humbled by what is smallest. In this state the vital tendencies are brought together, and Hölderlin's question then concerns what such a state would be and how it is to be understood. This is why we call Hölderlin's "speculative pro and con" an attempt at a "unification philosophy" (*Vereinigungsphilosophie*). Niethammer's program does not have the conflict of vital tendencies in mind. Nonetheless, he too, on what he took to be decisive metaphilosophical grounds, deemed the task of philosophical theory a task of *unification*.

We can now get a sense of why, in the two letters Hölderlin wrote to Niethammer in the year after his return from Jena, he referred to him as a teacher and philosophical mentor. Hölderlin writes that Niethammer had advised him to beware of "abstractions." This advice served Hölderlin well during his intensive studies of Fichte, and he must have limited himself to gaining some philosophical perspective on the problems concerning the subject in its knowledge and practice in general, without putting too much hope in the power of speculative reason. Hölderlin speaks in this connection of "fruitless efforts to which you bore witness" (*StA* VI, p. 202). Yet Niethammer could not have advised him to give up philosophical theory altogether. For at this point he still expects to receive essays from Hölderlin, and Hölderlin even sketches out the program of one of these texts for him in a way that thoroughly presupposes thoughts of the sort we find in "Judgment and Being." One can see, then, that Hölderlin embarks on this program, and would presumably have developed it further, in such a way that he could count on Niethammer's agreement on essential points.

Three such points of agreement stand out most clearly. First, for Hölderlin, too, the theoretical process of philosophical knowledge cannot be captured in any conclusive results. Second, the task of philosophy consists in the explanation and unification of every "conflict" within which we "think and exist." Finally, reference to some principle, an "absolute," is imperative for the fulfillment of this task. But it is inconsequential whether or not one conceives of this principle, with Fichte, as "I." One must only determine its status correctly, which for both Hölderlin and Niethammer (though of course in different senses) means that it must not be confused with the form of self-consciousness. In a letter to Schiller in this regard, Hölderlin coins a phrase that he would use again repeatedly and that corresponds perfectly to Niethammer's own formulation. In Niethammer it reads: "The subject, the spontaneity in us, the I (or whatever you want to call this unity . . .)."[6] Hölderlin speaks to Schiller of the unification of the subject and object in an absolute "I, or whatever you want to call it" (*StA* VI, p. 181).

Now all of these points of agreement are directly related to Niethammer's renunciation of the program of developing a theory on the basis of a single, highest principle. We can gather from Hölderlin's remarks in letters to Niethammer concerning his conversations with Schelling, moreover, that Hölderlin agrees with his "mentor" on this point. Since Niethammer had reached his position on the matter long before, and since it had even figured into the design of his *Philosophical Journal*, we must assume that Hölderlin was in fact following Niethammer's example.

Here then we can see an essential share of the profits afforded Hölderlin by his stay in Jena. Only in Jena could he have nourished himself on Fichte's teaching and Schiller's company, and the significance of whatever Niethammer was able to clarify for him pales in comparison. Yet through his friendship with Niethammer, Hölderlin gained access to a discussion in which Niethammer held a view in common with some of Reinhold's other students. It even verged on Reinhold's own new position, which was publicly nearly indiscernible. And so through the development of his own "specualtive pro and con," Hölderlin was soon able to achieve an independence, and above all a self-confidence, that allowed him to formulate a view against Fichte without either clinging literally to the words of Kant or straying off into amateurish lines of reasoning. New notions had arisen in Jena during the two years between the crisis of Reinhold's Elementary Philosophy and Fichte's arrival, and it was through Niethammer that Hölderlin became acquainted with them. And it is by means of them that we can explain how, in such a remarkably short period of time, Hölderlin arrived at a view that departed from Fichte's first-principle philosophy and gave rise to a new branch in classical German philosophy after Kant.

Hölderlin's Critique of Schelling

This explanation does not make the originality of Hölderlin's thought immediately obvious. For Hölderlin did more than just mimic Niethammer's doubts about first-principle philosophy. Going beyond that line of reasoning became possible, indeed unavoidable, precisely because of the sort of conceptual issues that had already taken on a decisive significance for Hölderlin. Moreover, this possibility now put him in a position to make use of the ideas of Jacobi and to draw connections between Fichte's theory of the opposition in the consciousness "I am" and Jacobi's basic insight. The text of "Judgment and Being" illustrates how these three threads could be woven into the pattern of a single philosophical program.

If one understands Hölderlin's program in this way, one can also explain why Hölderlin entered into a philosophical dispute with Schelling during the latter part of 1795, a dispute concerning foundational questions, not just the theoretical significance of art, as is often supposed. Hölderlin's occasional remarks concerning this dispute in his letters to Niethammer thus serve as indirect confirmation of our interpretation of Hölderlin's fundamental conception.

On December 22, 1795, Hölderlin writes: "Schelling, as you may know, has turned away somewhat from his original convictions" (StA VI, p. 191). On February 24, 1796, Hölderlin again refers to a *change* in Schelling's position: Schelling "with his new convictions, as you may know, has gone down a better road, without ever reaching his destination on the worse one" (StA VI, p. 203). These remarks are somewhat cryptic since they also apparently allude to conversations between Hölderlin and Niethammer. Hölderlin takes it for granted that Niethammer will essentially agree with his assessment of Schelling's work. And this presupposes that some exchange had taken place between the two of them regarding fundamental philosophical questions, and that that exchange had been thorough enough that Hölderlin could anticipate Niethammer's judgment concerning the new turn Schelling had taken. He is even sure of one point in particular, namely, that Niethammer will view the change in Schelling's position as a turn for the better.

In regard to Schelling, then, Hölderlin's remarks distinguish between two positions, both of which Niethammer must have been familiar with, and neither of which Hölderlin accepts, though he considers the more recent one preferable to the earlier. It must be pointed out that judgments of this sort could hardly be expected from someone who considered himself less competent to judge the matter at hand than the person he was addressing.

The fact that Hölderlin distinguishes between Schelling's two positions, and is critical of both, poses a problem that can only be resolved in connection with three of Schelling's early publications, written between the summers of 1794 and 1795. These include the treatise *On the Possibility of a Form of All Philosophy*, a short book entitled *Of the I as Principle of Philosophy*, and the first part of the "Letters on Dogmatism and Criticism." The "Letters" was written for Niethammer's *Journal*, and Hölderlin knew that the first part was already in Niethammer's possession by the time he wrote him regarding Schelling's change of heart. The problem therefore requires separating these three texts into two groups and then explaining the sense in which one represents a move away from the other.

It is, I believe, the two later writings that belong together in Hölderlin's mind, over against the first, and as evidence I would appeal to the different attitudes of the respective texts toward first-principle philosophy. In the treatise *On the Possibility of a Form of All Philosophy*, of September 1794, Schelling follows the plan of developing an elementary philosophy on the model advanced first by Reinhold and then by Fichte in his own programmatic work. Schelling's own contribution is an attempt to derive a conception of a first principle and principles following from it, from a purely formal concept of philosophy itself. Niethammer's introductory essay to the *Philosophical Journal* suggests that he may have read this piece already. So, if Niethammer and Hölderlin were of one mind concerning the failure of first-principle philosophy, we can assume they also discussed Schelling's first work.

It is also possible, though less likely, that Hölderlin had occasion to discuss Schelling's second piece with Niethammer as well. In it Schelling did not really dissociate himself from all forms of first-principle philosophy. This text, however, and the program it advances, makes only passing reference to first principles. Schelling later characterized the piece as an explicit attempt "to liberate philosophy from the stagnation into which it was bound to fall owing to ill-fated inquiries into a first principle." This sentence was written in October 1796, and so may be an overestimation due to hindsight. Still, one can already gather clearly from the "Letters" of the summer of 1795 that Schelling dissociated the ideas in *Of the I as Principle of Philosophy* from the realm of first-principle philosophy. He immediately goes on to explain that philosophy is not grounded in principles but in practical demands, and that the consciousness "I am," precisely because it is the consciousness of freedom, provides no basis for the formulation of highest premises for philosophical deduction.

Hölderlin knew that this turn against first-principle philosophy would meet with Niethammer's approval. And he himself could agree with Schelling about this much without then having to be "in accord" with him entirely. After all, Schelling went on to develop, short of first-principle philosophy, other ideas of Fichte's that Hölderlin had shown to be untenable in "Judgment and Being." Specifically, Schelling wanted to find something unconditioned in the consciousness "I." And for other reasons, which he may have already discussed with Hölderlin in the Tübingen *Stift*, he wanted to combine this unconditioned with Jacobi's certainty of being, which cannot be mediated by means of an inference. On the other hand, it would be necessary to distinguish between the notion of being and any form of subjective consciousness, both in terms of content and with respect to its role in philosophical reflection. So, if Schelling moved on to a better path, it was still one that called for a fundamental critique. And Hölderlin expected that Niethammer would understand the substance of his critique without further explanation, and that he would by and large concur.

We can now see the kind of arguments with which Hölderlin was able to approach his friend Hegel when, for the first time since they had left Tübingen, they found themselves reunited in Frankfurt at the beginning of 1797. We can also understand how the judgment he formed in Jena with regard to foundational questions, along with the conception based on it, could not only draw Hegel away from Kant but also lead him beyond both Fichte and Schelling's early writings and ultimately win him over to a unification philosophy. Hölderlin's ideas had gained an impetus from Jena and the discussion taking place there, an impetus capable of directing the swift development of philosophy after Kant.

Niethammer's mentorship is as crucial to an understanding of that impetus as is the philosophy of Fichte or the personal example of Schiller. Of course, the conclusions that Hölderlin drew from Niethammer's approach—notwithstanding their agreement in questions of metaphilosophy—led to designs going far beyond Niethammer's own horizons. To be sure, Hölderlin abandoned Fichte's foundationalist notions, but he held fast to Fichte's speculative developments, particularly his doctrine that subjectivity moves through oppositions and relative syntheses of oppositions. Encouraged by Schiller, but driven equally by his own early ideas, he saw the ultimate synthesis, insofar as it is possible in finite conscious life, in the aesthetic act. In Hölderlin's view, this principle combines the insight that philosophical theory as such can never be brought to completion and Jacobi's doctrine that the sense of the unity of all things must be understood not in the form of the I but only from a principle that precedes all consciousness—a principle that nonetheless manifests itself in consciousness, if only by means of a separation. The unification that not only springs from the one being but also corresponds to its oneness is of an aesthetic, not a theoretical, nature. For this reason, Hölderlin wanted to call his initial contribution to the *Philosophical Journal*, the one piece on which he had made the most progress, "New Letters on the Aesthetic Education of Man." The great ambition behind this modest title is unmistakable: Hölderlin would complete the project of Schiller, whom he so admired, but whose Kantian approach he would nonetheless criticize. And he would proceed on the basis of ideas he would bring to bear in a critique of Fichte as well—and not just as an afterthought but from the very core of his metaphilosophy. Niethammer was no doubt confident of his ability to carry out a project of this caliber and of the project's consistency with the aims of the *Journal*. It is understandable too, however, that Hölderlin was never able to finish it.

For by taking a retrospective look at the course of classical German philosophy we can see more clearly the status and significance a project of this sort would have attained had it in fact been carried out. It would have produced a philosophy of conscious life according to which consciousness and knowledge do not constitute the single, all-encompassing principle. Moreover, this philosophy would have ruled out from the beginning the program of an absolute science, to which Schelling and Hegel became committed shortly thereafter. It would have been speculative philosophy nonetheless. In order to describe the oppositions of life in their syntheses, it would have at least had to carry further the analyses with which Fichte had been able to penetrate more deeply than anyone before him into the dynamics of the unfolding of consciousness. In addition, it would have required a conceptual form that cannot be found in the kind of cognition that defines objects according to the rules guiding their transformations. Since metaphilosophy, which was decisive for Hölderlin, is neither the science of Reinhold and Fichte nor the science of the absolute later conceived by Schelling and Hegel, this conceptual orientation also would have had to be developed independently.

Hölderlin could not accomplish all this, and soon he no longer cared. To be sure, he continued to philosophize. But he now concerned himself less with foundational questions and more with the theory of poetry. It is possible to find in these later texts references to metaphilosophical problems, and deeper insights into them. Which is not to say these texts can simply be understood as metaphilosophical works themselves. Hölderlin's philosophizing cleared a path toward an understanding of the origin and the role of poetry in human life. And he let it stand at that. This does not mean, however, that his intellectual efforts, which nearly led him to a habilitation in the capital of German philosophy, were from the outset significant only as a means to an end. For it remains that the poet Hölderlin emerged transformed from his intense concentration on the philosophical problems of the day.

In the course of these reflections he was able to exert considerable influence at only one point in the development of classical German philosophy, a point we can determine with some precision. As a result, no history of the period can now afford to ignore Hölderlin's thought. Neither his own talent nor the questions on which he reflected allowed him to stand for more than a brief moment at the forefront of the philosophical movement that had taken its point of departure from Kant.

But the ideas of Hölderlin the philosopher remain present as more than just a theme in his poetry. His thinking is also literally "at work" in this poetry: in its universal scope, in the depth of its moving force, in the language carried along by the clarity and the strength of his ideas, and in the calculated architectonic of its construction—while the poetry continually seeks to reach out beyond any truth that can be articulated philosophically. In this respect the poetry itself is one of the immediate products of classical German philosophy. Only by focusing narrowly on its content, as Heidegger has done, could one suppose that it calls for a kind of thinking that classical German philosophy itself pushed aside. Still, it is up to us to ascertain and explore the potential, never in fact realized by Hölderlin himself, of a philosophy consistent not only with the outline of the conception he elaborated in Jena but with his later poetry as well. We can hear Hölderlin the poet too, then, in the lines he wrote to his brother on October 13, 1796: "Philosophy you *must* study, even if you scarcely have the money for a lamp and oil, and no more time than from midnight to the rooster's crow" (*StA* VI, p. 218).

Translated by Taylor Carman

SIX

Hegel and Hölderlin

HEGEL'S friendship with Hölderlin ended in silence. In all of Hegel's work Hölderlin is not mentioned once. And wherever his name does come up in letters, Hegel invariably gives only a scant reply. The period of their association, dominated by the "ideals of youth," seemed as far removed to Hegel, who had gone on to develop the idea into a philosophical system, as they did to Hölderlin himself, struck dumb by madness. In the absence of scholarly research, we would know nothing of the bond between them.

On occasion, of course, Hegel's old memories could come to life with astonishing clarity. He could then tell of his past with Hölderlin in such a way that those who listened found themselves transported back, much in the way Proust later described the remembrance of things past.[1]

Anticipating a renewed association with Hölderlin, Hegel once dedicated a poem to his friend, the only significant poem he would ever write. In it, anxiously awaiting their imminent reunion, he extolled the fidelity of their earlier bond of friendship.[2] And he gave assurance that he would need his friend's direction and guidance, just as Hölderlin, on the other hand, welcomed him as the mentor of his own, too often disturbed life.[3] What followed in the wider circle of their other friends was indeed a time that later seemed, to one of them at least, an "alliance of friends" with a "common view of the truth."[4]

For Hegel, however, this alliance fell through, with the rapid transformation of the historical setting of the age, which pulled the lives of these friends along with it, but in disparate directions; with his entering into the mundane routine of teaching at the University of Jena; with his growing conviction that the modern world could no longer recognize itself in the great mythic poetry for which Hölderlin lived; and also, no doubt, with the shock at the poet's appearance, once compared to the angels and the gods, now disfigured by madness. Thus the silence fell, deepened by the mood of the Metternich era, which always recalled, however reluctantly, the series of uprisings and crises through which it had finally secured a precarious calm. The silence was deepened also by Hegel's own self-presentation, according to which his system was to have followed from its predecessors with all the necessity of a logical inference. If he saw his own work as the quintessence of a thinking begun by Kant, Parmenides even, then it is no surprise that he would try to distance himself from the vital situation that in fact enabled him to understand himself as he did. It is the unlimited power of the Notion (*Begriff*) that brings forth its truth from the arbitrary and therefore indifferent conditions of the particular individual who first articulates it in its full determinacy—and that, for a good Hegelian, should constitute sufficient philosophical reasons for forgetting.

It has long since been clear, however, that we cannot regard the way from Kant to Hegel on the model of an ascent, leading step by step to higher levels of insight. The time has come to explain more precisely the extent to which the various formulations of a philosophy that appeared toward the end of the eighteenth century may be understood as so many competing attempts to resolve a singular complex of problems, each unfairly diagnosing and dismissing the others as historically obsolete or even as excretions of obscurity, naively applying the then novel resources of the philosophy of history to their originators. In the light of such a reconsideration, an image of Hegel's thought emerges that can no longer relegate the "alliance of spirits" with Hölderlin to a kind of inconsequential prehistory. The contours of this image, however, have remained indistinct until now.

I shall here attempt to trace these contours more clearly and to highlight the structures of thought at work in that personal encounter, an encounter that is especially moving since it forms part of Hölderlin's own treacherous ascent into his most inspired poetry as well as his descent into the darkness of solitude.

Hegel owed more to his friend than he could ever express, and this, indeed, in two quite distinct senses. First, he was indebted to him for the essential impetus behind the transition to his own thought, free at the outset from Kant and Fichte. From the time of their encounter in Frankfurt, Hegel remained on a continuous path of development, which he would not have found at all without Hölderlin's guiding influence. This is not to say that Hegel merely gave systematic articulation to an insight hit upon by Hölderlin. On the contrary, it can be shown, secondly, that Hegel soon recognized that he had to explicate Hölderlin's insight in a way Hölderlin himself never could. It was precisely the input from Hölderlin, then, combined at the same time with a rejection of it, that determined Hegel's early approach to his system. Received opinion has it that the mature Hegel always expressed what was peculiar to his own thought by way of a critical stance vis-à-vis Schelling. To some extent, of course, this cannot be denied, especially since Schelling's influence had become a public force that Hegel came to oppose. Yet it was not just consideration for his younger friend that at first prevented Hegel from mentioning Schelling's name. Hegel had to rediscover in Schelling's philosophy of identity a pattern of thought that he had already encountered earlier in Hölderlin, which had impressed him more deeply than Schelling's thought did during the period in Jena when Hegel was actually working out his system. Hegel learned to express what was most genuinely his own in connection with that pattern of thought while still among his circle of friends in Frankfurt.

We have grounds, then, for stressing the programmatic formulas of Hegel's thought, now on everyone's lips, in such a way that they both correspond to *and* militate against Hölderlin's insight. No less is required even to address the question of truth and priority to their projected lives and ideas, which became, if for different reasons, so unforgettable.

Selfhood and Abandon in Unification Philosophy

We have recently established with some certainty that it was Hölderlin who, in the light of Kant's theory of freedom, first challenged Kant's thesis that the unity of consciousness of the I as the subject of thought marks the highest point from which philosophy must proceed. It seems incredible that someone who saw himself strictly as a poet, and who justified his "speculative pro and con" (*StA* VI, p. 183) as simply being in the service of poetry, could earn such a place in the history of world philosophy. It is therefore all the more urgent to discover how such a thing was possible. Let us begin with this.

The consciousness of an age cannot always articulate itself completely in the philosophical theory that predominates at the time. Tributaries of thought consequently emerge that go long unheeded until they find occasion to join the mainstream, at which point they often alter the direction and current of that mainstream itself. One such tributary of the empiricism and metaphysics of the eighteenth century, though flowing from Platonic sources, was unification philosophy (*Ver-*

einigungsphilosophie). Hölderlin had already formulated the problem of his life in its terms, even before becoming acquainted with Fichte's thought. It gave him the strength to recast Fichte's ideas and, with their help, albeit in the new form he had given them, to set Hegel upon a course of his own.

The basic theme of unification philosophy is man's highest desire, which is satisfied neither by the consumption of goods nor by the possession of power nor by the recognition of others. In the Neoplatonic tradition, Shaftesbury had related this theme to the intuition of the beautiful, which is to be found principally in the power of the mind (*Geist*), whence beautiful works of art originate.[5] With this notion that the mind is the true seat of beauty, to which the highest desire attains, he remained close to the assumptions basic to modern philosophy.

Franz Hemsterhuis, however, soon came out more sharply against those assumptions. He maintained that desire cannot be conceived as the enthusiastic veneration of supreme creativity. Since desire impels us to attain full perfection, it must at once transcend all particularity and limitation. It is only satisfied when the boundaries fall away, separating the one who desires from that which he desires. The drive toward unification is thus a drive toward fusion, and cannot be the love for a highest being but merely an abandon to what is finite and external to us. Hemsterhuis conceived of God no longer as the power of love but only as the force that imposes the ungraspable fate of individuation upon a world in which everything strives toward totality.[6]

Herder then showed, in his influential essay on "Love and Selfhood," that this sort of surrender cannot be the meaning of love. The limits of love, which Hemsterhuis had located in our individuated existence, can never be superseded, lest the very *enjoyment* of love, and therefore love itself, vanish as well. Creatures must "give and take, suffer and act, attract to themselves and gently impart of themselves"— this is "the true pulse of life." Herder follows Aristotle in saying that friendship, which finds fulfillment in relation to a common end and which always seeks and preserves the autonomy of the friends themselves, must always be a component of love. "Friendship and love are possible only between mutually free, consonant, but not uniform, let alone identical, beings."

In this conflict between Hemsterhuis and Herder, unification philosophy was given its latest, indeed its specifically modern problem, a problem that determined Hölderlin's own original beginnings—in poetry as well as philosophy. Herder's Aristotelianism could not account for the experience of self-abandon that Hemsterhuis had taken to be, and convincingly presented as, the essence of desire. Herder was nonetheless convinced that when desire seeks surrender, love itself vanishes, and moreover the other definitive experience of modern life and modern philosophy—the inalienable right of the free subject—loses its legitimacy. In fact, it seemed necessary to strengthen Herder's arguments against Hemsterhuis, to acknowledge a higher claim for "selfhood," and *at the same time* to preserve Hemsterhuis's notion of abandon in the face of Herder's Aristotelian objection.

Much later, in his lectures on aesthetics, Hegel still recalled this problem in his explication of maternal love as a Romantic subject in art: "It is a love without desire, but it is not friendship, for friendship, however affectionate it may be, still requires some content, some essential issue as an integrating end. Maternal love, by contrast, has an immediate hold without any identity of ends and interests."[7]

But it was the young Schiller who made the first attempt to mediate between love and selfhood, in his *Theosophy of Julius*. He himself described that work as an undertaking to secure a "purer conception of love."[8] He interpreted love, contrary to Hemsterhuis, as the finite self's reaching over the entire world as it strives for perfection. What we mean by "love" is the eternal inner inclination to merge into another creature, or to absorb the other into oneself. It is therefore a misunderstanding to interpret love as a readiness for abandon. It is an act that aims at the reaching out of the self, although it tears down the self's barriers against the other.

It is easy to see that Schiller's interpretation, which seeks to preserve selfhood without denying the experience of abandon, can do so only because it transforms the meaning of abandon into its very opposite. Love, then, distinguishes itself only superficially from the struggle of all against all, inasmuch as it becomes the appropriation of what is in fact already its own and so is not an overpowering of something foreign or a mastery of mere means. It is hopeless to try to avoid the opposition between love and self by maintaining the pure identity of the two. What Schiller was the first to attempt, though, albeit with inadequate philosophical tools, is precisely what is formulated in the program of Hegel's speculative logic, namely, that self-relation must be conceived so as already to include the notion of a relation to another, and vice versa. But we can also formulate this problem so that it expresses Hölderlin's early problem of life, namely, that both love and selfhood must be conceived together, freed from their opposition, which seems hopeless—and this by means of a thought that neither denies nor robs either of its genuine sense by reducing it to a moment of the other. The novel *Hyperion*, together with some philosophical reflection, was to unfold and resolve this problem.

Both his natural aptitude and the early experiences of his life enabled Hölderlin, more than any other thinker, to see the opposition between the two equally legitimate tendencies designated by the words "love" and "selfhood." Sensitive to life and to the beauty of nature, ever devoted to his relatives, he had a willingness and even a felt need to open himself up to whatever he encountered. He learned early on, however, in the strict educational system of the schools, that self-preservation is possible only for one capable of relying on himself alone and, as Hölderlin put it, of finding something infinite within himself. As much as love and selfhood tend to be mutually exclusive, they nonetheless belong together, and only then constitute a life in its totality. This can be seen in that we feel ourselves to be free in both of life's tendencies and in that every system of power attempts to force the one as much as the other under its control. Yet it is not easy to bring them together in freedom, nor even to conceive of the unity in virtue of which they belong together. Precisely those tendencies that Herder sought to bring together in harmony nonetheless stand in mutual conflict, namely the drive toward the unconditional and the surrender to the individuated, particular existence—selfhood and love.

With regard to the opposition between the two, the principle of unification philosophy takes on an entirely new function in Hölderlin. No longer is the connection to be made between man and the beautiful powers of the mind, or between one person and another, but rather between life's tendencies, the very unity of which constitutes the person himself. Love then becomes a metaprinciple for the unification of opposites in man. The ardent longing for the infinite, the unlimited readiness for abandon, but most especially the drive to attain and to reveal the unity of these opposites—all this is now contained in the single word, "love."

"Unoppressed by the greatest, in awe of the smallest"—Hölderlin saw in this, the epitaph of Ignatius Loyola, the task of the kind of human life that is consummated in the unification of its own antithetical tendencies. It became the motto of *Hyperion*. But the integration cannot occur without conflict. For this reason it is conceivable only as the end result of a course of life extending through time. For Hölderlin, then, love is elevated into a force to be conceived of not statically but only in a movement through opposites. It becomes a principle of history. The conflict of the opposites leads some to try to escape the opposition itself along with the problem of unification, or at least to slacken their efforts. The historical course of man is thus threatened by a variety of possible aberrations. Hölderlin therefore applied it to the metaphor of a path with neither a center nor a fixed destination—an eccentric path.

He found, further, that life's integration into a totality is not only the aim of love but also the true meaning of beauty. It is thereby clear at the outset that this integration contains in itself the tension of multiplicity as well as that of opposition. But in what sense it can contain both, Hölderlin could not at first say.

Hölderlin's Approach to the Philosophical Foundations

Hölderlin's early philosophical sketches are so many attempts to offer a conceptual account of man's perturbed path with respect to his dual nature, beset by antagonism, as well as of the potentially harmonious resolution of the conflict. We know that he first attempted this with the help of Schiller's later philosophy, from the period in which the latter was a disciple of Kant. Schiller had at this point advanced beyond Hölderlin in seeking to derive the unity of man from the opposition of the law of duty and the inclination of the will. He too recognized "love" as a metaprinciple of the unification of the forces of life. In contrast to his early theosophy, however, his later work conceives of love not as beyond all opposition but rather as reconciliation, so that it appears more richly determined. Schiller describes it—in Kantian language, yet paradoxically cutting across Kantian distinctions—as the inclination of reason, according to the completion of its infinite task, to turn freely to its antagonist, the sensuous, in order to become aware, with surprise and joy, of its own reflection and to play with its own mirror image.[9]

We can easily see why Hölderlin remained dissatisfied with Schiller's paradoxical solution. For those tendencies that love unites likewise deserve the name of love, namely, the desire for the unconditional and the inclination toward abandon, whether it is to the smallest or to what is equal. So, one must understand not only how love bridges oppositions but also how it is already at work within them. Life's tendencies, inasmuch as they can be united at all, must be conceived as having the same origin, in spite of their opposition.

Hölderlin saw early on that for the sake of this goal he could not remain a Kantian as Schiller had. Kant had set the distinguishing feature of his thought in the fundamental difference between two kinds of human striving. He saw no sense in contemplating the possibility of their unification. Schiller contradicted him on this point, but without anticipating the kind of grounding unity that the opposition itself would prescribe. That effort too would necessarily have come to grief in the framework of Kant's theory, which reduces all knowledge to forms of subjectivity and leaves their origins in the dark—the darkness not just of unknowability but of indeterminacy. However much Hölder-

lin knew that this restriction had been imposed in the name of freedom, and however much he remained aware of his debt to the claim
and the impetus of Kant's thought, even into the period of his madness—nevertheless, he had to venture "beyond the Kantian frontier"
(*StA* VI, p. 137).

For a short time he enlisted the help of Plato, the founder of the tradition of unification philosophy. Plato had taught that the love of what is
beautiful in this world is to be understood in terms of a higher desire
that extends beyond the world into the ground of all harmony and into
the origin whence we ourselves emerge. This appeared to have preserved the duality and the unified ground of desire equally well. Plato's
doctrine can remedy the shortcomings of Schiller's effort only at the
price of compelling it to surrender its own merits. For if Schiller bridged
the antithetical directions of human striving without being able to identify the ground of their unity, then Hölderlin found that very ground
identified in Plato, though to the neglect of the opposition. For Plato
interprets joy in the appearance of the beautiful not as abandon but as
the first winged flight of the soul into the realm above the heavens.[10]
And so Hölderlin remained without a conceptual solution to the problem of life.

This situation changed completely and irrevocably during the few
months when Hölderlin began to grapple with Fichte's *Wissenschaftslehre*. Hölderlin took it up and transformed it almost immediately into
an answer to his own fundamental question. With it he then con-
fronted Hegel, who for his part was unable to appeal to anything of
comparable significance.

It is extremely important to get clear about how Hölderlin must have
read Fichte. With Plato he had ventured beyond all modes of consciousness and striving and had worked his way back to their transcendent
ground. With Schiller he had discovered the antithetical directions of
human striving and the need of their unification. But no one, neither
Plato nor Schiller, had been able to justify both for these together. Only
Fichte could do this.

From the earliest, as yet unpublished version of the *Wissenschaftslehre* one learns that Fichte arrived at his theory by way of two discov-
eries made in rapid succession. First, he saw, contrary to Reinhold's
thesis, that the fundamental act of consciousness cannot be an act of
connection and differentiation. For this presupposes, specifically, a
positing of opposites, which provides the very possibility of differentiation. It was Fichte's momentous thesis that consciousness can only be
understood in terms of opposition, not in terms of Kant's synthesis of
the manifold. Fichte's second step consisted of realizing that this con-

traposition itself calls for a ground of unity as well. This he could find only in the unconditionality of self-consciousness, which encompasses all posited opposition.[11]

One must be clear that these steps toward opposition and a principle of unity exhibit exactly the same formal structure as Hölderlin's unification philosophy—notwithstanding the basic difference between the two thinkers, namely that Fichte aims at understanding "consciousness," and Hölderlin "love." Two lines of thought that had evolved separately since the beginning of the modern period merge together, in Hölderlin's appropriation of the *Wissenschaftslehre*, into the problematic of idealist philosophy. These lines of thought answer to two related fundamental words: *unio* and *synthesis*—the key words of both the Platonic tradition and Kantian thought. Only in this way can we understand how from the awkward Frankfurt texts of the young Hegel, which seem to reduce Kantianism to sentimental rhetoric, the system emerged which subsequently became the world philosophy of the age.[12]

But Hölderlin could adopt Fichte's arguments only by modifying their meaning. If love is the unity and multiplicity of the directions of human striving, then its ground cannot lie in man's own selfhood. Talk of the I is at any rate only meaningful when related to self-consciousness. And that can only be conceived as the correlate of consciousness of an object—hence never as the sought-after ground of unity *beyond* all opposition. In this way, Hölderlin came to assume there must be a unity prior to consciousness and selfhood, which he conceived of, following Spinoza, as the being in all existence (*Sein in allem Dasein*), and, following Fichte, as the ground of all opposition. How such being could generate opposites through division Hölderlin could not at first say. Later he was able to avoid the question since for him the primordial unity is an absolute certainty but not an object of descriptive knowledge. Hölderlin thought that this kind of surmounting of consciousness could even be justified to the satisfaction of his Kantian conscience—for he acquired it from Fichte's theory of consciousness, which in turn recommended itself as the consequence of Kant.

Hölderlin was thus able to adopt a simple yet potentially significant philosophical theory, one that interprets the human condition along something like the following lines: man comes forth from a unitary ground to which he remains connected in the certainty of the presuppositions of his existence and of the possibility of a new unity. At the same time, he is bound to a world that, like himself, originates in opposition. For the sake of unity he strives actively beyond each of its boundaries. Yet in it he at once confronts the beautiful—an anticipation of the unity that is lost to him and that he seeks to restore. As he embraces the beautiful, the complete truth, which lies at an infinite distance, is realized for him within limits. He is thus captivated by it, and for good reason. But he must not forget that his active nature is called upon to overcome the finite. In the conflict of love and selfhood he runs his course, either errantly or with self-understanding.

Hölderlin had already worked out this philosophy by the year 1795. He must have spoken about it to Schelling in two conversations, which have been the subject of much speculation. Isaak Sinclair, Hölderlin's disciple and patron from Homburg, adopted the philosophy as his own. By 1796, Sinclair had put pen to paper and written his "Philosophical Reasonings."[13] We know the course—and the high points—of Hölderlin's thinking more from these than from Hölderlin's own texts. Hegel must have felt challenged by that thinking in the spring of 1797, possibly when he was already on his way to Frankfurt, where Hölderlin wanted to meet up with him.

Hegel's Understanding with Hölderlin

Hegel arrived in Frankfurt a devoted Kantian. Even at Tübingen he had wanted to contribute to the spread of the Kantian spirit of freedom by way of theological enlightenment. He thus attempted to think through the possible establishment of a public religion, which—unlike the existing one—would be a truly civic religion, promoting rather than suppressing reason and freedom. In 1793, shortly after his arrival in Bern, Hegel learned of the attack made by his theological professors upon the Kantian philosophy of religion. To fend off this attack, he had to give a fundamental twist to his critical writings against the church and traditional Christianity. This he did by dissociating the Kantian doctrine from any dependence on a transcendent God. The consciousness of freedom was for him now absolute, self-sufficient, and elevated above all hope of happiness and fortune in the ways of the world. In happy ages of freedom this consciousness can unfold in the direction of a harmonious public life. But it must also be able to withdraw into itself and surrender the natural existence of man to the fate of his life and times, and to acknowledge its own dependence on that fate without being dependent in itself. Stoic virtue and Rousseauian commonwealth are thus complementary elements of a humanity stemming from the power of freedom.

One can easily see that in terms of philosophical theory the scope of these ideas is rather narrow, since they rest entirely on the grounds and limits of knowledge laid down by Kant. Hegel knew this. He did not think himself able to accomplish more, nor did he see any pressing reason to do so—despite reports from Schelling concerning the latter's own movement toward Fichte, and even Spinoza. But in Frankfurt, Hegel could no longer limit his activities in this way. Hölderlin opened his eyes to the fact that the Kantian conceptual framework was incapable of grasping the shared experiences and convictions of their earlier years; that the Greek *polis* had been a *unity*, not merely a conjoining of free individuals; that freedom must be conceived not only as selfhood but also as abandon; that the experience of the beautiful consists in more than reverence for the law of reason.

All of this we can only infer from the abrupt change in Hegel's position that took place immediately in Frankfurt. We know, however, that the conversations between the two friends were very intense and contentious—Hölderlin's stepbrother reports this of a visit in Frankfurt in the spring of 1797. He recounts as well that Hegel received him with great warmth, but that the two colleagues soon forgot him when they engaged in a heated discussion concerning some philosophical question (*StA* VI, pp. 188 ff.). Hegel was not exposed just to the arguments of Hölderlin, since the latter lived among a circle of friends who all took after him in one way or another. Conversations with them too must have had some significance for Hegel, especially those with Sinclair, who had subscribed to Hölderlin's ideas completely and elaborated them in his own terminology. We have an account, in verse, of Hegel's first encounter with him during a visit in Homburg. It is a nearly literal report, and Sinclair published it many years later among his collected poems, possibly meaning to remind Hegel of their time together.[14] It is only by the most improbable accident that we are able to witness, as if with our own eyes, a circumstance of such great significance in the history of philosophy as Sinclair's poetic report makes possible.

Together with Hölderlin, Hegel entered the room of Sinclair, who was waiting, impatiently, for the older, more renowned figure, perhaps a bit anxious about whether he would be able to hold his own with him. They talked about the trip, moved on to more general observations concerning earlier trips, then on to the ethical relations of lineages and historical epochs—and finally to the beliefs of their elders. Sinclair, who might well have known already of Hegel's Kantianism, seized the opportunity offered by this subject to raise the fundamental question that had taken Hölderlin beyond Kantianism—namely, whether the beliefs of a people provide the ultimate point of reference for an understanding of their history, or whether on the contrary it might be possible to attain some knowledge beyond the subjective standpoint of the believers and their own freedom. What Sinclair held forth against Hegel is only a variation on the themes of Hölderlin's philosophy:

> Und ich stieg mit ihm zur Quelle
> Wo der Lauf sie noch nicht trübet
> Wies ihm da des Geistes Einfalt
> . . .
>
> Schwindet sie nicht da die Schranke,
> Die von Gott den Menschen scheidet?
> Lebt da Liebe nicht in Wahrheit,
> Wo die Wesen eint ein Leben?
> Darf man Glauben es noch nennen,
> Wo das hellste Wissen strahlet?
>
> With him I climbed to the source
> Not yet obscured by the path
> And led him to the spirit's oneness
> . . .
>
> Does not the barrier vanish there
> Which stands dividing man from God?
> Does love not live on in truth
> Where one life unites all things?
> And can it still be called belief,
> Where the brightest knowledge shines?

Sinclair says that Hegel did not contradict him. But since his philosophical convictions had been called into question, neither did he assent. Instead, he posed a problem for Sinclair that would have to be solved, if Hölderlin's view were correct—namely, how could that origin have developed to the point where the original truth came to be lost in mere appearance, so that now the only course open to us is the return into what was lost? Sinclair conceded that we cannot comprehend this beginning. But we can understand that the entire human race is bound up in one historical context of life that encompasses all deviations and errors, too—Hölderlin's eccentric course of life understood as the course of history. Hegel withheld any further reply and proposed to defer the distinction between belief and limitation on the one hand, and love and certainty on the other, to further study, further experience, and further discussion:

> Lieber, laß uns hier verweilen
> In dem Lauf des raschen Streites,
> Weiser die Entscheidung lassend
> Selbst der Wahrheit unserer Zukunft.
> Ob dem Geiste das gebühret,

Was du kühn für ihn verlangest,
Ob nicht besser ihm Beschränkung,
Die zu Höherem ihn weihet.

Allow us, friend to linger here
Amid the course of quickened strife,
And wisely leave the final verdict
To our own future's truth itself.
Whether it befits the spirit,
What you demand of it so boldly,
Or whether better were limitation
Ordaining it to higher things.

In this conversation the forces that moved Hegel along a course of his own or, more appropriately put, that held him to it, are already conspicuously present. Yet he had at first almost nothing with which to counter Hölderlin's speculation. It forced him at any rate to take up a critical distance from his own Kantianism, to enter into the conceptual arena of unification philosophy, and to posit "love" or "unification" as the highest ideal of a free life.

He initially conceived of this love in Kantian terms as a kind of attitude toward the world, thus as analogous to imagination.[15] But it soon became for him a unifying force as well, a force that binds nature and freedom, subject and object, in such a way that each remains what it is and yet merges with the other in an inseparable unity. Like Hölderlin, he now calls this unity "being"; and by this he means, with Hölderlin, "intimate unification." He maintains that it cannot be grasped by the understanding. He thus preserves a legitimate element of Kant's doctrine of faith, but in such a way that there is scarcely any discernible difference between that doctrine and Hölderlin's conviction concerning being.

Hegel's system emerged uninterruptedly from out of this adoption of the word "love" as the central term in his thought. The theme of "love" was for various reasons replaced by the richer structure of "life" and later by that of "spirit" (*Geist*), which has still wider implications. It would be wrong, however, to say that Hegel merely generalized and elaborated ideas that he was incapable of producing on his own. Such a presumption could hold only if, in considering the way Hegel was influenced by Hölderlin, one failed to make clear the characteristic difference between the two of them—a difference between their conceptions of theory, not just between their particular personalities. The difference is by no means obvious or apparent. But we must define it, for their work will not be remembered and judged just in terms of its enthusiasm and the impression it makes but as an articulated structure of thoughts and experiences.

A first step consists in observing that Hegel adopted Hölderlin's thought in merely abbreviated form. For Hölderlin, "love" was the unification of directions of *striving*, one of which tends toward the infinite, the other toward abandon. The one he understood in terms of a relation to the origin, the other in terms of a relation to that which had, like us, lost the unity of being. No trace of this duality is to be found in Hegel's concept of love. "Love" is simply conceived as the unification of subject and object. In its self-sufficiency it assumed the formal character of the Kantian autonomy of the will: it aims at nothing that precedes it, and it strives to produce nothing distinct from the power of unification itself.

At the same time, of course, it cannot be conceived as the "all in all." Yet it does presuppose the subsistence of a manifold of separation in relation to which it can take effect. Hegel initially took no notice of this aspect of his theoretical position, though Hölderlin had acknowledged it in his assumption of a separation in being. Only while editing his manuscripts on "love" in the winter of 1798–99 did Hegel take this into consideration, inserting simple arguments into the text:[16] love must seek to multiply itself in order to generate the greatest possible totality of unification.

Hegel's dependence on Hölderlin is thus evident inasmuch as he actually misunderstood one of the latter's most important reasons for going beyond Kant and Fichte. Characteristically, however, Hegel developed further on his own because of this very omission. How so? The reason can be given in the abstract: ultimately, all of the structures that Hölderlin understood in terms of primordial being Hegel had to interpret as modes of the interrelatedness of what is unified. The occurrence of unification itself, not the ground whence it derives, is the true absolute, the "all in all." It was for precisely this reason, as we shall see, that Hegel came to the conviction that the absolute must be called "spirit," and not "being."

In Bern, Hegel had already sung the praises of the independent consciousness that, as the very proof of freedom, defies fate by surrendering to it everything natural, under conditions in which the community of free agents itself remains unattainable. In contrast to this is the bad infinity of a belief that, in such circumstances, finds itself overcome by forces and objects. Even in the wake of Hölderlin's influence, Hegel sought to maintain this schema. But it was now no longer a sense of freedom but a true sense of unification that impels us to preserve the infinite within ourselves in worldly circumstances that bar unification.

Hegel had good reasons, then, for taking up Hölderlin's theory of love in reduced form—not out of ignorance, but because only in that way was it suited to the reformulation of the insights he had had in Bern. And this was a decision that would determine Hegel's subsequent course: for he could no longer understand the opposition between selfhood and abandon as an opposition between two impulses in the striving of love, each of which aims at a different form of unification in existence—namely, perfect and infinite unification on the one hand, and currently attainable but restricted unification on the other. If the I aims at the infinite, then it relies only on itself since it sees no possibility of a present unification with its world. Longing is a bad infinity, an abstract infinity that finds better expression in courage.

In order for Hegel's thinking to mature into a system, he had to treat and formally resolve two problems. First, the relation between finitude and the infinite had to be conceived such that the relata derive not from some third element but only from the internal conditions of their interrelation. Further, the manifold of that which is to be unified had to reveal itself from out of the essence of the unification itself—not, therefore, from some preconceived starting point or fundamental principle. This second problem is anticipated in Hegel's skeptical response to Sinclair, which led Hegel to ask how, given the primordial unity, the process of division and development is to be conceived at all.

Structures in Hölderlin's Later Thought

A further step is required before the profile of Hegel's thought can stand out clearly from that of Hölderlin. We must consider a few modifications that distinguish Hölderlin's later philosophy from his earlier one. In the speculative sketch that Hegel found so convincing, "beauty" functioned as a key concept alongside "love." The unified directions of human striving come together in the beautiful: to be unoppressed by the greatest, yet in awe of the smallest, is divine. However illuminating it may be to call the consummate beautiful and to find in it the strict beauty of the ideal, which does not exclude tension, this concept of beauty is nevertheless entirely indeterminate. It is in fact merely the postulate of the integration of the disparate tendencies of life combined with the aesthetic sensorium. It is incomprehensible how such an integration of life could actually occur.

We know that Hölderlin first began to philosophize again once he had been separated from Susette Gontard and had moved to Homburg. He now no longer worked on the fundamental problems of philosophy. The theory of poetry, the difference between Greek and modern verse, the relation between them, and the character of poetic language: these became his themes. It is plain to see that he was proceeding on the basis of what he worked out in his earlier "speculative pro and con" and what had been confirmed among his circle of friends. We can also see that what he had previously seen merely as the course of the individual life through its own antithetical tendencies began increasingly to serve as a conception of the history of mankind. Yet he introduced at least two important changes into his earlier draft, which taken together enabled him to grasp the concept of beauty more adequately and in greater depth.

Hölderlin consequently began by abandoning the notion of beauty as the simultaneous integration of life's tendencies. The highest beauty of poetry, at least, is based on an ordered *modulation* of acts in which each of the tendencies of life is momentarily released. From this follows the important point that neither present finitude nor the anticipated reunification can effect a static harmony. Art, like the consummate life, will but repeat harmoniously the *processes* of the actual, and deliver its oppositions from their conflict through completeness and order.

But if the path of life does not lead back into the origin, then one must distinguish within that process between its stance toward the origin and its stance toward the future. From the first transformation, then, a second follows necessarily, whether it in fact occurs for the sake of the consequence or for other independent reasons. Hölderlin replaced the dyad of life's disparate tendencies with a triad: on the one hand, man strives to overcome all finitude in order to achieve perfection actively. But he must also limit himself to the intuition of the finite. Finally, aware of the ungraspable origin, he must soar idealistically beyond everything and oscillate freely between his own drives. Idealizing and striving stand radically opposed to each other and can be united only through their common connection to the naïveté of an intuition satisfied in finitude. With these thoughts, then, Hölderlin, like Hegel, placed the unfolding of the oppositions above the idea of the restoration of original unity. And so it appears that he came very close, in the end, to what Hegel sought to maintain both early on and continually thereafter, namely, that truth is the path itself. On closer inspection, then, what seemed to divide them begins to fade. One might even be tempted to attribute this to the influence on Hölderlin of Hegel's notion of fate, an influence one can assume though it cannot be verified in any primary sources.

But one must not be misled by appearances. The difference stands out even in Hölderlin's Homburg writings, though it is a bit harder to detect there than in the Frankfurt texts. To see it, recall first of all that the very notion of a harmonious modulation was derived from Fichte's

Wissenschaftslehre. Even in Hölderlin's earlier turn against Fichte it came as a surprise that this notion developed out of some rather slight corrections made to the structure of Fichte's work. These corrections related to its opening paragraphs, concerning the relation of the unconditioned in the I to the opposition within it as it constitutes consciousness. When Hölderlin put the triad of modulation in place of the two directions of human striving along the eccentric path, he was not simply orienting himself by the triadic structures in the doctrine of categories, characterology, and poetic genres. At any rate, he knew that these could provide no justification. He found such justification, once again, in Fichte.

What he had in mind was the outcome of Fichte's presentation of the contradictions inherent in the concept of the self. Here Fichte had shown that a threefold distinction is necessary to conceive of the possibility of consciousness: the I, insofar as it is limited and related to objects; the objects, insofar as they are determined for the I and thereby limited, and these in reciprocal determination; and finally a third element, namely the unconditioned, which holds together the unified activity in both moments of limitation, and which is for its part grasped reciprocally as unconditioned along with the limitations of the other two. One can easily see that Hölderlin orients himself toward this triadic structure, but only so as to establish unity over against opposition, and such that each of the three, contrary to Fichte's intention, stands by itself as a tendency of life.

This connection with Fichte makes clear what unites Hölderlin's Homburg theory of beauty with that of his Frankfurt period. Beauty was for him initially an integration that could not be grasped. It then became the modulation of the moments of that integration. Even in this modulation, however, beauty remains something imponderable. For it is based only on the orderly relation of elements to one another in spite of their opposition. The sense of unity that manifests itself in this relation cannot be derived from those elements taken purely as moments. The fact that they come from a common ground alone marks them as aspects of a totality. It is for this reason alone that we must not only vary the differentiated elements but also "feel ourselves equal and at one with all things at the heart of all the works and deeds of men" (*StA* IV, p. 222).

Even with this constant reference to modulation, then, Hölderlin cannot forgo the grounding unity, though he regards the way leading into separation as definitive and the intimate original unity as lost, indeed well lost. The divine language of modulation speaks harmoniously from the unity of the origin, whose silence is still to be heard even where the modulation has become quick and has become a historical time of need.[17]

If Hölderlin maintains the notion of a binding element that does not itself arise from the modulating elements, then he could again find justification for this in Fichte. One can approach the most beautiful idea to be found in Hölderlin's Homburg drafts concerning poetry and history by way of a sentence from Fichte: "The positing I, through its most wondrous capacity . . . holds fast the diminishing accident long enough to have compared it to that which displaces it. It is this almost always unrecognized capacity that knits together unity out of perpetual oppositions, that intervenes between moments that would cancel each other out, and thereby preserves both; it is what alone makes life and consciousness possible."[18]

There must be more posited in the modulation than the modulating elements themselves, not only that it may be harmonious but also that it may emerge as a totality. Hölderlin shows that life and poem become one in *recollection*. The modulation of tendencies and their tones leads only to what is momentarily new. Thus in order to reveal the totality itself, an interruption must occur in the modulation. In this interruption the entire sequence is brought together, surveyed, and at once compared with what is new, which can already be sensed and which announces itself as the other of what has come to completion. This is the divine moment, the transcendental instant. The poet must know how to calculate and produce it. In life, however, it intrudes by its own fate. We can only preserve it and stay our future course more sensibly on the basis of the understanding it affords.

The theme of recollection is essential to Hegel's thought as well, though as the accumulation of forms from their external existence into the interior of comprehending spirit. For Hegel, recollection is always at once a transforming: turning inward (*Er-Innerung*), as the overcoming of the being-in-itself of the past; a new way of positing it as belonging to the recollecting I,[19] or to the general sphere of intelligence.[20] For Hölderlin, by contrast, recollecting is a preserving, subject to the demand of faithfulness, which therefore seeks and embraces the past in itself. For him there is no free striding into the future that might simply dispel past life instead of letting it—and those who shared its fate— live on effectively, in recollection, as the antithesis of its present self.

Hegel and Hölderlin in Contrast

In 1810 Hegel wrote to Sinclair that he was looking forward to the latter's main philosophical work: he was curious whether Sinclair was "still the stubborn Fichtean . . . and what role progress into the infinite plays in it."[21] This sentence easily lends itself to misunderstandings. It seems to suggest that Hegel must have argued in the Frankfurt circle in roughly the same way he did against Fichte in *The Difference Between Fichte's and Schelling's System of Philosophy*, of 1801. Yet Sinclair's manuscripts and all available documents indicate beyond a doubt that he occupied a different position altogether.

The sentence to Sinclair then takes on another, quite instructive sense. For Hegel was in agreement with Hölderlin's circle of friends concerning the need to go beyond that I as principle. Hegel had indeed learned as much precisely from them. The only point of contention might be whether certain elements from Fichte could still be maintained *after* this transition was made. In this sense, Sinclair insisted on infinite progress as an element of Hölderlin's doctrine of being, separation, and modulation. In this passage from the letter, then, we have it from Hegel himself that he had to develop his own insight not against Fichte directly but rather against the lingering Fichteanism of his anti-Fichtean friends.

One must therefore conclude that the shortcomings of Hölderlin's position served as an evidential basis for the later formulations of Hegel's system. The application of that evidence within the system is far more general and largely stands in the service of ideas more compelling than Hölderlin's own. But the critical starting point is still present. Hegel would not have been able to oppose Schelling's ideas with such resoluteness had he not already adopted this outlook during his conversations with the Frankfurt group.

Hegel's own distinctive idea is this: the relata in an opposition must always be understood in terms of a totality, but that totality does not precede them as being or intellectual intuition. Rather it is simply the developed concept of relation itself. He first worked out this idea in his analysis of the concept of life: one can understand life only by conceiving of the opposition among living creatures, and the organic unity within each of them, in terms of the generality of an organization that nonetheless has no existence prior or external to the living process of those creatures themselves. The same structure is again present in the idea of true infinity, for infinity is simply the relation between the finite and its negation, empty infinity—thus precisely not, *pace* Hölderlin, the common origin and end point of two tendencies. Nor is it any different with regard to the opposition of essence, say between positive and negative, each of which, in spite of their opposition, contains the concept of the whole relation, and thereby also its opposite. Thus the modulation between them is at once the modulation between identicals, not a modulation in or in relation to the ultimate ground or origin. Every category in Hegel's *Logic* is another example of this state of affairs, since in fact the entire work was written on the basis of an insight into this single structure. Hegel's beginning with the category of being must therefore be read as a direct opposition to Hölderlin's very different point of departure. For Hegel's starting point is not "being" in the absolute sense of the word, whence everything comes and in the intuition of which all unity resides. Rather, being is simply the immediate, the unfulfilled, the anticipation of concrete significance, and this *only*. The path of progress is therefore not separation but *determination*. Emptiness determines the totality—precisely *in virtue of* its emptiness—inasmuch as its indeterminateness becomes manifest, that is, through opposition. For this reason the opposition does not lead to modulation but to what Hegel calls "development": the working out of increasing determination on the basis of the indeterminate, that is, toward its production. There is no room in Hölderlin's thought for this sort of production. Everything is separation, modulation, and exchange, as well as measure or immeasure, and unity. Hölderlin could never have sung the praises of the "infinite power of the negative" in "opposition," since after all the power of unification arises through it, not from it; it alone is infinite.

For Hegel too, of course, production remains the self-enactment of the life without beginning or end, whence it came and to which it leads. Its consummation occurs in a reflective act in which it becomes complete for itself. Therein lies a relation to its beginning with being, a comprehending of its path, but again only as the process leading toward itself, which is grounded in nothing beyond itself.

Hegel's most famous proposition is perhaps that "everything turns on grasping and expressing the true, not only as *substance* but equally as *subject*."[22] The meaning of this proposition becomes more vivid and complete if we hear in it Hegel's rejection of Hölderlin. For it says that the true is the process, and only the process, which realizes itself in its end as the Notion of its own course leading to manifestation. And this is precisely the reason for describing the true as subject. That is, Hegel understands the essence of the conscious self in such a way that it is an active coming-to-itself, which presupposes nothing about this to-itself and for-itself. In this sense we can indeed speak of one coming to oneself yet know that a conscious being is in fact nowhere to be found prior to its coming to itself. For the awakening to consciousness first makes the human being a human being.

In this sense, a life that is not individual yet has the constitution of the subject may rightly be called "spirit," since it rests solely on itself and produces knowledge of itself through itself. Hegel therefore re-placed Hölderlin's "being," the term he himself was still using in Frankfurt, with the word "spirit." And this spirit is also substance, but only insofar as it is, as process, a continuum. Substantiality is thus only one moment of its actual structure, being an unconditionally self-producing relation to itself.

Hölderlin had replaced Fichte's highest principle with a new one, and had convinced Hegel of the necessity of no longer taking con-sciousness as the starting point. Hölderlin had nonetheless still em-ployed the methodological means afforded by Fichte's *Wissenschafts-lehre*. For Hegel, consequently, Hölderlin's thinking was still much too Fichtean to be what it aspired to be. Hegel developed it in a direction that corresponded completely with Hölderlin's later views, yet in a way that ultimately led him to see a new justification for Fichte's original idea, which Hölderlin had rejected early on—albeit in a wholly differ-ent sense than Fichte had intended it. To be sure, the totality in relation to which all opposition occurs is not our consciousness, nor an I, prior to the entire process of development. Rather, this totality, which exists as process only, is just the process itself, though conceived as selfhood, in accord with the structure of subjectivity. He best understands the meaning of Fichte's theory who abandons the Fichtean method. Hegel wished to be buried by Fichte's side.

Hölderlin provided the philosopher Hegel with his most important and final formative impetus. And for this reason one can say that Hegel is completely dependent upon Hölderlin—on his early efforts to grasp speculatively the course of human life and the unity in its conflicts, on the vividness with which Hölderlin's friends made his insight fully con-vincing, and also certainly on the integrity with which Hölderlin sought to use that insight to preserve his own inwardly torn life. The myth of Hegel as the autochthonous world philosopher must therefore be rejected.

This might seem to confirm those who suggest that Hegel mistook what was most profound in Hölderlin and just reduced everything he could to mere concepts. But this too we must reject. For Hegel's system is by no means a dry abstraction of Hölderlin's thought but rather a ges-ture in response to it, although the system preserves some convictions common to them both. It is hard to see how even Hegel's most general assertions could remain clear and intelligible except in this context. Be-fore his encounter with Hölderlin in Frankfurt, Hegel was a critic of the church and a historical and political analyst with connections to the Gironde. Only in relation to Hölderlin, and by the latter's influence on him, was he to become the philosopher of the age.

Still, none of this has addressed the question of truth—not even if we presuppose the limits within which the two found themselves, faced with the program of establishing a Spinozism of freedom. I think it can be shown that even Hegel's concept of the subject leads to aporias and that more sense can be made of Hölderlin's notion of modulation, as inaccessible to him as it may have been. But if one wishes simply to shed light on what united and divided Hegel and Hölderlin, then it remains an open question whether Hegel was entitled to exalt the power of the spirit to come to total self-realization, as he did upon his arrival in Berlin, or whether philosophy can only do what Hölderlin attributed in his last theoretical text to the language of Sophocles: "To represent man's understanding as walking in the midst of things unthinkable" (*StA* V, p. 266). Still, the spirit is never spared the effort that both Hegel and Hölderlin considered its very essence and to which they devoted themselves, providing a model of seriousness and inspiration: *se ipsam cognoscere*.[23]

Translated by Taylor Carman

THE COURSE OF REMEMBRANCE

To
Hans-Georg Gadamer,
with thanks

Translated by Taylor Carman

ONE

Preliminaries

The Resonance of the Poem

Of all Hölderlin's later poems, "Remembrance" is, for the uninitiated reader, the most approachable. One can read the poem in any anthology and fall under its spell without having any prior knowledge of the world of Hölderlin's thought.[1] Moreover, since its strophes evoke and sing the praises of a town and country along a river, one could say that "Remembrance" at once stands closely related to Hölderlin's river hymns yet in a sense continues the series of his odes and elegies of homage,[2] including especially "Heidelberg," "The Neckar," and "Stuttgart."

But this poem has also inspired the reflections of philosophers. Its very title makes reference to an idea, to something universal. Its meaning cannot be expressed or explained in just a few words.[3] And its final strophe, whose closing lines amount to nothing less than a summation of the poem as a whole, expresses something that could just as well be put forward as the conclusion to a reflection of the most general nature, comprising all philosophical questions. Neither the reader who is drawn in by the brilliance of the poem's poetic images nor the one who pursues the conceptual claims that it makes as such will fail to realize that its force and significance must be understood in terms of the way in which the work allows both imagery and reflective contemplation to unfold in a seamless and unforced manner. An interpretation must account for how this is brought off, and how it is possible given the poem's succinctness.

An initial assumption that might work against this impression would be to suppose that in the splendor and abundance of its images the poem seeks merely to depict the life of an actual countryside and its surroundings. Even when Hölderlin seems to breathe life back into his months in the Atlantic South of France through the use of poetic language, the landscape in fact emerges in that language with special significance as a construct of Hölderlin's own poetic experience. The wholly symbolic system of images in "Remembrance," then, would be decipherable only on the basis of some familiarity with the mythic view of the world that he had taken on board.

This view has much to recommend it, provided that it keeps Hölderlin's work at some remove from the sort of poetry committed to a conception of art stemming from some species of realism or impressionism. The themes of worldly experience that appear in Hölderlin's late hymns are also present in "Remembrance." It is reasonable and indeed crucial, then, to point out their presence in this instance. But at least equally worthy of the interpreter's attention is the fact that these themes do not come fully into view, that they work like a sounding board concealed in the poem's movement, that they are held in check by the very unity of scenic images and ideas. For this is what makes this particular late work of Hölderlin's what it is. It reveals a special quality of Hölderlin's poetry following the period of his hymns and "Songs of the Fatherland" (*vaterländische Gesänge*), which were modeled on Pindar's Victory Odes. One can even see new possibilities for lyric poetry taking shape in "Remembrance," possibilities that Hölderlin's creativity—at once reflective and poetic—would have been able to realize had it not been crippled by his illness and forced to retreat into the unimposing form of his last poems. To interpret "Remembrance" as simply falling within the web of meaning spun by the language of the hymns would be to rob it of its own special poetic character. Moreover, such an interpretation would then face the problem of having to differentiate unambiguously between image-motif and meaning. The hymns themselves each take up their own unique themes and follow their own particular laws of construction, so even they do not exhibit a manifest meaning that might serve as an element in an all-embracing world-picture common to all Hölderlin's works and ideas dating from the first few years of the nineteenth century. It is especially true in the case of "Remembrance" that the many resonances of meaning in the motifs produce an ambiguity that must itself be considered an important part of the very constitution of the text. If an interpretation ignores this and insists that the work is defined by those resonances alone, then it will miss the very point of the poem. It will fail to come to terms with the paradox of the text, namely, that its meaning is made manifest but is not progressively revealed as the text moves toward its conclusion. A different approach is required for the sort of account that could be brought into harmony not only with an unbiased reading of the text but with the course of the text itself.

Thus, while one challenge in interpreting "Remembrance" is un-doubtedly posed by its various mythical significations, significations that tie it to the corpus of hymns, there is another task that has yet to be brought to light. This task has to do with the unity of the modulation of images depicting the countryside along the Garonne on the one hand, and the poem's own articulation and embodiment of its closing thoughts on the other—the unity, one might say, of its central poetic and philosophical ideas. This task needs first of all to be clarified fur-ther.

Many of Hölderlin's later works in the form of the Hesperian hymn culminate in a final word that emerges from the entire course of the hymn as a resting point or full stop, as a summation of its unfolding meaning. The word, moreover, is often correlated with another word that has an approximately axial position in the whole of the progres-sion—just as in "Patmos" the "All is well" (*Alles ist gut*) is held constant over the extensive variations of the sacramental scene of the hymn.[4] By setting up the architecture of the hymn so as to accommodate such key words of contemplation as supporting elements, Hölderlin has estab-lished links with Greek models while preserving the conviction he ac-quired early on that poetry is the consummation of what is only begun in philosophy, inasmuch as it allows an ultimate and genuinely syn-thetic insight to emerge in pure expression from out of the experience of conscious life—refined in poetic form—through the sequence of that life's vital tendencies and conflicts.[5] That the "gnomic" statements of the hymns must be incorporated into the composition of the poems in such a way as to be supported by their architecture while elevating their structure is thus only in keeping with, and is in fact a simple con-sequence of, one of Hölderlin's basic philosophical and poetological in-sights.

In this connection, too, in virtue of the triad in the poem's closing lines, the relative brevity of "Remembrance" exhibits a continuity with the hymns, which are arranged in the grand Pindaric style. One may therefore assume that it was deliberately composed so that the closing lines would at once support and be supported by the structure of the poem at large. One might say that the reader of "Remembrance," espe-cially one who has returned to it over the years, tends to develop an intuitive sense that the triad in the short work's closing lines is not just as it were tacked on at the end. If these lines are referring to a poetry that is yet to come or yet to make itself felt, or to something poetically lasting (*ein Bleiben*) that has already been provided (*gestiftet*), then they are no doubt referring to the very poem that gives them voice. A cornerstone, similarly, points beyond itself through its inscription only by drawing attention to that which is unified and harmonized by it.

But if this is how matters stand, then we are forced to ask what features of the poem's design invest it with this kind of resonance. And this question entails an incremental investigation, a structural analysis, in order to make explicit the experiences of the reader who lets himself be drawn into the form and flux of "Remembrance." Its conclusion, which culminates in a proposition aimed at what philosophers called "the absolute," has its roots firmly planted in the poem itself, though this will remain obscure to anyone searching for hidden scaffolding or stabilizing forces supporting or underlying the poem, which might be discovered in Hölderlin's other works or correspondence. Clarity about what renders these lines poetic utterances is only to be expected once we have understood the wonder of the work itself, and with it the wake of its ideas, its "tone," the scenes it describes, as well as the manner in which they relate and refer to one another—and indeed as they reside within and constitute the work itself. Hölderlin himself was clear that this kind of form and structure is not just consonant with the meaning but is the meaning. What the poem says explicitly at the end emerges from what is already there to be understood in the poem's composition as a whole.

This task is complex enough, quite apart from trying to understand the poem in terms of its origin in Hölderlin's mythic world. His hymns are crafted with an acute sensitivity to the meanings of words. The words are woven together through their acoustic contours and through the affinities that unite the ideas and circumstances they present, as well as the distances that separate them. One can appreciate his principle of "the modulation of tones," which can be applied in a more or less thoroughgoing and literal way, in light of this unfailing sensitivity.[6] But Hölderlin is equally able to articulate reality and actual scenery in such a way that, between what is depicted and the flow of words and sentences, a whole of greater weight and as it were "expressive force" results. A work such as "Remembrance," which evokes a locality from real life and actual past experience and puts it into words, lends great significance to such a depiction of scenery. The form of the work as a whole, supported by and embodied in the triad in the closing lines, is irreducible to any clear and distinct understanding, regardless of the connections among the local images it evokes. A relation emerges, then, between the elucidation of the work's flowing succession of images on the one hand and an understanding of the form of the work as such on the other. An interpretation can in no way claim to have comprehended all aspects of "Remembrance" merely by arriving at an understanding of the various images in the poem. However, it cannot help but acknowledge that such an understanding forms an essential aspect and a necessary foundation for the elucidation of the work as a whole.

Now an interpretation that pursues this course will easily fall suspect of having confused the poetic work with what might be dismissed as a mere "reflection" of something actual.[7] This is to be avoided, one hopes, in virtue of the way the task has been introduced at the outset. Moreover, one has to consider that to view the poetically depicted landscape as the mere imagined interactions and conflicts in a mythically disclosed world would be to miss the peculiar force of Hölderlin's poetry, perhaps even more so than the impressionistic misinterpretation.

Dank ("thanks") and *Treue* ("faithfulness") are key words for Hölderlin.[8] They spoke to him, even in terms of the sites of his life's experiences. It is crucial, too, that he always experienced those places as being situated in a more universal world-historical setting. But it is not inconsistent with this that he nonetheless grasped and remembered them in their characteristic form and locality, and so as evidently real.

If one traces the development of his pastoral poems through their successive drafts, it becomes apparent that while he was searching for the words that best conformed to the sound and structure of the lines, he at the same time wanted to bring the image of the landscape into greater precision. And in the process of working with the words, he was able to make the recollections themselves more precise. The words had to live up to the recollection, and this likewise meant that he was forced to clarify that recollection itself in the process. As the poet reflected on the weaknesses of the choice of a word or a sound, he also had to apprehend the recollections themselves in greater sharpness and certainty as a result. Poetic depiction, being sober work, can admit of no dream images that might already have that sharpness and which could then become the basis of a mere "reflection," something in the manner of Guardi and Bellotto. Many of Hölderlin's key pastoral poems sprang from an engagement in active remembering, being written down from a distance, yet with a recollection that became increasingly precise in the course of the poiesis itself.[9] With regard to "Remembrance" it should be kept in mind that by the time Hölderlin lived in Bordeaux he had already long since completed poems such as "Heidelberg" and "The Neckar." He knew when he returned that he would probably never again set foot in the sphere of that city. And no extant source indicates that he tried at that time to capture the world of Bordeaux in a poem. The philosopher who had earlier maintained the reve-

latory significance of recollection for the constitution of a poetic totality,[10] however, could well have experienced and even explored, from his
permanent residence in later years, the layout and landscape of the
area, preserved as it was in a recollective vision. And he would thereby
be able to have right before his eyes, in retrospect, that style of composition that had characterized and perfected the odes, which had already
been published. It should also be pointed out that he only began composing "Remembrance" after his return journey, although this poem
seems even more closely related to the hymns and so seems to hark
back to the earlier odes in both form and content.

The recollection in which the poetic totality is constituted will therefore scarcely coincide with the mere transition from brute fact to an unfolding mythic experience of the world. And the intimacy with which
"Remembrance" allows the distant world to stand out in more vivid
presence is, in Hölderlin, more than just the concatenation and convergence of that world's sense and destiny as they are intimated in the
poem.[11] What is intimate above all is the poet's own devotion to the
reality he experienced, literally as well as in the sense associated with
love—a love that opens itself up to the essence of the beloved in all its
features, even the most trifling.[12] Hölderlin had early on granted the
same dignity to modesty in and before the most modest as he had to
aspiration toward the infinite. And he had chosen a sentence exalting
the unification of both as the epigraph for his novel Hyperion.[13] Hölderlin's devotion to the locality and country lost to him in his lifetime is
also intimate in this sense. And it is this intimacy that bears within it
the faithfulness that in turn tends toward and is borne by thanks. Such
faithfulness cannot allow either overlooking what is unique about the
depicted locality in the poem or translating it into an experience of reality to be found only in the life and thought of the poet. Rather, the opposite is what is crucial: the faithful depiction of the locality is what can
and should provide the force necessary to grasp the locality within a
framework of meaningful connections that situate it in a world, thus
bringing it to the fore and elevating it so that it actually endures. In
Hölderlin's poems of homage, consequently, one should not expect, nor
does one find, any tension between the concrete apprehension of the
local reality on the one hand—just as a master engraver would render
it in copperplate—and its poetic refinement on the other. Both aspects
become incomparable precisely through the unity of their faithful images with the meaningful order uncovered in them. The poems must
be understood in light of precisely this unity. In interpreting them,
however, we cannot consider ourselves above the task of clarifying the
sense of their images.[14]

One might suppose this to be the simplest task in the interpretation of Hölderlin's lyrical work, and so imagine that it must have long since been carried out to completion. That this is not the case will be made clear, to begin with, by means of some observations on the ode "Heidelberg." These observations themselves will at once suggest that in the case of the depiction of Bordeaux in "Remembrance," too, some information can only be gotten from a precise knowledge of the place where Hölderlin lived. It should perhaps once again be emphasized that such knowledge is not to be sought out for its own sake—though it may in fact be of interest on its own terms—nor on the presumption that the poetic work amounts to no more than a linguistic presentation of landscapes and picturesque scenes. However, it is on the basis of faithful depictions of actual settings that Hölderlin forges essential elements of the structure of the work, a structure that is made meaningful as such, and in which the meaning unfolds. We must know how to understand these depictions if we are to uncover the structure of "Remembrance," right down to the culminating triad in the closing lines.

To shed more light on this task and on the special significance it has in the case of "Remembrance," recall that in "Remembrance" the Bordeaux landscape is evoked *twice*: once in the two opening strophes, which would have been publishable as a poem complete in itself had they alone survived, and again at the beginning of the final strophe, immediately prior to the triad in the closing lines. The reiteration of this evocation is one of the poem's most striking features and must be heard as a dominant theme in its progression. But because a work of this stature can only arise out of mature poetic reflection, we must assume that the poet engaged in such reflection with some essential purpose in mind for the work. And since it constitutes a central feature of the poem's architecture, the interpretation cannot merely refer to it in passing or take it for granted as something obvious. The reiterated evocation instead calls for a special effort of the understanding—particularly if one is to understand why the poem as a whole even deserves the title "Remembrance." For this reason, then, the following reflections are informed specifically by an effort to uncover the significance of the reiterated evocation of the landscape along the Garonne with a view to the structure and the resonance of the poem.

However, it follows from this that we must understand the reiterated evocation not only as it impresses one simply upon reading the poem but also as it must have made sense to someone who could share with Hölderlin the actual experience of the place and hence its depiction in the poem from afar. For just as the poem "Heidelberg" is certainly not just the homage a well-traveled poet is paying to some place he wants to portray in an exotic light to a naive public,[15] so too—though it is more than just this—"Remembrance" is ultimately a poem for the times, and for the poet's contemporaries. Although its poetic intent was certainly not to create a kind of *veduta* in linguistic form, it nonetheless had to live up to the perceptions of an audience that was no less exacting.

Images and Movements: "Heidelberg"

In coming to an understanding of Hölderlin's images of the countryside and the city on the Garonne and of their role in the structure of "Remembrance," a few observations are in order concerning the images of that more familiar city on the Neckar in Hölderlin's ode "Heidelberg":

> Wie der Vogel des Walds über die Gipfel fliegt,
>   Schwingt sich über den Strom, wo er vorbei dir glänzt,
>   Leicht und kräftig die Brüke,
>   Die von Wagen und Menschen tönt.

> As the bird of the forest flies above the hilltops,
>   Over the river where it flows before you, the bridge
>   Lightly, sturdily vaults,
>   Loud with the traffic of coaches and footsteps.

Hölderlin's depiction of the city begins with this stanza about the bridge—one image that shows city and nature, shoreline and river, and human traffic, all in harmony, just as the engravings and gouaches of the time tried to do in their own way. A dominant presence is thus introduced at the outset into the subsequent series of images, which ultimately resolves restfully and harmoniously in the image of the narrow streets of the city blossoming out from the gardens. Even in the various preliminary drafts that have survived, Hölderlin wants us from the outset to see the trajectory of the bridge in terms of a bird's flight (presumably toward the city). The bridge itself therefore represents movement. In a series of further images of movement embracing the present and recollection, then, it can be the place where the poet, "once transfixed," first contemplated the movement of the river.[16]

But how is the movement of the bridge itself perceived in the poem? Interpreters have only belabored the obvious in pointing out the arch shape of the street and the side railing, that is, the uppermost profile of the bridge.[17] But this does not capture the precision of Hölderlin's image and simile; indeed it misses the essential point of the simile, namely to make the image of the bird's flight more concrete by comparing it with the bridge: it "vaults" over the river. Of course, one can see such "vaulting" in the single expanse of the bridge stretching from shoreline to shoreline. But this fails to capture the structure of the entire bridge in its unique form. Specifically, what is characteristic of this bridge is that its trajectory as a whole is built up from a series of individual arches. Thus a twofold movement is to be distinguished: that of the lower outline of the bridge, which forms a sequence of smaller and steeper arches; and that of the upper outline, in which the series of trusses makes up the overall profile of the bridge and the street leading to the city. The two outlines together, with their combined trajectory, determine the physical structure of the bridge, which always stands out so clearly against the light or in the luminous red of the sandstone. Both movements are "vaultings" in that they ascend and descend—the individual trusses no less than the single arch of the entire bridge, whose midpoint marks the apex over the water. The flowing series of trusses supports the high profile of the bridge, which is what first catches one's eye. Hölderlin, however, depicts it as it in fact ultimately appears if one focuses on the lines of the bridge, namely, as the flowing movement of two combined trajectories.

All small birds, and especially woodland birds, fly in just this manner. Their flightpath is not a straight line. With a few quick strokes they vault up into the air and forward at the same time. This trajectory then carries them farther along, at which point they glide downward slightly. They then catch themselves and vault again, often higher upward and farther forward. And they repeat this motion before finally setting themselves down to land at the spot toward which the arc of their flight had been oriented from the beginning. Their flight is thus a linear sequence of arcs—in short, an unbroken line and a series of arches.[18] This is especially true of woodpeckers, "birds of the forest" *par excellence*. Since they find their food in branches and treetrunks, they have developed a remarkable ability to maneuver quickly and safely up under branches and between treetrunks of varying heights, thus ascending to higher trajectories and descending to deeper arcs. When they fly away over the treetops, however, it is in these distinctive high and quick vaulting trajectories.[19]

One would be going too far in reifying Hölderlin's image if one were simply to make a positive identification between its presentation of the bridge and the flight of the woodpecker.[20] Being familiar as he was, however, with the forests of Germany from many walks, hikes, and journeys, Hölderlin must have observed the bird's flight with a surer eye than that of his interpreters. And even surer still is his perception of the distinctive character of the Heidelberg bridge. The image of the bird's flight captures the structure of the bridge in its totality, not just

its uppermost outline, the purpose of which is to support the street—
and hence in a more embodied aspect, as well as purely in terms of
movement. Also, we can scarcely perceive the bird in flight apart from
the very movement of its flight. Similarly, the body of the bridge itself
consists in a double trajectory, a vaulting movement, an arcing motion
extending from one bank to the other, which supervenes on the sequence of individual arches.

There is more to be said in deciphering the image that Hölderlin introduces with the simile of the bird's flight, namely, that the bird of the
forest flies "above the hilltops." One could say, then, that the bridge,
resembling the bird's flight, towers up high and free in its trajectory.
This flight above the hilltops, however, at once establishes a connection
with what the bridge is vaulting out over, namely the river's water. A
later, revised version offers some insight into Hölderlin's perspective
and into his effort to capture it in words. In this draft the bird vaults
"over the swaying tops of oaks" (*über die wehenden Eichengipfel*; *StA* II,
p. 410). It should be noted, if only in passing, that this draft also attempts to make the verb "flies" superfluous by directly combining the
"vaulting" (*Sich-Schwingen*) of the bird's flight with the profile of the
bridge in a single verb. Above all, however, we must try to see what
Hölderlin wanted to introduce into his image of the bird's flight with
this image of the "swaying tops of oaks."

The townscape of present-day Heidelberg provides no answer. The
river's waters have been made deep and calm by barrages for naviga-
tional purposes, as well as being kept narrow by the construction of
roads along the banks and their "walkways" (*Staden*). But the old engravings, watercolors, and gouaches can still show us what Hölderlin
himself had seen and what had come back to him in recollection: a
river with often fairly little water, which for the most part flows far beneath its present-day level and literally "runs out," leaving shoals and
reefs protruding as it washes and swirls around them, occasionally
branching out from the river. The river, the "youth," thus seems playful
and does not just flow by indifferently. It pours forth, as if hesitating
here and there as it goes, yet continuing out into the distant plain. The
movement of the older, wider river we find in these images, then, also
adds to the touching comparison with the "sadly glad" heart of the
young Narcissus. But the river's course must also be seen through the
image of the bridge in relation to the vaulting flight of the woodland
bird. Hölderlin wants to show the river's waters as "swaying tops of
oaks." Oak trees are crowned by jagged shapes. Their boughs move in
the wind, their leafy masses billowing and boiling, back and forth, to

and fro, changing color as the bottoms and tops of the leaves are blown about. The river moved with the same multiformity of current and visual effect. And so the water, over which the bridge extends in arching trajectories, may be compared with the forest, over which the woodland bird does the same. At the same time, a contrast is set up between the multiform movements of the waters, which are not always sure of the way out into the plain, and the clear, unambiguous form of the bridge, in its double trajectory. Moreover, one can see that at the peak of its trajectory the bridge is silhouetted by the hesitating, jagged movement of the river—indeed, that its trajectory is even heightened by the unfathomable waters, which could whirl and toss about wildly like oaks in a storm. But the proud trajectory of the bird and of the bridge has freed itself from them. If one bears in mind Hölderlin's early versions of this stanza, there can be no doubt that in the depiction the poetic process itself was geared toward a full and vivid apprehension of the place as it actually was and as Hölderlin actually experienced it.[21]

A second, less conspicuous image in the text of "Heidelberg," indeed the final image in the ode, will help to shed light on the accuracy of Hölderlin's apprehension of an actual place.

> Sträuche blühten herab, bis wo im heitern Thal
> An den Hügel gelehnt, oder dem Ufer hold,
>   Deine fröhlichen Gassen
>   Unter duftenden Gärten ruhn.

> Down to the luminous valley bushes blossomed where,
> Leaning on the hillside, embracing the bank,
>   All your happy alleys
>   Under fragrant gardens repose.

A draft of the first line shows that in this stanza Hölderlin wanted to bring the progression from the castle, over the castle into the valley, and into the city by the river, and thus to bring the entire movement of the ode to a final repose: "But on the river below, repose in the valley bright" (*Aber unten am Strom ruhen im heitern Thal*) (*StA* II, p. 412). At the beginning of the stanza, too, he takes up the motif of the repose of the streets in the valley and along the river. Other interpreters have seen that Hölderlin apprehended the exact image of the streets of the old city:[22] they run parallel to the river at almost no incline at all, perpendicular, but with an "inclination" determined by the terrain falling off toward the river. In this way, they "embrace" (*hold*) the bank. But what does it mean that they "under fragrant gardens repose" (*unter duftenden Gärten ruhn*)?

Again, one might rest content with a simple answer: the old city is surrounded by gardens, especially where it ends beneath the precipice of the hillside, which rises visibly above the houses along the alleys. But Hölderlin wants to guide the perspective of the poem from the river and the bridge out to the castle, and again up over the castle, finally bringing it to rest in the city along the river. And this he could not have done if in the end he had let the view settle at the foot of the hillside, from which the "gigantic castle" (*gigantische Burg*) hangs "heavily into the valley" (*schwer in das Thal*). And what does it mean that those alleys veering toward the riverbank in the middle of the city also repose "under" (*unter*) gardens, like the alleys running along the precipice of the hillside they "lean on" (*anlehnen*)? Are the gardens themselves on the hillside, with the alleys beneath them, approaching and embracing the river? The streets far away from the sloping hillside, which the alleys intersect on their way to the river, also "lean" on the hillside in this way, as their winding paths more or less follow the irregularities of the gently sloping hillside. Those more distant gardens might not surround the alleys near the riverbank, nor the others overlooking the river, in their "happiness" (*Fröhlichkeit*). But then the final stanza would just stop short and never fully arrive at the life of the city.

Anyone familiar with the city, however, will be able to decipher the image of the alleys under the gardens with incomparably greater precision—and indeed in such a way as to lend it greater weight in the interpretation of the city's appearance. For, except at its center, between the royal stables and the town hall, the old city was thickly interspersed with gardens, a few of which can still be found today. Some were planted on the ruins of houses that were never rebuilt after the destruction of the city by Melac. Others were the parks of aristocratic palaces that stood among the ruins, having fashioned level foundations on the sloping terrain by amassing soil atop the ruins behind retaining walls. The effect of both is that the alleys lie deeper than the gardens, which thus blossom fragrantly above them. Together with the gardens on the hillside, from different areas but in the same manner, they tower above the alleys in the city itself and often, with their blossoming trees, above the houses as well.[23] Hölderlin must have been struck by this peculiar feature of the city, rising up out of the ruins, and it must have stayed in his mind.[24] It may be that he also saw with his own eyes that an image can emerge from the catastrophe of such complete destruction in which the form and the life of the city, of which the alleys stand as an exquisite reminder, are embraced and contained by the conciliatory life of nature, which indeed "rejuvenates" (*verjüngt*) and "animates" (*belebt*) the demolished castle. The conclusion of the ode, the "repose" (*ruhn*) of the alleys, thus achieves an abundance of sense rich enough finally to let the sequence of images in the ode culminate in a silence and a security born of reconciliation.[25]

Now the reader of "Heidelberg" cannot be expected to discern this precision on the basis of the images alone, which came back to Hölderlin again in the course of writing the poem from his experience of keen observation.[26] Yet the poem itself gives one a sense of the valence of image and compositional arrangement. And if an interpretation is able to bring out Hölderlin's image again in all its exactness, then in so doing it makes the sort of unbiased reading that longs to resolve the image in such concrete terms all the more rich and secure. For such an interpretation simply corresponds to the poetic process in which the work was able to take shape for Hölderlin himself in the unity of imagery and circumstance. The precision of the images is in no way a burden on the poetic element in the work's creation. Indeed the very meaning of the work, which makes it accessible to philosophical interpretation, rests on the clarity and precision of the images themselves rather than being diminished by them. Just as the deepest thought makes it possible to love what is most alive (*StA* I, p. 260), so too that which is grasped in its living and moving form opens up the possibility of intimating a line of thought that leads to a peace and quiet corresponding to the repose of the alleys in the poem.

The Reiterated Evocation of the Landscape on the Garonne and the Presence of the City

We can expect one result of the interpretation of "Heidelberg" to hold in the case of "Remembrance" as well, namely, that it is sensible and indeed imperative to appreciate the unity this poem achieves between exact observation on the one hand and the disclosure of different levels of meaning on the other—to appreciate it not in order to forgo all consideration of the poem's architecture but precisely in order to prevent the interpretation from obscuring an essential source of the poetic force of the work. But this task presents a far greater challenge in the case of "Remembrance." The poem is much more complex than the ode to Heidelberg, partly because the themes are not just contained implicitly in its formal structure but also expressively realized and extended, Hölderlin having already elaborated them in philosophical prose. A further difficulty of an entirely different sort emerges from the fact that the only handwritten manuscript of different drafts of "Remembrance" to have been preserved is of the final strophe. As we have seen in the case of

"Heidelberg," these drafts provide the most reliable means of documenting the emergence of a precise memory in the poiesis of the work itself. A third difficulty, of yet another kind, has to do with the distance that separates the historical Bordeaux from anyone in Germany wanting to uncover the visual dimension in "Remembrance." In the case of "Heidelberg" we found that one is able to retrieve from the past the historical aspect of a place known to Hölderlin only by being long acquainted with it and with the source of the poem's images. Even with "Heidelberg" eminent interpretations have tended to be unsupported by any such familiarity. But if a German writer is at least in a position to acquaint himself with Hölderlin's Heidelberg, he has no hope of familiarizing himself from a distance with Bordeaux. So any new attempt to interpret "Remembrance," too, must remain tentative and qualified by certain reservations.[27] Such an attempt is nonetheless not uncalled for. For the architecture of "Remembrance" well rewards the effort to discover the scenes in and around Bordeaux in the poem in their purely visual aspect as well. Its composition allows one to attach a precise location and perspective to each image. Any attempt to bring the images Hölderlin evokes in the course of the poem to a kind of perceptual determinateness must remain true to the form of the whole work, which becomes ever clearer in repeated readings, but does not require any specialized knowledge. And, as with "Heidelberg," once the images in "Remembrance" are made fully concrete, the work must still be able to be read and understood according to its actual structural composition, for such concreteness may well enrich the poem without disturbing the sequence and structure of its sense. The images are essentially sense-determining and sense-determined elements of a whole. They can be grasped in and of themselves in understanding the work, but they may also provide the key to its constitution as a whole, to be tried and tested against the poetic work itself. The effort to illuminate Hölderlin's depictions of the banks of the Garonne must therefore remain thoroughly oriented to the genuine task of interpretation, namely coming to an understanding of the architectural and circumstantial dimensions of "Remembrance."

In his lyrical work Hölderlin developed a masterful ability to present open spaces as well as epoch-spanning stretches of time. Throughout the texts, broad, expansive lines of movement emerge, alongside rapid flights and distant voyages, but then with abrupt shifts in perspective.[28] To make a full study of the emergence of this masterful ability one would have to begin with Hölderlin's narrative technique in *Hyperion* and how it developed. It is, to my knowledge, wholly unique.[29] Neither can it be explained independently of Hölderlin's philosophical work in connection with Fichte's *Wissenschaftslehre* and its principles concerning the imagination, nor of Hölderlin's early theoretical writings, in which "recollection" (*Erinnerung*) already figures as a central concept. Hölderlin's odes and hymns, whose form encompasses this expanse of space, time, and movement, also deserve a place in the history of modern consciousness, in which the arts, music, and painting as well anticipated the collective experience and the development of technology and the sciences.[30]

But Hölderlin always puts this virtuosity in the service of a poetic realization of an insight in which the world and history as one-in-all unfold in the midst of catastrophes and in the direction of total intimacy (*Welt-Innigkeit*). Even the concise poetic form, then, held in harmonic order, can be composed of such forces. This is especially true of "Heidelberg." In this ode the movement of the bridge in relation to the landscape, the river, and the city occupies a central position that one might say dominates the poem and at once defines its spatial aspect. The poet's own place on the bridge is then discerned. From this point on, the ode is written in the preterite tense. The views follow first in the direction of the river, and then toward the castle and its ruins. Finally, the view follows the movement of the landscape over the castle, back into the valley. With this turn the poet's position on the bridge is also preserved. For it winds up in the city itself: the gardens blossoming over the alleys, which are said to "repose"—again the present tense, as with the bridge at the beginning of the poem. Throughout this series of movements, encompassing and yet preserving the poet's perspective from the bridge, the repose of the city and the surrounding landscape acquires a status that goes beyond time and is in this sense "transcendental." With this, the ode, along with the loving homage, comes to its all-embracing conclusion with a double level of intimacy.

Thus, by the art of bringing strands of movement into a coherent pattern, the ode form in "Heidelberg" exhibits the force of collected intuition, and of the sublimation of the celebrated city into its own everlasting place, with both sense and context,[31] the dimensions of which correspond to those in the landscape itself, which in turn underlie and inhabit the layout of the city. It is to be expected, then, that the more ambitious hymn form of "Remembrance" was crafted with the same technique, with an at least comparable force and intensity. What follows is an attempt to understand features in the construction of this poem as well in light of the sequence of its perspectives, and thus in terms of the actual countryside as Hölderlin himself actually experienced and remembered it.

Once again, "Remembrance" depicts the Bordeaux landscape twice, and this reiterated evocation must be of fundamental importance for the architecture of the work as a whole.[32] The view proceeds, along with the northeasterly itself, down to the river and to the gardens of Bordeaux, which rise up into the vivid presence of the landscape of the city and the river during the celebration of the spring equinox. This vivid presence breaks off at the end of the second strophe, since the poet's consciousness of his own situation bursts in upon what is not itself embraced and brought to a lasting repose by the gentle balance of day and night. Thus the image of the landscape, along with the linguistic tone proper to it, vanishes in another kind of reflection.

At the beginning of the fifth strophe, however, another image of the landscape acts as a supporting piece of the structure within which the movement of the poem and the course of remembrance unfold. Once the remembrance itself has broadened further, only then can the poem openly enter into this second image, that is, once the poet is no longer wholly at the mercy of the thought that he himself lacks the comfort of the southern celebration, and that he must endure life alone,[33] once he has been drawn into another reality, namely the life of the mariners and its fiery spirit, who endure loneliness in their own way and who in their voyage have gone out far beyond the place evoked by the image of the landscape.

But the landscape of Bordeaux is present not only in the two passages in which it emerges as an image and as part of the significance of the poem but also in the two strophes between those passages. These strophes deal with the landscape twice again, though without making it fully present visually. This occurs first at the beginning of the third strophe in the call for the "dark light" of the Bordeaux wine, famous for its fragrance and ruby-red luster. Between this and the second image of the landscape itself a connection is drawn in relation to the vineyard hills at the mouth of the Dordogne. A second relation is established at the end of the fourth strophe, which is a reflection on the mariners' journey across the ocean: they miss "the city's celebrations," the music and the dancing. One cannot simply identify this "city" with Bordeaux. The meaning of the definite article *der* vacillates, as Hölderlin in all probability intended it to, between the individuality of a particular city and the generic "city," which in the present context of course means seaport. But neither can one altogether avoid the specific reference to Bordeaux. The allusion to the previous passage in the second strophe and the celebration of the spring equinox are too obvious and important. It is also obvious that, as the poet says at the very outset of the fifth strophe, the mariners—the "friends" and the "men"—have set out to sea from Bordeaux, and that it is therefore this city and its festivities that they have left behind.

The fragrant cup, the vineyard hills. The celebration of the spring equinox, the city's celebrations. This double, alternating relation at the beginning of the third strophe and at the close of the fourth, between an allusion to the landscape on the one hand and its evocation in an image on the other, belong to the structure of the poem itself as much as does the reiterated depiction of the landscape itself. Anyone who listens to the poem with an impartial ear cannot fail to catch the double reference of the image and its echoes. One could even say that the landscape's first appearance in the two opening strophes and its second appearance in the final strophe combine with the third and fourth strophes to form a middle section whose position and perspective have yet to be determined. On the other hand, one might add that the thread running from the beginning of the middle section to the beginning of the final strophe, and the thread connecting the end of the middle section with the end of the opening section, draw the middle section into a movement throughout which the Bordeaux landscape, without being made manifest in images or determinate localities, nonetheless remains constantly fixed in consciousness, though nonvisually. And the wine and celebration motifs that play on the two visual images of the landscape correspond to this effect of movement produced by the arrangement of the strophes.

This may suffice to convince us that the composition, and with it the sense of "Remembrance," can only be grasped by attending to the artful reiteration in the evocation of the Bordeaux landscape and by acknowledging its importance for the structure and the content of the poem. This provides us with an initial approach to the way the landscape figures in the poem generally. One must have it before one's eyes in order then to appreciate in detail not only the poem's points of view but also its shifts in perspective through the Garonne countryside.

But first, a note on the methodology of interpreting poems composed of separate, integrated levels of meaning. Since they unfold temporally and linguistically, interpretations, like poems, have above all a linear structure. For this reason it seems fitting to match an interpretation to the poem itself so that the one follows the other from beginning to end. And interpretations of "Remembrance" have proceeded in just that way.[34] If an interpretation in addition aspires to serve as a commentary in the form of an ongoing exegesis, then such an approach can hardly be avoided. It is true, too, that every interpretation must have a sense of the way the poem progresses, which includes being able to trace out that progression in distinct stages. This does not require, however, that the interpretation march alongside the poem in lockstep. It might equally arrive at a cumulative understanding of the poem's progression through a series of preliminary discussions and explications, treating for example specific passages that, though separated by long stretches of text, stand in direct relation to one another.

Such a procedure will be more easily accommodated and better suited in the case of the polyphonic composition of a work of art. For it will be able first and foremost to rise above the references and relations that extend back and forth throughout the course of the text. The weight and the effect of the text, however, will depend more crucially upon those interconnections than upon its mere linear construction. And whatever the ultimate concern of the commentary may be, one could imagine it amounting to a single element within a comprehensive interpretation, an element that in part puts forward ideas concerning the whole, in part repeats and summarizes, but does not in every case attempt to recapitulate the text. Nor when it comes to highly integrative philosophical works can an interpretation hold to a purely linear form of commentary without thereby reducing the integrative character of those works, and with it their systematic constitution, to the status of a special problem. This would be to adopt an overly narrow focus from the outset. This danger, being the consequence of what might appear to be a natural point of departure, is to be avoided even more so in the interpretation of linguistic and musical works of art, which also exhibit a basically linear structure. Hölderlin's compositional technique especially, beginning as it does by working with the root words and laying out the space for a poem on an empty page, calls for a different approach. It will be more difficult to bring order and clarity to this sort of endeavor than to a linear account, for which such organizational problems are hardly an issue. The investigation here will undertake such an alternative approach. It will be made easier by the fact that the account, which would form a legitimate part of a complete interpretation, does not in fact reach its final destination. Every nonlinear commentary must indeed be addressed to a reader who has been familiar with the interpreted work itself for some time, who can see it as a whole, who perhaps even knows it "by heart," and who has had some prior experience with the difficulties that present themselves when one tries to capture an immediate understanding in reflective terms—not to mention some appreciation of the rather meager aid of commentaries that merely accompany the text or that speak of it very generally without explicating the specific dimensions from which its sense emerges as a whole.

These general observations on the method of interpretation are necessary here since they provide a rationale for focusing on the images and perspectival shifts rather than simply proceeding in the order of the strophes. It will also prove useful in terms of the exegesis of the images to gain an overview of the topography of the landscape that Hölderlin was remembering and that he depicted in the poem from various points of view. My attempt to clarify those points of view themselves, then, will begin with the second evocation of the Bordeaux landscape in the final strophe, and so proceed in reverse order of the text. One reason for this has to do with the contingent fact that only those earlier drafts of the text containing the second evocation of the landscape have survived. An interpretation that casts light on the point of view and the poetic intent in terms of the evocation itself is therefore possible only in the case of the second evocation in the fifth strophe. This is attested, moreover, by the fact that Hölderlin's depiction of the Bordeaux landscape was conceived from the outset in terms of its relation to that second evocation.

TWO

Observations and Interpretations

A Topographical Sketch of the Old City

Hölderlin was fascinated by the science of astronomy, and some knowledge of geography lies behind the wide-ranging spatial quality of some of his hymns, which is often more reminiscent of a line drawn across maps or globes than of a narrated journey. His keen perception of landscape scenes goes hand in hand with his sure grasp of their topographical features. An exact knowledge of the course of rivers, to cite just one example, plays as much of a role in Hölderlin's river hymns as does his familiarity with the landscapes through which they flow and which they "nourish" (*"urbar" machen*) (*StA* II, p. 190). Being a poem about the Garonne, "Remembrance" too takes its place among the river hymns. And in the text of "Remembrance" itself, in its various distinct scenes and allusions, Hölderlin has captured the entire course of the Garonne from Bordeaux out to the sea. The poem also plays on the topography of the Garonne landscape, at least in one of the undercurrents of its complex composition. But this will go entirely unnoticed if interpreters remain as vaguely and imperfectly acquainted with that landscape as they have tended to be.[35]

The Garonne enters Bordeaux from the south-southeast. There it bends in a semicircle not unlike, and indeed often likened to, the crescent of the waning moon, which is unusual in the lower reaches of an inland river. The city lies on the left bank of the river, along the outer edge of the crescent. At the beginning of the nineteenth century the opposite bank, on the inner edge of the river's bend, was still relatively undeveloped. There was no bridge leading over the river. To the east of the inside of the bend, some distance from the shore, loom the hills in the countryside between the Garonne and the Dordogne, known as the

Entre deux Mers. They range northward from the old city at the end of the river's crescent, down along the bank of the Garonne. There at one time lay the old village Lormont, which today makes up one section of the town. It thus lies to the north of La Bastide, the once small district near the river's bend, which gave rise to the present-day suburb of the same name; with its railroad and industrial works in what was then farm land along the east shore. The Garonne then runs more than 20 kilometers to the north. Its west side was once primarily swamp land; farther to the west were the southern wine-growing estates of the Médoc, and to the east, near the slope of the hills, scattered farms and vineyards. The Garonne then meets up with the Dordogne, which flows in from the east. The waters converge and form the Gironde. After another 75 kilometers, in a kind of coastal inlet that widens to over 10 kilometers, they pour into the Atlantic. The ebb and flow of the tides have a marked effect both on this "sea-wide" (*meerbreit*) stretch of water and on the Garonne in Bordeaux.[36]

The Dordogne flows together with the Garonne at an acute angle. The promontory on the point of the confluence bears the name Bec d'Ambès, and at one time had a small port on the Garonne. On the opposite side, set out in the river, is a narrow island a few kilometers in length: the Ile Cazeau. It is shaped like the head of a spear, pointing back up the river toward Bordeaux. Exposed to the winds coming off the river and from the west, its land has always been barren.[37] Next to the Bec d'Ambès and the bank of this island, the south slope to the north of the Dordogne forms the third boundary around the confluence of the rivers. The hill rises straight up from the bank. The peak and the island today bear the scars of oil exploration, but the hills still produce grapes. These yield a red wine of fair quality classed among those of the Côtes de Bourg region.

I shall discuss the "gardens of Bordeaux" in more detail. But first we should consider the following in our overview of the Garonne landscape: Bordeaux was, in the eighteenth century, France's most important international port. Ocean-going vessels could come to the city; up to 150 of them could drop anchor at once, often lining up in rows out into the middle of the river. The shipping route stretched for kilometers across the northern half of the bend in the Garonne, downriver from the city. Leading architects of the mid-century had planned, and for the large part carried out, the construction of parks, plazas, and avenues between the city, the port, and the surrounding countryside to the north. They thereby transformed the former layout of the city, giving it an entirely different emphasis, as was their intention.[38] This area of parks and avenues stretched from the northern border of the old quarter and the quays of the harbor down to the edge of the Garonne, and even into the meadow region, the "Esplanade" of the old fort of the Château Trompette, which was torn down not long after Hölderlin's stay. Joining the parks and avenues on the west and north were public gardens, and then the rural areas of the Médoc with their farms and vineyards. Here, as well as south of the city upriver along the Garonne, sat the country houses of the wealthy Bordeaux burghers, whose parks and gardens with their many elm trees were more or less open to everyone.[39] Hölderlin's host owned one such small palace in Blanquefort. It still stands there today, at a distance of some seven kilometers from the Garonne.[40] A series of the most varied kinds of gardens, then, ran from these estates in the Médoc over the city's parks and avenues down to the Garonne and out along the other bank with its farms, meadows, clusters of trees, and vineyards. They stretched out over a good twelve kilometers and yet were integral to the life and to the image of the city.

It is crucial in trying to understand the architecture of "Remembrance" to be clear about the fact that the only direct contact between the series of gardens to the north of Bordeaux's old center and the area around the confluence of the Garonne and the Dordogne is by way of the Garonne itself. The gardens all make up part of the life of the city. The confluence of the rivers, however, lies at some distance from it, just less than a quarter of the way to where the Gironde opens out into the sea. A comfortable day's journey in a boat at low tide would take one down to the mouth of the river, out among the ocean-going vessels. A report from Hölderlin's day tells of a trip lasting an hour and a half and leading out to a country house that lay halfway to the confluence of the rivers.[41] When in the course of "Remembrance" an image of the Bordeaux landscape on the Garonne is evoked a second time, then, we are not being drawn back into the same images that unfold in the first two strophes around the gardens of Bordeaux. The poem now evokes a *different* scene—somewhere along the river, but far away from the city, on the route of the mariners, inland, almost devoid of people, and unanimated by any of their celebrations.

But this landscape too corresponds topographically to the gardens of Bordeaux: these gardens lie for the most part in the network of avenues and plazas between the city and the harbor, extending north of the city out into the Médoc. They lie adjacent to the city, so they follow along to some extent in the direction of the Garonne and the shipping route from Bordeaux. In them too the city opens out onto the countryside, in the same direction in which the river flows out and spills into the ocean. The confluence with the Dordogne marks the next prominent though still distant point in the course of the river. The hills on the north bank of the Dordogne at this point extend far to the west, following farther along the bank of the Gironde. Looming over the outlet to the sea to the south-southwest, they form the horizon of the flat countryside to the north of Bordeaux. On old lithographs, drawn from a bird's-eye perspective, they actually represent the horizon itself. The countryside and the river at the "zephyrous peak" (*luftigen Spiz'*) on the one hand, and "the gardens of Bordeaux" (*die Gärten von Bourdeaux*) on the other, thus form distinct spheres of the Garonne landscape, separated and yet interconnected. Viewed from the gardens of the city, the other sphere lies "yonder" (*fernhin*)[42]—though not as just one part of the surrounding area among others. It is bound up in a special way with the beginning of the mariners' route and the life of the city in its contemplation of the world and the ocean, but so too with the characteristic features of the landscape.

We are now in a position to turn to the second evocation of the Garonne landscape in "Remembrance." But first there is a question whose answer will shed light on the train of images and, with it, the poetic form and conceptual structure of "Remembrance." We must ask, that is, in what manner and from what perspective Hölderlin evokes the sphere at the confluence of the Garonne and the Dordogne. The first line in the poet's evocation of the northeasterly wind reads, "There, where along the sharp / Bank" (*Dort, wo am scharfen Ufer*); that is, it begins with the locative "there" (*dort*). The second evocation of the landscape in the final strophe, "There on the zephyrous peak" (*Dort an der luftigen Spiz'*), begins with the same word. If the two passages were merely evoking different places, viewpoints, or aspects within one and the same sphere, then one would assume that the place *from* which they were being evoked should remain constant. And since the poem initially suggests a distant place in Germany situated to the northeast of Bordeaux, one would have to say that throughout its entire course the poem surveys the Bordeaux landscape from that original standpoint. Heidegger's interpretation makes this assumption as if it were self-evident. And yet, however inconspicuous the assumption may seem, everything Heidegger had to say about the tension between the location of the poet and that of the mariners, indeed everything he had to say about "Remembrance" as a whole, depends upon it.[43] If, on the other hand, we open our eyes as much as possible to the country and the landscape known to Hölderlin, the possibility of an entirely different sort of interpretation soon emerges. If one is familiar with the landscape in "Remembrance," as Hölderlin himself in fact was, one will immediately know that the vineyard hills and the "zephyrous peak" (*luftigen Spiz'*) can and indeed must be depicted in just this way *from Bordeaux itself*, that one can speak of them as a sphere lying "there," or even "yonder." This is not to say that in its second evocation of the sphere of the landscape "Remembrance" is orienting itself from this particular vantage point alone. As we shall see later, the "there" in the final strophe brings together a number of connections with the mariners' point of departure. But the distance between the gardens and the confluence, while the two are still situated in relation to each other within the Garonne landscape, opens up a space within which Hölderlin was able, artfully and eloquently, to shape the poem's movement, modulation, and perhaps a kind of suspension of relations, alongside one another—more eloquently, indeed, than the uncritical assumption underlying Heidegger's interpretation leads one to suppose. "Remembrance," being composed philosophically as well as poetically, not only fixes the location of the one drawn into the remembrance but is also able to *transport* us to another place and thus transform our own perspective. Saying this much is just to articulate the basic starting point for any interpretation undeterred by the false suspicion that the poet of "Remembrance" is merely depicting things literally. Quite apart from this, the attentive reader, letting himself be drawn into the poem's "intimacy" (*Innigkeit*), will be familiar with the transformative effect moving through the strophes of the work. It is hard, though, to preserve one's original impression of the artistic and conceptual force of the work itself in the face of Heidegger's own conceptually compelling interpretation, and in light of the contractions and displacements of meaning by means of which that interpretation tried—and failed—to capture the insight in Hölderlin's work.

The Outlet to the Sea: The Peak and the Vineyard Hills

Hölderlin's text of the final strophe has survived, together with the final phases of its composition. The manuscript affords some insights into the origin of the second evocation of the Bordeaux landscape. This evocation was the most thoroughly reworked passage in the strophe, and the one most elaborated in subsequent drafts. We shall be tracing these lines of the poem through their three stages of revision. They are well documented in the Große Stuttgarter Ausgabe.

The opening lines of the evocation were written twice. They read, first:

> Nach Indien sind
> Die Freunde gezogen.

> To India
> The friends have set off.

Since these lines appear at the top of the surviving page, we do not know whether the sentence continues in an enjambment from the previous strophe. The words *Die Freunde* occurred originally in the first line as *die Fr.* They were then deleted in the second draft. We needn't inquire here into Hölderlin's reasons for replacing *die Freunde* altogether with the words *die Männer* ("the men").[44] When he had decided to write *Männer* instead of *Freunde*, Hölderlin also happened to contemplate replacing *Indien* ("India"). In one draft, the stroke that crosses out *Freunde* in the second line also goes through *Indien* in the previous line. Why Hölderlin did not want to keep India as the definite destination of the journey needn't concern us here.[45]

In any event, instead of writing over either *Freunde* or *nach Indien*, he let the two short lines stand unaltered and drafted a new version. In it the line now begins with the *Nun aber* ("But now") that appears in the finished text:

> Nun aber sind zu Indiern
> Die Männer gezogen.
>
> But now to the Indians
> The men have set off.

Hölderlin then wrote *gegangen* ("gone") instead of *gezogen* ("set off"). The verb *ziehen* suggests a going away forever, as well as a migration (*Zug*) to another country. Moreover, the word *gegangen* corresponds to the departure on the way out to the ocean, as well as to the leave taken of those who have *just* been left behind. Thus the word *gegangen* also provides a succinct introduction to the subsequent second evocation of the sphere around the confluence of the two rivers. This evocation originally occurred alone in the following sentence, written in two lines:

> Fernhin, wo sich endiget
> Meerbreit der Strom.
>
> Yonder, where sea-wide
> The river ends.

These lines were probably already written by the time Hölderlin decided to replace *gezogen* with *gegangen*. For it is only in them that the scene at the mouth of the Dordogne, where the Garonne proper ends, has not yet been brought into sharp focus. Hölderlin surely felt that the double accent of the word *meerbreit* ("sea-wide") in conjunction with *Strom* ("river") expressed the finality of a departure off into the distance.[46] And the recollection of the long course of the Gironde out to sea, which already has the aspect of the sea itself, fused this finality with the image of the friends' initial route out to the ocean. And this fusion is captured in the very wording of the strophe.

But Hölderlin chose not to rest content with an evocation of the end of the river's course between the confluence and the sea. As the river passes by this transition point, the landscape was to emerge in the poem more vividly in its own right. Its poetic depiction probably began for Hölderlin with his recollection of the narrow, rugged island lying in the stretch of river that forms the transition into the Garonne, and with a memory of the cool breezes binding that stretch of river to a life at sea. It is also possible, of course, that he remembered the Bec d'Ambès promontory—the point at which the waters of the Dordogne first meet up with those of the Garonne. This is suggested by the fact that the French *Bec* is translated by the German *Spitz* ("peak"). The piecemeal composition of the text, on the other hand, suggests the contrary. For Hölderlin included the reference to the "zephyrous peak" in the text before he planned to make specific mention of the Dordogne. It is more plausible, then, to suppose that he had in mind the island marking the transition from the Garonne to the Gironde. Thus he wrote:

> Fern wo an luftiger Spize
> Meerbreit sich endiget der Strom.

> Far off, where on the zephyrous peak
> Sea-wide the river ends.

Here we must also attend to Hölderlin's choice of adverb in referring to the site throughout the poem. In the above passage, in the first draft of the text, the adverb is *fernhin* ("yonder"). The fact that this version has survived is a great help to an interpretation of the entire poem. For it makes clear that Hölderlin wanted to anchor the perspective of remembrance in the final strophe of the poem in Bordeaux itself. To say *fernhin* is to think at once of the route taken and of the place to which it leads. Only from the perspective of Bordeaux, the point of departure, can this dual extension of the recollection of the departure be understood. Nor does the contraction of the adverb to *fern* alter the identification of this perspective, once knowledge of the first version has made us realize that the poetic depiction emerged from it.

Hölderlin, however, modified the form of the adverb once again: *Dort an der luftigen Spiz'* ("There on the zephyrous peak"). The modification here is a consequence of the decision to evoke the sphere of transition in a concrete image. This decision had in effect already been made with the evocation of the "zephyrous peak." The adverb *dort* indicates a specific place, and even implies the possibility of identifying that place in all its specificity. Like *fern*, it presupposes that a distance intrudes, but it refers primarily not to the distance as such but to that which lies at a distance. Consequently, unlike *fern*, *dort* also presents the distance as not necessarily very great or difficult to overcome; it remains neutral with respect to magnitude. The word *dort* does not specify whether the thing lies "there" in the field of view or "there" in geographical space. By putting *dort* in place of *fern*, Hölderlin has begun to depict a place of transition that remains within the setting of the Bordeaux landscape. At the same time, however, he has drawn a connection to the first evocation of the landscape along the Garonne, the depiction of which is likewise introduced with the word *dort*.[47]

We may suppose, at any rate, that Hölderlin changed *fern* to *dort* only after he had resolved to depict the transition point in the poem more vividly than had been possible with the mere insertion of *Fern wo an luftiger Spize* ("Far off, where on zephyrous peak"). For with this line, written over the two lines of the first version, the direct link with the line already written, *Meerbreit sich endiget der Strom* ("Sea-wide the river ends"), has not yet been severed. Hölderlin then went on, however, to delete this line and to follow up the new line, *Fern wo an luftiger Spize*, which he placed above the old one, with two entirely new lines. In them the imagery of the evocation is fleshed out further. At this stage, then, the following text emerged:

(Fern wo an luftiger Spize)
Des Rebenlandes herab
Die Dordogne komt.

(Far off, where on zephyrous peak)
Down from the wine country
The Dordogne comes.

It is not difficult to guess why Hölderlin went on to elaborate in this way. One possibility has to do simply with the number of lines in the strophe; that is, Hölderlin wanted to depict the scene at the confluence of the rivers with greater precision simply because the last strophe had not yet grown to its proper proportions. But this explanation is not particularly compelling. For in the final version, too, the last strophe has one line fewer than the previous strophes. In a poem that has the free form of a hymn, this is undoubtedly justified by the impact of the concluding triad. It was in fact precisely the hymn form that would have allowed Hölderlin to increase the number of lines by dividing up individual lines. A more compelling suggestion, then, is that the concentration of meaning in the concluding triad, which must already have been conceived by the time the surviving manuscript was composed, demands of the immediately preceding section of the text that it too exhibit substantial content in itself. It would also require that in the course of its movement the text should come to rest in the line *Meerbreit sich endiget der Strom*. Supplementing and in fact outweighing this consideration is the fact that when he inserted the line *Fern wo an luftiger Spize*, Hölderlin had already begun an original depiction of the sphere of the confluence that was able to suggest a continuation. This sort of depiction was favorable not only to the conception of the inner balance of the final strophe but also to the balance of the poem as a whole: a return to the evocation of the Bordeaux landscape in another of its spheres would harmonize with the first evocation of the landscape with which the poem began. On the other hand, this means that through the inner development of its representation the second sphere will emerge more vividly and so accord with the first.

It is now easy to see how the decision to elaborate this second evocation allows the sphere of the confluence to emerge more vividly and succinctly, in Hölderlin's own memory as well. The second sphere of the landscape along the Garonne was first identified as the site of the departure, and therefore as the place where the river undergoes a transformation and loses its name. It was then further distinguished by the windswept peak, whether the spearhead of the island or the promontory between the two rivers. The depiction of this sphere then turns to the Dordogne, which flows from the right side into the Garonne and together with it becomes the sea-wide Gironde. The Dordogne comes "down from the wine country" (*des Rebenlandes herab*). This expression introduces the river's swift currents, bordered by hills on either side, as well as the fact that the Dordogne flows through the wine-growing regions. In this second aspect, however, the picture is supported by a knowledge of geography: the countryside and the river are presented as it were from a bird's-eye perspective, or even from their appearance on a map.

This sort of image must have seemed to Hölderlin overly abstract, too far removed from intuition. The sphere around the confluence, however, was still to be realized in the same imagery and concrete aspect in which Bordeaux itself had been depicted in the first evocation of the landscape. This intention becomes clear in the next state of the text, which Hölderlin undertook in rewriting the preceding lines:

Am Rebenlande wo herab
Die Dordogne kommt,

In the wine country, where down
The Dordogne comes,

What this version deals with is not the course of the Dordogne *through* the wine-growing regions but the scene *at* the confluence itself—a change that corresponds to the shift in view from the course of the Gironde to the confluence of the rivers. The talk of the "wine country" (*Rebenlande*), however, preserves some elements of the previous conception of the landscape that had been oriented in terms of geography. Hölderlin therefore felt compelled to abandon this way of evoking the sphere altogether and, in place of the geographical image, to produce an evocation that would bring out the full appearance of the confluence. Thus, by again rewriting the line *Des Rebenlandes herab* ("Down from the wine country"), he arrived at the final version:

> An Traubenbergen, wo herab
> Die Dordogne kommt,
>
> On vineyard hills, where down
> The Dordogne comes,

At this point, the text of "Remembrance" is still just a pure depiction of the sphere from which the seafarers will eventually depart. Hölderlin must have been familiar with the locale itself. He knew that the wine-growing mountains are situated across from the "zephyrous peak," mountains that lead up and onto the south face of the hills, which in turn project into the mouth of the Dordogne and into the currents of the Gironde. Traveling from Bordeaux down the Garonne, one's view is dominated on the left by the island's "zephyrous peak," and in front and on the right by the vineyard hills together with the converging Dordogne.[48] The fact, too, that the Dordogne comes "down" (*herab*) has acquired a wholly visual sense in the scene at the confluence. That it flows down into the Garonne from above is made clear by the fact that it extends to the river at Bordeaux together with the series of vineyard hills.

At the same time, however, it is clear that Hölderlin, who had himself long since taken leave of the area, was drawn back into the recollection of the landscape's visual aspect only gradually and in the course of the poetic process itself. For this strophe first took shape in mere fragments of recollection and geographical fact. The various revisions of the text coincide with the dawning of a vivid recollection of the place he had visited just the year before.

It has now become clear, however, that the visual perspective on this landscape became fixed only as Hölderlin's recollection unfolded along with the text of "Remembrance" in the emergence of the second evocation of the Garonne landscape. So long as these lines rested on mere geographical fact, it could still appear as if the perspective were that of a poet remaining behind in the distant Germanic northeast, sending greetings along with the wind to the river and the city. In the final version of the text, however, the sphere of the confluence is realized and depicted from Bordeaux itself. The mariners arrive with the Garonne at the confluence. And just as the landscape of the eventual departure then opens onto the "zephyrous peak," the Dordogne, which "comes" down, and the vineyard hills, so too the poem opens out before the reader. It is this line of sight from Bordeaux, not yet "far off" on the scale of a sea voyage around the world, which essentially makes it necessary to begin the evocation of this view of the sphere with the *dort* that also in fact introduces the evocation in the poem. We have noted already that this *dort* also acquires other meanings in the context of the entire poem. We shall have to reflect on them presently.[49] But whatever such reflections may yield, it is crucial at this point to emphasize that in its final strophe "Remembrance" aspires to a style or representation in which the location of the poet at the outset of the poem does not remain absolutely fixed. The place addressed in the initial greeting is now drawn into the course of remembrance and becomes one of the perspectives of the poem itself.

The City and Its Surroundings

The text of the second evocation of the landscape along the Garonne is separated from the first by a full two-thirds of the poem's length. Yet between them an equilibrium is established, not just between two discrete spheres but within the poem as a whole. The second evocation thrives on the presence of the countryside along the Garonne as it unfolds in the course of the remembrance, and thus emerges in rapid succession with an intuition of the sphere, as rich and various as the first. It is particularly regrettable that no handwritten manuscript of the two opening strophes, and thus of the more extensive text of the first evocation, has survived. For it is evident in the evocation of the second sphere in the final strophe that the successive versions afford us more than just an insight into the intentions of the poet. They also provide the best means of bringing the depiction found in the text itself into the kind of clarity and vividness that comes only with a knowledge of the actual place and of the perspectives in which it appears. Both the actual place and the perspectives on it figure into the poetic composition of the text. And each is most readily discoverable, or at any rate most reliably revealed, in the genesis of the text of the poem.

The general features of the landscape that appear in the second evocation at the confluence of the rivers can still be found there today, notwithstanding the damage that has been inflicted on the region. It is not altogether difficult to discover Hölderlin's meaning, and that of the poem, by looking at the countryside as well as the text. Things are different in the case of the first evocation, that of the sphere of the city on the Garonne. Here foliage and human artifacts play a larger role, and these provide less permanent fixtures than the system of rivers, hills, and islands. And as the example of "Heidelberg" showed, such things can indeed be reshaped by human hands in such a way that they no longer appear in the same context once known to Hölderlin and preserved in his writing. Still, the sphere at the confluence of the Garonne and the Dordogne has survived in its most essential aspects. Much of what Hölderlin bases his evocation of Bordeaux and its gardens on, however, is precisely what gets swept away most quickly as cities develop: gardens and even brooks are built over, trees are felled, mills are closed down and fall into disrepair. Only the rivers, in particular those that ebb and flow with the ocean's tides, go their own way unwaveringly through the epochs of a city's history. It is not easy, then, across this historical distance and on the basis of one's own impressions, to rediscover the sphere of the gardens of Bordeaux. In fact, such a task should be undertaken only by one who has lived in the city itself and is as familiar with its past as with Hölderlin's poetic methods.[50]

Nevertheless, we can begin to shed some light on the basic historical and visual features of the world that emerges in the opening strophes of "Remembrance," and so too something of Hölderlin's recollective poetic path as well. And it seems reasonable, in attempting to shed light on the evocation of Hölderlin's "Bourdeaux," to begin by considering some of the sources on which the following study has been based.

The present study, written far from Bordeaux, makes extensive use of the recent literature on the history of the city. Naturally it presupposes some knowledge of the city. The historical character of the Bordeaux of Hölderlin's day has not at any rate been captured explicitly in recent publications. It was therefore necessary to turn to contemporary sources. Of essential assistance in this respect is the *Revue historique de Bordeaux*, which has appeared semi-annually since the beginning of this century—an excellent journal, especially during its first three decades, dealing with the history of the Gironde province, and above all its capital city. This pointed the way to travel books written by foreigners in the decades around the time of Hölderlin's stay, sometimes nearly contemporaneously. As the first Hölderlin scholar, A. Beck deserves credit for having drawn attention to a report by the brother of Hölderlin's employer in Bordeaux: F. J. L. Meyer, *Briefe aus der Hauptstadt und dem Innern Frankreichs*, Tübingen: Cotta,

1802, in two volumes (see note 35 above). The account of Bordeaux occurs at the beginning of the second volume. It also appears in annotated excerpts in the *Revue historique*, vol. V (1912), pp. 164 ff., and vol. VI (1913), pp. 229 ff. Because of his proximity to Hölderlin's life situation, and because the visit he records in his book took place in 1801, Meyer is of particular importance, notwithstanding his all too cursory remarks on the topography. Yet his is only one of the larger group of such travel books. In 1804 the Dutch writer Adriaan von der Willigen stayed in Bordeaux from the end of September to the beginning of October. He reported on his stay in *Reize door Frankrijk in gemeenzame brieven, door Adriaan von der Willigen aan den Uitgever* (Haarlem, 1805) (available in Koninklijke Bibliotheek in The Hague, see pp. 433–503). This report was published in the *Revue historique*, vol. VI (1913), pp. 253 ff. But travel books from the period just before the Revolution also make an essential contribution to forming a clear image of the city Hölderlin visited. The single most important of these books should also be of interest, though for different reasons, to German specialists. For it comes from the pen of Sophie la Roche in the form of letters she wrote in 1785 in Bordeaux itself: *Journal einer Reise durch Frankreich* (Altenburg, 1787), see pp. 263–347. It too was published and discussed in the *Revue historique*, vol. IV (1911), pp. 169 ff and 253 ff. At about the same time a young Englishwoman, Mrs. Cradock, stayed in Bordeaux for nearly two months. Her travel book was published twice in France (in translation), the second time in Paris in 1911 (Perrin) under the title, *La Vie française à la veille de la Revolution, Journal inédit de Mme Cradock*, Mme Odelphin-Balleyguier, trans., printed in *Revue historique*, vol. IV (1911), pp. 9 ff. The first edition of 1896, entitled *Journal de Mme. Cradock, voyage en France (1783–1786)*, is in the Bibliothéque nationale in Paris. The second edition of 1911, used here, is in the City Library of Bordeaux, see pp. 199–213.

Further evidence is to be found in Henry Swinburne, *The Courts of Europe* (London, 1841) vol. 1, pp. 46–48 (on the occasion of his stay of 1774–75), and from Arthur Young's travel book, used here in German translation: *Reise durch Frankreich und einen Teil von Italien in den Jahren 1787 bis 1790*, from the English and annotated by E. A. W. Zimmermann, vols. 1–3 (Berlin, 1793, 1794, 1795) (see pp. 84–89 of the first volume). The differences among the four most extensive descriptions of travel may be characterized as follows. Meyer and S. la Roche had relatives in Bordeaux and so had access to the local customs and the news generally unavailable to foreigners. Meyer's main interest was in the city's political and pedagogical institutions. V. d. Willigen reports largely on its artists and ancient monuments. Mrs. Cradock is a tourist who also gives accounts of her excursions into the surrounding area. S. la Roche takes an active interest in and has a keen eye for the local habits of the people, and her literary education and her knowledge of French intellectual history allow her to investigate the historical sources themselves. Her account is consequently the most lively and productive.

Another important source is a description of the city written in 1785, also used by several of the travelers themselves, for example Mrs. Cradock: *Déscrip-*

tion historique de Bordeaux, avec l'indication de tous les Monuments, chef d'oeuvres des Arts, et objets de curiosités que renferme cette Ville (Bordeaux, 1785, de la librairie Paul Pallandre). This guide to the city, which describes itself on the title page as "indispensable aux Voyageurs, et trés-utile aux Citoyens," devotes considerable space to a commentary on the Roman monuments of Bordeaux. Further information is to be found in maps of the period, as well as paintings and other pictorial representations of Bordeaux from the second half of the eighteenth to the middle of the nineteenth century. These will be cited in the notes. Other sources, for example news sources, will not be listed separately.[51]

In making use of the contemporary sources one must always keep in mind the basic approach that underlies Hölderlin's city poems, and which is so characteristic of him. More so even than in "Heidelberg" and "Stuttgart," in "Remembrance" Hölderlin presents the city's landscape above all as a part of nature. Consequently, if one attends only to the primary and elementary meaning of the words and images making up the dominant thread of the text, it can seem as though Hölderlin wanted to put the life of the city proper entirely to one side. The river and its banks, the brook and the trees towering over it, the forest, the mill, and the mild breeze over the paths all meet as if in a kind of pastoral idyll imbued with deep mythic significance. It might indeed seem that the gardens of Bordeaux are depicted as if seen by the townsfolk of the port, who "on holidays" (*an Feiertagen*) bring their bustling activities to a standstill, wanting to preserve and enter into the peace and quiet of nature's embrace. The gardens adjacent to and leading into the city would then belong to the countryside of the "sweet Garonne" (*schöne Garonne*), but not to the city proper. The evocation of the city would then serve only to guide the elevating movement of remembrance up to the level of the Garonne as it passes by the city, thus leading it away from all the mundane business that reveals the city to those who in fact live there.

This impression certainly finds some warrant in the text of "Remembrance." The main thread of the poem's progression might even seem to confirm it, the pastoral scenes following upon one another as they do, into the serenity of the celebrations. But dwelling on this leads the interpreter astray from Hölderlin's approach to the layout of cities and urban life in general, as well as from the polyphonic conception of this, one of his consummate works. This poem does not just depict Bordeaux as a place situated in the surrounding countryside along the Garonne, where the townsfolk emerge. The distinctive life of the seaport is captured in tones that echo through the whole poem. Indeed, these tones are dominated by a language and an imagery that tends to conceal the city behind the natural world and the rural life bound up with it. The predominance of these images, however, is precisely the opposite of a detachment from the reality of the city. If one reflects on the verses further, letting them fuse together to form a general impression that leaves nothing out of account, then the very semblance of detachment will evoke the presence of the city all the more effectively and essentially. This is because the city seems at once embedded in yet elevated beyond the broader context situating it in its surroundings, situating those surroundings in their natural setting, and finally incorporating both the town and the country into the dynamic unity of the world and life at large through their relation to the ocean. A remark by Sophie la Roche concerning "what nature has done for the layout of this city, and how spirit and industriousness have put it to use"[52] suggests that this way of regarding the city on the Garonne was in no way peculiar to Hölderlin but had instead to do with notions concerning the effects of nature on the internal development of the city.

The gardens of Bordeaux remain the city's gardens, just as the celebrations in the poem itself are evoked as the city's celebrations. The "dark light" (*dunkles Licht*) in the fragrant cup, wherever one finds it, is brought in from the harbor. And it is the commerce of the port that brings together "what is beautiful of the earth" (*das Schöne der Erd'*) and sends the mariners off on their long years' voyage to India,[53] in which the nor'easter grants them a fiery spirit. By so skillfully bringing out the underlying voice of the poem, whose theme is the city itself, letting it sing out steadily so that its motifs do not break off into isolated images constructed in the language piece by piece, Hölderlin manages to strengthen rather than weaken its impact on the tone and significance of the poem—assuming that the interpreter is able to understand what is said in the poem itself and how it is expressed, apart from the explicit evocation of the images. The motifs that simply resound or echo, but which refer explicitly to the life of the city, stand in relation to the visual representation appearing at other points in the text and extending across several strophes.[54]

All of this must be kept in mind if the images of the Garonne and of the gardens of Bordeaux, which emerge in the poem like scenery visible to the eye, are to be brought into focus as they were in Hölderlin's recollection. The poem itself strives for this kind of clarity inasmuch as it seeks to speak with eloquence to Hölderlin's contemporaries too, who were able to share similar experiences and recollections—but even more so in that the poem is born of the gratitude and fondness of the visitor in thinking back on the sphere of life that once opened up before him. Once we as interpreters have understood that "Remembrance" makes the city itself manifest in the indirect way I have just described, we will no longer simply follow the initially plausible assumption that the gardens of Bordeaux must lie in the outskirts of the city and the surrounding area, or at the ends of country roads, or that they must be understood as mere *loci amoeni*. It would only accord with the inner structure of the poem, and the relation between city and nature that it seeks to impart, if the sphere of the river and the gardens were experienced and remembered as being drawn into the city itself and belonging to its own general aspect.

The ode "Heidelberg" and the elegy "Stuttgart"[55] testify to the fact that as his creative powers grew, Hölderlin developed the ability to capture a city in poetic language just by guiding one's view through its landscape, that is, by evoking the city through the features of the locale surrounding and feeding into its daily life. "Heidelberg" mentions none of the structures in the city, not even the church steeple, though it provides the city in the valley with a kind of counterpoint to the castle on the slope. The townsfolk appear only on their way to and from the city, and then only in the "traffic sounds" (*Tönen*) of their hustle and bustle on the bridge. The alleys among the fragrant gardens appear deserted, fixed only by their place in the landscape and by the foliage growing over the city. They are "happy" (*fröhlich*), and for that reason suited to a way of life that acquires a kind of happiness through them. Thus the city appears entirely in terms of its place in the world, and this in a poem that aspires simply to be a declaration of love to the city itself. "Remembrance," though an homage in its own way,[56] is addressed to Bordeaux in a more wide-reaching context from the outset— from the voyages of thought intertwined with the journeys of the mariners and the currents of the wind. But it is commerce and shipping, too, that make the city of Bordeaux what it is—essentially a port, and so a point of transition into the world at large. It is understandable, then, in a poem composed in and of a progressive course, which at the same time extends out beyond the spheres it depicts, that we should find the city and its urban routine fully situated in a latent yet all-pervasive presence, more so than in the earlier poems of homage.

One would have more of a sense of how to understand the images in the opening strophes of "Remembrance," and of how Hölderlin was able to situate the town within the country, if the various drafts of the text that have come down to us included more than just the final strophe. But we are now in a position to contemplate the polyphonic quality of the text itself, to shed light on the historical city itself, and finally to relate the one to the other. What follows is a series of observations leading to some conjectures concerning how one ought to see and understand the images of and the perspectives on Bordeaux in the text of the two opening strophes.

It may turn out to have been better to forgo such conjectures. On the other hand, in any case, we must suppose that Hölderlin's depiction of the first sphere of the countryside along the Garonne, which includes the city and the harbor, was just as calculated as that in "Heidelberg" and the depiction of the second sphere at the confluence of the two rivers. These lines, however, articulate the locality in its full significance precisely by stressing its visual form in a concise, "faithful" (*getreuen*) preservation of reality.[57] We cannot help seeing the same mode of representation at work in the strophes dealing with the Garonne and the city's gardens. And we must suppose that we have missed the concentration of the land and the life on the Garonne, and so too the unity of the poem as a whole, if the city fails to shine before our eyes in the opening strophes, standing out from the countryside both in appearance and significance. The reiterated evocation of the landscape on the Garonne corresponds not to a contrast between idyllic urban migration and heroic flight but to a contrast between two sorts of rest and repose: the one harboring the city of arrivals and departures, the other harboring the departures and farewells themselves.

The City Sphere: The Gardens and the Footpath

Thus far I have sketched out the topography of Bordeaux and the layout of the parks, meadows, and gardens in the foothills. The city, however, has a peculiar feature, to my knowledge unique, and that is that the beltway of lawns meets the Garonne at an almost perpendicular angle between the old city and the harbor. These lawns are mirrored by the grounds on the opposite shore. The reason for this is that the old Château Trompette (built on the site of a Roman temple) needed an open firing range for the cannons on its bastions. When the castle was built a wide, grassy area opened out between the region of the harbor and the northern outskirts of the town where the royal palace and the eighteenth-century stock market were located, near the river. The city planners of the eighteenth century had included this space early on as part of a grand scheme of avenues and plazas.[58] The architect Victor Louis had designed for it a concentric system of streets that would all run in one direction toward the Garonne and converge in a semicircular plaza, with a balcony looking out onto the river.[59] This array of boulevards was even drawn into the contemporary maps of the city.[60] But it was never installed. Shortly before Hölderlin's stay an alternate plan was adopted, being the winning entry in a competition in which architects from a number of different countries took part.[61] It corresponds, in essentials, to today's layout, namely that of the Esplanade des Quiconces, which was erected on somewhat narrow terrain. To this day it remains the largest public urban square in Europe. Perpendicular to the Garonne, it extends over half a kilometer. It ends at the shore in a semicircle and is accompanied on either side by wide avenues and promenades. Hölderlin was presumably familiar with both plans, for they were of great interest and much discussed in the house of the consul.[62]

Hölderlin was also able to examine both designs since the wide field of the Château Trompette presented itself in what was an obviously provisional state.[63] The avenues lining the park, on the other hand, had long since been constructed, for instance the Allées de Tourny, which with their four rows of trees on the right side (elms and lindens) were to cross over into the new park.[64] The *allées* led out of the old quarter to the northwest. The Grand Théâtre, completed in 1780, a symbol of the wealth and pride of the port city, was erected where the *allées* began.[65] At the other end, at a square called Place de Tourny—in honor of the architect, like the avenues—lay the palace[66] of Consul Meyer, who represented the city of Hamburg, one of Bordeaux's most important trading partners.[67] The palace was at that time the only building that stood with its facade facing the town. This is where Hölderlin stayed. "I'm living almost too magnificently" (*Fast wohn' ich zu herrlich*), he wrote to his mother, surely not just because of the luxurious interior of the palace and its architecture (*StA* VI, p. 430).

A few meters to the northeast lies the second avenue, which intersects with the Place de Tourny and continues the western border of the planned park in the region of the Château Trompette. On the left side of this avenue lies another park, which still exists today as the Jardin Public, though it now has a somewhat different layout. This was the old Jardin Royal, which must have been familiar to Hölderlin still as the "Champs de Mars," as it was called during the Revolution. Here, just a few years earlier, celebrations of the Revolution had taken place.[68]

Soon after the construction of the avenues, the path across the Allées de Tourny into the public garden became the preferred promenade of Bordeaux citizens. Consul Meyer's brother, who visited a year before Hölderlin's stay, reported of the holiday promenades in the park of the Champs de Mars that anyone who was beautiful, elegant, and generally noteworthy could be seen strolling through the grand avenues. On working days, however, on account of the marshy atmosphere, the garden, built in the old style of Lenôtre, was empty or was visited only by people of a lower class. The elegant world, he said, preferred to walk along the Allées de Tourny.[69]

While the Champs de Mars seems to have been well maintained in Hölderlin's day, shacks, huts, stables, and small fields and gardens were built and walks installed without authorization in the area around the Château Trompette. Along the avenues themselves a row of establishments catering to the entertainment of the passersby sprang up, again, in the form of makeshift shanties.[70] The upper floor of the house looked out over the mostly low-lying shacks and the field, out to the château and the Garonne. So the field presented itself neither in its former spaciousness nor in its future beauty.[71] But Hölderlin could see the area in terms of the construction plans. And the central location of this district from the beltway to the Garonne and out over the river had at any rate been preserved.[72] Immediately adjacent to the Champs de Mars, however, which lay nearby at the back side of Meyer's palace, were the vegetable gardens and pleasances of the citizens and suburbanites of Bordeaux, crossed by paths and extending out into the wine country of the Médoc. One might also stroll into the small villages nearby. Or one might cross over the Garonne, making one's way out to the little spots Lormont and Bouliac in the Entre deux Mers.[73] The routes of these walks and those of the promenades were thus bound up with one another in a single sphere.

It is not easy to form an image of the land on the other side of the Garonne as it existed in Hölderlin's day. In 1785 Sophie la Roche found the view across the river, with the masts of the ships, over to the towering poplars on the opposite bank highly attractive and described it in such terms.[74] A painting by Joseph Vernet dating from 1758, the first of two pictures of Bordeaux in his series *Ports de France*,[75] also shows part of the scenery on the opposite shore. One sees tall poplars and, in roughly the same numbers, other shorter trees scattered in a row. The picture of the harbor by Pierre Lacour, dating from 1804 and looking out from the point at which the area around the Château Trompette touches the Garonne, shows a scene on the other bank that also corresponds in essentials to the one in Vernet's work.[76] Lithographs produced some decades later suggest that the landscape on the right bank of the Garonne has changed rather little: to the north of the not yet visible La Bastide one sees large groups of poplars and other deciduous trees, perhaps at one time including larger oaks. Meyer looked out from the northern end of the roadstead over the river onto "fresh meadows and forest."[77] Vernet's paintings show a number of tall trees on the terrace of the Château Trompette, which according to the travel books featured an elegant garden in the French style, a *parterre*.[78] Whether there were oaks, and whether they were still standing in Hölderlin's day, is not known. According to Meyer's account, in 1801 "only a small portion of the castle was demolished."[79]

Maps indicate that a number of brooks fed into the Garonne, in the city proper as well as upriver and downriver from Bordeaux.[80] Water mills could only function in a brook with a strong current, or in the Garonne itself. It is certain that mills operated in some of the small tributaries into the Garonne and that there were even mills powered by the current of the Garonne itself.[81] Apart from these one should mention the Theynac mill project, which was installed at the northern end of the harbor and which had by Hölderlin's day already fallen into a state of disrepair. The installation was part of an attempt to make use of the tides of the Garonne. Its water was to be channeled through canals and over water wheels into a basin, and would then set the wheels spinning again in the opposite direction with the ebb tide. No one considered the possibility that the water from the Garonne would inevitably fill the canals with silt. But this ruin, testimony to the modern inventive spirit, clearly does not appear in Hölderlin's verse. I mention it here only as a monument that did not belong to the purview of the poem, which features the life and the industry of the city highlighted by the river and the countryside.

Enthusiasts of Hölderlin's poetry who live in Bordeaux and who happen to be connoisseurs of their own city's history might wonder whether the images of the trees, the brook, and the mill evoked in "Remembrance" can still be seen in the way Hölderlin remembered them as he worked the sphere of the river and the city into his poem. It must be assumed that the image of the brook and the trees and that of the bank and the footpath along the river, about which more presently, are directly interconnected. The two images must be united, just as the elmwood, the mill, and the fig tree, along with the stride of the women on the slow paths in the lulling breezes, are all brought together in a single image. The brook and the pair of trees, however, would not actually have to be visible from the perspective of the bank and the footpath. For the poet's greeting at the beginning of the remembrance is addressed to the Garonne and the gardens of Bordeaux, which are adjacent to or flanked by these other things. The brook and the trees, then, might lie elsewhere in the sphere of the river and the gardens, if that sphere is to emerge as a unified sequence of settings and perspectives.

The foregoing assumption must nonetheless take into account the fact that the bank, the footpath, the brook, and the trees, as they are evoked in the poem, stand closely connected with one another in the recollective image from which that evocation emerged. For all these things correspond to the subsequent scene evoking the mill, the elm-wood, the fig tree, and finally the stride of the brown women. The foot-path on the bank and the trees by the brook are bound together by the conjunction *und*. And the trees appear to be depicted not just as above the brook but also as "overlooking" (*hinschauend*) the footpath on the bank. If one could show that the path runs along the bank near the city itself, then the brook and the trees too would have to stand where the row of gardens meets up with the river. If this is the case, then it may well be that when Hölderlin speaks of the pair of trees, one need not have in mind two individual trees. The pair is a pair of "oaks and silver poplars" (*Eichen und Silberpappeln*), and this does not necessarily mean that Hölderlin had two individual trees of each kind before his eyes. Two clusters of trees rising up over the brook and the river, possibly from both sides, would be far better suited to the wording of the poem.

However that may be, we can at any rate no longer blindly assume that the brook and the cluster of trees, nor the elmwood and the mill, were in fact situated among the network of avenues, parks, and side-walks leading out to the country—a network that cut through the city itself and extended from the renovated center, between the downtown and the harbor, out to the country. Bordeaux, then, is dominated by the countryside along the Garonne in a way that corresponds exactly to Heidelberg's location on the river among the friendly forests and the gardens in bloom.

The sphere of the garden falls within the city proper and discloses its life while showing that life opening out onto the landscape. This emerges with greater plausibility and vividness here than in interpreta-tions that have focused exclusively on the motifs in "Remembrance" suggested by the poem itself and that give an impression of rural seclu-sion. One will have such an impression if one actually equates the evo-cation of Bordeaux with the picture in the opening strophe and sup-poses that the city's appearance grew hazy in Hölderlin's mind and so was put to one side.

But this has yet to be made plausible for the image with which the evocation of Bordeaux begins. This image provides the best test in de-termining the possibility, or even the inevitability, of regarding Hölder-lin's initial depiction of the landscape along the Garonne as a depiction of the city, with the river and countryside surrounding it:

> Dort, wo am scharfen Ufer
> Hingehet der Steg

> There, where along the sharp
> Bank the footpath goes

Hölderlin is no doubt talking about the bank of the "sweet Garonne" (*schöne Garonne*). In depicting the bridge in Heidelberg, he inserted a precise image of the distinctive trajectory of the entire structure into the very language of the poem. In his work Hölderlin became increasingly insistent on a careful, exact choice of words. We are obliged, then, for our part, not to assume that the evocation of the "sharp bank" (*scharfen Ufer*) plainly applies anywhere there are paths along the bank so that the waterline is not overgrown and the edge of the river stands out. But what does it mean to say that a bank is "sharp" (*scharf*)? This question requires some argument that, if persuasive, would shed light on the presence of the city in all its concision in the successive images of the opening strophes.

The port of Bordeaux was known to the Romans as *portus lunae* and to Hölderlin's contemporaries as *port de le lune*.[82] The apparent reason for this was its location in the semicircular bend in the Garonne, for in the Middle Ages it stretched out along the city in a continuous curve by the Château Trompette to the nearly two-kilometer-long Quai des Chartrons, a wide, level area that served both as a street market and as a shipyard and work area. Here businessmen resided in their mansions, though there were warehouses and a factory as well.[83] Now not just blades but also curves and bends are called *scharf*. The shoreline was sharp in precisely this sense. With the words *scharfen Ufer*, however, Hölderlin was able to bring this image of the river's bend together with yet another visual feature characteristic of Bordeaux, namely, that the Garonne is subject to the ebb and flow of the tides; its waters rise and fall with them daily. The highest point on the shoreline reached by the water, then, is generally exposed.[84] The paintings by Vernet and Lacour plainly show that the crescent-shaped bend in the harbor is formed by the banks dropping off steeply into the Garonne. Carts, harnessed with oxen and horses, would haul the ships' cargo up onto the level ground of the natural, unfortified quays, where more boats could be built. At the same time, the shoreline also resembles a slope extending out in a wide arc at the edge of the river on the quayside, visible from all vantage points, that is, from the city, from the quay itself, and from the opposite bank. Such a slope could also be described as *scharf*, that is, jagged or steep. The shoreline at the city, then, was *scharf* in two senses: with respect to the sharp bend in the river, and with respect to the jagged edge or steep slope of the bank leading down to the waters of the Garonne. Where the inclined area ended above the slope, however, is where the wide quay began, and all the traffic of the port had to make its way across it. But this is also where goods were being stored and boats were being built. In the days of the flourishing commercial activity of the city a hustling and bustling life predominated here, even more so than on the bridge in Heidelberg. Compared to those earlier years, however, the "chaotic" activity around the port had "settled down" by the time of Hölderlin's stay.[85]

Hingehet der Steg. ". . . the footpath goes." If the "sharp bank" means the sharply bending shoreline of the harbor on the Garonne, then the footpath that "goes down" it could be the level surface of the quay, which at the same time served as an avenue on the waterfront. One might think that this international commercial trade center would be just the opposite of the path on the shoreline described in such poetic terms—"not 'a' path, but *the* narrow, inconspicuous trail that stays close to the *sharp bank*, and in this closeness moves with the current of the river spirit."[86] But if we just take this for granted and suppose Hölderlin's meaning can be revealed by such a simple pronouncement, we will have missed the way in which the poem manages to capture a real-life context and reveal it in light of its place in a larger whole. "Remembrance," after all, is able to seize on the city on the river, ebbing and flowing with the tides, precisely by having risen above its mundane aspect, by making it visible from the perspective of the gardens, and by depicting its townsfolk on the day of the spring equinox. It is only fitting, then, that in the poem the everyday life of the city and the sea voyage emerge as if rising above the accompanying voice of the poem. The poem does not in fact speak of the city's shops and marketplaces, where "what is beautiful of the earth" (*Das Schöne der Erd'*) is gathered together. It does, however, speak of an ultimate context out of which the meaning of that life reveals itself in concrete terms. This is why it speaks not simply of Bordeaux but rather of the river and the gardens. Precisely in doing so, however, it says something about the city itself, depicting it in terms of its characteristic image, that of the harbor. It was just this image that stayed in the minds of tourists and painters too. Hölderlin, though, could see more clearly than any of them that the city's life itself, and so the life of the port, thrived on and was shaped by the course of the river and its waters coming and going with the ocean.[87]

To understand this much, to reflect on it, and even to incorporate such thoughts into an interpretation of Hölderlin's poem is not to spoil the poetic element of the work by imposing "transcriptions" and "descriptions" onto the poem, as opposed to letting it unfold in its own representational content. Such observations and considerations instead guard against the appearance that "Remembrance," even in its opening strophes, fails to enter fully or thoroughly into the lives of the men leaving the port for the wingèd war, but who all the while know of the city's celebrations going on without them. These considerations make plain, above all, something quite deliberately contained in the poem itself in virtue of its polyphonic construction, but which might easily elude the reader, namely, that the Bordeaux region is not being evoked and summoned from the outskirts of town, nor in images that might be hard to distinguish from idyllic renderings of the surrounding countryside.[88]

Of course, it would be a mistake to identify Hölderlin's own concrete experience of the city as the dominant theme of the poem. Any inquiry into the locale itself can only serve to articulate the strophes in their unique character and in the richness of their representation, over and above any comprehensive survey of the place. Whatever might be gained from such inquiries would again have to be reabsorbed into the depths of its poetic course. What must be conveyed explicitly in order to be seen is not the interpretation itself but an element in and a means to the understanding that in the end leads back to a free comprehension of the poetic work. In this poem the concrete image of the city on the river is elevated onto a higher plane. Anyone who has traced the visual appearance of the city back to its sublimation in the poetic text, which neither distorts nor suspends any part of that appearance, will be able to decide whether there remains a gap between one's familiarity with the actual Bordeaux and the depiction of its river and gardens in "Remembrance." Such a gap would indeed rule out, or at least fail to accommodate, any overarching coherence among the verses of the poem. And any talk of a transformation or poetic condensation of the actual into its deeper truth would then only conceal that gap. If any such condensation occurs in "Remembrance," it stems from a faithfulness to the memory of the city on the Garonne. Contemporaries familiar with the appearance of the city could bring its aspect and its everyday life to bear on the poetic depiction, while the poem itself allows the ground in which that life is rooted, shaped by the river and the landscape, to emerge from the life itself, pure and in its own terms.

Our recourse to maps and pictures of the old Bordeaux must remain partial. It is only a first step. Moreover, it has afforded no more in the way of conjecture than hints and traces, unlike our approach to the confluence of the rivers in the second picture in the final strophe of the poem. The relations between the views through the gardens and over the river and shoreline and the scenes evoked in the poem must remain peculiarly indeterminate and uncertain. In particular we have not managed to draw a connection between the view of the bank and footpath and the view of the brook and the pair of trees in such a way as to produce a composite image that might square with the testimony of Hölderlin's contemporaries. Apart from this, however, our excursion in and around the old Bordeaux has, I hope, made a convincing case that the presence of the city, which in fact dominates the poem throughout, must also provide a key to the images in the opening strophes. Anyone who tries to see the old city through Hölderlin's eyes must be struck by the fact that "Remembrance" does not simply pass over the city itself, only then to find its footing in the pastoral regions of the surrounding countryside.

Indeed, the range of evidence itself may yet be greatly expanded. One might ask why both the path on the shore and the slow stride of the walking figures are called "paths" (*Stege*). The answer should lie in their relation to the water and to the soil of the wetland parks, which makes the ground look soft and gives the springtime foliage a sheen, like that of silk.[89] One should recall the spring fair that Hölderlin must have witnessed. It was held at a time when the city was once again open to overseas trade during a brief period of peace between France and England, ripe with hopes of renewed prosperity.[90] Here the goods of Europe, the French West Indies, and the Far East were exchanged and shipped off.[91] Painters travel with sketchbooks and bring the vivid images from their voyages together in their permanent works.[92] The lines of the fourth strophe, then, with their allusion to wealth and commercial markets, must be explained in terms of this wonderful comparison:

> Sie,
> Wie Mahler, bringen zusammen
> Das Schöne der Erd'

> They,
> Like painters, bring together
> What is beautiful of the earth

The Polyphony and the Unity of Remembrance

But this is in no way meant to be a comprehensive commentary on "Remembrance." It has been shown that for the texts of classical German philosophy a direct approach or step-by-step exegesis cannot provide a basis for commentary that would illuminate the texts in light of the conditions shaping them. It has been shown, too, that in the case of those texts a number of preliminary considerations must be brought to bear in combination for the account to be a success, and that the scope and proportions of such a task have long been construed too narrowly.[93] Hölderlin's poems, too, belong to a domain of thought for which some sophisticated conceptual-theoretical developments may provide a criterion of intelligibility, namely, that thoughts have genuine contents and truth values. We should perhaps accustom ourselves to the task of explaining these poems with at least as much breadth and flexibility as we would bring to an account of the philosophical work to which Hölderlin always remained devoted. One approach would be to follow the work in the course of its structural development, another simply to catalogue the poet's words and then imperiously pronounce the truth of the poetry on the basis of the literal meaning of the ideas, but neither holds up in the face of a work of this form and stature. It matters little that this work is in fact the product of serious thought and that it demands an approach fully cognizant of the provisional status of any interpretation.[94] It is the concrete impression of the work that must accommodate the truth of its words and provide a basis for its full realization. The interpretation must itself assume a form suited to such an impression. And this is precisely why it must first make explicit the polyphonic dimensions of the work as such, which together shape its meaning. Only then can it bring its own resources to bear on the work itself, articulating them in its own terms.[95]

An approach in which the interpretation follows the poem itself, then, is only possible once some effort has been made to understand the poem and to do justice to its essential features. If we adopt such an approach straight away, we must see it as offering a merely provisional overview. Beyond that, it might also be taken as an endorsement of a method to be introduced into a common effort of understanding, or to be recommended as a set of observations for the future study of the work. Nonetheless, a complete interpretation of the work as a whole in terms of the course of its development must remain the essential aim and synthesis. In it there must be a convergence of the forces of interpretation driven by the energy of previous interpretive work.

All the clues and considerations leading us to the reiterated evocation of the landscape on the Garonne and the presence of the city have so far fallen within the range of only one such force. This shows just how far we are from being able to provide that final interpretive synthesis. Nonetheless, we are now in a position to take a larger step. We must return once again to the questions with which we began these considerations. Our aim was to understand the resonance of the succinct form of "Remembrance" and its impact on the triad in the closing lines of the poem. We have assumed that an answer to this question would require some consideration of the architecture of the poem as a whole. Now, in essential elements of its construction "Remembrance" is of a piece with the poems of homage, and its course leads twice into a depiction of the Garonne landscape. This reiterated evocation must be of crucial significance for the structure of that course. And it was this insight that led us to pursue more thoroughly what stood before Hölderlin's eyes in each case. Here two further insights proved crucial and found support in our observations on Hölderlin's "Heidelberg." First, Hölderlin does not sublimate the urban sphere into a poetic condensation that no longer corresponds to the city's real appearance. A certain elevation and condensation does occur when the poem depicts the city in the context of its place in the landscape and the world. But this is done while preserving its actual features. Second, the technique of leading one's view through the landscape is a means essential to Hölderlin's great poetic achievement in these depictions. By thus guiding one's view, the very pattern of the course it travels becomes manifest in such a way as to be grasped both as a system of meanings and as a place in a world comprehended in thought. Movements summoned up in the features of the landscape itself then often correspond to those perspectival turnings and repositionings. In them relations and references belonging to a single web of meaning become palpable in a unique way.

"Remembrance" is more than an homage to one particular place, though it does contain such an homage. It is a poem in which the direction and movement of the images is of the utmost importance. For, however we are to understand what Hölderlin in fact meant by the word, remembrance *is itself just such a movement*, containing in itself movements of a different sort. A recollection, that is, comes to us. We are drawn into it, images arise, forming a whole that encompasses us just as the world itself once did. Thoughts intrude upon the images and then reach out beyond the place, whose visible aspect retreats into obscurity. Yet the world into which we have been led can emerge anew and achieve a presence that holds fast even in the midst of those thoughts. Fichte attempted to elucidate the process by which the intuited present is constituted in acts of the imagination, in an analysis that sought to make the advent of such a pure presence intelligible in a series of steps.[96] Hölderlin's remembrance has a different meaning. If it is to be brought in line with philosophical concepts at all, it would correspond not to our most elementary relation to the world in perception but rather to the opposite, namely, the most comprehensive and all-encompassing form of understanding. But this too corresponds in part to what Fichte identified under the rubric of "imagination" as the structure of the intuited present in general. To this extent, too, even in the very conception of "Remembrance," Hölderlin remained a student of Fichte.

We need not at this point ask what it is about remembrance that makes it more than just intuition or recollection. We must first make a more thorough study of the form and the conceptual content of the poem that significantly bears that title. Nonetheless, in just now speaking of the course traveled by the depiction of a receding world, we have at the same time spoken of the course of Hölderlin's "Remembrance." Even if such allusions fail to identify what it is that makes the text a poetic text, still they point to something that belongs essentially to the very structure of the poem. We can follow these up now in order to get a view of the poem's layout as a whole.

The Change of Perspective and the Course of Remembrance

If the mode of representation in "Remembrance" is diverse and dynamic, and if the poem as a whole is conceived in terms of this movement, then much of it will become intelligible if we can ascertain the position occupied by the poet throughout the poem itself. The text of the poem determines this position, explicitly or implicitly. Heidegger based his own interpretation entirely on the rash assumption that the poet has returned from the South and is now greeting it from his home: he is alone, bearing the burden that has called him back to Germania, and there, on the way to the source and hence to the poetry that will prepare his people for the arrival of the gods, he is to found (*stiften*) a new life. "Remembrance," then, is the contemplation that grants the poet an enduring status at the site of his mission, a mission that imposes a solitude on him. At the same time it is the contemplation of the place and of the journey of his companions. They stand in yet another phase of the same course, not having returned homeward but having departed for the colonies where they will confront their true origin and their mission for the first time. For the poet, then, being among them and reflecting on their journey into distant lands together constitute one and the same course of remembrance. In it the poet at once necessarily depicts the world of the landscape in which he saw the qualities of the other and in which he came to understand the inevitability of the mission summoning him to return, a journey that has now attained its ultimate clarity in remembrance. The companions, that is, the mariners, are themselves the future poets of Germania. The South of France represents the Greek world the Hesperian poet must enter before being able to recapture what is most his own.[97]

This interpretation is based above all on the first letter to Casimir Ulrich Böhlendorff and on the late fragment on "Bread and Wine" ("Brod und Wein"), in which the relation between the colony and the homeland is conceived so as to correspond to the ideas contained in the letter.[98] There is good reason to object, however, that Heidegger is trying to understand the two texts only in their immediate relation to each other. Even more dubious is Heidegger's notion that the French Atlantic coast stands for Greece, since Hölderlin experienced things there as well as in his travels that brought him closer to Greek life, and since, being impressed by the simple life of the people under the "fire of heaven," he could say of himself that he had been "struck by Apollo" (StA VI, p. 432). Themes corresponding to Hölderlin's Greek world do indeed run throughout the poem—the fig tree, for example, recalls the tree of Achilles (StA II, p. 194) and of the grave of Semele (StA V, p. 41), just as the dark light from the vineyard hills recalls the birth and the journey of Dionysus.[99] It is true, too, that "Remembrance" concentrates the sphere around Bordeaux in such a way as to cast a special light on the "stillness of the people" and their "life in nature" (StA VI, p. 432). The life of Greece, as Hölderlin saw it, had once been born of this kind of life (ibid.). But "Remembrance" never presents this Atlantic lifestyle as that of the Greeks. It is Hölderlin, not the Southerners themselves, who has been so gripped by the heavenly fire that he needs the power of reflection to grasp it (ibid.). And Bordeaux never appears as a city in a Greek world. The city on the river figures as a place that, on a higher plane, marks a crossing and a departure out into the high seas. Therein lies the connection with Greece, which in any case pervades history quite generally. The city itself sits on Greek soil, atop the "ruins of the classical spirit" (ibid.)—and in that respect it bears a greater similarity to the setting of Hyperion's life, which is after all shot through with a knowledge that the Greek world has perished.[100] In returning from Bordeaux, then, Hölderlin has not returned from the Greek life that the Hesperian poet must know in order to grasp his own principles of composition. The real Greece is to be found only in a knowledge of the "word" that came to us "from the East" (StA II, p. 126). Any acquaintance with the world of the South amid the ruins born of the Greek spirit is of use only inasmuch as it leads to an understanding of that word. "Remembrance" accordingly presents the city and the regions along the Garonne in their true nature, depicting them amid the winds and gales of the Atlantic crossing in order to raise them to a higher consciousness of something whole and final, providing something "lasting" that transcends all historical process.

If this is the case, then it undermines one crucial presupposition guiding Heidegger's reading of "Remembrance." If the land along the Garonne does not simply stand for Greece, then neither can the poet be speaking from the Hesperian home from which the nor'easter blows toward the South of France. In any case, one would have to demonstrate in an interpretation of the poem as a *whole* that the poet's place throughout remains the place of one who has gone back home in order to clear a path to the source. But this is demonstrably infeasible, so Heidegger's approach fails to capture the movement of the poem and with it the true dynamism of "remembrance," as Hölderlin conceives it. To assume that the location of the poet, that is, the voice of "Remembrance" at its outset, remains constant throughout would be to ignore entirely the clear echoes and allusions crucial to the inner workings of the text. All our considerations of the images occurring within the poem itself, however, were but a preparation necessary to make this point in a convincing way.

Der Nordost wehet. "The nor'easter blows." At the beginning of the poem the poet stands in the current of the clear, cool breeze that drifts through his native land out to the French Atlantic coast. What is borne by the wind is a mood of early morning and departure, which "promises" the mariners the best of what they need. The poet is not among them, and the wind is moving over solid ground. Thus he is not setting sail in it. The wind is to go and greet the place where it is heading: the river and the city, precisely the site of the mariners' departure, where whether proudly or anxiously one cannot help but think of their voyages. In this way the poet stays behind. But to stay behind is not simply to pause before the current of the wind "dearest" to him, whose promise is so important to him. He is not just sending greetings to the distant coastal land. He is also thinking of the wind and the greetings blowing all around it and is thus traveling a path appropriate to who he is, where he is. The greetings are addressed to the Garonne and the gardens of the city. And just as the wind carries the greetings along with it, so too the poet's remembrance travels with the wind into the spheres of the river and the countryside, ultimately landing him there, once again enveloped by the landscape.

The course of remembrance and its arrival there are brought together in a series of four visual images in the two opening strophes of "Remembrance." The images of the bank and the footpath, and then of the brook and the pair of trees, are introduced with the first *dort*—a word whose double occurrence has a crucial significance for the structure of the poem, so that one can hardly avoid asking how the repetition of the word is to be understood. It points to that other distant place but without stressing its distance, let alone its withdrawal or absence. In this way it leads into the first image, taking its first step by fixing that distance in consciousness, albeit indeterminately.

The poet expresses this double consciousness at the beginning of the second strophe: *Noch denket das mir wohl* ("This comes back to me still"). The word *noch* ("still") imparts the distance, inasmuch as it suggests the danger of dissolution. But the fact that the land can draw him and his remembrance toward it, this is considered something genuine, something astonishing, indeed something comforting. That the land comes back "to me" (*mir*) establishes a connection to the poet's own situation, his life far from the gardens of Bordeaux. This distance poses a threat to remembrance. And yet it is not fading but developing a more fully embodied presence. What comes back to the poet is "how" the elm wood bends its broad tops above the mill—another visual image that seems to correspond to the figure and the movement of the tree-tops. The remembrance drifts over into the courtyard where the fig tree grows. Even when he saw this, it must have seemed to him the very focal point of a whole web of meanings: the tree at the foot of the wall of Troy, and at the grave of Semele;[101] the tree of Paradise at the threshold of the history of human knowledge. In one sense this explains the simple declarative sentence saying just that the tree stands there in the middle: *Im Hofe aber wächset ein Feigenbaum* ("But in the courtyard a fig tree grows").

But here the structure of the sentence gives it yet another meaning in connection with the course of remembrance, for it is the first sentence to stand by itself, not governed by a particle anchoring the representation to the starting point of the greeting itself. And it occurs before the final section of the second strophe, which speaks in the same absolute tone:

> An Feiertagen gehn
> Die braunen Frauen daselbst
>
> There too on holidays
> The brown women walk

Heidegger has keenly observed the effect of *daselbst* in, as it were, gathering the other visual images together in a single place.[102] More important, however, is the fact that unlike *dort* or even *fern*, *daselbst* picks out the place in its full determinateness. Moreover, the *da* of *daselbst* establishes a connection with what, in the word *dort*, had been a distance from what was being depicted. Owing to the *selbst* of *daselbst*, however, the place remains free of any relation to another place, in particular any place to the northeast. In this way *daselbst* opens the place up to the one approaching it on the path of remembrance. Of course, this *daselbst* at once imposes another sense of distance, for the one arriving at the depicted site does not really belong there. The place surrounds and protects him, but he remains a stranger there, just passing through. As long as it is a question of customs and occurrences taking place *daselbst*, then the stranger's sense of distance in that place is expressed so that it is as if the distance from the other place to this one were simply being transposed into a sense of distance in this place itself. In this way, having described a place to someone unfamiliar with it, one can tell of something strange or amusing that took place *daselbst*.

But the subsequent lines in the depiction extend across this second distance as well. The language of these lines, the sensuous texture of its tones and colors, is informed by the experience of a now-purer presence: the women, the silk, the golden dreams, and the breezes heavy with them. These are not the words of one merely "reminded of" a place, to whom pregnant images of the area have once again arisen, nor of one merely recounting what took place there. Rather, the sphere itself dawns and becomes present; the poet, and indeed anyone affected by his words, in whom they strike a responsive chord, is drawn into it— into a mood not itself a dream but giving rise to dreams. The remembrance builds up to this mood in the final lines of the depiction and then begins to reflect on the dream thoughts of the Atlantic coast in spring. Not only the blowing of the nor'easter but the lulling breezes of the South can now also be detected in the language and the tone of the verses.

These lines certainly touch on much more. On the other hand, it would be something of a digression to examine the whole range of meanings conjured up by them in terms of Hölderlin's world but without obscuring the structure of the poem by stressing its specific moments. This is what happens if the Atlantic holidays of the spring equinox are taken to prefigure the celebration of balance and harmony found in the Rhine hymns.[103] In "Remembrance" Hölderlin lets loose a range of experiences and a context of meanings that have their own horizons and that must be conceived and appreciated in their own right, on the basis of their own "totality," before one asks how they fit into Hölderlin's work as a whole. At the same time, one ought to ask whether Hölderlin's later work in general can be understood in terms of the unity of its themes and motifs, or even those of the songs of the fatherland (*vaterländische Gesänge*) proper. But such questions will have to be put to one side.[104] We shall not here pursue the context of meaning built up from the interconnected themes of the opening strophe of "Remembrance." Rather, our attention will remain focused on the movement of the poem, in particular its changing perspective. But this in no way leads us away from what is essential to the constitution of the work. Rather, it makes intelligible the constitution and the movement of remembrance itself, which would remain obscured and misunderstood if one assumed that an appreciation of Hölderlin's ideas concerning world history and their connections with the motifs in the poetry makes up the one and only legitimate approach to the poetic content of the work. Hölderlin's ideas, which are indeed crucial to his poetry, have more to do with the poem's structure and movement than with what it says, or what it alludes to as having been said or yet to be said in another place (*StA* V, pp. 195–97, 265–66). Nor would the triad in the closing lines of "Remembrance" be facilitated or enhanced by the content of what precedes it in the poem were that content not born of, and so grounded in, the movement of the remembrance itself.

The stride of the women on the silken ground in the lulling breezes in spring's balance of day and night[105] attains pure presence not by the hushed movement of the image alone but also by the elevated awareness and experience of the day lifted up out of the cycle of seasons, corresponding to the light, measured step of the women: to be attuned to one and all, where what has been, what is to come, and what at once pervades all reality are brought together—in dreams of the past and the future, in feeling at home with all things, calm in anticipation, safeguarded on all paths.[106] The second strophe then depicts the coastal river area in terms of the tranquility of its celebrations. The movement of remembrance drifts along until it too arrives at a sublimated state of repose. In this way the poem intimates that the movement and the tone of the final lines of the opening strophe now demand a stopping point, a pause in the text in which to abide and fade away. And in this moment of repose the course of remembrance, from its point of departure in the northeast to its transition into the sphere of the coastal celebrations, lingers and recedes. The quiet becomes most palpable when the northeasterly wind dies down. The poet is no longer caught up in it. It has ushered him to a place where not the wind itself but the lulling breezes pull. These breezes have neither place nor determinate direction on the wind rose of the Greeks. The poet has now been transported to the place he sent his greetings. Nor will "Remembrance" subsequently send him back to his own point of departure. He will, however, arrive at a place encompassing not only his departure but also the gardens of Bordeaux.

But the repose of this first balance is not definitive; it is the repose of the city's celebrations only and does not prove lasting. It bursts forth like the pure presence of the countryside on the holiday, into which the first image of the remembrance had led. This repose is not a knowing repose but is simply burdened by dreams. For this reason the poet is in a foreign place there, and again ultimately leaves. His speaking of the "brown women" may also hint at the fact that he remains excluded from their celebrations. Like them, he walks along the footpaths, but those paths are not meant for him. They are delightful, to be sure, but they belong to the countryside, as one might find in images drawn by

Macke and Munch. And this is why the self-containment of the belea-
guered life can and must break in upon the tranquility of the first stage
in the course of remembrance.

But the poet needs the tranquility conducive to an experience of the
southern holiday. He would like to be able to rest. So he calls out to a
comrade in the festivities who might lead him with the wine of the
region toward another resting place under the trees—toward sleep,
hence toward the repose not of transcendence but of forgetfulness, a
repose in which he might forget the anxious thoughts of things unfamiliar and lonesome, a repose in which he could stay close to the
golden dreams on the footpaths.

Unreconciled anxiety breaks in—and so the poet refers to himself
(*mir*), as in the opening of the first strophe. But it would be wrong to
suppose that this also takes him back to the place of his departure. He
is lonely not just in leaving but also in the country where the remembrance has taken him. At the beginning, with the early morning greetings and the departure with the wind, his loneliness was not obvious.
Now it stands out. And though the loneliness itself may be exactly the
same, the poet now experiences it in the sphere of the city on the Garonne. Hölderlin makes this so palpable that for anyone familiar with
the poem there can be no doubt: the dark light with the renowned bou-
quet of the Bordeaux grape is indeed the local wine. It flows during
the city's holidays and is therefore not an import product of Swabia.
Moreover, in March no one in Germanic Hesperia would want to rest
in the northeasterly breeze, in the shade and the open air. This sort of
prosaic observation has serious implications, for if Hölderlin's poem
leads to a lasting repose, it is not by remaining rooted in the place
where the poet sets out on his remembrance to begin with.

The loneliness initially lacks all contemplation of anything universal. It longs for wine and sleep. Yet it finds its way into a reflection soon
wholly dominated by anxious self-absorption. As if begging out of the
celebration that has excluded him, the poet explains his longing for
sleep: anxious thoughts are not a good thing since they threaten what
might make life secure and lasting. It is this explanation, this reflective
knowledge that leads into more wide-ranging contemplation. What
would do him a lot of good is precisely what one who need not be lonely
on a holiday might enjoy, namely a conversation not dwelling on wor-
ries and anxious requests, where you can say what is really on your
mind, and where, being together with one another, everyone just
wants to talk about the way things were and about what is important to
them. Something "lasting" (*ein 'Bleiben'*) can already be found in what
animates such a conversation as it spins itself out effortlessly.

Yet the friends, the companions traveling common paths, are no longer close by. The poet knows this, so he does not call after them. The thought that their company would be good is attended only by the poet's faint lament, though it now leads into the question why they have gone away. They go no farther along this path with him, for it is not or is no longer the path of the mariners.[107] He too is well on his way, but in the course of remembrance, and that course traveled with the wind, to the harbor, though already knowing it would not find them there.

Mancher / Trägt Scheue, an die Quelle zu gehn. "Many / Are shy of going to the source." This line more than any other must be read in the context of Hölderlin's work taken as a whole, in particular the river poems with which "Remembrance," a poem about the Garonne, is associated.[108] Again, this is simply to identify the task, not to undertake it. But if one attends just to the connection the poem itself draws between shyness and the source, there is plainly enough there to be understood on its own terms, namely, that the source and the sea stand in contrast. The sea brings wealth. He who has turned to the source is truly rich because no longer in need, yet grasps things at their origin. This is made plain by the fact that in the poem the source corresponds to what is lasting—for on the one hand the way to the source separates the poet from the companions with whom he talks about the deeds of mariners and the days of love, while on the other hand there is no return from the source, yet from it all things come into being. To know the source and to see all things derived from it are one and the same. The way to the source, then, is blind without some other experience that could survey all other paths. For this reason it is the path of one whose path has always been the course of remembrance.

The sentence about the way to the source, then, must in the end be understood in terms of its position in the poem at the outset of the contemplation taken as a whole, which first reflects on the journey of the mariners and the companions and then depicts the place of their departure in order finally to bring together everything said and done in the poem in an all-encompassing insight. From this point on, the contemplation remains free of any intrusion of anxiety. The poem speaks with a clear vision free of all self-absorption and culminating in a triad in the closing lines, which are the product of ultimate perspicuity and insight.

We must ask, however, where the poet's contemplation actually takes place. It is not hard to give a partial answer: clearly not in the native Hesperian land, the starting point of the remembrance. The anxious longing for wine and sleep erupts in such a way as to anchor it to the Bordeaux region, so it is even less plausible to imagine the poet having returned home while contemplating the journey of his companions. If talking about the source means talking about the source of a river, one would have to imagine the source of the Garonne in the Pyrenees, and of course the poet is certainly not on his way there. But he has arrived at the city on the river. The river, like almost no other pathway, is associated with the voyage out to sea, hence with the sea itself. Thus it is the river of the mariners. Going to the source means not sharing one's path but standing in contemplation of it through one's own actual deeds. In this way the poet is speaking from the very place to which his poem pays homage. Once his remembrance has drawn him into the place, of course, though loneliness and alienation overcome him as well, he is now no longer intimidated by the city's celebration. His contemplation aims at the spirit of the men who on their journey are bound to the Garonne just as the ships are bound to their home port.

The contemplation is introduced through the searching question, still haunted by loneliness, of where the friends have gone, where they might have landed. But inasmuch as the contemplation then begins to grasp the nature of all their paths, which is possible only in an understanding that knows a source this side of *any* river, it at once reaches out beyond the place of the mariners' arrival at the river—it has freed itself from the alienation and from the longing for sleep and conversation among friends. The poet's thoughts follow the lives and the journeys of the mariners. And those thoughts depict their sea voyage with a clarity and collectedness owing as much to its opposition to the course leading to the source of all paths, which is not included in the journeys of the mariners, as to the fact that the poet whose thoughts followed the nor'easter all the way to the harbor did not go with them on their journey.

In the collectedness of his thoughts the poet has now turned to something universal, namely the life of the mariners. These thoughts at once allude to the memory (*Gedenken*) that introduced the course of remembrance, when the poet felt the nor'easter around him as a wind for mariners. This initial thought too here unfolds and reaches full expression. But this only forms a continuity with the beginning of the course, not a return to it. For the sea voyage is depicted just as it stands before the eyes of those who have remained behind in the harbor, on dry land. The contemplation of the essence of the mariners is thus anchored in the city on the Garonne, though in the distinctive clarity and universality of the thought of the mariners' life it is not bound to this city alone. This is why it can follow upon the greetings sent from afar.

Moreover, insofar as the contemplation is rooted in the harbor, it stands removed from the life of the sea voyage. The port city is associated with the life of the mariners without actually taking part in it: it prepares the ships, sends them off, and awaits the goods and treasures they bring back, which are the source of its wealth as a commercial center. The poet's contemplation in the city naturally, indeed essentially, bridges the distance separating the harbor and the high seas. It does indeed take up the city's perspective on the ships' journeys. But the stranger's contemplation of the place is what lets one grasp the mariners' journeys in contrast with other life courses, including the way to the source, and with a clarity detached from all the vital interests of the city.

It is this fine but therefore asymmetrical balance that first makes it possible for the poem to contain the entire course of remembrance within itself. At the outset of the remembrance there is a balanced diversity among the unfamiliar parts of the city and the ground of the contemplation in the city's essence itself. The poem consequently leads directly into the depiction of a second sphere in the countryside along the course of the Garonne, and to an entirely new way of entering into it. This in turn leads to another sort of contemplation encompassing all paths in life and thus detaching itself from all the places, stages, and regions into which the course of remembrance has flowed, thereby drawing it to a close and bringing it clearly into view.

In the contemplation of the mariners' voyage Hölderlin has brought out their intimate connection with the city as well as the distance separating them from it. The contemplation commences with a thought conceived from the perspective of the city, its wealth beginning in the sea, brought back by the mariners:

> Sie,
> Wie Mahler, bringen zusammen
> Das Schöne der Erd'

> They,
> Like painters, bring together
> What is beautiful of the earth

As we have seen, this image represents the several weeks of the city fair, sublimating them through the metaphor of artistic exercise (cf. p. 186 above). But then the contemplation turns to the mariners' battle in and against the elements, the wind and the water. These thoughts obscure the presence and the appearance of the city—as do the mariners' own attempt at a quick, safe voyage. It is the course of the mariners, and so their very lives, that find such pure expression in these thoughts. In the long struggle of their voyage, however, the memory of life at the port will come back to them. So the contemplation once again conjures up images of the harbor. The mariners miss its celebrations:

> wo nicht die Nacht durchglänzen
> Die Feiertage der Stadt,
> Und Saitenspiel und eingeborener Tanz nicht.

> where the city's celebrations
> Do not penetrate the night,
> Nor music of strings, nor native dance.

The beginning and the end of the contemplation thus fall between two images of the city left behind by the mariners. In the second of the two, Hölderlin at once clears the way for the depiction of the second sphere in the Garonne countryside, the site of the final departure, for which the perspective in the city must again be fixed.

Hölderlin leads into the second view of the Garonne landscape by simple yet highly refined artistic means. For the contemplation of the mariners' courage ends with a contemplation of what they have to relinquish in their voyage. Here the city's celebrations emerge as they must appear in the recollective gaze of the mariners. The thought of the origin of wealth was conceived from the point of view of the city. The memory of its celebrations, by contrast, is seen from the high seas where the mariners carry on a life wholly their own. Between the opening and the closing of the contemplation, then, there is an inversion of perspective corresponding in part to the mariners' changing experience on their long voyage.

But since the images alluded to on the high seas are images of the city's celebrations, they at once point toward the city's presence on the holiday, which is where the poet's anxiety and contemplation had arisen in the first place. They came over him while he was still basking in the warmth of the holiday, after drinking and sleeping. The celebration remembered by the mariners, the subject of the contemplation, lies in the lights and the dancing by the river that evening. This leads the contemplation back to the life of the mariners, and then away from their perspective back to the place where the contemplation of them began. Thus the contemplation ends with the dawning of a clear awareness of a new presence and the reappearance of the poet in the city. And it ends with a knowledge of the mariners' journey that sheds light on the stranger's loneliness but that remains fixed in consciousness precisely as it had just now taken place.

The course of remembrance thereby interrupts the temporal continuity of the celebration from which the contemplation of the mariners' journey first arose. This temporal break along with the turning of remembrance toward a new presence is significant on two related grounds. First, it provides a segue into the second evocation of the landscape on the Garonne. Second, in the counterposing elements of the poetic form, it heightens the impact of the final strophe, which itself effects a kind of twofold transition. But the unfolding of the course of remembrance is not itself disturbed by this break in temporal continuity. It is in virtue of that break, in fact, that its inner unity continues to develop. For the course of remembrance has its own temporality and its own logical consistency through the changing presences corresponding to the views of the various spheres of the river. Moreover, the temporality can be broken off along the way precisely because the course of remembrance once again finds its way back to the city's celebrations—though now from the perspective and the recollection of the mariners traveling away from them on the high seas. They emerge no longer with the pure presence they had in the previous strophes, but only in the accompanying voice in the contemplation of the mariners' journey, in which they nonetheless clear the way for the conclusion and the transition into a new presence. In the contemplation of the celebrations that the mariners think back on, and in the very contemplation in which the temporality of his own life diminishes, the present moment of the one who stayed behind is transformed into the moment when he must say farewell: *Nun aber . . .* ("But now . . ."). In his wakefulness at the place of their departure the poet can now say:

> sind zu Indiern
> Die Männer gegangen
>
> to the Indians
> The men have gone

That is, they will acquire for the city new wealth from the East. In this wakefulness, which anticipates the clarity of the triad in the closing lines, the second occurrence of the word *dort* introduces the second sphere around the flowing Garonne. The perspective of the poem is thus fixed to this sphere, to the beginning of the mariners' voyage in the port city. The day and night of the holiday, too, are connected by a discrete thread to the new presence within the city and to the mood of the mariners' departure when the sound and the spectacle of the parties have faded away. One almost feels that the mariners have gone on to *another* party the next morning, or that a convoy has accompanied them to the "zephyrous peak" and taken leave of them there.

This sort of association alone would make a compelling case for supposing the depiction of the second sphere in the Garonne countryside to be centered in the city. But since that depiction takes its point of departure from the contemplation of the journey and the life of the mariners, the manner in which the perspective shifts from the city to the confluence of the rivers will also be governed by the sort of universality aimed at in the contemplation. The new image, then, makes up one stage in the course of remembrance, which now falls within the scope of an all-encompassing insight.

We have seen how Hölderlin drew this second sphere, and how it acquired precision and stability in the unfolding of the poem itself. So, we also know how through the successive drafts the image and the movement of the perspective were bound together as the point of view itself took shape in the city and in the currents of the Garonne. The sense and the urgency of remembrance, then, issue from its very course through the poem as a whole. The landscape along the Garonne marks a point of transition out to sea. The contemplation within remembrance has now arrived at that transition and grasped its significance. In the depiction of the place where the transition is definitively made and leave is taken, there is repose and the farewell no longer occasions grief.

This is also because the Dordogne flows into the Garonne in such a way that their waters together make up the route of the mariners, and because the hills towering overhead bear the wine whose dark light signifies something lasting, shining forth in unity through all distance and division. The breezes too converge at this place. The northeasterly wind and the lulling breezes in the gardens of Bordeaux come together on the "zephyrous peak" while scattering and transforming themselves. The breeze at the confluence is not the breeze of the fiery voyage, nor the breeze lulling one to sleep. It is a breeze of clarity and endurance, a breeze that touches and embraces all winds. It is the breath of knowledge, "blowing" now and ever more.

Dort an der luftigen Spiz' ("There on the zephyrous peak"). This *dort* is spoken from the point of view of the city on the Garonne, out toward the passage onto the open sea. It therefore alludes to the first image yet does not correspond to it, at least not in terms of the direction the view takes. But at the same time it connects up with the place where the remembrance commenced and where it entered into the first sphere of the river and the city's gardens. That first entrance into the landscape erupted in anxiety, going on to launch the voyage of remembrance on a more far-reaching contemplation and a deeper tranquility in all pathways. The second *dort* alludes to the first, then, inasmuch as the first embarcation of remembrance hooks up with the clarity that has now dawned on the outlet of the river and the departure of the mariners. Having followed the poem thus far, one can hardly arrive at the second depiction of the countryside along the Garonne without at once recalling the path leading into the first sphere on the Garonne, the friends mentioned there, and the passage into the clarity of remembrance, now all the more fertile. The second *dort*, too, is spoken from the point of view of this course of remembrance. And what gets depicted in the second view appears in the same clarity and repose drawn from that course as a whole. The landscape at the confluence is deserted once the mariners have disembarked. Yet the landscape intimates neither loneliness nor estrangement.

Nor is one drawn into the landscape at the confluence the way one was drawn into the city's gardens during the holidays. For the waters, as for the mariners, the confluence is a place of transition. The poet's arrival there in the course of remembrance nonetheless accords with its significance, just as the entry into the sphere of the city accorded with its gardens and its holidays. The path into the sphere of the city enters into the very lifeworld of the harbor, which cannot be preserved and so fails to transform the loneliness into something lasting. The path into the point of the departure, by contrast, leads to an insight grounded in the place of transition and extending beyond all human paths. The poet arrives at the second sphere from a course that leads to the origin, hence to the source of all pathways. This explains why the depiction of the landscape does not become detached from the *dort* that introduces it and that is spoken from the perspective of the city on the Garonne. The same is true in the case of the second strophe in the first image, in which the perspective of the first *dort* vanishes and transports the speaker into the footpaths and breezes of the city's holiday. The place of transition, the place of the insight, is not so easy to reach that one arriving there must necessarily have left his point of departure behind. The origin and the vantage point of remembrance are contained in the depiction of the third place, which is essentially a point of transition and, for the one caught up in the course of remembrance, a crossing over into the sea and into insight.[109]

One can therefore understand the images in which "Remembrance" depicts the spheres of the Garonne as they open up for readers not already familiar with Hölderlin, and in light of that understanding we can try to grasp those images more precisely and explicitly. Only then will we see, in addition to the poem's architecture, the context unfolding within it and flowing into the triad in the closing lines. The Garonne landscape is evoked twice and is viewed in such a way that the distinct spheres draw the path and the movement of remembrance into themselves in their course, each in a manner peculiar to it so as to preserve it while at once fostering the essential insight. The distinctions and connections between the two tacks as well as the sequence in which they occur make it clear that the course of remembrance reaches out beyond the two spheres toward a conclusion that transcends the countryside along the Garonne, as does the source underlying and uniting all paths and currents. Hölderlin's poem thus stands fast through the repeated depiction of the landscape, which supports, prepares, and preserves it for the insight contained in the closing lines.

These lines find us at the place of departure, and they are only possible given an understanding of its significance. What they have to say is no longer spoken from any determinate place. But they are surely the summation of a remembrance leading directly to this place, into these two parts of the river, which bear within themselves the tension of transition and departure. The view of a departure, a departure bringing with it a sense of the world at large, is essential to the location. The one who experienced that place, even as a stranger, and whose thoughts return to it, will be drawn back into a world-encompassing contemplation embracing both the point of departure itself and the eventual passage and repose. The gratitude paid as homage to the locality and the countryside therefore cannot linger there. It has to turn away, whether in lamentation or in favor of some other more essential place. To be sure, the contemplation extends beyond the city and the river, but only so as to comprehend the place as a whole, whose all-pervasive and even placeless presence had disclosed itself to the poet precisely there, in the spheres of the landscape.

The movement of remembrance does not come to rest with a sense of certainty concerning the place and the task the poet has rediscovered in his native Hesperian land. Remembrance is insight, and hence departure, ascent, and transcendence, all in one. Formally speaking, the triad in the closing is independent of time and place precisely because it conveys a truth encompassing all places. Nonetheless, the movement of remembrance reaches them from the city, where it had previously arrived with the wind from the north. The stranger, thinking back on this place with gratitude, is led back by the place itself into the region of the mariners' departure and from there into a final contemplation. It is a contemplation of the place, and at once comes to a repose that the poet could as little find in the life of the city itself as in any mundane locality—regardless of what that life could offer him, even in the way of reflection.

If one considers the matter purely in terms of the continuity of bodies and persons, then of course the poet, who stands in the Hesperian northeast, cannot travel with the wind and arrive at the destination of his greetings. One would have to conclude, then, that the poet in fact stays behind. And so it would follow that the movement of remembrance must be an understanding arising from the divergence of places and pathways, hence an understanding suggested especially by the unbridgeable yet mutually intimated gap separating Hellas and Hesperia. But the place where the poem begins is from the outset itself a place within the course of remembrance. Hölderlin sought to make it vivid by letting it appear from the northeast of Bordeaux. And the wind, the nor'easter, is from the outset taken to be the wind of the mariners. The poem says nothing in memory of the rivers back home. To be sure, this other country is present inasmuch as the spheres of the Garonne emerge in their own characteristic South Atlantic features, and since they are portrayed not as home but in terms of the "magic" (*Zauber*) that draws the stranger toward them. But the stranger does not find clarity and repose in rediscovering and understanding his own native land. On the contrary, he gains that clarity at the place of departure farther out to sea, and in a turn of understanding that allows him to comprehend what it means to be a poet in renunciation of the ocean and of love. This—the moral, the theme, and the course of the poem, all in one—is not itself bound to any particular locations. It is certainly not indifferent to them; rather it looks over them in faithfulness and gratitude. As such, inasmuch as it comprehends the essence of a place, it attains a true collectedness. But it springs entirely from a movement of remembrance transcending all places, without its support thereby falling out from under it.[110] In "Remembrance" more than in any of his other poems, Hölderlin captured the course and the very heart of poetry in such a way as to incorporate the conceptual themes of the brand of thought that called itself "transcendental." That thought provided him with insights he never abandoned. The stranger rises to his task precisely at the point where he no longer stands in need of a home in the mundane, where he stands as a poet with a knowledge of the very ground from which and upon which all paths proceed.

And it is not just the poet who arrives at this all-convergent perspective through the sequential views of remembrance. For his work opens up that view to anyone who would follow its course. The triad in the closing lines, then, culminates in words neither about the poet himself nor about the poets of Hesperia, himself included. Wherever something lasting has been, is, or will be overcoming all lamentation, it is the poets who have established it and held it fast. The sentence, then, speaks of all true poetry. It may well pertain to a poetry of Germania yet to come. But first and foremost it speaks of the work springing from the insight to which the movement of remembrance has led. At the same time it speaks of the poetry of the Greeks, which sprang from just such a movement. But above all it speaks of the poem itself, whose course and construction culminate in such an insight. Were this not the case, "Remembrance" would have to be read as a poem merely preparing the way for true poetry. But it already is true poetry itself. And this is why the final line in the triad appears in the poem at all, like a cornerstone completing and perfecting its overall composition.

This also points up the fact that it remains possible to take the second occurrence of *dort* in the depiction, which first and foremost points the way from Bordeaux toward the confluence of the rivers, as alluding back to the first *dort* in the opening strophe. For in the movement of remembrance both indicate a place where the poem takes one of its crucial steps. Both sites lie along the French Atlantic coast where the nor'easter blew. In this way a connection also obtains between the sphere of the zephyrous peak and the departure at the outset of the poem. And the concluding insight that pulls the poem together as a whole also unites its beginning and its end. Still, it remains decisive for the poem's path of remembrance that the second sphere of the Bordeaux countryside is that of the men's departure from Bordeaux. The progression from that point to the actual arrival of remembrance, and then out to the point of no return, is what constitutes the structure and the resonance of the poem. All this will be lost on us if we hear the recurrence of the word *dort* as nothing more than the reiterated gesture of a poet who has returned home to his native land. To do so would be to empty the poem of all the transformative effect of remembrance, from which alone its final contemplation arises—and thus to rob it of its very poetic sense and above all of the force of its underlying idea.

The Unity of the Spheres: The River

There is another matter to attend to, however. It is very difficult to discern the change of perspective and so the path of remembrance without some prolonged preoccupation with what after all reveals itself spontaneously in the poem. It is therefore easy to miss the complexity of the allusion at work in the recurrence of the word *dort*.[111] In investigating the images underlying Hölderlin's initial evocation of the Bordeaux landscape, it became clear that he was drawing on a very precise perception of the city on the Garonne. It became clear, too, that that evocation pushes the everyday lifeworld of the city back into a kind of latent state and draws the city's features purely in terms of how it situates itself in the landscape. If we cannot share in Hölderlin's perception and if our interpretation cannot find all the keys that spontaneously unlock the path of its remembrance in the course of the poem, then the Garonne countryside will take shape before our eyes in a single image, which will inevitably come across as vague, even muddled.[112]

We have seen how Hölderlin understood the essence of a city in terms of its surrounding landscape. He practiced this poetic technique for quite some time, and it had its roots as much in his contact with nature as in his ideas concerning its relation to human life. In "Remembrance," however, Hölderlin had special reasons for depicting the life of the city and its celebrations as mere background for the images of Bordeaux, though in fact they constitute a pervasive presence throughout the poem. Namely, Bordeaux is a port city. It is thus wholly bound up with the arrival and departure of the ships and their crews, thus with the sea and the wealth it provides. The departure itself, however, has a sphere and a locality of its own along the river, that is, at the point where the river blends into the sea. At the same time, the sphere of the city and the site of the departure are intimately interconnected through the essence and the course of the voyage. It is the countryside, then, in its diversity and expansiveness, that surrounds and shapes Bordeaux in this special way. And if both the repose in the city's celebrations and the passage out to sea were to be depicted in one unifying context, this had to be done with careful attention to their interconnection within the landscape.

This is also why it is to the Garonne that the poet initially sends his greetings. The two spheres as well as the journey out to sea are disclosed around it and through it. Moreover, it is the river that is depicted in the evocation of the second sphere. It is no accident that in the first evocation it is called "the sweet" (*die schöne*) and in the second "glorious" (*prächt'ge*). In the sphere of the city the river is much narrower and, being a harbor, at the service of the land along its banks. What "Remembrance" depicts from the standpoint of the river is the world of those shores, the world of the gardens. In the evocation of the second sphere the river widens, flowing around the island of the "zephyrous peak"[113] and directly spilling out seawide with the Dordogne. There, like all things glorious, it dominates the scene and is now more of a passageway than it was near the city where the ships drop anchor and the gardens open out around it, making room for the city's celebrations. This is why the second evocation of the Garonne countryside ends with the river itself. Unlike the first evocation, the second begins by depicting the land of the peak and the vineyard hills, only then relating it to the river, which nonetheless already appears from the very beginning of the evocation since this is where the men, the mariners, have set sail.

We must not lose sight of this thread that runs through the complex pattern of "Remembrance" if we wish to comprehend the architecture of the poem in full and bring it out in our interpretation. In virtue of the dominant presence of the Garonne in the two depictions, the repeated evocation using the single word *dort* helps to realize something like a total image, a sphere of spheres, centered by and rooted in the river, which is where the first evocation commences and which is finally named in the second. If one failed to grasp the unity of these two evocations, held together as they are by the river, then one might well be tempted to view them as if they were both situated in a single place with a single perspective, and so be inclined toward the preconceptions underlying Heidegger's interpretation.

To see what lies behind this tendency, however, is at once to guard against it. Going along with it would mean missing the essence of what the Garonne lets us see and reflect on in the two spheres it describes. Its course, that is, can in no way be seen as composed of two aspects along a single line of sight extending as it were perpendicular into the area from the distant northeast. One has to follow the course of the river in its own direction. In doing so one must indeed arrive at the Garonne, but also above all from a perspective anchored in its own course. The view out to sea, toward the outlet of the river at the confluence with the Dordogne, belongs no less to the life of the city on the Garonne than does the sphere of the "gardens," which unites the river and the harbor and reaches out to the opposite bank. Consequently, if by means of the dual relation to the river Garonne "Remembrance" seizes upon the two spheres evoked in the poem as a single landscape, then the line of sight from the city to the river's outlet is as much a genuine feature of the life and landscape of Bordeaux as the river itself.

The Triad and the Insight

There is a differentiation in the line of vision, then, and a connection between the one view that lingers but leads to no lasting tranquility and the other that makes its way toward something lasting. Therein lies the structure and content of the poem. The triad in the closing lines, which rises above all mundane places and all times, and at the same time points up the work as a whole, warrants our hearing the two occurrences of *dort* as interrelated. And the fact that in the juxtaposition of its two spheres the landscape of the Garonne is evoked as the landscape of the river already brings to the first occurrence of the word *dort* a hint of the second—especially by the time the poem has reached its second evocation and come to an end. Once we recognize and acknowledge all this it becomes perfectly clear that in light of its two occurrences the word *dort* is not being uttered from some fixed site to which the poet has allegedly returned. The *dort* is itself still subject to the movement of remembrance, and to the very sort of synthesis effected

by the poem itself. And if it could be said that the first *dort* already anticipates the second, then so too one could say that the second, whose
perspective in the Garonne countryside is fixed by the city and the
course of the river, alludes back to the first. This reciprocal relation between the two evocations is in keeping with the fact that the remembrance initially enters into a sphere in which the celebrations offer
nothing lasting, and yet this sphere points the way toward the point of
the departure where the farewell itself leads over into something genuinely lasting. To imagine the perspective centered in the northeast,
then, is to undermine the significance and the very unfolding of the
course of remembrance itself. What makes the nor'easter palpable
throughout the work as a whole cannot be its relation to Germania and
its distant view of Bordeaux. It is instead a connection with the spirit
and the voyage of the mariners.[114]

It is with them that the triad in the closing lines also emerges in the
course of remembrance, so bringing it to a close. Short of interpreting
those lines here, let us consider the way in which they lie in the course
of remembrance and in the structure of the poem. The mariners to
whom the poet bids farewell at the confluence of the rivers have on their
voyage to India left harbor and home behind them and followed the
promise of the voyage and the distant land. Once far away, they will be
drawn into memories of home, and remembering the city's celebrations
they will journey back again. The departure and the spheres it navi-
gates will then be present to them as well. The town and the country
along the Garonne too will dawn on them with greater clarity, imbued
with their own special significance.[115] Yet their course extends far beyond this constant back and forth movement, which cannot accommodate what is lasting.

Love remains constant in a different sense. That the course of the
mariners is guided by love and only love underlines this reciprocation
as an essential possibility of human life. There is no mention of love in
"Remembrance" up to this point. The talk of "days of love" (*Tage der
Lieb'*) in the conversation of the friends does bring it into the essential
domain of remembrance. One might also discern it in the reference to
the sweet Garonne, or hear an echo of it in the dreams on the breezes
sweeping the paths where the women walk, or in the dancing in the
city's celebrations. And the greeting sent to the Garonne and the gardens, like all remembrance, arises from a sensibility attuned to love.
But only in the final triad does the poem mention it directly—precisely
at the point at which it sums up the spirit of the mariners approaching
and following remembrance on their journey as they reach the river and
the city on the Garonne. It is of the essence of love not to let one's vision

embrace a totality but rather to be "captivated" (*befangen*) by the beloved. To be bound to what is smallest, to the form and the singularity of the life of the other, is divine: this was already the epigraph of *Hyperion*.[116] But no space open to love can be entirely closed off to lamentation since it must at once embrace separation—and yet not embrace it, for the one captivated, the young love,[117] must shy away from death and separation in order ultimately to be swallowed up by it. To be sure, love goes beyond the hither and thither of life at sea. Thus it has a duration that surpasses mere memory, which can only be given once it has been taken away and which thus naturally points the way back home. The duration of love lies not in the gaze that ventures outward but in those that have found each other and become inseparable. In its total devotion to and captivation by what is smallest, however, love and its gaze know the whole of life as well—precisely by turning away from it.

The remembrance that bids farewell to friends heading off to war must speak of love too if it is to grasp the course of the mariners and the farewell itself as it takes leave of them. For their long, restless journey is precisely the complement of love, which keeps the eyes "fixed" (*heftet*) and holds one's gaze on the world. To think of the course of the mariners, but of nothing else, nothing supreme yet finite, is to contemplate the finitude of love, which alone might be thought able, even removed from the heroic spirit, to emerge complete from a finite life. But to identify with the mariners is to forgo the hope that would find fulfillment in love. Separation is equally essential to both, but so is the emergence of something genuinely "lasting,"[118] something that endures precisely because it is cut off from nothing and so terminates nowhere.

Yet this truth is articulated with specific reference to poetry, which discloses something lasting in just this way. It was Hölderlin the philosopher who became convinced that only poets could achieve this (*StA* VI, p. 293 *et passim*). Only in a knowledge of the whole is there something lasting. But this knowledge does not spring from the sort of detachment that would approach life on a merely conceptual level (*StA* IV, p. 237). It must instead issue from an exploration of essential human possibilities, moving with them and at the same time experiencing separation and acknowledging its inevitability. This movement, cognizant and yet deflected from its very course, aspiring to a knowledge in which something lasting, with thanks, reigns even in separation—this is remembrance.

In its closing lines this late poem, "Remembrance," enters into the philosophical domain Hölderlin had worked out years before. Like it, the poem puts in perspective those dimensions of life that all human existence knows as its own essential possibilities. In this way it dis-

closes their internal limits along with the necessary departure they intimate. One must therefore also take leave of those dimensions of life
themselves, inasmuch as they seemed absolute. It must be pointed out
incidentally that in "Remembrance" Hölderlin no longer conceives of
those dimensions of life as he had in his earlier thought, and that the
poetry enters in to shape the contemplation where thought would posit
some third element, the ideal form of life, which like the others is still
defined by an inevitable departure.[119]

We need not take "Remembrance" as just one more stage in Hölderlin's philosophical development. We have merely sought to understand
how in its course and structure the poem provides a point of departure
for the culminating lines that seem to project so far beyond it, and how
it at once supports and embodies them in itself. Since these lines could
just as well stand as philosophical propositions, and since what they
express properly belongs to that realm, our task is from the outset as
urgent as it is demanding. It must be made clear, however, that these
lines have their roots firmly planted in the poem taken as a whole. In
them the course of remembrance culminates in a contemplative work
that the poet has fashioned into something lasting, something that
shows the origin of the repose that is life itself and that is neither fearful
nor forgetful of separation.

THREE

Reflections

The Title and the Claims of the Poem

Considerations thus far have led us to ask how the poem gradually acquires the force necessary to support the triad in the closing lines by
depicting the landscape along the Garonne and by shifting perspective
through the spheres of that landscape. This concentrates that force in
a concise form, quite apart from its thetic moment, while integrating it
into the course of the poem and into the claims the poem makes. An
answer now suggests itself, but in turn raises further questions. For we
have not yet said precisely what remembrance itself is, such that it
might provide a basis for the articulation of the poem's closing lines.
Those lines, after all, and the final line in particular, can as easily be
understood as the culminating reflections of a general philosophical
orientation.

This question, if taken up in earnest, would entail an extensive
study of Hölderlin's fundamental ideas, the philosophical as well as the
poetological, their development, and the theoretical sketches he drew
from them at various times from various points of view. Hölderlin
probably never set down a general theory that would shed light on his
theoretical texts in relation to one another and in terms of their common
aim. At any rate, no such text nor even the trace of one has survived.
His theoretical writings come to us as an ensemble of reflections, arguments, and inquiries, all referring to one another and all guided by a
few basic problems and insights. But unlike the collected works of a
philosopher, they cannot be taken as a system of mutually supporting
arguments forming a whole.

Such inquiries would also have to relate the theoretical texts to the ideas at work in Hölderlin's poetry. The composition of his poems must be understood in terms of a form of thought exhibiting great philosophical sensibility, though it unfolds in mythopoetic language and hence largely according to its own laws. Hölderlin is probably the only poet in any language for whom philosophical insight is itself an underlying condition for true poetic form. But this never renders the poetic insight derivative, as if it were the mere transcription of discourse into poiesis. We are not yet in a position to provide a detailed interpretation that would account for the singular unity of Hölderlin's thought and poetic work.

Yet given the autonomy of Hölderlin's poetry, even within the philosophical horizons defining it, there is good reason, short of such an exhaustive study, to pursue the question concerning the nature of remembrance in conjunction with a consideration of the poem bearing that title. Each of Hölderlin's theoretical texts represents a more or less self-contained line of inquiry within a broad horizon of problems, and for these a few fundamental insights have provided us with a general framework and orientation. The poems, however, especially those in the form of hymns, and notwithstanding their interrelatedness, must be understood even more as self-contained structures rich in meaning. An interpretation of these structures would be suspect were it not able to relate them to the motivating concerns of the theoretical texts and the other poems. But above all such a reading must live up to the concrete dynamics of the work whose formal aspects it seeks to uncover. We can in no way regard the work as a mere function or application of some antecedent understanding that might be arrived at quite apart from the work itself.

"Remembrance," in virtue of its unique literary form, is a poem whose own internal dynamic culminates in an insight, as is generally the case with Hölderlin's thought and poetry. Consequently, considerations concerning the conclusion of the poem will not necessarily have any novel scholarly implications for Hölderlin's work as a whole. Here, in a series of sketches, we shall turn our attention to the way in which the poem itself constitutes a course of remembrance and how we are to understand its title. Discussions of this sort have to be fairly wide-ranging. They should help us to see previously unrecognized aspects and interconnections within Hölderlin's work as a whole. For that work is at once philosophical and poetic, and in both respects springs from original achievements that are brought together in the later poems. Just as the closing line of "Remembrance" could pass for a philosophical proposition, so too the title of the poem could be seen to name a philosophical problem. Reflecting on that problem will shed new light on the poem and point up in a new way the grounds for its preeminence.

Hölderlin mentions remembrance in the title of the poem only. And in all his work it is only in this poem that he employs the Swabian idiom *Noch denket das mir wohl* ("This comes back to me still"). One must assume, then, that the title and the lines of the poem are meant to stand in close relation to each other, producing a kind of mutual resonance and so encouraging us to reflect on their significance. Hölderlin could be sure that both expressions, especially in this particular context, were unusual enough to dispose the careful reader to attend closely to the meaning issuing from the poem and not merely to be enthralled by the brilliance of its images.

It should be noted that the only sense of the word *Andenken* still current among modern German speakers, that of a souvenir from a journey, was only just coming into use in Hölderlin's day.[120] It is not among the several meanings conveyed by Hölderlin's title. On the contrary, the word *Andenken* was commonly used in the sense of abiding thoughts and warm regards for a person or an event, though this sense soon became archaic. In letters one assured friends of one's remembrance and entrusted oneself to theirs in greetings and best wishes. The conciseness of the title, with neither definite nor indefinite article and with no object, would seem less conspicuous and of little importance if it had to do with a souvenir. But Hölderlin speaks of a kind of remembrance that for his contemporaries had a sense close, but not reducible, to that of *Gedenken* ("thinking of"). The concise title, then, has wide-ranging significance but also seems rather peculiar, indeed baffling. We do not know whether Hölderlin originally considered other titles as well, as he did in the case of "Mnemosyne."[121] If one had to guess, titles like "Bordeaux," "The Mariners," or "The Garonne" might suggest themselves. Some such title as this would also have described the course of the poem as a whole. One of Hölderlin's reasons for choosing the title he did was plainly to indicate that the work itself is making a claim on which a philosophical inquiry could be based. In this sense, the title itself is able to clear the ground for the poem's conclusion in its closing lines.

Nor can we overlook the way in which a context is set by the very choice of the title, as between "Remembrance" and "Mnemosyne"—about which more later.[122] For the title "Mnemosyne," given its concise form and its heightened significance owing to the use of the Greek, also names a fundamental preserving act of knowledge. Of course, Mnemosyne is the name of the mother of the muses. And, consistently enough, she is expressly summoned in the final strophe of that poem. Considering the significance of the title "Remembrance," and now bearing in mind its connection with Mnemosyne, it becomes clear that the poem extends into the realm of philosophy.

The multifaceted theme indicated in the title unfolds in the course of the poem accordingly, for there is a kind of recollective thinking at work in the poet's greeting to the city on the Garonne. The opening line of the second stanza, *Noch denket das mir wohl*, is meant to facilitate a more precise grasp of the peculiar presence of the distant land, and to serve as an introduction to the continuing course of remembrance by which the poet is ultimately drawn into the sphere of the city on the Garonne. The sameness of day and night is itself the mark of a holiday of recollective contemplation, which is at the same time an anticipation of the future. The conversation with friends too is a collective remembering, itself recollected by the poet no longer in their company. If we have correctly understood the presence of the city along the mariners' route, then we must see their voyage as one rich with memories—in its bringing together "what is beautiful of the earth" and in its forsaking "the city's celebrations." It is of course only at the destination that the recollections become memory, and memory is what marks their point of return. The fifth strophe ties this all together in speaking of a farewell experience, of the memory that the ocean takes and gives back again, of the inevitable loss of love, and of what is lasting, which poetry affords by its unique evocative power. Remembrance, in the sense indicated by the title of the poem, is precisely that evocation. If the poem itself is a course of remembrance, through its train of images and changing perspectives, then each of its strophes articulates one aspect of remembrance, as do the words and images of the final strophe itself in the conclusion of the poem.

Angedenken, Erinnerung, Gedächtnis

In Hölderlin's mature poetic work, three words associated with *Andenken* are given a refined sense: *Angedenken* ("remembrance"), *Erinnerung* ("recollection"), and *Gedächtnis* ("memory").

Angedenken, which is "sacred," preserves what was "dear" to us in the past, lets the heart repose amid life's labors and is itself preserved in the "lyrestrings" of poetic song.[123] Being near the beloved devotionally allows those dear to each other to "think of" one another (*aneinander denken*). So there is more to *Angedenken* than merely "not having forgotten." We think of those whose memory we preserve, or as it were "carry in our hearts"—we think fondly of how they are and of who they are.

Erinnerung, by contrast, can be a burden. The recollection of suffering withstood may indeed be "sweet." But recollection in this sense also leaves us "shaken." It may be hard to endure, and though we are in need of it, it may be burdensome, so that it weighs on our shoulders like a "load of logs" and so confounds us that we can no longer even "pull ourselves together."[124]

Gedächtnis too is "sacred." It directs itself toward the "highest" and the "best." This much is evident in Luther's use of *Gedächtnis* in rendering *anamnesis* in the words of institution from the Eucharist. "Bread and wine" are therefore present wherever there is memory—including the Socratic symposium, in which Plato calls the highest knowledge by the same name found in the words of institution according to Luke. Memory, then, means holding fast to what is most essential—unlike *Angedenken*, in which one is moved and in which one's thoughts are thoroughly immersed. In memory some single thing is held fast in the weight and clarity of its essence, for instance the Platonic Form or the divine sacrifice. Though in them lie the "abysses of wisdom," they are nonetheless to be "preserved," "in fixed, ingenuous eyes."[125] This "preserving," of course, is the sort that opens up one's own life for the sake of the thing preserved, and so for that inner awareness (*Innesein*) that Hölderlin calls "inwardness" (*Innigkeit*). Out of this inwardness come thanks, wholehearted thanks, that is, the thanks to which the hymns are attuned.[126]

Some progress may be made in trying to understand remembrance in Hölderlin's sense if we keep in mind its proximity to these three other memory words. There is no question that *Andenken* too is a way of preserving something in memory. Its closest neighbor is *Angedenken*, and not simply in virtue of the formal similarity between the two words. *Andenken* is distinct from *Erinnerung* in that it cannot be a curse or a burden. It is closer to the fiery spirit of the mariners and the slow course under golden dreams than to the thorny paths between the flight into independence and the chains of devotion. It is different from *Gedächtnis* in that it essentially charts a course of its own. It does not hold fast intimately to a single, particular thing. It *discloses* as it recalls—just as *Angedenken* is continually occupied with thoughts of the beloved, whom one's thoughts embrace when parting is "sweet sorrow." This aspect of disclosure figures in all the more conspicuously when in the title "Andenken" the prefix *ge-* of the more common *Angedenken* is dropped. Wherever the prefix appears, something like a terminus or definite state of affairs resulting from a deed or an event is intended as well. In *Gedenken* and *Angedenken* ("thinking of" and "remembering fondly") this determinateness is rooted in a relation to something definitely past. Although it occupies our thoughts and moves us, it is nevertheless distant, lying in the past, like all things that have come to an end or that have been decided at some point in time. *Erinnerung* and *Gedächtnis* too must be directed toward something fixed in the past, which we think of as always having been what it is now. By contrast, *Andenken* appears to be free of any such definiteness. Though also a form of *Gedenken*, it is above all a process in which that toward which it turns first emerges in its full determinateness. Whereas the thoughts involved in *Angedenken* merely encircle the beloved, *Andenken* at once represents a renewed emergence of the person remembered in the mind of the one drawn into it.

It is this aspect of *Andenken* that brings it—more so than *Gedenken* or *Angedenken*—into proximity with *Denken* ("thinking"). Both thought and remembrance constitute events, or the products of events, and as such processes with results, though results determined by those processes themselves. Thinking does not merely grasp thoughts, it develops them, unfolding their contents and implications—and so too does remembrance. But in remembrance these thoughts can be neither entertained freely nor taken up at one's pleasure. Remembrance instead sets a course of its own and is set going by what it is directed toward, "shy" in the face of it. Although, like thinking, it follows a directed course, it is subordinated to the course it takes. One could say, then, that it corresponds at every step to that course alone. Its course, then, leads to the emergence of what is depicted in thinking and to that from which thinking acquires its thoughts. It is nonetheless something enacted, which must be completed, such that in its completion that which dawns on thought, that which one remembers (*ihm wohl denket*), is also transformed—not by means of a free mental act, but in such a way that it is apprehended in remembrance in its pure form and significance, and thus "grasped." This much remembrance has in common with memory, which is able to comprehend more than was experienced in the event itself. It may be argued, then, that Plato's Forms are actually first taken up and grasped in *anamnesis* itself, so that no original intuition could ever provide a fully adequate knowledge of them.

Although remembrance proceeds from something past, it can also aim at what was "always already" and at that which is inherent in or underlying it; at what is as well as what was, and so too at what is to come. In this way, remembrance grasps through depiction what lies in the past and the order of events surrounding what is pictured, and can thus reveal in the process of depiction something wholly general and ultimately all-encompassing.

That remembrance is subordinated to what it reflects upon, however, means more than that it proceeds from what lies in the past in order to preserve and transform it. Remembrance is devoted in inwardness to what it reflects on, an inwardness characteristic too of memory in its devotion to the "best" and the "highest." Remembrance is in this sense very close to what in religious practice are called "devotions" (*Andacht*). The thought involved in remembrance, then, could be called "devotional"—dedicated to what is thought of, and so elevated at once through it and toward it. But Hölderlin's poetry shuns the word. For him it is associated too much with bound and bridled religiousness and too little with the free course of thought. Still, remembrance has much in common with devotions, in contrast to thought understood as discourse or consideration. For these latter do not involve inwardness. They do not, as Plato put it, allow the whole soul to attain knowledge. For they do not orient the stream of moods and emotions toward what is attended to in remembrance, and thus require neither "composure" nor "collectedness," nor what is felt as "uplifting" in devotions. Remembrance, on the other hand, consists in an attunement to that which is depicted in its course. Thus its course is also a course through a series of moods belonging to the spheres and forms of life that reveal themselves in remembrance. And this is just to say that the course of remembrance is carried out through a "modulation of tones," which for its part follows from a principle concerning the essence of poetry. But since the modulation is reflective, and since each of its steps preserves that from which it emerged, the modulation is perspicuous, with a growing clarity, and so collects conscious life as a whole and encompasses its "emotions" and tendencies. This modulation aims at bringing together everything from which and in which this life finds its orientation and, in it, clarity. Hölderlin's "Remembrance" attains precisely this collectedness in the triad in the closing lines.

Remembrance is therefore really and truly a form of thinking: *Andenken* is a kind of *Denken*. For it is an ordered course aimed at clarity and self-awareness. At the same time, inwardness belongs just as much to remembrance as it does to the other modes of thinking of. And because it constitutes a course of inwardness, remembrance guides conscious life through a series of moods in which it collects itself, as in devotions, but with the anticipation of the kind of collected clarity that comes from final insight and perspective.

If one wished to exercise a kind of will to theory in investigating and shedding light on what has here only been laid out schematically, one would come across a field of problems as yet uncultivated and unsurveyed. Only a few such problems can be dealt with here. For example, when Hölderlin speaks of remembrance, he means the conscious unification of what in theoretical language we call discourse and meditation. Discourse involves the transparent and autonomous ordering of thoughts, meditation the collectedness and clarity of conscious life. But the course of remembrance takes us through a depiction of spheres, their moods, and the experiences of conscious life that "resound" with and are borne by feelings. Remembrance must gain intimate access to these as well. It must therefore extend farther than the mere unity of ordered thought and meditative concentration, which is difficult enough to grasp already. If we are to explain how remembrance is possible, then we ought to be able to conceive of discourse, the concentration of consciousness, and emotionally charged experience all as a unity and all constituting a kind of thinking. But then we also ought to be able to say more about what thinking is in general, and about what thinking in the form of remembrance is in particular. For such thinking cannot be mere cognition or the reflective application of rules, yet it must be an ordered, controlled sequence of steps, which we might also call layers or stages. It cannot be mere discipline or reflection because its course holds fast only to what it itself represents—and also, above all, because it follows only that inner progression of mood that emerges within the representation. The law guiding remembrance is just the law governing that inner progression itself, not the law of critical inquiry.

Remembrance relates to recollecting in another sense, then, inasmuch as it does not spring from the mere emergence of a recollection. For recollection too follows its own rules of representation in proceeding from image to image, from thought to thought, and from one perspective to another. There is, however, also a kind of thinking that follows this mode of progression and yet cannot properly be called "associative." For it constitutes the constructive form of rationality, in contrast to the critical. Such thinking opens up and brings to consciousness new domains of inquiry and makes their significance felt, at which point critical reasoning can then apply itself. Once such problems have arisen, it is again in virtue of this kind of thinking that they fall into substantive constellations, so that they can—again as Plato said—play off one another. But above all, often suddenly, yet only after long contemplation, such thinking opens new paths of insight that seem clear and compelling, however poorly they may fare in the long run. This kind of thinking makes immediately clear what would otherwise appear to be no more than an unfounded assumption, namely, that thought and consciousness constitute a unity, not in a trivial but in an emphatic sense. Moreover, both unfold with the same swiftness—consciousness like a sudden awakening and spontaneous thinking in a mode of increasing wakefulness, beyond reflective comprehension.[127]

And given that consciousness and spontaneous thinking produce or maintain insight, it is no accident that such insight was once understood as something emerging in a flash (ἐξαίφνης).

This provides an occasion, finally, to note that this sort of thinking, inasmuch as it takes up a course and sketches out a path in spite of its own rapid pace, must stand in some relation to what are known as "transformations of consciousness." Consciousness is essentially modifiable, and moreover already attuned, never simply governed by moods imposed upon it and shaping it in advance. If the swift course of spontaneous thinking moves through distinct stages toward clarity and insight, these stages will also bear traces of distinct forms of awareness, which, being embedded in the course of thinking with its unique wakefulness, never settle into a single fixed position. If these different stages of thinking had no impact upon the collectedness of consciousness itself, neither would the insight yielded by that thinking, namely the insight that elevates conscious life into a collected state and allows it to emerge transformed.

That Hölderlin must have had all of this in mind is clear from the fact that he saw remembrance as bound up with the essence of poetry, which for its part does not stand opposed to thinking but in fact frees it for its own ultimate possibilities. We are still a long way from seeing how poetry, by way of remembrance, is able to combine the forms of spontaneous representation, all of which, notwithstanding their interrelatedness, follow separate paths—first, recollecting, in which once familiar but now distant spheres of the world come to light; second, the inwardness of entering into the moods of those spheres; third, the course of their emergence, which at once aspires to something universal in the understanding; and finally, the transformation of consciousness into a collected state of clarity and ultimate insight. But there can be no doubt that Hölderlin did indeed bring all these currents together in composing his poetry—in particular one of his greatest poems, "Remembrance." There is just as little doubt that his poetic achievement lay in a mastery of the rules of composition, which he thought fell under a "calculable law" (*StA* V, p. 265). With this formula, reflected in the beginning of his notes to the Sophocles translations, he perhaps concedes too much to the element of craft in poetic composition. For his theory proceeds entirely from the conviction that in poetry the spontaneous modes of conscious understanding attain their highest potential only in expressiveness and unity. What kind of "calculus" (*StA* V, p. 195) could form the basis of poetry is a question that must itself be worked out in the context of this enterprise.

The Theory of Recollection

The foregoing discussion was intended to facilitate some understanding of the meaning of, and the fundamental problems raised by, the fact that Hölderlin called his poem "Remembrance." We began by considering Hölderlin's use of memory words in his later poetry. We then reflected on the problems relating to the kind of thinking that could be seen to share a common course with recollecting, inwardness, and the modification of consciousness. And since that thinking has such decisive significance in determining the essence of poetry, we must now consider Hölderlin's attempts to formulate a theory of poetry.

Here too we must preface our investigation with a few remarks. Our inquiry will not, of course, lead to the discovery of a conceptual definition of remembrance in Hölderlin's own theoretical writings. Nothing in the poetic works corresponds exactly to the poem's title, nor do the theoretical works ever say explicitly what is meant by it. The ideas bound up with the architecture of the poem and with the claims of its title are to be found nowhere else. Once again, and in a new way, then, it becomes clear that this work was bound to excite philosophical reflection and that it will continue to do so—precisely according to its own intent. The theoretical writings do nevertheless provide further information and greater clarity with regard to the associations that guided Hölderlin through the poem toward a conception of remembrance that at once means thinking, remembering, intimacy, and a course of transformation. For *Erinnerung* ("recollection") is also the central concept in some of the most important sketches of his thought. In those sketches, more than in the poetic works, it becomes evident that this sort of recollecting relates to a supreme insight, which is philosophical as such. In this way, the poet's philosophical manuscripts too can help us to understand the course of remembrance in the poem, including the triad in the closing lines.

It is easy to see that recollection brings things together, and thus that it constitutes a kind of synthesis. What happens, including what happens to us, stands in a comprehensive interconnection of events and motivations. We presuppose this interconnection at every moment and think we have some knowledge of it, or traces of it, and in our conscious experience. But we could never take up an attitude toward it, could never ask about it, if all events were forever past and gone with the very flow of time. What was, however, can be made manifest as such. And since this holds in principle for everything that has ever been, memory is able to bring together things that in reality never would have occurred together, or at the same time, or observably. And this, again, is what makes it possible to conceive and to understand them in a context of interconnectedness. For they come into the world by way of dependencies and manifold exclusions, ultimately standing fixed in an insight built entirely upon recollection and yet surpassing it.

Only those who can recollect are able to foresee. For foresight is not a mere apprehension of future events; rather we are always anticipating the future in relation to what lies in wait for it. This is why foresight is always the foresight of something soon to be past, and so of a recollection to come. And to this extent the inner form of memory does not restrict it to an apprehension of what was. It is as such universal, extending over the entire course of conscious life, whatever end that life might be directed toward. And it is just this universality that is assumed wherever recollection figures as the fundamental dimension of experience, making possible the higher form of understanding proper. Kant builds on this insight when he defines knowledge as spontaneity, and spontaneity as synthesis. Fichte followed it too, in his own way, when he sought to understand the form of consciousness, and with it the forms of all understanding, in terms of acts of the imagination, in which that thoroughgoing interrelatedness arises by which recollection becomes a universal faculty of conscious life.

This new philosophical doctrine defined and guided Hölderlin's thinking entirely, as it did that of his young friends. The doctrine does not, of course, undertake to reveal the nature of the elementary acts of conscious life, of concept formation, or of our knowledge of objects. Rather, it enters in at the highest level of those problems addressed by the thesis concerning recollection's constitutive significance for the essence of insight: its initial problem is posed not by perception and the acts of synthesis contributed by the imagination but by the orientations of conscious life and the question of how they can be brought together.

Accordingly, this thinking does not amount to a self-contained theory of knowledge but is from the beginning grounded in a metaphysics. That is, the orientations of conscious life may be thought of as so many sketches of the ways in which that life itself might establish some relation to its own origin. The origin as such is necessarily distant, or withdrawn. For the unity of the origin shatters to the extent that life goes on. Wanting to let that unity simply reappear would amount to relinquishing consciousness altogether. The metaphysical principle itself shows this to be impossible. And in any case such a regression would be not knowledge but the overcoming of all knowledge, an act that conscious life could only perform by way of its own dissolution, and hence not from within itself or as a realization of itself. These orientations of conscious life, then, which are at once struggles to organize that life in itself, are all reactions to the lost origin, once it has withdrawn.

The next step in Hölderlin's thinking leads to the insight that the tendencies of conscious life are mutually irreconcilable yet equally legitimate and indispensable. A life that aims at actively overstepping all boundaries (such as the life of the mariners) cannot be the life of love, which sees in the finite a reflection of undivided and now lost plenitude and whose steadfast gaze is "kept fixed" on a single essence. Conscious life, then, can never be wholly satisfied in any of its orientations or tendencies, since a renunciation of what is essential is what constitutes each of them. Conscious life must therefore encompass a whole that straddles this opposition, comprehending and affirming all its tendencies but not thereby relinquishing the knowledge of order, origin, and truth. Such knowledge is not bound up with just one of those tendencies but rather admits of entering into all of them. It is in this sense "transcendental." And since it can unite the tendencies and their moods only as they resound with feeling, it is therefore not thinking but poetry alone that is the locus of genuine transcendental insight.

On metaphysical grounds, then, this, Hölderlin's fundamental idea, leads immediately to a theory of consciousness as well as to a theory of poetry. It follows that no insight is to be expected of poetry over and above its insight into the very order in which the tendencies of conscious life hold sway through their successive oppositions. In this way the transcendental perspective of the whole takes on a pure form only in the immanence of conscious life, but in such a way that this immanence is for its part thought to spring from an origin that cannot be disclosed as such or in itself. Philosophy may well show that we entertain true thoughts concerning this origin. But if philosophical knowledge never crosses over in any way into the experience of conscious life, then it never makes the sort of progress that brings life itself into equilibrium. Philosophical knowledge then never attains certainty in the form of an insight springing from the course of thinking that takes shape in conscious life itself. In this way philosophy itself requires that poetry take up its own course and that philosophy move in its own reflection toward its end, though now in a different, more appropriate way. What had merely been intimated in philosophy is now actually borne out in poetry inasmuch as the latter cultivates a consciousness that grasps life's tendencies in harmony—though never resolving them into a unity free of all opposition. Only when those tendencies emerge united in a form that preserves their respective moods, so that they can occur pure and unperturbed, only then can abstract thought emerge in conscious life, borne out by that life itself: "so that, at the root of all the works and deeds of men, we feel equal to and one with all" (*StA* IV, p. 222).

These are the basic elements of Hölderlin's thought.[128] Since he never formulated them in a compelling theory it is no wonder that they are never clearly spelled out in any of his texts, or that these texts pursue ideas that resist any straightforward organization. And his thinking remained in motion even after his work largely ceased to be explicitly philosophical. In his theory of tragedy, with its conception of history and of the path of the spirit from Asia to Hesperia, and above all in the development of his mythic world-picture, Hölderlin worked out new and important lines of thought in connection with his fundamental ideas. It is not immediately clear if they fit neatly with his early philosophical ideas. But Hölderlin never went back on those early ideas. His commentary to the Pindar fragments, as well as his notes to the Sophocles translations, can only be understood if one sees at work in them a thinking consistent with the foundations of his early, truly philosophical writings.[129]

Keeping in mind the essential elements of his thought, it is easy to see why and in what sense the concept of recollection came to play such a crucial role for him—crucial indeed for that realm in which the idea of a self-withdrawn, life-pervading, and fractured origin acts as a guiding light in the analysis of life's dynamics. Although Hölderlin does not say so explicitly, he assumes that the Kantian theory of the universality of recollection applies in essence to the internal structure of perception itself. To this theory he then adds a counterpart that regards the collectedness of differentiation as an achievement of the highest as well as the most primitive form of consciousness. Recollection thus comes to be the act through which everything that forms a true whole emerges in consciousness.

In three theoretical manuscripts, all addressing widely different issues, Hölderlin attributes decisive force to this one fundamental idea. (1) From recollection comes a perspective whose entire course is condensed in a "divine moment" in the formal *construction of the poetic work*, and as a constitutive moment of that form (*StA* IV, p. 251). (2) The *new lifeworld* arising out of a historical catastrophe can achieve a secure and independent status only by traversing its own path toward a recollection in which the world lost, as well as the necessity of traversing the path itself, are made manifest in undaunted clarity (*StA* IV, p. 284). (3) But *religion* too springs from recollection, indeed a recollection that fixes not on something past but on the whole everyday human context defined by the necessities of life. If one pays heed to life and to how it unfolds, one grasps the "spirit" in the world in its more subtle, "infinite" connections. This grasping is recollection—not a mere abstract representation or a repetition of the everyday in what one pejoratively calls merely keeping-in-mind. Rather, recollection is an internalization in which man is at once thankful for life as a whole. Indeed recollection is itself religion and must above all be understood in poetic and mythic terms (*StA* IV, pp. 275, 280–81). At this point the theory of religion is a continuation of the idea underlying the theory of poetry. For there it was shown that only poetry is able to make us aware of the context of life as a whole, in the moods of life's conflicting tendencies.

Here it becomes apparent how the constitution of remembrance and its course, which makes up Hölderlin's poem, can be elucidated in terms of the key elements of the theoretical writings. For those manuscripts foreshadow Hölderlin's poetic use of a special word for recollection derived from the root word for thinking: *Denken*. This word, of course, brings together various aspects of the meaning of thought, what is characteristic of it, and what marks it as the basis of supreme insight. The significance of these aspects, and the fact that they constitute only one mode of understanding, is evident in the form of the word itself. Notwithstanding the fact that it refers to thought in a unified sense as precisely as possible, the use of the word also suggests that any account of the notion of remembrance would itself lead the way to unexplored philosophical terrain. For the word *Andenken* as Hölderlin uses it is an unusual one and will seem mysterious, though its primary meaning suggests clear, intimate knowledge.

One can nonetheless grasp its central significance without being forced to relegate Hölderlin's philosophical writings to metaphysical oblivion and then substitute for them some unique and more original thinking to which his poetry would answer.[130] The fact that Hölderlin's thinking and poetic work are so mutually illuminating has lent plausibility to this brief account of the construction of Hölderlin's thought from the ground up.

Imagination and Infinitude

But it remains to relate this thinking to the direction and construction of the course of remembrance, in terms of which the structure of the poem by that name is to be understood. Our analysis of its series of images of the landscape along the Garonne showed two things. First, the shifting perspectives of these images are not tied to a single point of view but are instead sequential. Second, this series of viewpoints is laid out so that at the end, from an image of the point of departure from the route of the mariners, an insight is achieved that is in itself bound to no specific location. The course is consummated in a thought that encompasses all paths and so settles on a place, but no longer belongs to any particular path or place. If, in granting central status to the concept of recollection, Hölderlin's thought provides an essential point of departure for the constitution of the course of remembrance, then some connection to and some account of the course of remembrance must be available from within it.

The first of the two claims concerning the constitution of the course of remembrance can be clarified and supported if we see it in relation to the philosophy of Fichte. There the theory of imagination occupies a central place; indeed it was Fichte's theory that initially afforded Hölderlin the prospect of making his conception of recollection the key concept of his theoretical sketches.[131] We have seen that recollection in this sense means holding fast to events, knowing all in one. In this respect it is in accord with Fichte's theory, given that every important event, particularly in the historical process and in the construction of works of art, is in view of its continuity destined from the outset to enter into memory, and given that *qua* event it relates to its own progression as well as to its own representation. Hölderlin did not in fact subscribe to Fichte's epistemological idealism. But he did follow it to the extent that he understood the structure of all events according to their possible representation and conceived the form of representation for its part in accordance with Fichte's idealist theory of constitution.

But this yields an initial result that is important for the interpretation of Hölderlin's poem, namely, that the course of such a depiction cannot be conceived of as bound to a fixed starting point. It is crucial to Fichte's theory of imagination that this fundamental act of consciousness proceeds solely from its own continuous dynamic yet does so in stages: it constitutes a point of mediation between contrary acts of consciousness, and this in such a way as to prevent it from ever falling into a static state. It then lifts itself up from that point and proceeds to constitute a new point of mediation, yielding a series of such points, through which the particular site of mediation shifts and moves foward.[132] Depiction too assumes such a course, and indeed spontaneously, with no explicit instigation, and solely on the basis of its own essential nature. And this again corresponds to the fact that the course of remembrance *delivers one* to the place it anticipates at its outset.

From this it follows that the course consummates itself in a mood akin to the mood Fichte attributed to the imagination—at least to the minds of his readers, by deeming it a kind of "oscillation" (*Schweben*).[133] This has a double meaning. At each point of mediation, the imagination is in constant transition between the moments it mediates. But at the same time, it maintains a constant relation to that in virtue of which the mediation is evidently given—namely, according to Fichte, to an ongoing activity extending over all the points of mediation and contrary moments, from the beginning into infinity. From this it would have to follow that the course of remembrance too, were it to conform to this line of Fichte's analysis, could only depict a specific location on two conditions. On the one hand, it would have to enter into the sphere and emphasize vividly those aspects from which it emerged, in their relation to one another. On the other hand, it would have to reveal each place in terms of its relation to something all-encompassing—not something of which it was only a part but something that was already present in it, in the whole of its very structure and significance. Of course, "oscillation" should not be construed to mean a kind of dream state, though one only understands consciousness if one defines it in such a way that dream-consciousness is taken to be one of its modifications. For Fichte, "oscillation" is constitutive of all consciousness of reality. In order for Hölderlin's notion of depiction to correspond to this oscillation, he would have to claim that it is precisely in depiction that the true reality of any given place is disclosed. On the other hand, this means that consciousness enters into the place in a manner that corresponds to its true reality.

The infinite, which according to Fichte the imagination must insert into each of its mediations, is different from the infinitude of the all-encompassing unity to be found in Hölderlin's philosophical sketches. And this difference must have some effect on the constitution of the course of remembrance. Before going into this, however, we ought to highlight another element of Fichte's theory, an element Hölderlin incorporated into his own thought. The mediating function of the imagination is necessary because consciousness is possible only where an *opposition* develops. But an opposition as such can only exist in consciousness if its moments are "unified," which means in the first instance being compared with one another. Comparing means interrelating, hence determining. As such, it presupposes relatability, and thus unity. The mediating function of the imagination, then, is the simplest, the irreducible form of the unification of consciousness in general.

The notion of determination through opposition can be traced as a leitmotif through the whole of Hölderlin's work, a theme clearly recognizable in its many manifestations. Even in the text accompanying Pindar's fragment, which Hölderlin entitled "The Highest," the notion is formulated explicitly in the form of a principle (*StA* V, p. 285). It leads to the idea found in Hölderlin's first letter to Böhlendorff concerning the relation between Greek and Hesperian poetry, and concerning the inner opposition from which both poetic forms derive. It is presupposed in the poetic theory of the modulation of tones. Even the forms and movements of the landscapes Hölderlin's poems depict are viewed in terms of oppositions and arranged in harmonious resolution with one another. The form of the landscape and its poetic evocation, then, are related in a manner that corresponds formally to what Fichte sought to show to be characteristic of imagination and thus of recollection.

More significant for the course of remembrance, however, and for the infinitude in which and toward which it progresses is the fundamental opposition of the tendencies of conscious life. The poem "Remembrance" is also a contemplation of one of these modes of life, namely the heroic life of the mariners. The course of remembrance leads first to their city where their route is interwoven with the spheres of the river and so with other modes lived in passing. These spheres contain in themselves more than what belongs to the passage of the mariners, for here there are gardens and festivals and the dark light growing from the vineyard hills. In this way one can see that these spheres, where remembrance comes upon the river of the mariners, fit into a whole that goes beyond the life and the passage of the mariners themselves. The structure and significance of that life and that passage are nonetheless bound up and held secure in the overarching whole.

If this is the case, then one can understand in other respects why a negative image of the mariners' form of life can and must emerge from a contemplation of the entire path, from the departure with the route of the mariners to the very end of the poet's course of remembrance. One also understands that the image is expressed in language just as the life of "love" is made a negative image juxtaposed to the life of the mariners by way of a common limit: neither can be genuinely lasting. Thus the contemplation reaches its final stage. Remembrance has taken shape and become clear and perspicuous about itself in virtue of the form of the poem. Yet in its very understanding of the modes of life, it is at once bound to and cut off from them both.

The infinite emerges as such in this insight contained in the triad in the closing lines, and from it the course of remembrance takes shape. Interpreters consequently have the task of making intelligible, on the basis of Hölderlin's notion of the underlying whole, the relation between the place where the ultimate insight is gained and the content of that insight itself. The insight transforms the one drawn into the course of remembrance and brings that course to a close at the place to which it was leading. In virtue of its inner form, however, the insight at once supersedes all connection to this or indeed to any determinate locality. For the line of thought that is taken up from Fichte with respect to an

understanding of the stages of remembrance, but that belongs to speculative metaphysics in virtue of the fundamental idea on which it
rests, the problem arises of grasping that relation, and this is a metaphysical question itself. An answer to the question would have to provide a definitive account of the course of remembrance, in particular
its final stage.

Hölderlin remains close to Fichte in seeing what is first and foremost, the origin of all knowledge, present and at work in the form and
function of knowledge itself. He is close to Fichte too in denying that
this true foundation of knowledge can be grasped in a pure mental act
isolated from all other acts of the understanding. Already in his Jena
manuscripts Hölderlin had come to the conclusion that the infinite One
is conceivable only on condition of being defined in terms of an irruption into difference and interrelation. Thus it can be realized and at the
same time grasped not by means of a regression but rather in a new
mode in the understanding itself, a mode that it in turn alters. But this
now requires and accounts for the fact that all knowledge is derived
from it solely on the basis of and in terms of opposition. From this it
follows that the emergence of knowledge is subject to process, that it
must be conditioned, perhaps arising only from upheavals and catastrophes, and that knowledge remains in this respect a kind of making
certain (*Vergewisserung*), bound as such to finitude and so never going
beyond the finite to attain the sort of clarity one might be tempted to
call "otherworldly."

Yet what one comprehends in such knowledge is nonetheless the
ground that transcends everything finite, and moreover its emergence
from out of itself into the world, the forms of life oriented around it,
and the path leading to an insight into what is lasting, an insight that
falls within the world and is at once poised before its own foundations
and its own meaning. In this way, then, such knowledge, precisely in
virtue what it knows, lies beyond everything finite, beyond all the
places whose local features give rise to it. It is as it were concentrated
in the placeless ground of all places and of all meaning.

On the other hand, it is not placeless in the sense of being removed
from all places and so from its own origin. For it points forward and
backward along the worldly paths where it alone reveals itself, toward
all the places that are origins of insight and whose own significance
reveals the ground of what is lasting. And yet this conclusive perspective is such that the place where the insight was gained is no longer
included in what is itself placeless and primordial. For just as in the
insight itself the place is contained in that which distinguishes it as the
place of transition to what is placeless and primordial and to what is

lasting, so too are all the other places where paths of remembrance might arise or resolve, and so too the pattern of these paths determined by the tendencies of conscious life and the remembrance that follows them. Thus in the concluding insight, and in what is lasting, now no longer imperiled by oppositions, the place of transition, together with all such places, is reintegrated into the ultimate, or is rather itself made lasting in the whole of its course of insight arising from remembrance.

No existing texts in fact indicate that Holderlin ever advanced or even entertained these lines of thought. But some of his manuscripts and correspondence from the period following his stay in Bordeaux express very clearly things that reason might well yield on its own simply by following up Hölderlin's fundamental ideas. Moreover, these texts attach great significance to a consciousness binding an ultimate insight to the place where the insight emerges. This is made clear by three otherwise unrelated texts that—not to go into the differences between them here—speak of the possible gathering of all in one, in one single place. In a draft of one of the hymns, not yet fully clear in its conception, Hölderlin depicts a place in Germany in such a way as to suggest echoes of John's Cave on the island of Patmos:

> Ein wilder Hügel aber stehet über dem Abhang
> Meiner Gärten. Kirschenbäume. Scharfer Othem aber wehet
> Um die Löcher des Felses. Allda bin ich
> Alles miteinander.

> But a wild hillside stands above the slope
> Of my gardens. Cherry trees. But a sharp breath blows
> About the crevices of the cliff. And there am I
> Everything at one.

This passage expresses a kind of consciousness embracing all modes of life as one in their differences in terms of the experience of primordial unity.[134]

In the second letter to Böhlendorff, written shortly before the period in which "Remembrance" was composed, we read: "that all sacred places of the earth are together in one place, and the philosophic light in my window, this is now my joy." This sentence expresses the same consciousness, but in connection with all places brought together in a consciousness of the One, and for someone who has attained that consciousness in some place.[135]

Finally, in the commentary on the Pindar fragment entitled "The Asylum," Hölderlin generalizes this experience of a light in his window in the Nürtingen asylum: "the asylums of man, the silent resting places, to which nothing foreign came, because there the work and the life of nature was concentrated, and about them something prescient, like remembering" (*StA* V, p. 288).

Actuality and Transformation

In the interest of philosophical precision, one would do well to reflect on the nature and possibility of this kind of final consciousness. For the thought crucial to the development of such a consciousness, in which it is grasped and conveyed, leaves to one side the ideas standing at the center of the speculative systems worked out by Holderlin's young friends, Schelling and Hegel. Hölderlin did not make the thought systematically clear, nor did he set it down in writing with any attention to alternative lines of argument. But even his friends who occupied themselves with pure theory articulated their ideas, very much in accord with Hölderlin's own, in the sort of style that leaves the greater part of the effort of clarification up to the interpreter who tries to follow along.[136] That job will not be taken up here.

In any case, that task would have to draw clearer connections between knowledge of the One and knowledge of the course of remembrance that leads to the One. It would have to clarify further how the insight, in itself indeterminately placed, into what is primordial at once grounds and yet includes the place where it emerges in a knowledge of the paths of remembrance, without however simply proceeding from there directly to the insight itself. It would need to clarify how this place is as one with all such thresholds to the insight. It would have to suggest some account of the fact that one can reach the threshold of the insight in the course of remembrance without in fact traveling to the region itself. It would thus relate the problems addressed in Fichte's theory of imagination to an understanding of the inner construction of the resolving insight of remembrance. For the poet in Hölderlin's poem has arrived at the sea-wide confluence of the rivers *solely* through the course of his remembrance, and this in a movement that originates in the sphere of the city on the Garonne, in which the course of remembrance alone has borne him along. The course is consummated, then, in a dual transformation of consciousness, with its corresponding discontinuous temporal constitution (cf. p. 200 above)—and indeed such that the first part is divided in a series of steps: from the Hesperian site under the northeasterly wind to the sphere of the city on the Garonne, and from there in a rejuvenated present out to where the mariners disembark. Here emerges the indeterminately placed insight that embraces the course itself, its place, and with it all places.

It is hard not to be suspicious of one who pursues such a course in earnest, a suspicion tied to empirical knowledge and the identity conditions definitive for it. The identity of places is, from the point of view of empirical knowledge, no less rigidly determined than that of the one who travels throughout the world, bound to the real contours of countries and countrysides, and thus bound to the continuity of the passage of time. So it is only by actually arriving at some place that one is able to attain a world-transcending insight, as Hölderlin did in Bordeaux, above the "intersecting heights of Auvergne" (*StA* VI, p. 429). Where we are, so says scientifically grounded empirical knowledge, is just wherever our cerebrum happens to find itself, and there can be no question of transformation apart from this simple truth. Any paths or insights departing from this are just so many fantasies, derivative of the places and paths that are, by contrast, within reach of one's sense organs. As far as this empirical knowledge is concerned, it will certainly not be convincing to claim, as Heidegger does, that "Remembrance" is located in the poet's return to his Hesperian home.

Otherwise, it is true: the course of remembrance is for its part presented *solely* as the course of a poem. Unlike children's fairy tales, the poem does not aspire to a fantastic journey, lulling us for a few moments into our dreams and becoming real. For the course of remembrance that it initiates can only be comprehended in sober reflection and can only lead to a transformation of consciousness, which does indeed take place, where the triad of the poem's closing lines culminate in an insight. To this extent, the place where the poet was actually standing when he fashioned the work is in truth a matter of indifference, just as it is a matter of indifference where it happens to be read and understood. All the places in it belong to the course of remembrance, which is carried out within the poem. The advent of remembrance in the poem, then, cannot be approached realistically by bracketing the preceding course as something merely intended or as present only in the imagination.

Moreover, in the poem itself the course toward the river of the mariners is explicitly conceived as a course of remembrance. For this reason, too, it is not a course contained in representational consciousness alone. It unfolds precisely *as* a course of remembrance. One might always be tempted, then, to infer that it does indeed stand in brackets up to the point of its concluding insight, brackets referring one back to its starting point. But to concede this would be to underestimate the nature of thinking. Even so-called "naive" realism assumes the possibility of our knowing the world around us although the known object, to the extent that it is known, may not be present directly before us and may be known only in its relation to the place where we happen to be standing. And the determinate location of that place, or of some successive place, is for its part known only with reference to a spatiotemporal coordinate system not constituted stepwise on the basis of some prior consciousness. Thus anyone wanting to reject from the outset the possibility of the movement of remembrance as some abstruse notion would have to be suspicious of even the simplest realism in natural consciousness. It may indeed be less obvious that a wide-ranging knowledge of the most sublime form of world-orientation would have the same eventfulness in connection with every fixed human habitat that affords some access to it. But neither is there any compelling argument to the contrary. The path toward the final insight on the one hand, and the unfolding of primordial world-consciousness on the other, have this in common, that neither can be understood as a line intersecting actual regions of space-time. The final insight, in which we grasp our own life on the basis of an understanding of all life, cannot therefore be conceived as an insight simply projected or extrapolated from its own genetically fixed point of view.

For this reason, where Hölderlin's work gets its inspiration from Fichte's theory of imagination, we may follow him without any such reservations. For just as the imagination involves a transition not necessarily bound to any fixed point in space, so too the course of remembrance is able to *deliver* us. We may also follow Hölderlin in his mature philosophical thought according to which, for the course of remembrance, the transition is made by way of an insight that is, in virtue of its content, in itself placeless. Both sorts of transition constitute essential stages in the course of remembrance. Thus we can only pursue this course by being in accord with it, in the absence of external, mitigating factors. And this is precisely what we do whenever we hear and understand Hölderlin's poem.

This of course implies, on the other hand, that we ought to grant the poem the status of philosophical reflection. To the extent that we take up questions of philosophy, we cannot forgo questions in the theory of knowledge, nor the problem of determining the origins of consciousness. And so too the possibility remains of giving a rational account of the internal constitution of thought and insight on grounds that are neither simply Fichte's nor those Hölderlin would have regarded as decisive. It is enough to get clear about the fact that, when it comes to offering such an account, nothing under consideration amounts to an objection to understanding the course of remembrance as a deliverance and transformation of consciousness in a final insight. Nor does anything stand in the way of taking up this course in the earnest pursuit of truth, and understanding its achievement of that insight as a kind of truth in which conscious life is illuminated and takes a stand on itself and its origin. By itself this decides nothing. But neither does it set anything decisive against Hölderlin's claim that such insight is grounded in poetry, which leads the course of remembrance into ultimate clarity.

It is nonetheless perfectly in order, in the interest of hermeneutical and epistemological clarity, to draw a distinction between the inner form of the course of remembrance and the various other conditions of identity with which an analysis of the poem as a medium of insight would have to concern itself.

Since the course of remembrance is laid out in a poem, then, and inasmuch as its unity and constitution are accessible to the understanding, there appear to be *five* conditions for attributing to it a kind of identity. These conditions must first of all be differentiated. For an analysis equal to the demands of theoretical poetics, however, such a differentiation would offer no more than a point of departure for the more important task of contemplating the complex relations that figure into these dimensions of identity, the way they overlap and interweave, in the construction of the poem and in their effects on anyone familiar with it. For although the poem, in virtue of its structure and its unique universality, forms a conclusive whole by moving into its course of remembrance, it nonetheless speaks in thoughts and experiences to a concrete orientation of conscious life. Its structure in particular anticipates its consummation in a single word and as a complete unit, a whole that is borne out and that promises to endure in this life.

The several senses of identity can be laid out simply as follows: (1) The actual *reader*, whoever and wherever the person is, in whatever biographical context he or she turns to the poem, moves with the course of remembrance unfolding in the poem, holding it in view. One would assume, with a poem of this stature, that the work will only reveal itself to a reader acquainted with it for some time, so that one's understanding of it will be bound up with different periods in one's own life as one becomes more and more familiar with it. But in fact what one has to do is to grasp the insight to which the course of remembrance leads and apply it to one's own self-understanding, which will in turn be bound neither to the place where one reads the poem nor to any specific spatiotemporal locale.

(2) *The author of the poem* (the historical Hölderlin) must answer for a work of this kind. We take it that his own life and thought bore witness to the course of remembrance as it is laid out in the poem. So, in addition to wondering about the authenticity of a poem making claims to thinking in the context of a life's struggle for true understanding, we

can also turn our attention to the place where we know it occurred to Hölderlin, and to the significance it had for his own understanding. On the other hand, the place itself must remain indeterminate with respect to the information *in* the poem itself concerning the course of remembrance, nor does the poem make any attempt to rescue it from that indeterminacy.

(3) *The poet in the poem* is himself wholly caught up within the course of remembrance. But it moves with the greetings and with the wind. It delivers the poet into the sphere of the river, the sphere of the mariners, and leads him toward the indeterminately placed insight revealed within the poem both to him and to the reader. The poetically constructed poet can ride the current through the poem's shifting perspectives, since insight and remembrance follow laws other than those governing movement in actual space-time. But the identity of the poet is no different from that of anyone whose course describes an orbit of insight. Consequently, it is a matter of indifference whether or to what extent the historical poet was pursuing a course of remembrance in the very poiesis of the work, and whether it corresponded to the one in which the poet within the work is drawn. The conditions of the poetic composition itself stand in an especially complex relation to the course of the insight followed through the work.

(4) *The text of the poem* has identity conditions of its own. These conditions are fixed not by location but by the text's linguistic and aesthetic form, which has been able to transcend linguistic boundaries and which in fact has also been realized successfully in other parts of the world.

(5) But the text unleashes and brings into view *the course of remembrance itself*. Its identity is that of a self-moving form, indeed the form of the movement of that thinking in which (according to Hölderlin) the whole of conscious life can become cognizant of its own path and origin. After all, the poem, in accordance with the constitution of remembrance as such, charts the course not (*à la* Fichte) through a clarification of abstract rules but rather as an actual act of remembrance, which as such is able to reconcile life's drives. For remembrance follows the route of the mariners into the sphere of the river. Moreover, it is by means of its structure that the poem sets the course in view in explicit and thoroughgoing relation to itself. This must be distinguished from the self-relatedness already essential to remembrance as such. In the context of the poem, then, remembrance itself must be taken as a conjunction of the fourth and fifth senses of identity.

If in approaching the poem one unwittingly lets one of these senses of identity infiltrate one's questions where one of the others would have been a better guide, then the poem's sense and structure can easily become obscure. Indeed, this can stem from preconceptions that seem irresistible precisely because of their own obscure origins in the connections among the world, conscious life, and the poem itself. And this in spite of the fact that for any comprehensive interpretation it is not the distinctions themselves but precisely those conjunctions of different senses of identity that are of primary importance.

Still, the considerations of Hölderlin's poem developed here have undertaken no such broad commitment. Here the effort has been simply to uncover the course of remembrance as such in the manner in which Hölderlin's poem unfolds it—and indeed in the context of the ideas worked out by Hölderlin himself, as well as those that make sense of the structure of the poem and its philosophical dimension. Our considerations have consequently remained focused on the third and fifth sorts of identity conditions mentioned above, and on the clarity and perspective into which they are brought in virtue of the poem's structure, which as such falls under the fourth sense of identity.[137] Getting clear about this may help to motivate as much as possible the thesis that the course of remembrance is able to deliver the poet in the poem, and with him the reader, into the spheres of the countryside along the Garonne, and thereupon at once to effect a transformation of consciousness. That such a transformation illuminates the poem, as well as the person who reads it, is bound up with the fact, emphasized above in connection with the first sense of identity, that the identity of a person at best only indirectly determines the identity within the course and construction of that person's conscious history, and does so only in relation to two relatively independent variables. One would more readily say that the train of thought and understanding in the course of one's life can depart from the place where one actually lives it out. The very concept of a person includes the capacity for this sort of departure and extension of the understanding. If that understanding transforms consciousness, then it can and will impinge upon the outlines of identity into which a life moves in the real world, a life that in the end also changes and is transformed further in various ways.[138]

The Insight and Structure of the Poem

It is the poem itself that sets out the course of remembrance and brings it into harmony and perspective so that it can be consummated in and bear witness to a final insight. Once this has been accomplished in a reflection on the inner constitution of the sort of thinking remembrance is, it then becomes possible to address the question that motivated our consideration of Hölderlin's poem to begin with. That question had to do with the way the structure of the poem secures and supports the triad in the closing lines.

Hölderlin never turned his attention away from the question concerning the structure and significance of the poetic work.[139] The later texts that have come down to us deal for the most part with the cultivation of the mythic language of the hymns and with the relation between Greek and Hesperian poetry, yet the architecture of poetry remains one of their abiding themes. This preoccupation at the time "Remembrance" was written is best attested by the second letter to Böhlendorff. There Hölderlin offers some insight into the thoughts awakened in him by his "beholding the ancients" in Paris. They helped him to understand "the highest in art, which, even in the highest movement and phenomenalization of concepts, and of everything meant in earnest, nonetheless sustains everything upright and for itself, so that in this sense certainty [Sicherheit] is the highest form of the sign." We may assume Hölderlin is here speaking not just of what we call the "fine" arts but also the art on which poets lay "fateful hands" (StA II, p. 66).[140] This passage in the letter leaves a number of things to interpretation.[141] We can put them to one side and still see that Hölderlin's analysis of the construction of plastic works also applies to the structure of his own poem.

The poem containing and consummating the course of remembrance enters into each of the spheres so as to let them emerge pure, each in its peculiar character, differentiated yet at the same time tied to one another. The poem, inasmuch as it constitutes a course of remembrance, draws together its differentiated moments into a whole in such a way that its structure corresponds to the movement of remembrance itself, holds it thoroughly in view, and so lets it emerge. This is how we should understand the "calculative" reflection with which Hölderlin unveils the landscape along the Garonne in both spheres. It is also why the unveiling of the two spheres is composed so as to focus on the initial revelation in the mind of the reader—weighing each line in order to stress that the second summoning, in contrast to the first, is connected with the foregoing depiction of the city's spheres.[142] But there is more underlying this connection than the fact that the first image had already delivered us into the landscape. More than this, it means that the first sphere, inasmuch as it is the mariners' sphere of the city, also points toward the second sphere, the point of their departure. Here one can only contemplate for oneself the balance achieved, in virtue of the structure of the poem, between the two depictions of the landscape along the Garonne, although the first spans two complete strophes while the second makes up only half the final strophe.

The depiction of the first sphere leads only indirectly into the second, and only through a discontinuity in time (cf. p. 200 above). And this is so on more than merely formal grounds having to do with the poem's composition according to the oppositional modulation of tones.[143] That modulating form itself is grounded in what it brings to expression: it must be understood in terms of the relation between life's conflicting tendencies, the modes of consciousness governing and guiding life and their harmonious interweaving, which must occur so as not to obliterate the opposition between them. In the poem, however, this principle of composition, which remains crucial to the poem's structure, accords with a more significant feature flowing directly from the constitution of the course of remembrance. The analysis of the two summonings of the Bordeaux landscape has already brought it to our attention, so we need only remind ourselves—remind ourselves in such a way, however, that it becomes apparent how the feature relates to the whole of our considerations concerning the constitution of remembrance.

Remembrance is not the same as a retrieval in reproductive memory. It leads back into the withdrawn sphere so that remembrance is what first discloses that sphere's actual constitution and significance. But since this significance must be understood in terms of worldly paths, remembrance is from the outset contained in a consciousness bound up with the origin of all paths, and is therefore open to an insight into the universal. Such an insight, if it is to prove itself explicitly and as a kind of knowledge, can nonetheless only be achieved through stages in the course of remembrance. One might even conclude that the course of remembrance must be set out in a manner that corresponds to the movement of the poem of that title, namely from the point of departure into a sphere whose significance is disclosed in such a way as to fall short of affording something lasting, from which distress and the recollection of need, which are familiar to conscious life, irrupt. Further reflection arising in this need, however, again leads back into a sphere or a place that supersedes the significance of the first, into a whole that in turn becomes the point of departure for an insight encompassing all paths and places, and so allows for something truly lasting. Only then does the course of remembrance come into the unity that lies at its core, and indeed in such a way that it both encompasses and comprehends all oppositions. The course must lead into those oppositions since it is always a course of conscious life's own understanding of itself, a course whose dynamics are rooted in the experience of such dichotomies.

One might even attempt to express this in a formula. Such a formula would have to represent the course of remembrance and the perspective that it achieves in the poem as a fivefold unity: point of departure, initial entry, irruption and initial reflection, second entry, and finally the insight into what is lasting. The sequence of steps is at each point grounded in a notion characteristic of Hölderlin's thought, namely, that without the irruption of the subjective, the insight into what is genuinely lasting would lack the *opposition* from which that insight first gains its special significance. Without the second entry, the insight would not be an insight obtained in remembrance, which as such is also *recollection*. Moreover, without the deliverance from a point of departure into the sphere of the initial entry, remembrance would not amount to depiction, which is presupposed in its being a genuine *inner awareness*. The concluding insight must make the course of remembrance intelligible in its *unity*. And this happens inasmuch as the course of remembrance, as it proceeds, merges with what is understood in the insight, namely the origin and interrelatedness of all the places of the world and all the paths of conscious life.

But we must guard against putting too much faith in such formulas. They encourage the idea that Hölderlin's work could in the end be derived through philosophical deductions, just as Fichte's *Wissenschaftslehre* sought to derive the fundamental synthesis of conscious life. We have no reason to suspect that Hölderlin pursued any such program, nor do we have any grounds for assuming that his central ideas could be developed and refined so as to allow such a program to be carried out. The very idea breaks down anyway in light of the fact that Hölderlin drew the basic tendencies of conscious life from life's own experience of itself, and relied on principles only in arranging them in relation to one another. Indeed, in the end, such a procedure has a greater degree of philosophical legitimacy.[144] But neither is it just an indifferent game to show that the fundamental ideas of Hölderlin's philosophical manuscripts make it possible to understand the constitution of the course of remembrance in relation to conceptual forms of speculative thought. For the consistency of a compellingly constructed form can arise from consistent thinking without any guidance from a reflection bound to the formation of concepts. In the case of Hölderlin's poetic work, however, a different path opens up, insisting in its own way on its affinity to the philosophical understanding with which it was associated and which it left in its wake. That understanding is preserved and at work in the mode of thought from which the poem acquires its structure and force in bringing conscious life to an intimate clarity as something lasting.

A course of remembrance, if it is to correspond to what Hölderlin's philosophical manuscripts have to say about recollection and determination in oppositions, must then take on a certain inner order, an order reflected in the architecture of Hölderlin's poem. The problem of interpreting the poem has been informed by the question of how such a short work acquires the strength to support and contain the triad in the closing lines. For this to be possible, even according to the principles of formal aesthetics, the work must have an inner diversity to support and balance the universality, and thus the significance, of the closing triad. But the order and diversity of its distinct moments cannot simply be taken as a formal structure. For the course here in question is the course of remembrance. Its order must therefore consist in a series of representations, culminating in an emergent awareness. That awareness, however, must be grounded in and borne out by the construction of the course itself.

The course of remembrance corresponds to the course it takes in its double entry into the landscape along the Garonne. The first entry delivers, but is unable to preserve in a lasting way. A reflection thus emerges from it, generated by need yet also tending toward something universal: for it recollects the works and deeds of men, and contemplates the mariners' route, into whose city the first passage had led. This contemplation makes room for the farewell to the mariners, a farewell that no longer calls for preservation and a final destination. Remembrance thereby frees itself for the second depiction of the Garonne landscape, a depiction of the confluence at the vineyard hills. Remembrance is then free to enter into this sphere, where it takes its leave of the mariners. This entry no longer aims at remaining in a single place.[145] The place itself is just a point of transition—on the route of the mariners out into the ocean, and along the course of remembrance toward the placeless insight encompassing all places, including those that have determined the very direction of that course. In answer to the question with which we opened the interpretation, then, we may say that the structure of the poem is able to support the triad in the closing lines as much in virtue of its formal arrangement as through the specific ordering of the stages of remembrance occurring within it.

In addition to these two, there is yet a third principle determining the resonance of these supremely universal lines: the course of remembrance amounts to an awareness of the city and the route of the mariners. The course leads, with the wind and the city, into the vicinity of their lives. The distress of the foreigner, with which the first depiction concludes, leads to an actual meditation on the mariners' route. The second depiction, then, follows them into the sphere in which they take leave of the city and in which the course of remembrance takes its leave of them. Insight into the actual constitution of their life's course takes

shape in the ongoing depiction and meditation: "But the ocean takes /
And gives memory." Since all understanding "is possible only through
opposition" (StA V, p. 285), this insight already lays the ground for
grasping the mariners' route as a whole, and this brings all the paths
of conscious life together in their very opposition. The triad in the closing lines expresses this insight. One sees it all the more vividly if one
sees how these lines at once express the fundamental idea of Hölderlin's
philosophical thought. But anyone who follows the course of the poem
itself needs no such explanation. That the poem culminates in these
lines is evident in its very structure. And this, again, is what constitutes the preeminence of the work. An interpretation provides us not
with the key to some secret meaning but simply with an explicit account of what the poem says and what it gives us to understand.

These three principles, in terms of which the poem's culmination in
a final insight is to be understood, converge in such a way that the first
also presupposes the last. The formal composition of the poem is for
its part grounded in the sequential structure of remembrance. But it is
the unity and differentiation of the city and the route of the mariners
that give content to the course of remembrance and indicate the special
awareness of the ground from which everything lasting emerges. The
resonance of the poem, then, must be understood in terms of a single
principle. That principle, though, has an inner complexion that again
corresponds to the complexion characteristic of the constitution of remembrance itself.

There is, finally, a fourth principle determining the resonance of the
work, discernible on the basis of the constitution of remembrance. The
universality of the insight contained in the triad of the closing lines
does not constitute a mere terminus in the course of remembrance.
Each point along the way has the meditative and visual clarity that it
does solely in virtue of its place in the course of remembrance as a
whole. This is evident already in the fact that the course of remembrance unfolds within the framework of the poem and that it can be
interpreted clearly only from within the poem. Its status within the
poem is carefully determined to be at the service of what it depicts and
what it affords an awareness of. So, each point along the way is, above
all, related to the points that have preceded it. The structure of the
poem allows it to lead a depiction into one sphere in such a way that
remembrance is drawn into it and enveloped by it, without forcing its
connection to the previous spheres back into a merely latent state. Since
the depiction occurs in language in the strophes of the poem, it always
occupies a place within a whole, without thereby restricting the intimacy of the emergence itself. Consequently, each point along the way

moves beyond itself in reverse direction. Each line and each strophe proceeds in virtue of the ongoing movement of the course previously laid out in a precisely structured series, bringing with it, throughout the poem as well as at its conclusion, the anticipation of a larger and as such comprehensible whole.

The poem is therefore the pure consummation of remembrance, since in it the movement of remembrance is carried out in thorough perspicuity, and in anticipation of a totality that itself affords a perspicuous view of the course as a whole. This perspicuous view is the indispensable precondition for the triad of the closing lines belonging in the poem, so that with them the meditation does not run free of the poem itself. Although they ground the departure from the route of the mariners, which the course of remembrance had initially followed, and take on a kind of finality, they do so nonetheless as a consequence of what the course of remembrance had itself realized. The poem is therefore the very opposite of a means that one could forget about or dispense with upon reaching one's goal. If it were, it would be no more than a prolegomenon to philosophical certainty. But on the contrary, the poem taken as a whole is the ground that supports its closing lines, indeed the ground of the determinacy and intelligibility of its unique meaning. This is why Hölderlin thought that poetry, even or rather especially when it culminates in lines that could as easily be philosophical statements, in fact surpasses philosophy in thought and certainty. This is why one can say that the closing lines can be read only as lines of verse. They are supported by the poem only because they fit flush with its overall structure.

Remembrance, as we have seen, is at once the course and the retrospective connection to the whole of the course. The course leads to its goal only if at the same time it leads to an understanding of itself as a course. Without the structure of the whole, the course would not arrive at any such perspicuous view. And without that perspicuous view, its concluding insight would remain groundless and unsupported. It is therefore in virtue of the structure of the poem that the course of remembrance is able to proceed as it does, harboring its conclusion within itself. What is lasting, what stands firmly rooted in the concluding insight, is as much the basis of conscious life as it is the basis of the structure of the work. And since the basis of life lies in remembrance, which is cultivated by and culminates in the poetic work, the basis of life too is grounded in and supported by the structure of the work. The conclusion of Hölderlin's poem is to be understood in this threefold sense: *Was bleibet aber, stiften die Dichter* ("But what is lasting the poets provide").[146] It is this threefold sense that explains why the work bears the title that it does. For it indicates the essence of certainty, whose course it makes manifest in its pure form and dynamic as a work of art.

"Mnemosyne" and "Remembrance"

All our considerations concerning the course of remembrance and the formal structure of Hölderlin's poem thus come to a close. In them we have tried to understand how this poem of Hölderlin's relates itself to and lays claim to philosophic thought. They have also shed light on Hölderlin's notion of what poetry is and what it can achieve, and of the kind of thinking that pursues its own authentic course and, as poetry, achieves its own clarity. It would appear, then, that the interpretation of this one poem ought to shed some light on the whole of Hölderlin's work.

In fact the interpretation of the poem must also delve down to the very foundations of the development of his work taken as a whole. What one discovers in the process are some basic features that all of Hölderlin's great works have in common. One must keep in mind, however, that the present interpretation assumed a limited scope from the outset: our initial question led us to a study of the poem's structural form. To understand this structure one has to see why the poem depicts the landscape along the Garonne twice over. The series of images is grounded in the movement of remembrance. Remembrance is a course leading through various spheres toward an insight of indeterminate location—not a back-and-forth movement between homeland and colony, coming back to an understanding of the original point of departure.[147] Our attempt to understand the constitution of this course itself gave occasion to grasp the unique quality of the thinking that constitutes remembrance, a thinking that culminates in the poetic work. Our considerations have thus centered around an effort to give an account of the structural form of Hölderlin's poem.

For this reason we had to omit from the interpretation a number of things that have hitherto preoccupied interpreters of Hölderlin's poem. As a result, none of the motifs relating to Hölderlin's mythic view of the world have been dealt with or accounted for here. Of course, such motifs and interconnections are thoroughly interwoven with the course of remembrance. Any interpretation seeking to be comprehensive would have to apply to them as well. When Hölderlin evokes wind, river and brook, oak and poplar, night and celebration, dream, departure and "dark light"—there is a hint of meaning that unites them all in the setting of a world in which the Heavenly appear and withdraw and in which a poet speaks, saying of his song that it is "the work of gods and men" (*der Götter und Menschen Werk*). We shall not belabor this dimension of the poem here by hunting down further notes and fragments. Our interpretation will come to rest at the limits we have set for it.

Of all Hölderlin's poems, "Remembrance" is also the one that departs most radically from the rest of his hymns.[148] Connections to the hymns are hinted at but not put directly into words; consequently they form a kind of background or sounding board for the course of remembrance, which calls for a mode of interpretation specially suited to it. One should not expect that simply by grasping these connections an interpretation could arrive at the same insights that such a special effort would have brought to light through its own observations and reflections. Interpretations that have sought to understand Hölderlin's thought and this poem in terms of the world of the hymnal poetry have suffered either by obscuring the structure of the poem entirely or else by presenting it in a distorted and impoverished form. Remembrance and its course do not form some ephemeral thread in Hölderlin's poem that could simply be deduced from deeper principles. Still, there must be some account of how Hölderlin's poem lays out the course of remembrance without any mention of gods or God, whose radiant beam the poet offers to the people, veiled in song (*StA* II, pp. 119–20), or whose word he fosters in the "firm letter" (*vesten Buchstab*) of the poem. If this cannot be explained by saying that the course of remembrance moves only on the surface of the actual act of poetic composition, then the proper account must have to do with a certain inner limit Hölderlin's poem imposes on the way in which it carries the course of remembrance to its conclusion. Only thus does one begin to understand that the structural form of this course reveals an insight that lies at the very heart of Hölderlin's work, but that it nonetheless neither contains nor expands on essential elements in that work. Taking all this into account means bringing a new perspective to bear on all considerations of Hölderlin's poem. The perspective extends far beyond the point at which such considerations converge and so presents them with a new challenge.

Remembrance, in the poem by that name, moves through dichotomies toward a final insight, but is essentially *harmonious*. This is due to the basically lyrical tone of the work. That tone lets pure visual images emerge in such a way that "Remembrance" is not just a great work but also a "beautiful" sounding poem in a straightforward sense. To be sure, it is shot through with a sense of loneliness. That loneliness, however, does not rise to the point of despair but instead remains a muted lament. It is the anguish of the unsheltered subject; it lacks the seriousness associated with apocalyptic experience. The subsiding of this anguish in the final insight emerging from the course of remembrance, then, is also bound up with philosophical certainty inasmuch as it is neither a deliverance from danger nor an end to the darkness of the age.

We have seen that the constitution of remembrance, and the insight at its conclusion, are predicated on an idea basic to Hölderlin's thought, namely, that the One, the origin, has withdrawn forever. But it has left its mark on places and paths in the world, and in the drives of conscious life. These can therefore be located in relation to one another and brought together in the unity underlying them. And yet the way loss and unification take place has not been fully elaborated in these reflections that have helped us to understand the constitution of the course of remembrance. Still, Hölderlin had already begun to develop his theory of tragedy before even beginning the hymns. In its final form, which must be viewed in connection with Hölderlin's translation of Sophocles, the theory seeks to show that the One, pervading all fates, reveals itself not in free insight but only in the demise of the individual. The derivation of this tragic dimension of conscious life figured into the various poems and into the drafts of the hymns.

For its part, however, that derivation proceeds in a different context. It is bound up with Hölderlin's ideas concerning the nature of historical transformations in which insight and catastrophe occur simultaneously. This gives rise to further thoughts concerning the relation of the grounding One to the world, and to the becoming of worlds, in which the One at once loses and transcends itself. The tragic realization of life cannot be conceived apart from an awareness of danger, nor the latter apart from a familiarity with the bewilderment and disorientation of conscious life. What that life seeks to hold onto thus slips through its fingers. This suggests, on the other hand, that the grounding One is able to *withdraw* by crossing over into the world of *Ur-teilungen* (judgments of original divisions). And this in turn is bound up with the idea that the concealment of the One is one of its essential aspects—and hence that the world, constituted on its basis, is pervaded by darkness, and that its paths may therefore lead into an abyss.

Again, this is no more than a rough sketch of one line of thought. It still needs to be carefully worked out. Moreover it would need the following crucial supplement: not only the experience of deprivation and withdrawal but also the experience of the divine and talk of the gods—and from the gods—which is all-important in the hymns, would have to be analyzed in terms of their possible connections with Hölderlin's fundamental metaphysical ideas. The opposition of life's drives, the anguish of deprivation and withdrawal, the presence of the with-drawn god—it is within these three recurring, interconnected motifs, alternating between mundane and elevated meanings, that the very heart of Hölderlin's poetry after 1800 moves and develops. This sort of supplement and elaboration would shed light on the way Hölderlin's thought figured into and indeed contributed to the development of his mature poetry.

But even an incomplete sketch of this sort may convince us that the basic elements of the experience informing the worldview in Hölder-lin's hymns were not imposed from without onto the fundamental ideas evolving in his philosophy, ideas that have afforded us an under-standing of the course of remembrance. Neither must we conclude that Hölderlin abandoned these fundamental ideas, and in doing so at-tained his true poetic thought. If that were so, then "Remembrance" would either have to be excluded from that body of work, or else be-come obscure in any interpretation that ignored or failed to appreciate its structure.

But the course of remembrance can itself flow in different directions from the harmonious one that leads Hölderlin's poem into the country-side along the Garonne and to the triad in its closing lines. A different course would yield works of a different tone. In them the distress in which the ground reveals itself as "annihilating force" (*vernichtende Gewalt*) would itself become language. And the memory would not re-main wholly within the intimacy of evocation but would become the burden of a recollection no longer able to bear its own weight. It would therefore remain within the One from which all paths extend, so that the force too could be transformed into the insight that affords some-thing lasting. Yet the opposition that emerges in these tracks and traces of remembrance would be different from that into which the mariners are led in their wind-blown journey. One might say that it would be driven not by the wind but by the storm of history.

This brings us to another of Hölderlin's poems, one that is related to "Remembrance" by its title: "Mnemosyne." On the basis of our knowl-edge of the various drafts of this work, we can take it to be the one most closely related to "Remembrance," even in its formal structure. It would be going too far simply to trace the conception of the work, which is not yet fully understood, back to the structure of remem-brance. But one can nonetheless see the two works as forming a kind of diptych. They fit this description insofar as they relate to each other precisely by standing in such sharp contrast. Nor is the contrast simply between their respective tones or the mood of their recollections.

Of the two poems, "Remembrance" is the one that might be deemed "philosophical"—not just because it contains an account of the constitution of remembrance, nor because its title could also refer to a philosophical problem, nor because it culminates in the triad in the closing lines, which could themselves qualify as philosophy. More than this, its basic tone is closer to the tone in which one would arrive at and elaborate a philosophical insight. But this too may be misleading. For if conscious life as such knows the distress that determines the basic tone and course of "Mnemosyne," then any thinking incapable of grasping it would be lacking seriousness and truth. Hölderlin, of course, was of the view that any thinking arising from such seriousness can be consummated only in poetic thinking.

In "Mnemosyne" the course of remembrance comes under the sway of fate, a burden to be endured, not grasped or manipulated. The poem's title places it in the realm not of thought but of the catastrophes of a world to whose destiny we remain bound. This poem is therefore related to "Remembrance" just as Hölderlin's basic notion of the One is related to its unfolding in conflict, a process that was to lead from the theory of tragedy over into the myth of the hymns. For this reason one can in the end also characterize the relation between the two poems as follows: "Remembrance" is composed against the background of Hölderlin's fundamental idea in such a way that the One, in which all paths are grounded, and the insight into it, which brings each life into what is lasting, can be attained within a harmonious course of remembrance. The poem thus relates to unity precisely by itself embodying that kind of harmonious course, safeguarded by the differentiation into which the One itself is drawn. "Mnemosyne," by contrast, is defined by differentiation inasmuch as it is a destiny and must tend toward need before any lasting totality could be disclosed to remembrance.

This classification, which is admittedly a bit facile, nonetheless shows the way in which the two poems figure as counterparts within a single basic idea and the conceptual framework that idea is able to disclose. It also shows that this poem more than any other, though its mode of composition stands in need of explanation, helps one to understand Hölderlin's thought—the philosophical as well as the poetic. The relation between the two poems, however, also indicates the problem that any interpretation of Hölderlin's work must now confront. Namely, Hölderlin's thought must be understood in terms of its foundations and in light of the transformations it underwent, both in its potential and in its actual process of composition, that is, in its proper setting. And it is in this context that an approach must be found to the poetic work in which Hölderlin's thinking was begun, carried out, and "borne out" (bewährt) in Hölderlin's sense, so that it might speak truth.

Such an approach should also afford some insight into the design of the hymns following "Patmos." In general they, along with "The Ister," are no longer structured with a view to a totality. In this way, moreover, they are informed by an insight into the grounds of the impossibility of genuine song, the kind that could stand alongside the songs of Pindar. "Patmos" had reached its formal conclusion in that very insight. Some of the later drafts can be understood as attempts to combine the essential features of the poems "Remembrance" and "Mnemosyne," which after all share a common fundamental orientation. Thus the draft entitled "The Titans" says that song "fails" (*der Gesang "fehlet"*), and this in conjunction with images of the memory of Bordeaux. These images introduce a mood untroubled by need. Its depiction is successful when the hymn is still able to speak beyond the boundaries the age would impose upon it, and within which it would fall silent. An insight into this situation will already have made apparent the diptych of "Remembrance" and "Mnemosyne." What this connection indicates is a poetic possibility that would have remained open to Hölderlin had he not succumbed to illness. The traces of that insight, however, can still cast light into the recesses of the disturbed consciousness that produced his very late poems.

An understanding of the course of remembrance, then, brings us face to face with the much broader aspects of Hölderlin's poetic work as a whole.

Afterword

IN conclusion allow me to say again what the aims of this text on Hölderlin's poem "Remembrance" have been. They are distinct but not separate. I have tried to show how Hölderlin preserves and reveals the concrete reality of a landscape as such by representing it in terms of the significance inherent in it. That he does this successfully is a presupposition for realizing the main objective of this text, namely to make the architecture of "Remembrance" intelligible and to show how the structure of the poem supports and makes possible the broad scope of its final lines, which could also figure as the conclusions of a thinking of universal scope. Together with this I then wanted to answer the question, what does the thinking that proceeds as remembrance consist in, and what kind of philosophical consciousness brings it about and makes it intelligible? These reflections have thus also been intent upon demonstrating that Hölderlin transposed his philosophical thought into the poetic construction of the course of remembrance, and that it therefore remains effective within it. These reflections are also intended to contribute to our seeing Hölderlin's work as a whole in the domain of the possibilities for thought and experience opened up by classical German philosophy, so that steps can be taken against Heidegger's interpretation. Finally, they have been an attempt to test a method of interpretation that aspires to complete insight without thereby claiming to have examined a poem of Hölderlin's in every aspect.

The present essay arose from the preparation for publication of a short lecture, prompted by Cyrus Hamlin, for a collaborative colloquium at the annual meeting of the Hölderlin-Gesellschaft in 1984. The task only came to completion, however, in the form of a book. How the ideas in it stand in relation to the philosophical problems I have been pursuing is made clear by the book itself. Studies dating back to 1970 have informed the observations in the first two parts. Since the observations concerning the old Bordeaux and the opening strophe of "Remembrance" had to remain largely tentative and incomplete, and in some respects sought only to give impetus to future research, less tentative studies of Hölderlin's "Heidelberg" and the opening section of the final strophe of "Remembrance" prepared the way for, and so made possible, my claims concerning Hölderlin's way of poetically depicting a landscape and above all the principal thesis concerning the construction of the poem's architecture.

I would like to thank Cyrus Hamlin and Hilary Putnam for their input; Bernhard Böschenstein, Jacques D'Hondt, and Christoph Jamme for an initial reading of the manuscript; the Hölderlin Archives and the collections in Bordeaux, especially M. Avisseau of the Municipal Archives, for various information; and Ursula Martin for her valuable secretarial assistance.

This text is dedicated to Hans-Georg Gadamer. I met him long ago when I was a young student, only just of age, in a discussion and over a game of chess in Marburg. In our many conversations since then we have always been closest to each other in those concerning poetry. I thank him for the early and ever-renewed confidence that one is able to find one's own way in thinking, and for every possible encouragement. Above all I thank him for setting an example of a man whose work is borne out by an ability to find the right words in and regarding important life situations, a teacher, that is, not just of theory but of philosophy in the true sense of the word.

> Doch mit der Zeit erfährst Du dieses sicher.
> Es zeigt die Zeit den rechten Mann allein.
> An einem Tage kennest Du den schlimmen.

> But you will see this sure enough in time.
> For time alone reveals an honest man.
> You'll come to know a scoundrel in a day.

> Sophocles, *Oedipus the King*
> Hölderlin's translation (620–22)

Appendix: Texts of "Remembrance" and "Heidelberg"

ANDENKEN

Der Nordost wehet,
Der liebste unter den Winden
Mir, weil er feurigen Geist
Und gute Fahrt verheißet den Schiffern.
Geh aber nun und grüße
Die schöne Garonne,
Und die Gärten von Bourdeaux
Dort, wo am scharfen Ufer
Hingehet der Steg und in den Strom
Tief fällt der Bach, darüber aber
Hinschauet ein edel Paar
Von Eichen und Silberpappeln;

Noch denket das mir wohl und wie
Die breiten Gipfel neiget
Der Ulmwald, über die Mühl',
Im Hofe aber wächset ein Feigenbaum.
An Feiertagen gehn
Die braunen Frauen daselbst
Auf seidnen Boden,
Zur Märzenzeit,
Wenn gleich ist Nacht und Tag,
Und über langsamen Stegen,
Von goldenen Träumen schwer,
Einwiegende Lüfte ziehen.

Es reiche aber,
Des dunkeln Lichtes voll,
Mir einer den duftenden Becher,
Damit ich ruhen möge; denn süß
Wär' unter Schatten der Schlummer.
Nicht ist es gut,
Seellos von sterblichen
Gedanken zu seyn. Doch gut
Ist ein Gespräch und zu sagen
Des Herzens Meinung, zu hören viel
Von Tagen der Lieb',
Und Thaten, welche geschehen.

Wo aber sind die Freunde? Bellarmin
Mit dem Gefährten? Mancher
Trägt Scheue, an die Quelle zu gehn;
Es beginnet nemlich der Reichtum
Im Meere. Sie,
Wie Mahler, bringen zusammen

REMEMBRANCE

The nor'easter blows,
Dearest to me of winds
Because of the fiery spirit
And safe passage it promises mariners.
But go now, go and greet
The sweet Garonne
And the gardens of Bordeaux
There, where along the sharp
Bank the footpath goes down and deep
Into the river falls the brook
But over them a noble pair
Of oaks and silver poplars looks;

This comes back to me still, and how
The broad tops of the elm wood
Bend above the mill,
But in the courtyard a fig tree grows.
There too on holidays
The brown women walk
On silken soil
At a time in March
When night and day are the same
And over footpaths slow,
Burdened by golden dreams,
Lulling breezes pull.

Someone then
Pass me the fragrant cup
The goblet filled with dark light
So I may be still, for sweet
Is sleep beneath the shade.
It is not good
To be soulless
With mortal thoughts. But good
Is conversation, and to speak
The heart's conviction, to listen to tales
Of days of love
And deeds once done.

But where are the friends? Bellarmine
And his companions? Many
Are shy of going to the source;
For wealth begins
In the sea. They,
Like painters, bring together

Das Schöne der Erd' und verschmähn
Den geflügelten Krieg nicht, und
Zu wohnen einsam, jahrlang, unter
Dem entlaubten Mast, wo nicht die Nacht durchglänzen
Die Feiertage der Stadt,
Und Saitenspiel und eingeborener Tanz nicht.

  Nun aber sind zu Indiern
Die Männer gegangen,
Dort an der luftigen Spiz'
An Traubenbergen, wo herab
Die Dordogne kommt,
Und zusammen mit der prächt'gen
Garonne meerbreit
Ausgehet der Strom. Es nehmet aber
Und giebt Gedächtniß die See,
Und die Lieb' auch heftet fleißig die Augen,
Was bleibet aber, stiften die Dichter.

What is beautiful of the earth
And scorn not wingèd war
Nor to live alone long years beneath
The leafless mast, where the city's celebrations
Do not penetrate the night,
Nor music of strings, nor native dance.

But now to the Indians
The men have gone,
There on the zephyrous peak
On vineyard hills, where down
The Dordogne comes,
And together with the glorious
Garonne sea-wide
The river spills. But the ocean takes
And gives memory
And love keeps the eye attentively fixed,
But what is lasting the poets provide.

HEIDELBERG

Lange lieb'ich dich schon, möchte dich, mir zur Lust,
   Mutter nennen, und dir schenken ein kunstlos Lied,
     Du, der Vaterlandsstädte
      Ländlichschönste, so viel ich sah.

Wie der Vogel des Walds über die Gipfel fliegt,
   Schwingt sich über den Strom, wo er vorbei dir glänzt,
     Leicht und kräftig die Brüke,
      Die von Wagen und Menschen tönt.

Wie von Göttern gesandt, fesselt' ein Zauber einst
   Auf die Brüke mich an, da ich vorüber gieng,
     Und herein in die Berge
      Mir die reizende Ferne schien,

Und der Jüngling, der Strom, fort in die Ebne zog,
   Traurigfroh, wie das Herz, wenn es, sich selbst zu schön,
     Liebend unterzugehen,
      In die Fluthen der Zeit sich wirft.

Quellen hattest du ihm, hattest dem Flüchtigen
   Kühle Schatten geschenkt, und die Gestade sahn
     All' ihm nach, und es bebte
      Aus den Wellen ihr lieblich Bild.

Aber schwer in das Thal hieng die gigantische,
   Schiksaalskundige Burg nieder bis auf den Grund,
     Von den Wettern zerrissen;
      Doch die ewige Sonne goß

Ihr verjüngendes Licht über das alternde
   Riesenbild, und umher grünte lebendiger
     Epheu; freundliche Wälder
      Rauschten über die Burg herab.

Sträuche blühten herab, bis wo im heitern Thal,
   An den Hügel gelehnt, oder dem Ufer hold,
     Deine fröhlichen Gassen
      Unter duftenden Gärten ruhn.

HEIDELBERG

Long it has been I have loved you, and would to my delight
　　Call you mother and make you a gift of an artless song,
　　　　You, of homeland cities
　　　　　　I have seen, the most lapped in beauty.

As the bird of the forest flies above the hilltops,
　　Over the river where it flows before you, the bridge
　　　　Lightly, sturdily vaults,
　　　　　　Loud with the traffic of coaches and footsteps.

As if it were sent from the gods, a magic once transfixed me
　　On the bridge, as I was making my way across,
　　　　Up then into the hills
　　　　　　The radiant distance shone before me,

And the youth, the river, ran out into the plain,
　　Sadly glad, as the heart overflowing with itself
　　　　Perishing with love,
　　　　　　Plunges into the torrents of time.

Sources you had given, had given cool shadows
　　To the fugitive one, whilst the banks looked on
　　　　After him, and their lovely
　　　　　　Trembling image rose from the waves.

Heavily though, looming into the valley, the gigantic
　　Fate-acquainted castle, to its very foundations,
　　　　Crumbled by rough weather;
　　　　　　Yet the eternal sun poured down

Her light of rejuvenation upon the bastion's bulk,
　　Growing old, and all around the living ivy
　　　　Thrived, and friendly forests
　　　　　　Rustled over the castle walls.

Down to the luminous valley bushes blossomed where,
　　Leaning on the hillside, embracing the bank,
　　　　All your happy alleys
　　　　　　Under fragrant gardens repose.

NOTES

Foreword

1. Friedrich Nietzsche, *Sämtliche Werke*, Kritische Studienausgabe, ed. Giorgio Colli and Mazzino Montinari (Munich: Deutscher Taschenbuch Verlag, 1980), vol. 1, p. 171.

2. Alessandro Pellegrini, *Friedrich Hölderlin. Sein Bild in der Forschung* (Berlin: de Gruyter, 1965) p. 39.

3. Wilhelm Dilthey, *Gesammelte Schriften* (Stuttgart: Teubner, 1957–62), vol. 5, p. 144.

4. In 1867, the 34-year-old Dilthey had already published—under the pseudonym Wilhelm Hoffner—an article titled "Hölderlin und die Ursachen seines Wahnsinns," *Westermann's Jahrbuch der Illustrirten Monatshefte* (May 1867), in which he contrasted Hölderlin's "great genius" with the almost total absence of recognition of his achievements in Germany.

5. See Wilhelm Dilthey, *Poetry and Experience*, trans. Joseph Ross, ed. Rudolf A. Makkreel and Frithjof Rodi (Princeton, N.J.: Princeton University Press, 1985), pp. 303–83.

6. See Ernst Cassirer, "Hölderlin und der deutsche Idealismus," in *Idee und Gestalt* (Berlin, 1921).

7. Stefan George, "Hölderlin," in *Blätter für die Kunst*, 11th and 12th series (1919), p. 13.

8. *Hölderlins Sämtliche Werke*, ed. Norbert von Hellingrath, vol. 4 (Berlin: Propyläen Verlag, 1916), p. xi.

9. Martin Heidegger, "Das Wesen der Sprache," in *GA* XII, p. 172.

10. Martin Heidegger, in an interview with the German magazine *Der Spiegel*, Sept. 23, 1966, published posthumously in *Der Spiegel* 23 (1976), p. 214; English translation by M. P. Alter and J. D. Caputo in *Philosophy Today* 20 (Winter 1976), p. 281.

11. Martin Heidegger, "Beiträge zur Philosophie (Vom Ereignis)," in *GA* LXV, p. 422.

12. In this volume, p. 74.

13. In 1985 Henrich himself initiated the "Jena Program," an extensive,

government-supported research program dedicated to the reconstruction of the philosophical and intellectual situation in Jena during the years 1789–95. Unfortunately, only a few of the results have been published so far. For Hölderlin's Jena period, see "Hölderlin in Jena," in this volume, and Dieter Henrich, *Der Grund im Bewußtsein. Untersuchungen zu Hölderlins Denken (1794–1795)* (Stuttgart: Klett-Cotta, 1992).

14. Hölderlin to his mother, June 18, 1799, in Friedrich Hölderlin, *"Hyperion" and Selected Poems*, ed. Eric L. Santner (New York: Continuum, 1990), p. x.

15. Quoted in David Constantin, *Hölderlin* (Oxford: Clarendon Press, 1988), p. 20.

16. G. W. F. Hegel, "Vorlesungen über die Philosophie der Geschichte," in *Werke in zwanzig Bänden* (Suhrkamp: Frankfurt, 1970), vol. 12, p. 529.

17. Heidegger's lecture course of 1941–42 was published as *Hölderlins Hymne "Andenken," GA* LII. His essay "Andenken" appears in *Erläuterungen zu Hölderlins Dichtung* (Frankfurt: Klostermann, 1971).

18. Dieter Henrich, *Konstellationen* (Stuttgart: Klett-Cotta, 1991), p. 16.

The Path of Speculative Idealism

1. M. Brecht, "Die Anfänge der idealistischen Philosophie und die Rezeption Kants in Tübingen (1788–1795)," in *500 Jahre Eberhard-Karls-Universität Tübingen, Beiträge zur Geschichte der Universität Tübingen 1477 bis 1977* (Tübingen, 1977), pp. 381 ff. Brecht has worked out an admirable survey of the works of the *Repetenten* during the period of Hegel's studies. His theme is not, however, concerned with coming to understand the significance and consequences of their positions for the development of speculative-idealistic philosophy.

2. U. J. Wandel, in *Verdacht von Democratismus* (Tübingen, 1981), has brought to light new documents suggesting that Schelling was also involved in political conspiracies as a student. Diez seems to have limited himself to a Kantian attack on the teachings of the church.

3. See D. Henrich and J. L. Döderlein, "Carl Immanuel Diez. Ankündigung einer Ausgabe seiner Schriften und Briefe," *Hegel-Studien* 3 (1965), pp. 276 ff.

4. This emerges from Reinhold's letters to J. B. Erhard, which are published in the edition of Reinhold's letters. I thank the editors for this information.

5. Twenty years ago I called attention to Schelling's Plato commentary and the commentary on Paul in his unpublished writings, and obtained permission from the Literary Archive of the Academy in East Berlin to have them published. Hannelore Hegel then prepared a transcription, and I undertook the arduous study of the contemporary Plato interpretations that Schelling had for the most part known and made use of. Once the Bavarian Academy began preparing the complete edition of Schelling's works, it seemed to me superfluous to publish the Plato commentary outside that edition. Since work on the unpublished writings has been delayed in the edition, however, some preliminary indication of the content and value of the commentary seems appropriate in the context of the present survey.

6. Ch. Jamme has pursued this development in *Ein ungelehrtes Buch* (Bonn, 1983).

7. Important investigations in this area have come out of the Academy editions of various collected works—from the Hegel edition, those of H. Kimmerle and K. Düsing; from the Fichte edition, those of R. Lauth. Nevertheless,

it seems to me that these studies have not yet worked out the conceptual and theoretical connections guiding the development of Hegel's mature speculative thought clearly enough. I have attempted to develop them *in abstracto* in "Andersheit und Absolutheit des Geistes," in *Selbstverhältnisse* (Stuttgart, 1982), pp. 142 ff. A second draft of my extensive manuscript dedicated to this subject, which the publisher has already advertised under the title *Das Andere seiner selbst*, has unfortunately not yet been completed.

8. See H. Timm, *Gott und die Freiheit*, vol. 1 (Frankfurt, 1974).

Dominant Philosophical-Theological Problems in the Tübingen Stift

1. H. E. G. Paulus, "Das theologische Stift in Tübingen in Beziehung auf die neuesten für dasselbe getroffene Verbesserungsanstalten," in *Neues theologisches Journal*, ed. C. F. Ammon, H. C. A. Hänlein, and H. E. G. Paulus, vol. 5, part 1 (Nürnberg, 1795), p. 70.

2. The letter was written on February 26, 1791, in Göttingen. It will be published in the (unfortunately already long-delayed) edition of the correspondence and writings of Diez from the years 1790–94.

3. G. C. Storr, *Pauli Brief an die Hebräer erläutert* (Tübingen, 1789); also *Doctrinae christianae pars theoretica e sacris litteris repetita* (Stuttgart, 1793). This biblical dogmatics, which Storr distinguishes from ecclesiastical dogmatics (he taught both subjects in alternation), appeared in a German translation by C. C. (the younger) Flatt as *Lehrbuch der Christlichen Dogmatik* (Stuttgart, 1803)—an edition considerably enlarged through explanations and references to the literature which were supervised and approved by Storr himself. In 1807, the Latin dogmatics appeared posthumously in a version enlarged with additions from Storr's manuscripts. In the following discussion, passages will be cited from the first edition, but in the translation of 1803 by C. C. Flatt, under the title *Dogmatik*.

4. G. C. Storr, *Annotationes quaedam theologicae ad philosophicam Kantii de religione doctrinam* (Tübingen, 1793); published in German as *Bemerkungen über Kants philosophische Religionslehre* (Tübingen, 1794), translated and with remarks in relation to Fichte's *Versuch einer Kritik aller Offenbarung* by F. G. Süsskind. This translation will be cited as *Bemerkungen* in the following discussion.

5. Storr, *Dogmatik*, Preface, p. xx.

6. F. I. Niethammer, *Philosophische Briefe über den Religionsindifferentismus* (n.p., 1796), p. 13n. This is a special edition printed after the original publication in the *Philosophisches Journal*.

7. C. F. Stäudlin, "Von dem Zwecke und den Wirkungen des Tods Jesu," *Göttingische Bibliothek der neuesten theologischen Literatur* (ed. J. F. Schleusner and C. F. Stäudlin) 1 (1794–95), pp. 875–96.

8. Ibid., p. 876.

9. Ibid., p. 877, with explicit reference to Storr.

10. Carl Christian Flatt, *Untersuchungen über die Lehre von der Versöhnung der Menschen mit Gott*, 2 vols. (Göttingen, 1797–98).

11. M. A. Landerer, *Neueste Dogmengeschichte* (Heilbronn, 1881), p. 168 and n. 2.

12. Cf. J. F. Flatt's letter to F. H. Jacobi of Sept. 29, 1807, in *F. H. Jacobi's auserlesener Briefwechsel in zwey Bänden* (Leipzig, 1825–27), vol. 2, pp. 402–3. In it, Flatt speaks of his wish "to show" Jacobi "his great reverence in person" as one

of his "most heartfelt wishes." And he sends Jacobi the edition of the sermons of "my unforgettable and always dear teacher and fatherly friend, Storr" that he and Süsskind had prepared.

13. Carl Friedrich Stäudlin, *Ideen zur Kritik des Systems der christlichen Religion* (Göttingen, 1791).

14. Published anonymously as *Über Religion als Wissenschaft zur Bestimmung des Inhalts der Religionen und der Behandlungsart ihrer Urkunden* (Neustrelitz, 1795).

15. All the evidence for these claims is to be found in the edition of the letters and writings of C. I. Diez, forthcoming.

16. Ibid., the letters from Diez to Niethammer of June 19, 1790, and July 12, 1791.

17. This is based on an unpublished letter of Reinhold's to J. B. Erhard of June 18, 1792, for knowledge of which I thank the editors of the edition of Reinhold's correspondence.

18. The evidence for this is F. G. Süsskind's response of Feb. 26, 1791, from Göttingen.

19. Cf. D. Henrich, "Leutwein über Hegel," *Hegel-Studien* 3 (1965), pp. 56–57.

20. Cf. Storr, *Dogmatik*, § 107, p. 673, n. 2. Cf. also Storr's essay "Über den Geist des Christentums," *Magazin für Dogmatik und Moral*, ed. J. F. Flatt (1796), pp. 103 ff., esp. pp. 163 ff.

21. Storr, *Dogmatik*, p. 675, from which the following quotation is also drawn.

22. Cf. note 4 above.

23. Cf. note 7 above.

24. Storr, *Bemerkungen*, p. 237.

25. Ibid., pp. 238–39.

26. Ibid., p. 223.

27. F. G. Süsskind, "Über die Gründe des Glaubens an eine Gottheit, als außerweltliche und für sich bestehende Intelligenz, in Beziehung auf das neueste System der absoluten Identität," in *Magazin für christliche Dogmatik und Moral, deren Geschichte und Anwendung im Vortrag der Religion*, vol. 11 (Tübingen, 1804), pp. 143 ff.; vol. 12 (Tübingen, 1805), pp. 24 ff., esp. pp. 150 ff.

28. I have developed the following reflections in connection with the "Jena Project," for which the Bavarian State Ministry for Education and Culture furnished special financial assistance.

29. In a review of Fichte's *Versuch einer Kritik aller Offenbarung*, in *Neue allgemeine deutsche Bibliothek. Des zweiten Bandes erstes Stück* (Kiel, 1793), pp. 3–48, the possibility is already considered that "Herr Fichte may not be altogether in earnest with his theory of revelation" (p. 43). Hegel's remark on the danger connected with Fichte's work, like Schelling's suspicion, may be derived from this review alone, which was probably written by Gottlob Ernst Schulze. (Cf. J. G. Fichte, *Gesamtausgabe*, ed. R. Lauth et al., vol. 1 [Stuttgart-Bad Cannstatt, 1964], p. 13.)

30. Cf. K. Rosenkranz, *G. W. F. Hegels Leben* (Berlin, 1844; photomechanical reprint, Darmstadt, 1963), p. 40.

31. Cf. D. Henrich, "Hölderlin's Philosophical Beginnings," in this volume. Hölderlin's excerpts from the "Spinoza book" are based on the first edition. Hölderlin may also have possessed the second edition (cf. *StA* IV, pp. 397–98. The copy on which this supposition is based was barely, if at all, worked through

by him. When, how, and on the basis of what copy Hölderlin studied the second edition will not be discussed here. If, however, one considers the importance accorded the second edition and its appendix VII in Tübingen, the supposition is well founded that precisely this text did not escape Hölderlin's attention. Jacobi himself also, in the course of the second edition, refers repeatedly to this appendix.

32. The version in the *Werke* of F. H. Jacobi, published in 1819, is revised and does not reproduce all the notes of the second edition. The reprint in H. Scholz, *Die Hauptschriften zum Pantheismusstreit* . . . , *Neudrucke seltener philosophischere Werke*, edited by the Kant-Gesellschaft, vol. 6 (Berlin, 1916), does not include the whole of the preface, which is important in this context.

33. Cf. also note 12 above.

34. J. F. Flatt, review of Jacobi's *Spinoza* in *Tübingische Gelehrte Anzeigen*, Nov. 8, 1787, pp. 713 ff. That this review was written by Flatt is clear from, among other things, a self-quotation on p. 718.

35. J. F. Flatt, review of Jacobi's *Spinoza*, 2nd ed., *Tübingische Gelehrte Anzeigen*, Apr. 29, 1790, pp. 266 ff. That this review too is by Flatt is shown by its style and the central points of the questions it addresses to Jacobi. Flatt was responsible for the reviews of the philosophical literature at least until Abel came on the scene in 1791. At the time of Flatt's transfer to the theological faculty (Spring 1792) at the latest, the quality of this part of the *Anzeigen* declined noticeably.

36. F. H. Jacobi, *Über die Lehre des Spinoza*, second, expanded edition (Breslau, 1789), p. 415A.

37. In this line of thought there emerges for the first time a model for theories that became crucial for the speculative idealism of Hegel, Hölderlin, and Schelling: finite consciousness can be grasped only through a principle that neither has the status of a Kantian idea nor can be defined in terms of the form of consciousness as such. It is nonetheless "present" in this consciousness as its ground of possibility in a fashion that it is one of the most essential tasks of philosophy to define.

38. Kant did this himself in his letter to Jacobi of Aug. 30, 1789. *Kants gesammelte Schriften*, Akademie-Ausgabe (Berlin, 1900 ff.), vol. 11, p. 75.

39. Hegel to Schelling, Nov. 2, 1800. See *Briefe von und an Hegel*, vol. 1, ed. J. Hoffmeister (Hamburg, 1952), p. 59.

Hölderlin's Philosophical Beginnings

1. Information about the editions then available is given in Friedrich Gottlieb Klopstock, *Werke und Briefe*, Historisch-Kritische Ausgabe (Berlin and New York, 1981), pt. 3, vol. 1, pp. 115 ff.

2. To determine the precise edition is a task for students of Hölderlin's relation to Klopstock. It should be noted only that Hölderlin in the fourth line writes *Sehn's* and *glauben's* ("see it" and "believe it") with an apostrophe, so the apostrophes must have been copied. Editions of the day differ in their manner of writing these two verb forms and also in the spelling *Glük* ("happiness"); the Hamburg edition of Klopstock gives the verb forms without apostrophes and writes *Glück*.

3. Cf. *StA* II, pp. 141 and 715. F. Beißner's explanatory notes to the hymn

and also the interpretation of its closing lines by W. Binder (*Hölderlin-Jahrbuch* 21 [1978–79], pp. 170–205, esp. pp. 202 ff.) can thus be supplemented with some knowledge resulting from the inscription in Niethammer's *Stammbuch*. It should also be mentioned that Heidegger closed his lecture cycle of 1941–42 on Hölderlin's hymns with precisely these final verses from "Die Wanderung"; cf. Martin Heidegger, *Hölderlins Hymne "Der Ister,"* GA LIII, p. 206.

4. Niethammer's *Stammbuch* is in the possession of the family of Freiherr von Haniel-Niethammer in Schloß Tunzenberg in Lower Bavaria. The author came to know of it almost twenty years ago while engaged with Johann Ludwig Döderlein in a search for the widely scattered but considerable literary remains of Niethammer. Thanks are due to the owners for their permission to publish the material discussed here. I would also like to thank Maria Kohler for providing much information in the course of editing. The *Stammbuch* (from which one entry, presumably in Schiller's hand, is missing) consists of two parts, distinct in format, with respectively 171 and 68 almost continuously numbered loose single pages. It is full of entries for the years 1786 through 1794, but for the years thereafter it contains only sporadic entries. Along with many other informative entries is one by Novalis, with the early date of April 16, 1791. (This entry has been made available for the Novalis edition.)

5. The entry should be compared with the almost contemporaneous *Stammbuch* entry for C. C. Camerer, which is published as an appendix and thereby hidden away in StA III, p. 569. Hölderlin signed it, too, "C. Hölderlin" ("C." for *candidatus*).

6. On Niethammer see M. Schwarzmaier, *Friedrich Immanuel Niethammer, ein bayerischer Schulreformator,* in *Schriftenreihe zur bayerischen Landesgeschichte,* vol. 25 (Munich, 1937); E. Hojer, *Die Bildungslehre F. I. Niethammers,* in *Forschungen zur Pädagogik und Geistesgeschichte,* vol. 2 (Frankfurt u.a., 1965); G. Lindner, *Friedrich Immanuel Niethammer als Christ und Theologe,* in *Einzelarbeiten aus der Kirchengeschichte Bayerns* (Nürnberg, 1971). None of these works has fully evaluated the available biographical sources (to be found primarily in Tübingen and Stuttgart). Schwarzmaier's account provides an essentially correct report of Niethammer's development. Materials now no longer available are used in a manuscript biography by F. von Lupin, on which in turn J. Döderlein, *Unsere Väter* (Erlangen and Leipzig, 1891), is based. The von Lupin work was also used by Schwarzmaier. From Niethammer's own curriculum vitae in *De persuasione pro revelatione . . .* (Jena, 1797), which was also used by Schwarzmaier, a connection can be drawn to Hölderlin's entry in the *Stammbuch* that is essential for the present reflections.

7. Cf. the chart of family relationships in the appendix to H. W. Rath, *Regina, die schwäbische Geistesmutter* (Ludwigsburg, 1927), supplemented and expanded by H. Decker-Hauff in a later edition (Limburg, 1981).

8. Cf. StA VII, p. 401, esp. ll. 14–18, and app. A, pp. 22 f.

9. Niethammer, in *De persuasione . . . ,* pp. 6–7 of the curriculum vitae.

10. Niethammer's diploma, received after the theological examination of summer 1789 (Landeskirchliches Archiv, Stuttgart, A, 13 no. 1, vol. 4), says only "studia philosophica et philologica non neglecta." The contrast with Hölderlin's diploma of 1793 is striking. The latter contains the well-known remark "Philologiae, inprimis graecae, et philosophiae, inprimis Kantianae, . . . assiduus cultor" (StA VII, p. 479, no. 129).

11. On the position of such "senior students" in the *Stift* see the letter from

Süsskind of Dec. 2, 1790, second paragraph, in the forthcoming edition of Diez's letters and writings.

12. Schwarzmaier, *Niethammer*, gives parts of the passage in translation, and citations are from his text.

13. There are, however, a number of clues for identifying Niethammer's benefactor: one can formulate a hypothesis regarding the patron even from the dedication of Niethammer's work, *Philosophische Briefe über den Religions-indifferentismus* (n.p., 1796), to the city secretary Krais in his hometown Beilstein (Krais was an uncle of Niethammer's, see von Lupin, manuscript biography of Niethammer, p. 29). Further, according to von Lupin, Niethammer later supported Krais's grandson during his studies. From Diez's letters to Niethammer in Jena it further appears that Niethammer wrote letters to Krais that he sent to him via Tübingen.

14. See von Lupin, manuscript biography of Niethammer, pp. 10–11. Fischer made an inscription on page 36 of Niethammer's *Stammbuch* on July 5, 1786, and renewed the entry in Jena on July 5, 1790. Other natives of Tübingen, too, went to study in Jena; cf., e.g., M. Brecht, "Die Anfänge der idealistischen Philosophie und die Rezeption Kants in Tübingen (1788–1795)," in *500 Jahre Eberhard-Karls-Universität Tübingen, Beiträge zur Geschichte der Universität Tübingen 1477 bis 1977* (Tübingen, 1977), pp. 381–428, 390. And Schiller and Paulus taught there, two of the best-known Schwabians of the time.

15. Diez's entry of March 23, 1790, reads: "People judge gladly and often, but they are reluctant to investigate matters and seldom have the information necessary for doing so. A comforting remark, if we allow it the influence it deserves on our disposition to oppose received judgments! Let this be said without any reference to what YOU, my K. [Klett] have said on the other side. It applies to us, my friend N.! Your true friend, Diez." This text, which already shows Kantian influences, is an indication of the task that Niethammer and Diez set for themselves: a thorough examination of the foundations of theology and dogma. (In the *Stift*, Niethammer was a year ahead of Diez.)

16. Niethammer, in *De persuasione . . .* , p. 8 of the curriculum vitae.

17. See *StA* VI, pp. 48 f., letter 29, and A. Beck, "Hölderlin und das Stift im November 1789," in *Glückwünsche aus Bebenhausen. Wilhelm Hoffman zum fünfzigsten Geburtstag am 21. April 1951* (privately printed by Dr. A. Kelletat, Schloß Bebenhausen, 1951), pp. 18 ff.

18. See Document 72, in *Briefe von und an Hegel*, vol. 4, ed. F. Nicolin (Hamburg, 1977), p. 89.

19. Niethammer, in *De persuasione . . .* , p. 6 of the curriculum vitae.

20. See Diez's letters to Niethammer of June 19, 1790, in the forthcoming Diez edition.

21. *StA* VI, pp. 190 f., letter 111, ll. 4–6.

22. *StA* VI, pp. 202 f., letter 117, ll. 6–9.

23. See the author's "Hölderlin on Judgment and Being," in the present volume.

24. *StA* VII, p. 579, ll. 10–12.

25. Niethammer had already become a *Privatdozent* in 1792, and in 1793 *professor extraordinarius* in the philosophical faculty of Jena.

26. In the Tübingen theological faculty this was the domain of Professor J. F. Maerklin. Niethammer's diploma (see note 10 above), like his curriculum vitae (see note 6), does not mention Maerklin as one of the professors with whom

Niethammer had studied closely. It would nevertheless be possible to establish with fair probability, through an analysis of Maerklin's position and doctrines, which of the numerous compendia must have received particular attention in Niethammer's examination on the foundations of moral theology. For the contemporary literature see E. Luthardt, *Geschichte der christlichen Ethik seit der Reformation*, vol. 2 (Leipzig, 1893).

27. See, e.g., "Lebenslauf Hegels aus dem Konversationslexikon von 1824," in Nicolin, ed., *Briefe von und an Hegel*, document 107, pp. 127 f.

28. The first qualifying essay (1785) with an unambiguously Kantian theme was that of the later tutor to a prince, professor of law and luminary Karl Heinrich Gros. It was the second of Gros's three qualifying essays and had the title "Entwurf einer Prüfung des Kantischen Systems." Gros had also attended Flatt's lectures. See also Brecht, "Die Anfänge der idealistischen Philosophie," p. 389, and, for the research on the *Stift* with regard to Hegel and Hölderlin, Brecht's articles in *Hegel-Studien* and in the *Hölderlin-Jahrbuch* cited there.

29. Niethammer, in *De persuasione . . .* , p. 7 of the curriculum vitae.

30. *StA* VI, pp. 63 ff., letter 41. The Stuttgart edition (*StA*) contains Hölderlin's notes on Jacobi's Spinoza book in vol. 4, pp. 207–10, as well as dates for Hölderlin's studies of Jacobi and Spinoza in vol. 4, pp. 397 ff., and vol. 6, letter 41, l. 34; letter 94, l. 48; and above all in the commentary on these letters.

31. See Schwarzmaier, Hojer, and Lindner (note 6 above). After the middle of the year Diez began to draw the radical conclusion from the Kantian limitation of all knowledge to possible experience and quite simply denied altogether the possibility of certainty based on revelation. This position could be defended only with difficulty after Fichte's *Attempt at a Critique of All Revelation* (1792) and Kant's own book on religion (1793). This explains Niethammer's speedy reception of Fichte's work.

32. *StA* I, pp. 114 f. and 414. On the Alderman's Days see *StA* I, p. 406.

33. See, however, *StA* VI, p. 54, letter 33, ll. 12 ff.

34. *StA* VI, p. 470, letter 34a, ll. 15 ff. Hölderlin opens his statement on the importance of philosophical study for him with the intimation "There is still a great deal more I intend to do."

35. Diez states in his letter to Niethammer of June 19, 1790: "From the beginning of February, with the exception of a three-week interruption and a few little trips, Reinhold, Kant, and Schulze occupied me almost entirely."

36. One can suppose that Hegel's rapid conversion to Hölderlin's position—which Hölderlin had worked out in Jena in 1795—after Hegel's arrival in Frankfurt in the beginning of 1797 was at least favored by Hegel's knowledge of Hölderlin's philosophical intensity since 1790. (Their common philosophical reading included, aside from Plato, precisely Kant and Jacobi; cf. K. Rosenkranz, *G. W. F. Hegels Leben*, [Berlin, 1844; photomechanical reprint, Darmstadt, 1963], p. 40). Hegel's change of direction in Frankfurt can certainly be explained above all through the inner power of Hölderlin's new position and through the credibility that it possessed by being a product of the milieu in Jena—and also through Hegel's philosophical sympathy for its contents insofar as they were capable of being given theoretical form. But Hegel also trusted Hölderlin from their Tübingen experiences to "lead" and "guide" him (*StA* VI, p. 222, letter 128, ll. 41 ff., and the commentary to this passage). Hölderlin, on the other hand, sees Hegel as his mentor in situations in which his "temperament" made him "into a stupid youth." Hegel's formulation, however, points more in the direction of help with theoretical problems (cf. Maria Cornelissen, *Hölderlin's*

Ode "Chiron" [Tübingen, 1958], p. 103), although Hölderlin also calls Niethammer "Mentor," and in this case with an eye to the philosophical guidance he had received from him (cf. *StA* V, p. 203, letter 117, l. 24). We could make more assured conjectures on this matter if we could set Hegel's first steps toward a philosophical system in relation to those of Hölderlin with respect to both content and chronology. But the documents from Hegel's studies of philosophy in the narrower sense are meager for the Tübingen and Bern periods. And current research is—with grave consequences—disoriented by the preconceived notion that in the materials that, for special reasons, have come down to us, one can find a full and complete picture of Hegel's philosophical development. But it is rather to be assumed that the young family tutors, when they set out on their long and expensive journeys, could not take with them—nor thus preserve—everything that had been committed to paper. For that reason it is possibly not even an accident that Hölderlin's letters to Hegel are more completely preserved than the letters of Hegel to Hölderlin. Thus the volumes of correspondence in both collected editions need perhaps to be reviewed anew with an eye to the preservation of letters that were received and the particular reasons the recipients could have had for keeping precisely these letters.

37. Cf. *StA* VI, pp. 49 ff., letters 30 and 31 and their dates (*StA* VI, pp. 550 f.).

38. Cf. M. Brecht, "Hölderlin und das Tübinger Stift 1788–93," in *Hölderlin-Jahrbuch* 18 (1973–74), pp. 20–48, esp. pp. 38 ff.

Hölderlin on Judgment and Being

1. The present study was originally intended for Karl Löwith's *Festschrift* and thus was written exclusively for philosophical readers. Since that volume grew beyond the limits set by the publisher, it was possible to issue this essay in the *Hölderlin-Jahrbuch* and thus to lay it before a wider circle of the friends of the philosophical poet.

2. See the author's "Historische Bedingungen der Philosophie des deutschen Idealismus," in D. Henrich and J. L. Döderlein, "Carl Immanuel Diez. Ankündigung einer Ausgabe seiner Schriften und Briefe," *Hegel-Studien* 3 (1965), pp. 276 ff.

3. Ernst Cassirer, "Hölderlin und der deutsche Idealismus," in *Idee und Gestalt* (Berlin, 1921), pp. 109 ff.

4. Wilhelm Böhm, *Hölderlin*, vol. 1 (Halle, 1928), pp. 141 ff.

5. Kurt Hildebrandt, *Hölderlin, Philosophie und Dichtung* (Stuttgart, 1939), pp. 82 ff.

6. Johannes Hoffmeister, *Hölderlin und die Philosophie* (Leipzig, 1942), pp. 4, 55, 68, *et passim*.

7. Ernst Müller, *Hölderlin. Studien zur Geschichte seines Geistes* (Stuttgart, 1944), pp. 2 ff., 6 ff.

8. Dieter Jähnig, *Vorstudien zur Erläuterung von Hölderlins Homburger Aufsätzen*, Ph.D. diss. (Tübingen, 1955); Lawrence Ryan, *Hölderlins Lehre vom Wechsel der Töne* (Stuttgart, 1960); Ulrich Gaier, *Der gesetzliche Kalkül* (Tübingen, 1962).

9. Friedrich Hölderlin, "Urtheil und Seyn," in *StA* IV, pp. 216–17; cf. p. 738, ll. 4 ff.

10. *StA* III, pp. 309 f., and Maria Cornelissen, *Orthographische Tabellen zu Handschriften Hölderlins*, Veröffentlichungen des Hölderlin-Archivs no. 2 (Landesbibliothek Stuttgart, 1959).

11. Hölderlin writes *Seyn, Bewußtseyn*, but at one point also *Bewußtsein* (*StA*

IV, p. 216, l. 13); alongside *Theilung* and *Urtheil* we also find *Gegenteil* (ibid., p. 217, l. 3); we also find the old spelling *Wahrnemung*.

12. Hölderlin twice (ibid., p. 216, ll. 27, 28) corrected *Sy* to *Seyn;* the pressure to write in the new way made him hurry over the *e*. At one point he corrects *oneh* to *ohne*, and thus in the first instance used the old version as at p. 217, l. 4. (Cf. p. 738, ll. 17, 20.) I am indebted to Maria Cornelissen for this clarification of the dating of the sheet by means of its spelling.

13. Schelling's preface is signed "Tübingen, 29 März 1795." This was the date of Palm Sunday that year. Therefore the earliest the work could have been available for printing and for binding was Easter Week. The Tübingen bookseller Heerbrandt was Schelling's publisher. If one assumes that he worked very fast and that Schelling wrote his preface after the rest of the work, several weeks must still have passed before the work could have come into Hölderlin's possession. Schelling's preceding work, *On the Possibility of a Form of Philosophy in General* has an afterword that was finished on September 9, 1794. Schelling, however, sent Fichte a copy only on September 26. He certainly sent it off as quickly as possible. The publisher, then, needed something over two weeks for production. One therefore has to assume the same for Schelling's work *Of the I as Principle of Philosophy.* It was indeed slated to appear at the Easter fair, but when the fair actually took place is not clear. It was the general custom, however, to deliver many of the works announced in the catalogue only after a certain delay. Probably a great deal more time passed before the book was available. Schelling did not send the copy set aside for Hegel until July 21. This date may be owing to the timing of their correspondence. Fichte, too, wrote on July 2 to Reinhold: "Schelling's work is, as far as I have been able to read it, wholly a commentary on my own." This remark seems to imply that the work had not been in Fichte's hands for long, but Schelling had certainly sent it to him as soon as possible. His cover letter has unfortunately not survived. (In the edition of Fichte's correspondence, edited by H. Schulz [Leipzig, 1925], vol. 1, p. 481 n. 2, is based on a mistake.) Furthermore, announcements and reviews of the work did not appear any earlier. It remains to note that the book in which Hölderlin wrote his reflections later titled "Judgment and Being" cannot have been Schelling's *Of the I,* for the format of the latter work is smaller than that of the sheet of paper. Fichte's *Wissenschaftslehre* was issued by the sheet and therefore needed to be bound later. It is impossible, then, to draw any conclusions from the type of paper used. Its format does not exclude the hypothesis that Beißner proposes in *StA* IV, p. 402, l. 20.

14. The part of the text printed second was probably the first in order of composition. Cf. below.

15. *Briefe von und an Hegel,* vol. 1, ed. J. Hoffmeister (Hamburg, 1952), p. 25.

16. L. Ryan, *Hölderlins Hyperion* (Stuttgart, 1965), p. 37; cf. also pp. 36, 44, 55, *et passim.*

17. Schiller's letters appeared in three series in *Die Horen,* nos. 1, 2, and 6 (1795).

18. *StA* VI, p. 137, letter 88, ll. 96–97.

19. The prose sketch for the metrical version, the metrical version itself, and "Hyperions Jugend," *StA* III, pp. 186–206.

20. *StA* I, pp. 189–90, l. 488; cf. *StA* VI, pp. 135 ff., letter 88, ll. 99–100.

21. Cf. D. Henrich, "Der Begriff der Schönheit in Schillers Ästhetik," *Zeitschrift für philosophische Forschung* 11 (1956), pp. 527–47. English translation in T. Cohen and P. Guyer, eds., *Essays in Kant's Aesthetics* (Chicago, 1982).

22. At *StA* IV, p. 217, l. 4, Hölderlin corrected the beginning of the question

"May I . . . ?" to "How can I say: I! without self-consciousness . . . ?" The manner of correction ("May" is written over with "How," and "Can" is inserted before "I" over the line) suggests that the correction took place after the whole sentence was already written down and there was no more space to cross out what had been written and to replace it.

The correction signifies a change in the mode of thought: the question "May I say . . . ?" seems to demand some discussion; the question "How can I say . . . ?" is clearly just rhetorical—it already implies a negative answer. And Hölderlin's next sentence in fact presupposes such an answer: if "I" is not to be thought without self-consciousness, one must ask how such self-consciousness is possible in order to discover that it comes to be by means of opposition. One can of course also read the question "May I . . ." in light of what follows as merely rhetorical, as in "May I then do it at all? . . . Indeed not." The correction, on this view, would have aimed at making as clear as possible in the very form of the question the absurdity of the assumption that there could be an I without self-consciousness. Thus arose the formulation "How can I . . . ?" with the unequivocal sense of "How can one possibly . . . ?" This correction is hard to understand if one does not see in it the hand of the author. If Hölderlin had copied out the text, he probably would not even have noticed the mistake. The line of thought we are led to expect by the question "May I . . . ?" would not have been altogether absent in the following sentence, and so the usual motive for subsequent changes would have been lacking. The author of these ideas, on the contrary, had good reasons for making the correction. For it relieves him of the task of securing the evidence that "I" is conceivable only as self-consciousness.

This one instance alone warrants the assumption that Hölderlin presents himself as the author of the theses concerning judgment and being. That does not exclude the possibility that there had already been another written text before this one. In that case the text on the flyleaf would be a summary, perhaps even in part a compressed abstract from his own writing—possibly from his own notes. It could equally well be the record of thoughts Hölderlin arrived at and gave voice to in the course of a conversation. The author thanks Friedrich Beißner for a long conversation about the sheet "Judgment and Being" which resulted in this note.

23. It also accords with this view that the three errors in spelling occur in the second part (*StA* IV, p. 216, ll. 27 and 28; p. 217, l. 4). In the first part Hölderlin's hand seems to have gotten surer. As far as the content and argument of the text is concerned, the present second part can be read without difficulty as the first.

24. These observations are based on a photocopy of the original, which is in the possession of the Hölderlin Archives in Stuttgart.

25. *StA* VI, p. 159, letter 95, l. 99; cf. also p. 711, ll. 31 ff.

26. Sinclair's letter to the University of Jena of November 25, 1795, Archive of the University of Jena, Fach 161, no. 2224a.

27. *StA* VI, p. 198, letter 114, ll. 17f.

28. *StA* VI, p. 185, letter 106, l. 60.

29. See *StA* VI, p. 185, letter 106, l. 60, and ibid., p. 189, letter 109, l. 24.

30. *StA* VI, p. 198, letter 114, l. 16; *StA* VI, p. 201, letter 116, l. 18; and *StA* VI, p. 210, letter 121, l. 86

31. *StA* VI, p. 201, letter 116, l. 19.

32. *Varnhagens Tagebücher* (Leipzig, 1861), vol. 2, note for Tuesday, June 11, 1844, *et passim.*

33. "Philosophische Raisonnements und zusammengereihte Sätze," in the

Varnhagen von Ense Collection in the Königliche Bibliothek in Berlin, indexed by Ludwig Stern (Berlin, 1911), p. 764.

34. For this there is reliable evidence, which will be made public at the appropriate time. [In 1977, Henrich published his findings in "Beethoven, Hegel und Mozart auf der Reise nach Krakau," *Neue Rundschau* 88, no. 2, pp. 165–99. Subsequently, the Polish authorities made the autographs accessible again in the Bibliotheka Jagiellońska in Krakow, Poland.—Ed.]

35. After his book *Der Hochverratsprozeß gegen Sinclair* (Marburg, 1949), W. Kirchner was preparing further studies of Sinclair.

36. Kirchner's literary remains were donated to the Hölderlin Archives by his widow. There the present author noticed the importance of Sinclair's manuscript and was generously given permission to examine and publish it by the director of the archives, Herr Dr. Hoffmann.

37. Walter Lotz, "Die Beziehungen zwischen Friedrich Hölderlin und Issac von Sinclair und ihr Verhältnis zu Hegel (Ph.D. diss., University of Basel, 1924).

38. The material for the proof of this thesis will be available in the abovementioned monograph by Hannelore Hegel. [See now Hannelore Hegel, *Isaak von Sinclair zwischen Fichte, Hölderlin und Hegel* (Frankfurt, 1971). In the meantime, the originals have been rediscovered; see Christoph Jamme, "Isaac von Sinclairs 'Philosophische Raisonnements.' Zur Wiederauffindung ihrer Originale," *Hegel-Studien* 18 (1983), pp. 240–44.—Ed.]

39. Ludwig Strauß, "Jacob Zwilling und sein Nachlaß," *Euphorion* 29 (1928), pp. 368–96, cf. p. 388. These literary remains regrettably disappeared without a trace after the end of the war. Despite the efforts of Adolf Beck and the present author, the search for it in Bad Homburg has not yet been successful.

40. See *StA* VI, pp. 180 f., letter 104 (to Schiller); *StA* VI, pp. 202 f., letter 117 (to Niethammer); *StA* III, pp. 235–37 (preface to *Hyperion*); and *StA* I, pp. 197–98 ("An die Unerkannte").

41. *StA* VI, pp. 180–81, letter 104, l. 14. Like this one, the following references from letters are not mere reformulations. They also serve the purposes of interpretation in that they bring out the direction of Hölderlin's thought more clearly.

42. In the original, of course, there is a question mark at the end of the poem.

43. *StA* VI, pp. 155–56, letter 94. Hölderlin had felt from the outset that Fichte's thought and language needed an interpretation that he had not yet himself provided. This is not just the result of the difficulty in comprehension that all readers of Fichte found themselves having. Hölderlin felt his language to be irreconcilable with his explicit, considered convictions. What it sought to communicate, however, seemed to him of extraordinary importance. Compare the tone of the remarks in letter 94, ll. 48 and 65–66; letter 97, l. 76; letter 103, ll. 54–55; letter 104, l. 14; and *StA* III, p. 190, ll. 20–21.

44. *StA* VI, pp. 155–56, letter 94, ll. 57 ff.

45. Hölderlin derived original being by apparently legitimate means from the principle of critical philosophy, i.e., consciousness. His derivation of being relied on means that cannot in principle be distinguished from those found in Fichte. Thus Hölderlin could believe that the way to the thought of "Judgment and Being" remains more faithful to Kant's *Critique* than did the return to Plato, which seemed to signify a further step beyond the Kantian frontier (*StA* VI, p. 137, letter 88, l. 96). Consequently, in the Jena version of *Hyperion* Hölderlin's

concern is to disarm Kantian objections to his ideas (cf. *StA* III, p. 192, l. 4; p. 202, l. 3).

46. See the author's "Fichtes ursprüngliche Einsicht" (Frankfurt, 1967), translated as "Fichte's Original Insight," in D. E. Christensen, ed., *Contemporary German Philosophy*, vol. 1 (University Park, 1982), pp. 15–53.

47. Even during the period of Hölderlin's madness Kant was Hölderlin's only philosophical memory. The few words that have come down to us will admit of interpretation only on the basis of an understanding of the role of philosophy in Hölderlin's work.

48. In the following I shall merely indicate in a series of assertions the thematic areas about which more extensive studies have become possible and urgent.

49. *Briefe von und an Hegel*, vol. 1, p. 22.

50. Schiller to Goethe, October 28, 1794; see *Fichte in vertraulichen Briefen seiner Zeitgenossen*, ed. Hans Schultz (Leipzig, 1923), pp. 50–51.

51. This can be inferred from K. A. von Reichlin-Meldegg, *Heinrich Eberhard Gottlob Paulus und seine Zeit* (Stuttgart, 1853), pp. 97 and 226.

52. *Kritische Friedrich-Schlegel-Ausgabe*, ed. Ernst Behler (Munich, 1963 ff.), vol. 18, pp. 4 ff.

53. Isaac von Sinclair, "Über dichterische Composition überhaupt, und über lyrische insbesondere," in *Glauben und Poesie*, edited by Lucian (Berlin, 1806), reprinted in Norbert von Hellingrath's edition of *Hölderlins Sämtliche Werke* (Berlin, 1922), vol. 3, pp. 569 ff.

54. *Briefe von und an Hegel*, vol. 1, pp. 322, 354.

55. *StA* VI, p. 191, letter 111, ll. 36–37; ibid., p. 203, letter 117, l. 42.

Hölderlin in Jena

1. Immanuel Kant, *A New Exposition of the First Principles of Metaphysical Knowledge (Nova dilucidatio)*, trans. John A. Reuscher, in *Kant's Latin Writings*, ed. Lewis White Beck (New York: Peter Lang, 1986).

2. F. H. Jacobi, *Über die Lehre des Spinoza*, second, expanded edition (Breslau, 1789), p. 424.

3. C. L. Reinhold, *Versuch einer neuen Theorie des menschlichen Vorstellungsvermögens* (Prague and Jena, 1789).

4. F. I. Niethammer to F. P. von Herbert, June 2, 1794, published in Dieter Henrich, *Der Grund im Bewußtsein. Untersuchungen zu Hölderlins Denken (1794–1795)* (Stuttgart, Klett-Cotta, 1992), pp. 828–34, 832.

5. F. I. Niethammer, "Von den Ansprüchen des gemeinen Verstandes an die Philosophie," *Philosophisches Journal* 1, no. 1 (May 1795), p. 39.

6. F. I. Niethammer, review of J. C. C. Visbeck, *Die Hauptmomente der Reinholdischen Elementarphilosophie*, *Philosophisches Journal* 2, no. 3 (Nov. 1795), pp. 257–58.

Hegel and Hölderlin

1. Cf. the entry in the diary of Princess Marianne of Prussia, in Werner Kirchner, *Hölderlin, Aufsätze zu seiner Homburger Zeit* (Göttingen, 1967), pp. 120–21.

2. In the poem "Eleusis," printed in (among other sources) *Briefe von und an*

Hegel, vol. 1, ed. J. Hoffmeister (Hamburg, 1952), p. 38. In what follows, only explicit quotations and a few important less-known passages will be cited. Otherwise, since reference is made throughout to the writings of Hegel and Hölderlin during their Frankfurt period, further documentation has been omitted.

3. Hegel's insistence is to be inferred indirectly from Hölderlin's reply. Cf. *StA* VI, p. 222.

4. Hegel, *Briefe,* vol. 1, p. 322.

5. See especially Earl of Shaftesbury, *The Moralists,* pt. 3, sec. 2.

6. Cf. Franz Hemsterhuis, *Sur le desire,* concluding paragraphs.

7. G. W. F. Hegel, *Vorlesungen über die Ästhetik,* in Hegel, *Sämtliche Werke,* ed. H. Glockner (Stuttgart, 1927–40), vol. 13, p. 152.

8. Schiller to Reinwald, April 14, 1783, in F. Schiller, *Werke,* Nationalausgabe, vol. 23 (Weimar, 1956), pp. 78–82.

9. Concerning the paradoxes resulting from Schiller's use of Kant's terminology contrary to Kant's intentions, see D. Henrich, "Der Begriff der Schönheit in Schillers Ästhetik," *Zeitschrift für philosophische Forschung* 11, no. 4 (1958).

10. Plato, *Phaedrus* 250a ff.

11. Fichte's *Eigene Meditation über Elementarphilosophie,* out of which the rise of his *Wissenschaftslehre* can be fully reconstructed, will soon appear in the Fichte edition of the Bavarian Academy of Sciences. [Fichte's text has since appeared in vol. II, 3, of that edition.—Ed.]

12. So it is dubbed by Karl Marx in a letter to his father, November 10, 1837. See *The Marx-Engels Reader,* ed. Robert C. Tucker (New York, 1972), p. 8.

13. These arguments are interpreted in D. Henrich, "Hölderlin on Judgment and Being," in this volume.

14. Isaak von Sinclair, "Die Bekanntschaft" [The Acquaintance], in *Gedichte von Crisalin* (Frankfurt am Main, 1812), vol. 2, pp. 188 ff. Note in the volume title that "Crisalin" is an anagram of "Sinclair." Hannelore Hegel first drew attention to this poem. [That Sinclair's poem refers to Hegel has been challenged effectively by Otto Pöggeler, "Sinclair-Hölderlin-Hegel," *Hegel-Studien* 8 (1973), pp. 19 ff.—Ed.]

15. This view is expressed in the second part of Hegel's text that Herman Nohl gave the heading "Moralität, Liebe, Religion" [Morality, Love, Religion], in Hegel's *Theologische Jugendschriften,* ed. H. Nohl (Tübingen, 1907), p. 376.

16. Two drafts lie behind the fragment bearing Nohl's title "Die Liebe" [Love]. Only in the second does Hegel pose the problem of the origin of the manifold.

17. Cf. Hölderlin's "Der Archipelagus" [The Archipelago], final stanza.

18. *Fichtes Werke,* ed. I. H. Fichte, vol. 1 (Berlin, 1971), pp. 204–5.

19. G. W. F. Hegel, *Jenenser Realphilosophie,* in *Sämtliche Werke,* ed. G. Lasson (Leipzig, 1931), vol. 2, p. 182.

20. G. W. F. Hegel, *Encyclopedie,* secs. 452 ff.

21. Hegel, *Briefe,* vol. 1, p. 332.

22. G. W. F. Hegel, *Phenomenology of Spirit,* trans. A. V. Miller (Oxford, 1977), Preface, sec. 17, p. 10, translation modified.

23. Hegel, *Sämtliche Werke,* vol. 19, p. 685.

The Course of Remembrance

1. Cf. Norbert von Hellingrath's observation in his edition, *Hölderlins Sämtliche Werke,* vol. 4 (Berlin, 1916), p. 303.

2. "Remembrance" is not strictly speaking a poem of homage since it does not actually evoke and celebrate Bordeaux and the Garonne landscape.

3. Cf. p. 213 below.

4. *StA* II, pp. 167, 175, 182, 186.

5. This view is first formulated in the preface to "Fragment of *Hyperion*," *StA* III, p. 163.

6. The effort, under way by 1960, to clarify Hölderlin's doctrine of the modulation of tones, along with its applications in his work, has made essentially no progress since that time. The following proceeds from one manifestation of the modulation in the poems that does not really follow strict laws of succession. Such laws would be strict if they involved a rule of combination for all possible poetic forms in general. The distinction becomes clear in light of the difference between the work of L. Ryan, *Hölderlins Lehre vom Wechsel der Töne* (Stuttgart, 1960), and that of U. Gaier, *Der gesetzliche Kalkül* (Tübingen, 1962).

7. M. Heidegger, *Hölderlins Hymne "Andenken," GA* LII, p. 51. Only since the publication of his three Hölderlin lectures has it become possible to see how Heidegger's interpretation of "Remembrance" relates to his reading of Hölderlin and to his own philosophical work. See Heidegger's *Erläuterungen zu Hölderlins Dichtung* (Frankfurt, 1944), expanded in 1951 and again in 1971 and finally published as *GA* IV (Frankfurt, 1981); *Hölderlins Hymnen "Germanien" und "Der Rhein," GA* XXXIX; and *Hölderlins Hymne "Der Ister," GA* LIII. It is important to keep in mind that Heidegger's interpretation of "Remembrance" is guided not just by his own thought, above all his theory of truth as it had developed by the early 1930s, but also by earlier interpretations of other hymns, and that it took shape under the influence of F. Beißner's reflections on the relation between Greece and Hesperia. See Friedrich Beißner, *Hölderlins Übersetzungen aus dem Griechischen* (Stuttgart, 1933; 1961), which is in turn based on the fragment of "Brod und Wein" on the relation between the colonies and the fatherland, published by Beißner (*op. cit.*, pp. 147 ff.). The critique of Beißner's interpretation is summed up in A. Beck, *Hölderlins Weg zu Deutschland* (Stuttgart, 1982), pp. 180 ff. H.-G. Gadamer very early and convincingly addressed it ("Hölderlin und das Zukünftige" [1947], in his *Kleine Schriften II* [Tübingen, 1967], p. 52 A), in spite of Beißner's critique (*StA* II, p. 621). See also H. J. Kreutzer, "Kolonie und Vaterland in Hölderlins später Lyrik," *Hölderlin-Jahrbuch* 22 (1980–81), pp. 18 ff.

8. Cf. R. Zuberbühler, *Hölderlins Erneuerung der Sprache aus ihren etymologischen Ursprüngen* (Berlin, 1969), p. 88.

9. This is certainly true of the depictions in "Heidelberg," "Remembrance," and in the second stanza of "Der Ister," though not of those in "Stutgart." Still, it should be pointed out that any attempt to interpret Hölderlin's work, which is a considerable task, would have to aim at understanding the way he depicts localities and landscapes he never set foot in, in contrast to his depiction of things he actually experienced. Notwithstanding its promising title, D. J. Constantine's *The Significance of Locality in the Poetry of Friedrich Hölderlin* (London: Modern Humanities Research Association, 1979) has contributed little to this question. However, there are some interesting topographical research to be found concerning Hölderlin's poetic depiction of landscapes familiar to him in D. Sattler's *Friedrich Hölderlin: 144 Fliegende Blätter*, 2 vols. (Köln, 1981), e.g., vol. 1, p. 109. Cf. P. Bertaux, "Hölderlin in und nach Bordeaux," *Hölderlin-Jahrbuch* 19 (1975–77).

10. Cf. pp. 220 ff. below.

11. Cf. Heidegger, *GA* LII, p. 91 (see also *GA* XXXIX, pp. 248 ff.). Among the many things that Heidegger's interpretation of Hölderlin's work leaves out is Hölderlin's faithful preservation of the intimate language to which he had become accustomed at home in the company of his loved ones. Such intimacy is the tenderness of being close that lets lovers feel happy together and that brings out their true nature in easy, tender words. Such intimacy contains within it the strength of the heart that wants to open itself to and take in the other, the life and nature of the one to whom it opens itself; and an experience of the fact that lives opened up and embraced in this way has found an ultimate and everlasting ground of lives bound together and interwoven. Intimacy, then, theoretically speaking, is subjectivity, openness to the world, and metaphysical certainty all in one. A thinking that thinks itself able to address what it calls *das Seyn* (being) only once it has already exposed the movement of subjectivity as a self-referring forgetfulness of being belongs, from a historical point of view, among the short-lived attacks on the formative experiences that gave rise to the very lifeworld of the Germans as well as to the fundamental notions of classical German philosophy. Hölderlin's thought, which grants poetry the last word, together with the poems, which bring together what is referred to today as the "culture of inwardness" on the one hand and the rational form of that fundamental notion on the other, taken together amount to a key to the self-understanding of a possible form of life. Heidegger was never close to this—neither in the phenomenological-Aristotelian orientation of his thought nor in the experiences he regarded as decisive. But Hölderlin's work goes beyond cultural boundaries and casts light on the substance of such experiences. It can attest to them as possibilities for life wherever it finds resonance with a similar experience that has not sunk under the weight of inhibition. For that reason, however, it might also happen that a people, helpless in the face of an embroiled history and a present marked by uncertainty and readjustment, and having retreated into sheer superficiality, will one day no longer have an ear for the language of Hölderlin.

12. What one might call the speculative sense of intimacy is associated throughout Hölderlin's work with connotations of a kind of devotion and togetherness of conscious life, above all at the beginning of "Grund des Empedokles" (*StA* IV, p. 149), in the essay "Über den Unterschied der Dichtarten" (ibid., p. 268), and in the letter to Sinclair of Christmas Eve, 1798 (*StA* VI, p. 299), but also for example in the sketch entitled "Gestalt und Geist" (*StA* II, p. 321). The speculative concept of this relation, which means a (generally reciprocal) being-in-one-another or a being-contained-in-one, can also quite easily be combined with the humane sense of a closeness that opens up and reveals the conscious life of the other without interruption or reservation. One might say that the word itself, which refers to the way human beings devote themselves to and concern themselves with one another fully and from the bottom of their hearts, could only develop from such a formal sense of relation. In Fichte's work, too, *innig* has a formal systematic meaning, indeed it means a synthesis that makes a differentiated activity into a single act, or lets it be understood as such (cf., e.g., J. G. Fichte, *Sämtliche Werke*, ed. I. H. Fichte, vol. 1 [Berlin, 1971], p. 124). Hölderlin, who along with Fichte did not want to give up "subjective experience" as the site for the unfolding of the speculative principle of all reality, once again reunited intimacy in conscious life with the systematic sense of a speculative concept. It is all the more inappropriate, then, that Heidegger

should deliberately set out to undermine the substance and richness the philosophical poet brought to this "fundamental word" of speculative thought. Cf. R. Guardini, *Hölderlin* (Munich, 1955), p. 203. It should be kept in mind that these remarks can only point in the direction of the pending analysis of the uses of *Innigkeit* in Hölderlin's work.

13. Cf. the epigraph of the first volume of *Hyperion*. [*Non coerceri maximo, contineri minimo, divinum est*. "Not to be confined by the greatest, yet to be contained by the smallest, is divine."—Trans.] It should be understood in light of the main ideas of Hölderlin's unification philosophy.

14. One could describe Hölderlin's way of poetically transforming landscapes, in connection with his own theory of poetry, as the construction of a "metaphor" (*StA* IV, p. 266). Everything would then rest on understanding this "metaphor" as a translation that *preserves*—not as a hypersophisticated elevation that strays from its roots in an experience grounded in sober contemplation.

15. Heidelberg was a postal station with a generally lengthy stopover on one of the most important routes of the day, namely that between Frankfurt and Stuttgart.

16. The movement of images dominates the transition from present to preterite tense and back to present in the last line. Through the present tense in the depiction of the bridge and the present tense of the last line, a latent but significant division is established between the bridge and the city streets. And in contrast to the preterite tense of the other evocations, the present tense stresses the "repose" of the streets with which the poem concludes. Any continuation of the poem (*StA* II, p. 412) could only have attached further present-tense images to this structure, which is already self-contained, even in the modulation of its tenses. Any such continuation was deliberately avoided; cf. p. 157 below.

17. This way of understanding the depiction of the bridge is only implicit in the most important interpretations. Indeed the issue is often raised only to suggest that Hölderlin's image of the trajectory of the bird's flight is in no need of interpretation, and need only be repeated. This is true of the most important interpretations of the ode: E. Staiger, "Hölderlin: 'Heidelberg,'" in *Gedicht und Gedanke*, ed. H. O. Burger (Halle, 1942), more readily available in E. Staiger, *Meisterwerke deutscher Sprache aus dem 19. Jahrhundert* (Zurich, 1943), pp. 14–15; A. Beck, "'Heidelberg': Versuch einer Deutung," *Hölderlin-Jahrbuch* 2 (1947), p. 51; also C. Hamlyn, "Hölderlins 'Heidelberg' als poetischer Mythos," in *Jahrbuch der deutschen Schillergesellschaft* 14 (1970), p. 442; also clearly R. Guardini, *Form und Sinn der Landschaft in den Dichtungen Hölderlins* (Tübingen, 1944), p. 26. Attempts to clarify the intuitive substance of Hölderlin's image, though not fully adequate or precise, are found in R. K. Goldschmit, *Heidelberg als Stoff und Motiv der deutschen Dichtung* (Berlin, 1929), p. 16 ("delicate power of the line"); H. Chr. Schöll, "Wie von Göttern gesandt," in *Merian*, Heidelberg volume (Hamburg, 1949), p. 50 ("in gentle ascent and corresponding dropping off of the bridge, that trajectory"); and Otto Pöggeler, "Hegel und Heidelberg," *Hegel-Studien* 6 (1971), p. 71 ("which vaults itself over the pillars in the river"). One aspect essential to any reading is discussed by W. Schneider, *Liebe zum deutschen Gedicht* (Freiburg, 1969), p. 89 ("the comparison highlights not the building material but the form . . . the series of arches from shoreline to shoreline"). See also *StA* II, pp. 407–8, 412–13.

In studying the historical illustrations of the bridge, I was able to avail myself of the collection of the Kurpfälzischen Museum in Heidelberg. Concerning the structure of the bridge, incidentally, compare A. v. Oeschlhäuser, in *Die Kunst-denkmäler des Großherzogtums Baden*, vol. 8, part 2: *Die Kunstdenkmäler des Amtbe-zirks Heidelberg* (Tübingen, 1913), pp. 102–3.

18. "Trajectory" (*Schwung*) generally indicates the elevating and energetic movement up and over something, from one point to another. But the trajec-tory of the bird's flight reaches from point to point across a series of trajectories in which the "vaulting" strokes position the whole. A similar unity is found in the physical structure of the bridge, conceived as movement. A detailed exami-nation of the genesis of the text, of course, shows that Hölderlin first posited only the unified trajectory of the entire bridge in the linguistic form of the po-etic lines. For after *StA* II, p. 410, l. 9, he at first wrote "(schwingt sich) . . . *der* Bogen der Brüken" (emphasis added). This rendering, however, was rejected and replaced by a more precise image: "(schwingt sich) . . . leicht und kräftig die Brüke" (l. 10). If one does not take the genitive *der Brüken* to mean the series of arches and thus to be the genitive plural, one can just as easily infer from the origin of the lines some grounds for doubting whether, in comparing the bridge to the bird's flight and speaking of its "vaulting" (*Schwung*), Hölderlin had the construction of the trajectory out of the individual arches in mind from the very beginning. One can also doubt whether he wanted to introduce this construct into the image of the poem at all. The switch to *leicht und kräftig* ("light and sturdy") might then be explained as a mere reification of the language and desire to dispense with the use of the abstract term *Bogen* and instead more accurately characterize the unity of a single trajectory. It should be added that, in doing so, Hölderlin again took up both of the first two characterizations of the trajectory of the bridge and the bird. The draft of the first line had originally begun with the word *Majestäti*. This was immediately crossed out. But another characterization was added to the beginning of the second line: *Stolz und kräftig* ("proud and sturdy"). With the new addition of *leicht und kräftig* to this motif in the third line, which at once replaces the *Bogen der Brüken*, Hölderlin achieved a successful characterization that satisfied him in the end since it omits all predi-cates that are not purely descriptive. That he replaced *Bogen der Brüken* can be explained by reasons of poetic economy for the ode, an economy that was not realized in the first version. In the series of characterizations, however, Hölder-lin attempted above all to capture in language the height and clarity of the arch-ing trajectory up and over the hilltops.

On the other hand, with regard to the second ground for doubt that might arise from these examinations of the genesis of the text, it should be noted that the course of poetic evocation consists not just in the choice of words but also in the precise delineation of a remembered view. The fact that such a delinea-tion can proceed, and the way it does so, deepening the memory as it goes, can be clearly recognized on several levels in the origin of the final strophe of "Remembrance" and in the second evocation of Bordeaux. Such a remembered view, however, can be perfectly exact without also being reflectively and lin-guistically organized to full satisfaction. We can no longer determine which of these two modes of a memory, made precise, corresponds most to the genesis of the bridge stanza. At any rate, the correspondence of the bridge's movement with the trajectory of the bird's flight first emerged fully concrete in the final choice of words. Hölderlin therefore worked out the complex substance of the analogy, which had at least occurred to him from the start, first gradually and then into the full correspondence of images in which the height, clarity, and double trajectory of a movement are all grasped as one. And this is the best reason, in view of the version of the stanza ultimately accepted, why in it the singular *Bogen* was stricken—a word that does immediately capture the unity and the effect of the vaulting motion, though not the constitutive series of arches (at least not definitively). The version that thus emerged still satisfied Hölderlin when he made a revision resulting in an even more precise image of what the bird was passing over in its flight. This revision implies that Hölderlin concerned himself further with the image of the birdlike trajectory of the bridge as a whole. The image of the text that then corresponded with the double aspect of the trajectory of the bridge also withstood these revisions—in contrast to the talk of "hilltops" (*Gipfeln*), which seemed to Hölderlin in need of greater precision. So, what is to be viewed as an objection can also serve as grounds for a deeper insight into the dynamics of the evolution of the poetic representation.

The final revision of the same draft (a page in the Heidelberg Kurpfälzsichen Museum), which aims at rendering more precise the image of what the bird passes over in flight (and which is interpreted above, pp. 151–52), probably predated the fair copy that went to press. And the preliminary version of this copy has been preserved as well. Consequently we must assume that Hölderlin rejected the final revision in the end. It remained a merely programmatic effort and so belongs to a kind of elucidation of the work by its creator, rather than a version that might appear in an edition of his works. A study of Hölderlin's handwriting would require color photographic reproductions.

19. One can read about the flightpaths of individual species of birds in volume 13 of Brehm's work on animal life in the new edition by A. Meyer, and about the flight of birds in general in M. Stolpe and K. Zimmer, *Der Vogelflug* (Leipzig, 1939), and in K. Lorenz, *Der Vogelflug* (Ph.D. diss., University of Vienna, 1933; Pfulligen, 1965). More than a decade ago I was able to correspond with K. Lorenz concerning Hölderlin's image of the bridge. As an expert on the subject of bird flight, he found the reference to the flight of the woodpecker quite plausible.

20. What might count against attributing the image to the flight of the woodpecker is that woodpeckers—accustomed to flying below the hilltops—only rarely vault "over hilltops" as high as the trestles of the bridge. Speaking in its favor, however, is the fact that the woodpecker is, after all, the great "bird of the forest." The bridge is an important structure whose grandeur mirrors the breadth of the river. It is visible from afar and is evoked in the poem from a distance. So one has to consider the "bird of the forest" capable of a flight that can be called "majestic" at first sight. Hölderlin begins this stanza with the word *Majestäti* (*StA* II, p. 410). This characterization finds no corroboration in the flight of small woodland birds. But neither should we think of the other great birds, as well as birds of prey (which are not forest birds, with the exception of the wood grouse, the cuckoo, and the owl). For their flight is not an arching trajectory. And it cannot be called, as in the definitive version of the stanza, *leicht* (light) and sturdy. Among the bridges known to Hölderlin, the Heidelberg bridge, in spite of its massive stature, is striking in its gracefulness and in the clarity of its lines. So it is entirely possible that Hölderlin also tried to capture its uniqueness by means of a simile with an uncommonly high-flying woodpecker.

21. The beginning of the revision (see n. 18 above) also makes it clear that Hölderlin must have seen the continuous trajectory of the bridge from the north bank of the Neckar through to the city. For the modified text reads "across the river toward you vaults" (*so schwingt über den Strom sich dir*). One ought not to suppose, for example, that the woodland bird should be thought to be literally flying toward the city. In Hölderlin's day too, wine, not forests, thrived on the slopes of the north bank—just as on the hills at the confluence of the Dordogne and Garonne. The image of the flight is an image of the pure dynamism in the structure of the bridgeworks.

22. Cf. Staiger, *Meisterwerke deutscher Sprache*, p. 15, and A. Beck, "'Heidelberg': Versuch einer Deutung," p. 59.

23. Eichendorff has perhaps captured this peculiarity as well, in that other great poem about Heidelberg, if with a precision not quite equal to that of Hölderlin's language and imagery:

> Geblendet sahen zwischen Rebenhügeln
> Sie eine Stadt, von Blüten wie verschneit
>
> Dazzled, they saw between the vineyard hills
> A city covered as if in a snow of blossoms

I have referred to Hölderlin's view of the streets beneath the gardens in "Kein Abschied von Heidelberg," *Heidelberger Jahrbücher* 27 (1983), p. 61.

24. To begin with, it should be pointed out that Hölderlin's image of the gardens above the streets of Heidelberg should be understood in connection with the following interpretation of the "gardens of Bordeaux." I shall also show that these gardens belong to the city proper and that their appearance makes an unmistakable impression. I shall claim, too, that these two interpretations substantiate each other. It is inconsistent with neither of them that Hölderlin tends to evoke cities with reference to their landscapes and to the movements within them, toward the city. In the gardens of Heidelberg and Bordeaux the landscape itself is assimilated into the life of the city in such a way as to impress one with a clear image. A cultural-historical study could be made of Hölderlin's experience of the division between the gardens and the life of the city, a study that would have to clarify the meaning of incorporating the gardens into the life of the residents of the city in the closing years of the eighteenth century. For a good portion of intellectual life was taking place somewhere in the gardens and houses of Jena during the time of Hölderlin's visit. (Cf. R. Zuberbühler, *Hölderlins Erneuerung der Sprache*, p. 93.)

25. Hölderlin's line that has the castle "heavily . . . looming into the valley" (*schwer in das Thal hieng*) also rests on a precise image: the castle sits high atop a promontory on the steep slope of the Königstuhl. Before the view from the riverbank to the castle had become obstructed, one could see the castle in this way as it hung over the city on the steep slope from which it might otherwise slide down.

26. One cannot leave entirely out of account the fact that Hölderlin had also seen engravings of Heidelberg, which were common at the time. The interpretation of "Remembrance" will show, however, that the evocation of the landscape along the Garonne could only have come to him from memory. There was, moreover, no contemporary depiction at all of the "zephyrous peak," according to the generous information of M. Avisseau at the municipal archives of Bordeaux.

27. The following interpretation is based on my visit to Bordeaux in the summer of 1972. Such a visit can shed some light on that city's general topographic conditions. Yet the image of the city and the harbor has so changed that the more important insights are to be gained only by studying the contemporary and historical literature, including old postcards and engravings. I obtained some information in the municipal archives of Bordeaux, above all from M. Avisseau, and from J. du Pasquier in the Musée des arts décoratifs, which was recommended to me by W. Walz (cf. note 35 below). Citizens of Bordeaux, above all the secondhand-book seller Bernard Picquot, offered friendly and very helpful advice. Hölderlin's visit is a well-known fact to many citizens. Picquot was immediately able to identify the site of the landed estate of Consul Meyer in Blanquefort and to report that it just stood there empty, so that it was possible to familiarize oneself with all the rooms in the house. Efforts to work with F. G. Pariset by mail have unfortunately come to naught (cf. note 50 below).

28. Recall the "flight of the eye" from the Neckar and the Rhine to the "golden Pactolus" in "Der Neckar" (*StA* II, p. 17); the evocation of Stuttgart from a course toward Lauffen and back (ibid., pp. 87–88); the eagle's flight in "Germanien" (ibid., p. 150); the transformation of the place the poet speaks of in "Die Wanderung" (ibid., p. 140); and the flight in the abduction of Germania to Asia Minor in "Patmos" (ibid., pp. 173–74). "Die Wanderung" articulates the capacity of such journeys to move the poet over wide distances in the course of a poem (*StA* II, pp. 138–39):

> Ich aber will dem Kaukasos zu!
> Denn sagen hört' ich
> Noch heut in den Lüften:
> Frei sei'n, wie Schwalben, die Dichter.

> But I am off to the Caucasus!
> For I heard it said
> Just today on the breezes
> That free as swallows are the poets.

29. This is the result of a comparative study of Wordsworth's "Intimations of Immortality" and Coleridge's "Dejection" in relation to Hölderlin's "Remembrance," for which I am grateful to a seminar at Harvard University and to the stimulating remarks of C. Hamlin.

30. A little-known example of this is the fantasy images of the English painter John Martin. See F. Baumgart, *Vom Klassizismus zur Romantik 1750–1832* (Köln, 1974), pp. 196–98.

31. In what follows I shall rely on these two terms without analyzing them, though they stand in need of analysis. Sense (*Sinn*) is that in virtue of which the actual is open to interpretation; significance (*Bewandtnis*) is the way in which that sense points to other senses.

32. Cf. pp. 149–50 above. Pp. 189–205 below concern themselves with an interpretation of this double evocation, along with the use of the word *dort* ("there") in both cases. The interpretation is elaborated in note 111 below in connection with an account of why both evocations and both occurrences of *dort* are preceded by an *aber nun* ("but now") or *Nun aber* ("now though").

33. See *StA* II, pp. 92, 173, 217–18, 244, 263, 340.

34. In addition to Heidegger's reading one should mention above all those of J. Schmidt, *Hölderlins letzte Hymnen* (Tübingen, 1970), and Zuberbühler, *Hölderlins Erneuerung der Sprache*. B. Böschenstein has recently made important observations on "Remembrance" as a document pertaining to Hölderlin's understanding of Dionysus: "Geschehen und Gedächtnis," *Le Pauvre Holterling*, no. 7 (Frankfurt, 1984), pp. 7–16. In the still rather limited literature, these three studies especially deserve notice. (The interpretive efforts of E. E. George, *Hölderlins Ars Poetica* [The Hague, 1973], and R. Unger, *Hölderlin's Major Poetry* [Bloomington, Ill., 1975], though noteworthy in their own right, make no mention of "Remembrance.") The Hölderlin Archives furnishes a bibliography, including all passing references to "Remembrance" in publications, which I have used extensively without finding any further information relevant to the formal structure of "Remembrance" or the questions posed in this investigation. In this study I have had to forgo any comprehensive consideration of that literature and of the three publications mentioned above. In orientation, and with regard to fundamental questions concerning Hölderlin, my views are close to those of Schmidt, with whose observations concerning the poetic form of "Remembrance" I am in agreement. Schmidt himself (pp. 12–13n) notes an agreement with Zuberbühler, which is surprising in light of the entirely different approaches and orientations of the two studies. The agreement lies in the conception of "Remembrance" as a "celebration of the most elevated consciousness" (Zuberbühler, p. 87), or as a vision of the "harmonic coherence of life" (Schmidt, p. 47). It is my intention to show how such a consciousness can be derived from the constitution of the course of remembrance in the formal structure of the work, and indeed from the double depiction of the countryside along the Garonne. C. Hamlin's interpretation has not yet appeared and so has not been included. I have mentioned the works of Schmidt, Zuberbühler, and Böschenstein only in passing because it seems more important to challenge Heidegger's reading directly and to present "Remembrance" with a knowledge of its themes and assumptions so as neither to neglect Hölderlin's thought nor simply to foist ideas ascribed to him onto his work. I shall refer to this debate as far as possible in the notes. In advancing his own interpretations Heidegger ignores all inappropriate and uninfluential approaches to Hölderlin. An interpretation driven and inspired by Hölderlin's work ought not to be kept constantly on its guard against every polemical distraction. Still, anyone who departs fundamentally from Heidegger's reading must at the same time take account of his own thought in terms of its formative conditions, as the mode of thought inherent in "Remembrance" allows it to become explicit. The difficulty of this task stems from the fact that until now, in spite of the considerable influence of his readings (even on W. Binder, for instance), Heidegger has for the most part only been contradicted from a respectful distance, here and there, but never radically. This is true, too, of the occasional corrections in B. Allemann, *Hölderlin und Heidegger*, second edition (Zurich, 1956). Exceptions include Adorno's essay on Hölderlin, which in spite of its valid objections to Heidegger warrants even stronger opposition (cf. note 139 below), and B. Böschenstein's apt critique of a number of details, which in addition correctly stresses the limitations of Heidegger's reading, considering the time frame to which it belongs ("Die Dichtung Hölderlins. Analyse ihrer Interpretation durch Martin Heidegger," in *Zeitwende* 48 [1977], pp. 91 ff.) A critical overview of the literature on Heidegger's Hölderlin interpretation can be found in Ch. Jamme's

"Dem Dichter Vor-Denken," *Zeitschrift für philosophische Forschung* 38 (1984), pp. 191 ff.

35. Heidegger initially made no effort whatever to take into account the second evocation of the landscape along the Garonne in terms of Hölderlin's actual experience of the country. The hasty note near the end of the lectures of 1941–42 (*GA* LII, pp. 183–84) is repeated in the essay on "Remembrance" and elaborated in a few tentative notes (*GA* IV, pp. 140–41). But even A. Beck, who was able to explain so much in terms of the experiences of Hölderlin's life, failed to shed any light on the spheres evoked in "Remembrance." Beißner's commentaries of 1951 (*StA* II, pp. 802–6), too, have no further information to offer. In "Kleine Zufallsfunde," *Hölderlin-Jahrbuch* 7 (1953), pp. 67 ff., A. Beck then tried to give a more detailed account of Hölderlin's depictions in light of the travelogue of Consul Meyer's brother F. J. L. Meyer. This involves the mistaken association of the depictions of the confluence of the Garonne and the Dordogne with one of Hölderlin's visits to the Blanquefort estate. At that time, from Meyer's country house one had a good view of the pennants on the high masts of the seagoing ships but not of the quite distant mouth of the Dordogne on the "zephyrous peak" (Beck, "Kleine Zufallsfunde," p. 72). The same inaccuracy can be found in *Hölderlin—eine Chronik in Text und Bild*, edited by A. Beck and P. Raabe (Frankfurt, 1970), p. 401. It becomes more serious still in *StA* VII, p. 197 (1972), where Beck speculates that Hölderlin reached Blanquefort via the waterway described by Meyer's brother. Blanquefort is scarcely closer to the Dordogne than is Bordeaux itself (cf. p. 164 below). This does not, of course, imply that Hölderlin traveled along the waterway to the mouth of the Dordogne. Schmidt, *Hölderlins letzte Hymnen*, and Zuberbühler, *Hölderlins Erneuerung der Sprache*, draw no connection at all between Hölderlin's imagery and his personal experience. An essay by I. Koschlig-Wiem, "Hölderlin in Bordeaux," *Atlantis* (1943), p. 277, called attention to pictures of the Meyers as a married couple. In "Auf der Suche nach Hölderlin. Drei Wochen in Bordeaux auf des Dichters Spuren," *Der Literat* (1967), pp. 35–36, W. Walz makes some observations concerning Meyer's house and events occurring during Hölderlin's stay. The film he mentions in his piece was shot for Saarland Broadcasting by Georg Bense (*Bordeaux, Notation einer Stadt*). I was able to see it on Hessian Broadcasting. It gives no precise information concerning the depictions in "Remembrance." More significantly, during the German occupation of France a series of newspaper articles concerning Hölderlin and Bordeaux appeared, which I found and looked through thanks to the bibliography at the Hölderlin Archives, though I found no further information concerning the relation between "Remembrance" and the topography of Bordeaux. Suffice it only to quote H. Herrmann's "F. Hölderlin in Bordeaux," *Armee-Nachrichten 1943*, from March 10, 1942: "In a lovely poem, virtually inscribed in the ears and eyes of the soldiers who know Bordeaux, Hölderlin has given incomparable expression to the image of the city as it lay in his memory."

36. The *Plan de la Ville de Bordeaux* of 1823 records the water levels at the ebb and flow. The tides cease to be of great importance for shipping around Langon, some 40 kilometers upriver from Bordeaux.

37. Old maps even represent the island as two islands alongside each other, which would indicate that the high tide was able to wash over the middle of the island. Even today the northern part of the island is still called "Île du Nord." Maps of the wine country show only two tiny vineyards on the south-

ern half of the island in the eighteenth century. Cf. F. G. Pariset et al., eds., *Bordeaux au XVIIIᵉ siècle* (Bordeaux, 1968), p. 161. On the Bec d'Ambès, see p. 168 below.

38. Literature containing reports of their work is cited in notes 59–91 below.

39. P. Butel and J.-P. Poussou, *La Vie quotidienne à Bordeaux au XVIIIᵉ siècle* (Paris, 1980), p. 258. The *Plan de la Ville de Bordeaux* of 1808 makes clear the layout of the parks and gardens in the heart of the city.

40. Like Meyer's palace, it was built by Louis Combes. Cf. Pariset et al., *Bordeaux*, p. 689.

41. Cf. F. J. L. Meyer, *Briefe aus der Hauptstadt und dem Innern Frankreichs*, 2 vols. (Tübingen: Cotta, 1802), vol. 2, pp. 156–58, and Beck, "Kleine Zufallsfunde," p. 68. The journey to the mouth of the Gironde onto the ocean could take up to fifteen hours (cf. A. v. d. Willigen, *Reize door Frankrijk in gemeenzame brieven, door Adriaan von der Willigen aan den Uitgever* [Haarlem, 1805], p. 501); the trip to Blaye, about twice as far from Bordeaux as the Bec d'Ambès, with a favorable wind, four hours (cf. Mme. Cradock, *La Vie française à la veille de la Revolution, Journal inédit de Mme Cradock*, trans. Odelphin-Balleyguier, in *Revue historique de Bordeaux* 4 [1911], p. 221).

42. Hence the first draft of line 51 of "Remembrance," *StA* II, p. 801.

43. Heidegger's reading is guided entirely by this assumption; the passages cited here are a nearly random selection: *GA* LII, pp. 55, 129–30, 137. Heidegger understands the whole of the poem in terms of the greetings at the beginning, and he has valuable things to say in that regard in terms of his own thinking, which leads him to associate it with letting beings be (*das Seinlassen des Seienden*), and thus with what he calls "truth" (ibid., pp. 49 ff).

In this connection he even grants that such a greeting contains "moments of transition from one to another" (ibid., p. 51; cf. pp. 91–92). But this is not borne out in his interpretation, and consequently the location of the poet remains what it is at the outset when the greeting is sent off with the wind. But "Remembrance" is not a greeting from beginning to end. In his lecture Heidegger says the greeting comes to an end in the second strophe (*GA* LII, p. 136). But he is unable to make clear what role the following strophe plays in the unity of the poem as a whole. And even in the two opening strophes there is a passage that concerns itself with the greeting. In the later essay Heidegger regards the second depiction too as a greeting—an arbitrary reading that marshals inadequate forces to remedy the weakness of the interpretation found in the lecture concerning the unity of the poem (*GA* IV, p. 141). Notes for a draft of the lecture course, reproduced by the editor, make clear just how little attention Heidegger paid to the entirety of "Remembrance" (*GA* LII, p. 197). A number of allusions to the themes of the lecture course, above all *GA* LII, p. 136, indicate that the ideas contained in the notes determined in large part the direction of the lecture course and concentrated on a reading of the first two strophes.

44. The poet speaks of "friends" when he still feels close to them and holds out hopes of a conversation with his companions. The mariners are "men" in the life course reserved for them and in their courageous years of solitude. This way of referring to the ones previously called "friends" can already be found in the transition to the insight into the meaning of their path among all life's paths as a whole (cf. p. 208 below).

45. The men are on their way not to India proper but to its ports to trade goods. They will return and then disembark once again, and although they will meet foreigners there, "Indians," they will have no friends.

46. This tone contributed to the switch from *sich endiget* ("ends") to *ausgehet* ("goes out"). *Ausgehen* implies coming to an end, as in the extinguishing of a candle that "goes out" (*ausgehet*), as well as going out in the sense of people leaving the house and "going out" (*ausgegangen sein*), or "stepping out" (*Ausgang haben*). *Ausgehet* is therefore more fitting in this double sense, if the depiction of the course of the Garonne near the confluence with the Dordogne is to be made more precise.

47. Cf. pp. 200 ff. below.

48. Moreover, if one assumes that the "zephyrous peak" is the Bec d'Ambès, the journey on the Garonne provides the most perspicuous view for the depiction of the sphere at the mouth of the river: one reaches the mouth, which is bordered on either side by the peak and the vineyard hills. Hölderlin surely knew it was possible to accompany the sailors to the confluence of the rivers. Perhaps he even had the opportunity to take part in such an escort. But Hölderlin could just as easily be remembering one of the walks he loved to take along the opposite shore. In the interest of thoroughness, it should be mentioned that the best map of the day, the *Carte de la Guyenne* by Belleyme, also contains highly detailed information concerning the landscape along the Garonne, as well as the forests, the clusters of trees, and the vineyards. Leaves 27 (Bordeaux) and 20 (Libourne) were published in 1785. Unfortunately, I was not able to gain timely access to leaf 20, which covers the confluence of the rivers. But leaf 27 contains the portion that includes Bordeaux (but without the suburb by the quay). It can be found more easily in F. de Dainville, *La Carte de la Guyenne par Belleyme 1761–1840* (Bordeaux, 1957), plate 14. The composition of the closing strophe of "Remembrance" in fact establishes, however, that Hölderlin depicted the confluence by drawing on his own memories and not by recourse to whatever map he may have had at his disposal (cf. note 26 above).

49. Cf. p. 169 above. Pp. 189–205 interpret the form and direction of "Remembrance" taken as a whole.

50. The Bordeaux art historian F. G. Pariset often promised to publish a study of Hölderlin's stay in Bordeaux. Cf. Pariset et al., *Bordeaux*, p. 689n; also Pariset's "Louis Combes," *Revue historique de Bordeaux*, n.f. 22 (1973), p. 18. Unfortunately, Pariset has in the meantime died.

51. The sources could probably be multiplied further still. Thus one could track down the names of the no doubt many tutors in the foreign families, provided their letters could be found. We do not even know who Hölderlin's predecessor or successor was. In *Hölderlin-Jahrbuch* 4 (1950), pp. 80 ff., A. Beck quotes a few passages from the letters of Karl F. Reinhard from Bordeaux to K. F. Stäudlin, letters that in the German literary archives of Marbach date from the years 1789–90. Another student of the Tübingen *Stift* by the name of Weber, whose identity I have not been able to determine, was active during the same period. Just to show the sort of information these sources could provide, one might have another look at a passage from Hölderlin's second letter to Casimir Ulrich Böhlendorff (*StA* VI, p. 432). In it Hölderlin mentions "the shepherds of the South of France." From this remark, Beck suggests that Hölderlin "perhaps" saw the shepherds along the coast of southern Bordeaux (*StA* VI, p. 1087; see also Beck and Raabe, *Hölderlin—eine Chronik*, p. 64). No hike to the coastal region, which would have taken several days and would have indeed satisfied Hölderlin's desire for a "view of the sea" (*StA* VI, p. 427), is recorded, nor are there any hints in the texts dating from after his return from France. Since the second letter to Böhlendorff about the encounter with the shepherds is quite

straightforward, and since the structure of the letter mirrors his tracing the way back to Bordeaux in his memory, Beck's suggestion is not a plausible account of the remark concerning the shepherds at the beginning of the letter, where they appear in the countryside around Bordeaux. A simple explanation can be found, however, in S. la Roche, who offers a detailed report of her visit to Montesquieu's castle, La Brède, which could be reached in a day's journey traveling southeast from Bordeaux, and from which one could return late the same evening: "I set out at five o'clock in the morning . . . through the deep sand and dry heath around Bordeaux" (*Journal einer Reise*, p. 283 ff.). She describes the herds near La Brède, the dress of the shepherds and their simple way of life, and mentions the frequent pilgrimages of foreigners to the place where *Spirit of the Laws* was written. Whether Hölderlin was there himself or not—Montesquieu is never cited in his oeuvre, and phrases such as "spirit of the states" (*Geist der Staaten*, StA V, p. 272) are not specific enough to establish any explicit connection to Montesquieu—still the shepherds' domain stretches out into the vicinity of Bordeaux, and in French their heathlands are called *landes*. Willingen tells of their presence on one of Bordeaux's markets that dealt in mutton, charcoal, venison, and even oysters. Shepherds could also cover great distances very quickly traveling on stilts (*Reize door Frankrijk*, pp. 496–99). So, the passage from the letter to Böhlendorff provides no evidence of a trip (of more than 40 kilometers) to distant regions, then already referred to as Departement "Landes," today known as the pine forest region of "les Landes." It should also be pointed out that Willigen regarded the people from the "heath," whom he knew only from the market, as "degenerates" (ibid., p. 499), unlike la Roche, who met them in their homes.

52. See la Roche, *Journal einer Reise*, p. 272.

53. The poem actually speaks of a sea voyage to India, not the "West Indies," that is, French colonies in the Caribbean, as is often thought. Bordeaux's trade in the West Indies was one of the main sources of the city's wealth. But the ships' voyages there and back each took only about three months; cf. P. Butel, *Les Négociants bordelais, l'Europe et les Iles au XVIIIe siècle* (Paris, 1974), pp. 225 ff. The Marquise de la Tour du Pin (*Journal d'une Femme de cinquante ans*, ed. A. de Liederkerke-Beaufort, 2 vols. [Paris, 1913], in the collection of the Universitäts-Bibliothek Heidelberg) gives reasonably exact travel times for the trips from Bordeaux to Boston (about two months) and from New York to Cadiz (May 6 to June 10, 1796) (vol. 1, p. 370, 386; vol. 2, pp. 105–6). During the last third of the century, however, Bordeaux firms made increasing use of the possible trade with Indian and Chinese ports, which had resulted from the special privileges of the Indian Commercial Company (cf. Butel, *Les Négociants bordelais*, p. 39, and Pariset et al., *Bordeaux*, pp. 239 ff.). A vivid picture of the course of one such Asian journey that lasted at least a year can be found in R. Cruchet, "Le Voyage en Chine de Balguerie Junior (1783–85)," *Revue historique de Bordeaux*, n.f. 1 (1952), pp. 213–36. Preparations for the voyage of *La Diane* to East Asia were under way during Hölderlin's stay—probably a topic of conversation in Consul Meyer's house (cf. Butel, pp. 43–44). On the significance of a journey to India in Hölderlin's world, cf. Schmidt, *Hölderlins letzte Hymnen*, p. 31, and Böschenstein, "Geschehen und Gedächtnis," p. 13. Incidentally, both sea routes, the one to the West Indies and the one to Southeast Asia, served above all in the trade of luxury goods, especially the one to Asia (cf. Butel). Prime imports were tea and porcelain, while West Indian trade for the most part

brought coffee, sugar, and indigo to Bordeaux ("They . . . bring together / What is beautiful of the earth"; cf. p. 186 below). On Bordeaux's merchant shipping see in addition P. Butel, "L'Armement en course à Bordeaux sous la Révolution et l'Empire," *Revue historique de Bordeaux*, n.f. 15 (1966), pp. 17 ff., and Pariset et al., *Bordeaux*, pp. 221 ff. It should be possible, both from archives and from the daily Bordeaux papers of the period, to find out more about the ships that disembarked and returned during Hölderlin's stay, and about Consul Meyer's connections with the tradesmen.

54. The final line of the fourth stanza comes very close to a concrete image: "Nor music of strings, nor native dance" (*Und Saitenspiel und eingeborener Tanz nicht*). Perhaps one should think of the ocean voyage of the mariners, on which they encounter no island where, as on the "sweet Ionian island, in the green night, kettledrum and cymbal sound to the labyrinthian dance" (*StA* II, pp. 17–18). Yet it is especially the "city's celebrations" that the mariners miss—*their own* city, Bordeaux. Sources tell of the people of Bordeaux and of their passion for dance. On Sundays and holidays people danced in the open air and along the waterfront at the harbor (cf. p. 184 below) amid garlands and certainly late into the night. The young people of the city and the surrounding area took part in these folk dances. The light and joy of the dancing "penetrated" the evening gardens and the avenues, and penetrated too across the river where the ocean-going vessels would drop anchor. Cf. Butel and Poussou, *La Vie quotidienne de Bordeaux*, pp. 227 ff., esp. 229; Cradock, *La Vie française*, p. 207; and la Roche, *Journal einer Reise*, pp. 276–77. Butel and Poussou, however, probably misunderstand la Roche in thinking she was referring to an open-air dance floor in the road on the waterfront. La Roche tells of another dance at a farm, amid the foliage that lay in the fields behind the dock area (see her p. 306). Hölderlin, too, must have had an experience of the dancing amid the garlands very similar to that of la Roche; cf. *StA* II, p. 237:

wo
Des Sonntags unter Tänzen
Gastfreundlich die Schwellen sind,
An blüthenbekränzten Straßen

where
Of a Sunday amid the dancing
The gates are welcoming
Along garlanded streets

Cf. further Willigen concerning a dance floor near the Jardin Public called "Tivoli" (*Reize door Frankrijk*, p. 486), and another dancing garden that was called the "Plaisance" (p. 495); see especially the city guide of 1785: *Déscription historique de Bordeaux*. This describes the Bordeaux custom of hanging wreaths above the streets. This activity took place in May, so la Roche and Hölderlin both knew of it (see her pp. 138–39). See also Pariset et al., *Bordeaux*, p. 449. Mrs. Cradock also tells of the Bordeaux flower festival, *La Vie française*, p. 208.

55. Cf. note 9 above.
56. Cf. note 2 above.
57. Cf. pp. 147 ff. above.
58. It should be noted here that Hölderlin had no difficulty depicting more

modern cities as being at one with their natural surrounding. Even the Heidelberg bridge had only been erected a few years before and was the newest structure in the city.

59. Cf. X. Védère, "Les Allées de Tourny," part 4, *Revue historique de Bordeaux*, 24 (1931), pp. 167 ff.; Pariset et al., *Bordeaux*, pp. 633 ff.; L. Desgraves, *Évocation du vieux Bordeaux* (Paris, 1960), pp. 431 ff.

60. Cf. Pariset et al., *Bordeaux*, plates 29 and 30, p. 704, and the additional plan of 1808 pictured on page 4, the photograph of which was provided by the municipal archives of Bordeaux.

61. Cf. P. Lavedou, "Concours pour l'aménagement de la place du Château-Trompette à Bordeaux," in *Archives de l'Art française, Études et documents sur l'art française du XIIe au XIXe siècles* (Paris, 1959). The controversies relating to the renovation of the area around the Château Trompette, which can be traced back to a petition by a citizens' group seeking to profit from housing construction, are also chronicled by M. de Lapouyade in his essay on F. J. L. Meyer's travelogue in *Revue historique de Bordeaux* 5 (1912), pp. 180–81. According to M. Bernadou, *Le Viographe Bordelais* (Bordeaux, 1844), p. 90, the sale of the château and its property in 1785 by the king to the citizens' group was voided after two years. Louis Combes, the architect of the palace of Meyer's brother, Hölderlin's employer, was among the competitors in the design competition.

62. Cf. previous note. La Roche (*Journal einer Reise*, p. 273) already knew the plan of Louis by the year 1785.

63. Cf. p. 180 below.

64. Cf. X. Védère, "Les Allées de Tourny," parts 2 and 3, in *Revue historique de Bordeaux* 23 (1930), pp. 231 ff., and 24 (1931), pp. 75 ff. Also cf. P. Courteault, "Les Arbres des allées de Tourny," ibid. 6 (1918), pp. 103 ff., and with it, concerning the intentions of the theater manager Tourny to join the city and the port suburb, P. Chavreau, "La Formation topographique du quartier des Chartrons," ibid. 22 (1929), pp. 181–82.

65. The architect of the theater was Victor Louis, who was also active in Paris. He could consequently claim special qualification for planning the bordering esplanade.

66. Concerning the palace, see Védère, "Les Allées de Tourny," part 4, pp. 178–80; Pariset et al., *Bordeaux*, p. 688; and Pariset, *Louis Combes*, pp. 17 ff.

67. Concerning Consul Meyer see the travelogue of his brother, *Briefe aus der Hauptstadt*; the contributions of Beck and Koschlig-Wiem, *op. cit.* (cf. note 35); and M. de Lapouyade, "Voyage d'un Allemand à Bordeaux," *Revue historique de Bordeaux* 5 (1912), pp. 164 ff. (correspondence concerning the travelogue). Concerning the brother himself see K. V. Riedel, *F. J. Lorenz Meyer 1760–1844*, Publications of the Society for the History of Hamburg (Hamburg, 1963). The leading role of Hamburg in Bordeaux's trade is documented by M. Oudot de Dainville, "Les Relations commerciales de Bordeaux avec les villes hanséatiques aux XVIIe et XVIIIe siècles," in *Mémoires et Documents pour servir à l'histoire du commerce et de l'industrie en France*, 4e série (Paris, 1916), pp. 213–69. This source also explains why, even in Bordeaux itself, this trade was conducted by German businessmen. See also Butel, *Les Négociants bordelais*, pp. 48 ff. There are only two references providing information concerning Meyer's political opinions and attitudes. I therefore refer the reader to one hidden allusion to his political convictions: cf. La Tour du Pin, *Journal d'une Femme*, vol. 1, pp. 376–77, concerning Meyer's assistance in the flight of an aristocratic family from Bordeaux in 1794.

68. Desgraves, *Évocation du vieux Bordeaux*, p. 355. Hölderlin's stay occurred during the time when the new revolutionary calendar was still in use, in which the Christian Sunday was once again granted a limited role. (It is significant in this regard that, on the occasion of the death of his grandmother, Hölderlin dates his letter to his mother, "Good Friday, 1802.") The original series of revolutionary festivals was in the meantime reduced to just four. The celebration of the spring equinox was no longer among them. I was unable to discover which celebrations were held, and in what manner, during Hölderlin's stay. Cf. Pariset et al., *Bordeaux*, pp. 449–50, 458, 477 ff. The draft "Die Titanen" (*StA* II, p. 218) makes clear allusion to one of the military exercises or deployments in the Jardin Public, a victory celebration with a parade in which children marched with their fathers' weapons to the sound of trumpets. It is almost certain that these lines flow from Hölderlin's own experience, which provides corroboration, significant for "Remembrance" too, of the connection between the "gardens" and "footpaths" and the Jardin Public. Cf. the interpretation that leads far afield of Hölderlin's experience in A. Häny's "Hölderlins Titanenmythos," in *Zürcher Beiträge zur deutschen Literatur- und Geistesgeschichte* 2 (Zurich, 1948), pp. 73–75. An overview of the revolutionary calendar and the revolutionary festivals is readily accessible in the articles of the *Grande Encyclopédie*, vol. 8, pp. 908 ff., and vol. 17, pp. 352 ff. On the use of the Champ de Mars at the outset of the Revolution, see M. Lhéritier, "Les Vieux arbres du Jardin-Public," *Revue historique de Bordeaux* 9 (1916), pp. 236–38, esp. p. 237, and J. Marchand, "Le Voyage de François Jacques Delannoy à Bordeaux," *Revue historique de Bordeaux* 37 (1944), pp. 33–34; and for its use during the consulate see P. Courteault, "Promenade historique à travers le Jardin Public," *Revue Philomatique* (1933), pp. 130 ff. A notice from the summer of 1793 records the exact course of events of a revolutionary festival; cf. *Revue historique de Bordeaux* 13 (1920), pp. 57 ff. See also Pariset et al., *Bordeaux*, pp. 677 ff.; Courteault, "Les Arbres des allées de Tourny," part 3, p. 110; and the *Déscription historique de Bordeaux*, pp. 133–34.

69. F. J. L. Meyer, *Briefe aus der Hauptstadt*, vol. 2, p. 32, and Willigen, *Reize door Frankrijk*, p. 456. Otherwise see Cradock, *La Vie française*, pp. 202, 205. On this point especially refer to note 24 above. The observations concerning the way in which the gardens of Bordeaux are integrated into the life of the city, and the way they shape the impression it makes, can be seen in close connection with the observations concerning the gardens over the alleys of Heidelberg. Also cf. Védère, "Les Allées de Tourny," part 4, pp. 173 ff., and Willigen, *op. cit.*, p. 455, who, as noted, also describes a Sunday in the Jardin Public.

70. Willigen, *Reize door Frankrijk*, pp. 494–95, tells of the entertainments offered in the shanties (small theater, also with marionettes, performers, live human curiosities, dice games, etc.). A map of the parks bordering the avenues of 1794 can be found in Védère, "Les Allées de Tourny," part 4, p. 172. See also Desgraves, *Évocation du vieux Bordeaux*, pp. 332–33. The illustration of Meyer's palace in *Revue historique de Bordeaux* 5 (1912), pp. 176–77, shows next to the palace the two-story Théâtre de la Gaieté, which was erected in 1798 and torn down in 1821. Already in 1785 Mrs. Cradock visited a "shanty" on the way back from the harbor to the hotel by the Jardin Public, which may have been located elsewhere. She saw wax figures representing Judith and Holofernes. These figures could be opened up to serve as demonstrations of human anatomy (*La Vie française*, p. 206). Performance and entertainment were apparently typical professions in this port city as well.

71. The avenues themselves came under the care of the municipal authority

shortly before Hölderlin's arrival: the dead elms were replaced with newly planted ones; cf. Courteault, "Les Arbres des allées de Tourny," p. 112.

72. The Marquise de la Tour du Pin reports that in 1793, late in the revolutionary period, eight hundred to a thousand young Girondists were able to stop military exercises taking place on the glacis of the Château Trompette (*Journal d'une Femme*, vol. 1, p. 310). It may therefore have been only partly built over at that time.

73. Cf. Butel and Poussou, *La Vie quotidienne à Bordeaux*, p. 257. Mrs. Cradock tells of a Sunday outing to a place where people would drink, sing, and play cards (*La Vie française*, p. 206).

74. La Roche, *Journal einer Reise*, p. 266. La Roche speaks in the same breath of a "poplar island," which unfortunately doesn't correspond to anything in the topography. Since she wrote her report in the form of a diary, and this text was written entirely on the day of her arrival, she would not yet have had a sure sense of the course of the river.

75. Cf. Ingersoll-Smouse, *Joseph Vernet, peintre de Marine*, 2 vols. (Paris, 1926), vol. 1, plate 7. Illustration no. 159 likewise offers the *Première vue de Bordeaux* of 1759 (in the possession of the Louvre).

76. Lacour seems to have taken three years to complete his work. Cf. *Revue historique de Bordeaux*, n.f. 4 (1955), p. 124. The best reproduction of this painting (in the Musée des arts décoratifs), so often reproduced in the Bordeaux literature, can be found in C. Jullian, *Historie de Bordeaux* (Bordeaux, 1895), plate 28, opposite p. 703. Willigen tells of a visit to the studio of Lacour and of the origins of the painting, *Reize door Frankrijk*, pp. 481–82.

77. F. J. L. Meyer, *Briefe aus der Hauptstadt*, vol. 2, p. 36. According to M. de Lapouyade, *Revue historique de Bordeaux* 4 (1911), p. 172 n. 1, the promontory in the moon-shaped bend in the Garonne is called the Pointe de Queyries. According to de Dainville, *La Carte de la Guyenne par Belleyme*, the region on the bank dense with trees north of La Bastide in the bend in the river is called "les Queyries."

78. On the image of the castle, see also la Roche, *Journal einer Reise*, pp. 273–74, 325.

79. F. J. L. Meyer, *Briefe aus der Hauptstadt*, vol. 2, p. 29.

80. La Roche tells of a brook that flowed by her host's garden, which was directly adjacent to his house on the quay. The question concerns the water referred to in the maps of 1823 and 1831 as "Estey Grebat." J. du Pasquier (cf. note 27 above) tells of brooks and small rivers that used to flow into the Garonne and have now either dried up or been built over by the city (letter to the author of January 3, 1975). A report of the erstwhile pattern of streams that flowed through the city can be found in a manuscript of the Abbé Baurein (from the late eighteenth century), in *Variétés Bordeloises* (of Baurein), new edition, vol. 4, ed. v. G. Méran (Bordeaux, 1876), pp. 38–43. One would think that a brook that "falls deep" would plunge from some height into the river almost like a waterfall. The topography of Bordeaux would only accommodate such a scene near the village of Lormont on the farther shore. (Mrs. Cradock gives an impressive report of an excursion to Lormont and the gardens there; *La Vie française*, pp. 213–14). Even there, of course, the scene can no longer be corroborated by sources, nor is it to be found today. And in all likelihood in Hölderlin's day, too, at most only a few inclined banks bordered the river. It should be noted, however, that even in the city itself a brook could fall into the river only

if, taking account of the tides, the surface of the river generally lay below the highest embankment, so that a stream would have at least a moderate "drop" near the shore (cf. *StA* II, p. 879, the variants of line 65n of "Kolomb"). According to the maps, both of the somewhat larger waters opening into the Baronne in the city in 1823 flowed concealed beneath the quay. The brook and the "noble pair" of trees therefore remain unaccountable for the time being (cf. pp. 185–86 below). M. Avisseau reports in a letter to the author of July 1, 1985, that he looked for the brook with Pariset, his teacher, but to no avail (cf. note 50 above).

81. The first point emerges from de Dainville, *La Carte de la Guyenne par Belleyme*, which, like the earlier *Carte de Cassini*, indicates the mills of the tributaries; the second from Young (*Reise durch Frankreich*, p. 87), who incidentally, though for the wrong reasons, predicted the financial ruin of the Moulin Theynac, which I shall mention presently and which Meyer also discusses (the name is also often written "Thaynac"). On mills in the brooks, see also Baurein, in Méran, *Variétés Bordeloises*, vol. 4, pp. 39–40.

82. *Déscription historique de Bordeaux*, pp. 27, 36; Young, *Reise durch Frankreich*, p. 85; la Roche, *Journal einer Reise*, p. 271, and her emphasis on the semicircular form of the quay, pp. 266–67; F. J. L. Meyer, *Briefe aus der Hauptstadt*, vol. 2, p. 22, and Willigen, *Reize door Frankrijk*, p. 450: "een halve cirkel."

83. On the history of the harbor district, cf. P. Chauvreau, "La Formation topographique du quartier des Chartrons," *Revue historique de Bordeaux* 21 (1928), pp. 208 ff.; 22 (1929), pp. 110 ff., 173 ff., 222 ff.; 23 (1930), pp. 17 ff.

84. The city plans of 1821 and 1831 indicate the water levels at their highest and lowest points.

85. Cf. F. J. L. Meyer, *Briefe aus der Hauptstadt*, vol. 2, p. 24.

86. Cf. M. Heidegger, *GA* IV, p. 98.

87. See the quote from la Roche on my p. 176 above.

88. It is possible to give an even fuller intuitive sense to the line about the "stage" or "path" (*Steg*) by the bank. Engravings from the middle of the eighteenth century show that along the quay a dense row of façades was constructed. Their purpose was to allow the boats that were used to load and unload ships to berth in the rising and falling waters (cf. Pariset et al., *Bordeaux*, plate 5). These mooring places, which we would call "landing stages," are not to be seen in the painting by Lacour, nor are they mentioned by la Roche. Lacour shows the loading being done on planks that likewise made it possible to effect a stable surface on which to work while the water level was constantly changing. La Roche tells of the skillfulness of the scrubbers doing the work (*Journal einer Reise*, p. 267). In the same context she tells of a row of arbors that the businessmen built for the sailors (and scrubbers) and that were shaded by two lime trees (ibid.). These arbors are easily recognizable in Lacour's painting, too. These small areas were surrounded by walls built chest high. From a distance they formed an additional line along the sharp bank, which as a whole was a mooring place for boats and to that extent also a landing "stage."

The harbor shore, then, which today is overrun by train stations and warehouses, had at that time an altogether different appearance that was integrated with the beauty of the natural surroundings. One can always point out that Hölderlin's lines depict the works of men and their means of production pure and detached from actual practice, wholly in terms of nature. But if one thinks of the concreteness of the images, and at the same time sees the way in which

Hölderlin places them in a whole shaped by nature, without abandoning them, then it is plain that the poetic spirit of his approach remains faithful to the experience of the city.

89. "Damp meadows" have a significance for Hölderlin because of a place where the waters linger before being led away by the river (*StA* V, p. 289, and *StA* II, pp. 233–34). There is a connection, then, between the harbor in the river and the sheen of the soil in the gardens of Bordeaux. Cf. F. J. L. Meyer, *Briefe aus der Hauptstadt*, vol. 2, pp. 93–94. Another observation may be added concerning his point that the "paths" (*Stege*) (of the gardens and of the Jardin Public) and the silkiness of the soil can be explained in terms of the water that flows over the land in Bordeaux, namely, that the images of the first strophe, which evoke the city on the Garonne, are all images relating to bodies of water. However, they ought also to be reconstructible as images revealed to particular points of view. Once this has been done successfully, it will turn out that the images of the first strophe, which still depict Bordeaux from a distance, correspond to a variety of scenes around the Garonne and the city. The second strophe, in which remembrance emerges in the city, would then be deliberately speaking in terms of images of a single concrete set of surroundings, and so in terms of the real presence of the city's gardens.

90. In March 1802, during Hölderlin's stay, England and France concluded the peace agreement of Amiens. In it France returned most of its overseas territories, and the trade routes were once again open to Bordeaux. The peace led to great hopes and to a faith in the future in the port city after the long period of crisis (cf. Jullian, *Histoire de Bordeaux*, p. 702), but they were short lived. Cf. Butel, "L'Armement en course à Bordeaux," p. 18, and Pariset et al., *Bordeaux*, p. 497.

91. On the fairs in Bordeaux, which began on March 1 and October 15, see *Déscription historique de Bordeaux*, p. 101; P. Butel, *Les Négociants bordelais*, pp. 145 ff.; and Butel and Poussou, *La Vie quotidienne*, pp. 171 ff. The most important imported goods from the West Indies were sugar, coffee, and indigo; tea and porcelain were imported from India and China (cf. note 53 above); northern Europe supplied ore, wood, fish, and fur; while Bordeaux exported above all wine but also other products such as honey and dried fruits (to as far away as Russia). The fairs, however, furnished domestic and foreign trade with wares of all kinds. P. Butel and J. P. Poussou are also good sources on this point (but see also la Roche, *Journal einer Reise*, p. 279). P. Courteault, "La Vie des foires bordelaises," *Revue historique de Bordeaux* 11 (1918), pp. 15 ff., esp. pp. 23, 27, 29, reveals that the fairs continued even during the period of economic crisis, hence during Hölderlin's stay. The products specially offered at the fairs are reported there on pp. 28–29 (materials, jewelry, tableware, pets, weapons, etc.). One should bear in mind above all in this regard Hölderlin's lines from the period when he wrote "Remembrance" that attest to his memory and his affection for Bordeaux as a center of trade (*StA* II, pp. 218–19):

> Und die Werkstatt gehet
> Und über Strömen das Schiff
> Und es bieten tauschend die Menschen
> Die Händ' einander, sinnig ist es
> Auf Erden und es sind nicht umsonst
> Die Augen an den Boden geheftet.

And the workplace thrives
And the ship across the currents
And people reach out their hands
To one another, it is fitting
On earth, nor are their eyes
Cast down in vain at the ground.

92. Cf. fragment 53 (*StA* II, p. 331):

Und der Himmel wird wie eines Mahlers Haus
Wenn seine Gemählde sind aufgestellet.

And the sky is as a painter's house
With all his paintings on display.

Concerning "what is beautiful of the earth" one should also take note (besides "The Archipelago," *StA* II, p. 105, l. 75) of fragment 54 (*StA* II, p. 331), evidently a draft of one of the poems shaped by the Bordeaux experience, which is marked by a sense of thanks for the experience and by a depiction of the happiness that emerges from the voyage of the mariners. Its close relation to fragment 53 becomes apparent when one considers that this fragment and the beginning of the draft of fragment 54,

Süß ists,
und genährt zu seyn vom Schönen
Der Welt

Sweet is it
and to be nourished by the beauty
of the world

are bound together in the lines of "Remembrance" about the painters who bring together what is beautiful of the earth. It would be entirely possible, then, to give a far more precise explanation not just of the way in which his stay in Bordeaux was present in Hölderlin's poetic manuscripts but also of what surrounds "Remembrance" and, if exact dates could be determined, perhaps also the story of its emergence and subsequent fate. There is all the more reason to take up the task since the circle of themes of "Remembrance" and the Bordeaux experience are also present in, and indeed lend structure to, drafts of "The Titans" (*StA* II, pp. 217 ff.), "Whatever Is Nearest," ("Das Nächste Beste," ibid., pp. 233 ff.), and "For from the Abyss . . ." ("Vom Abgrund nemlich," ibid., pp. 250 ff.). Other notes make reference to individual lines of these drafts. The layout of the drafts allows abundant confirmation of the considerations of the presence of the mariners' city in the depiction of its landscape, and of the observations concerning the gardens of Bordeaux. One would hope, and in view of the bulk and quality of Hölderlin research it is also highly likely, that the fragments and drafts will be made the object of another study, which would have to include and indeed focus on "Remembrance."

93. I have shown this in the case of small pieces of text by Kant in *Identität und Objektivität, eine Untersuchung über Kants transzendentale Deduktion* (Heidelberg, 1976), and for a short passage of text in Hegel in "Hegels Logik der Reflexion, neue Fassung," in *Die Wissenschaft der Logik und die Logik der Reflexion,* ed. D. Henrich, *Hegel-Studien,* suppl. vol. 18 (Bonn, 1978), pp. 203–324.

94. Heidegger would indeed like his interpretations to be taken only as suggestions (*GA* LII, p. 1) and experiments (*GA* XXXIX, p. 8; LIII, p. 1). But those interpretations, which give the appearance of a kind of rapprochement, conflict with the attitude the author brings to bear on the text and so too therefore with the character of his questioning and argumentation. Heidegger is no help at all in methodically uncovering Hölderlin's approach or the kind of thinking from which it derives. He speaks instead with the conviction of someone in touch with Hölderlin's ideas from the outset and is therefore imperious rather than thoughtful and reflective. We can thank Heidegger for contemplating Hölderlin's work in relation to real philosophical questions, and here we can agree with him. But depth without flexibility in questioning can easily distort and obstruct; moreover it encourages mindless imitation.

95. Cf. pp. 159 ff. above.

96. Cf. pp. 225 ff. below.

97. This much is by way of calling to mind the whole of Heidegger's interpretation and the intentions behind it.

98. *StA* II, p. 608; *StA* VI, pp. 425–28; cf. note 7 above.

99. E. Staiger, "Das dunkle Licht," in *Festschrift für die Feier des 350jährigen Bestehens des Suso-Gymnasiums* (Konstanz, 1954), pp. 134 ff.; also in *Hölderlin: Beiträge zu seinem Verständnis in unserem Jahrhundert*, ed. A. Kelletat, Schriften der Hölderlin-Gesellschaft 3 (Tübingen, 1961), pp. 336 ff.; and Böschenstein, "Geschehen und Gedächtnis," pp. 12 f.

100. In the years during Hölderlin's stay, more Roman monuments came to light in Bordeaux, in addition to the countless ones already known (cf. Willigen, *Reize door Frankrijk*, p. 484). Willigen tells with particular interest of the Roman buildings and other finds (pp. 454, 462, 465). The plans of the city, which were printed a short time later, show the presumed layout of the Roman fortifications.

101. Cf. p. 190 above and F. Roland-Jensen, "Hölderlins Mnemosyne," *Zeitschrift für Deutsche Philologie* 98 (1979), pp. 222 f., who shows that Hölderlin's association of the death of Achilles with the fig tree is not supported by tradition.

102. *GA* LII, p. 82; IV, p. 108. We must bear in mind here that Leo v. Seckendorf may have altered the text. His letter to Justinus Kerner (*StA* II, p. 585) deals with the first four poems of Hölderlin's that he published in the *Musenalmanach* in the year preceding the issue in which "Remembrance" appeared. But whatever moved him to alter these poems, he would have had all the more reason when it came to the drafts of "The Rhine," of "Patmos," and of "Remembrance." The deviations from the manuscript in the concluding stanza, which are the only ones we can detect since the other stanzas have come down to us only through Seckendorf, must however be regarded as undeleted reader's or printer's errors. Since the concluding stanza, a draft of which is still extant, was printed correctly in its essentials, an interpretation focusing not on individual words but on the structure of the whole is therefore on firm ground, though individual words were altered by Seckendorf. The very printing also presupposes the existence of a fair copy that must have been prepared by Hölderlin himself.

103. Cf. *GA* LI, pp. 59 ff., in connection with Heidegger's reading of "The Rhine" of nearly seven years earlier, in *GA* XXXIX, pp. 282–83, in which the interpretation of the significance of the "celebration" has not yet been elaborated.

104. More recent studies of Hölderlin's texts from the period after his return from Bordeaux and of the fragments from the second Homburg period showed that signs of a new mode of poetic competition was to be found in them. "Remembrance" too, inasmuch as the mythic motifs are introduced in latent form and the philosophical ones take on new significance, may be counted among the signs. It is even possible that it should throw some light on the efforts Hölderlin later made in Zimmer's tower in Tübingen (cf. pp. 246–47 below). It cannot be maintained that after completing his work Hölderlin simply became "deranged."

105. It should be pointed out that the sameness of day and night is the celebrated beginning of spring, as well as the midpoint of and the transition between the ages, in which the relation of the past to the future hangs in the balance. In the revolutionary calendar the celebration was above all conceived as a celebration of spring. But Hölderlin stresses, along with the old name of the day, the harmony of the seasons. In this way the holiday in the poem is associated with arriving at an encompassing insight at the end of the second depiction of the country along the Garonne. This insight is "transcendental" in Hölderlin's sense, hence free of the place and the time in which it was attained. It is also an insight into the harmony of the conflicting vital tendencies, just as the celebration rises to meet the harmony of the positions of the sun and so the harmony between the seasons. Unlike the insight of remembrance, however, the celebration of the movement from the one astronomical orbit to the other does not give life the status of something genuinely lasting.

106. One is tempted to follow Bertaux, "Hölderlin in und nach Bordeaux," p. 97, in his claim that the "golden dreams" are based on an intuitive image of the pollen from pine trees drifting through the air. But the claim would need to be made compelling—on the one hand in light of the fact that the rough draft of the (earlier) "fragment," "Beginning of Spring" ("Frühlingsanfang"), a poem that was originally to be called "Vengeance of Spring" ("Frühlingsahndung") (*StA* II, p. 937), begins with the words "Golden dreams" (*Goldne Traume*) (*StA* II, p. 936, just as in "The Archipelago," *StA* II, p. 104, l. 37), and on the other hand in light of the fact that the pollen of the conifers of the Bordeaux countryside, above all the maritime pine (*Pinus pinaster*, syn. *Pinus maritima*), is out within about three weeks of the rainy season in April and May, but not in March, and so not on the day of the spring equinox (according to information kindly provided by the Botanical Insitute of the University of Munich). Hölderlin's memory of the chain of yellow vapors therefore must have become imprecise in the course of the year beginning around the time he had the experience. To this one could reply, albeit not very convincingly, that before it refers to the celebration of the equinox, "Remembrance" uses the more general plural "on holidays" (*An Feiertagen*). Bertaux has recently reiterated his observation for French readers in the Bordeaux chapter of his Hölderlin biography, *Hölderlin ou le temps d'un poète* (Paris, 1983). In it he rightly remarks against Heidegger that the true poet, as Cocteau said, does not play with symbols but rather "donne à voir"—he lets us see something (ibid., p. 241). In his interpretation, however, Bertaux observes this principle too superficially. First he maintains that the fragment from "Brod und Wein" passed on by Beißner (*StA* II, p. 608; see also note 7 above) is to be related to the Bordelaisers' practice of letting their precious wine ripen faster so they could send it along on the journey to the Indies on their ships (ibid., pp. 235–39). He then envisions, though entirely on the basis of his own imagination, a visit of Hölderlin's to an inn beyond the

Garonne that is supposed to supply the first three stanzas of "Remembrance" with their intuitive content (ibid., pp. 240–41). Bertaux's commentary on Hölderlin's poem, however, suffers most from his effort to relate the whole of the work to the death of Susette Gontard: "To be soulless / With mortal thoughts" are the lines forming the middle axis of the poem; and the words "mortal thoughts" (*sterbliche Gedanken*) have the same initial letters as the name of the beloved, showing them to be thoughts of death—her death. One need not marshal too many objections against this argument since in any case it can make no contribution to an explication of the structure of a poem that takes us from a series of depictions of life on the Atlantic coast around the river and the city of the mariners to an insight in which the diffidence and worry of personal life have vanished. So, if Hölderlin wished to leave a hidden clue in this work in reference to his own love, it would certainly not have been in order to let it steer the very course of remembrance. Moreover, imagining there to be a clue does not corroborate the possibility that Hölderlin already learned of the death of his beloved in Bordeaux.

107. The question of where "Bellarmine and his companions" are links the closest of the "friends," namely Bellarmine, to another friend, or to other mariners, since he calls this other friend, or friends, "companions" (*Gefährten*), which is what those traveling with Odysseus on his voyage are called. Cf. F. Beißner, *StA* II, p. 804 and—in a bold conjecture—Sattler, *Friedrich Hölderlin: 144 Fliegende Blätter*, vol. 2, pp. 459–60 and 609–10. The poet thereby radically detaches himself and his old friendship from the path that is now theirs alone. And this also means that the poet's friendship with them was not based on the shared experience of an ocean voyage. It becomes clear, then, that the friendship goes back to a time when the friends had not yet gone their own ways. This accords with the fact that already in the opening lines of the poem the "mariners" are referred to as men leading a different life, one dear to but at the same time distant fom the poet. And this further anticipates that the course of remembrance leads into the city, not into the surrounding area and not into something lasting, and furthermore that in the depiction of the departure the friends are now called "the men" (*die Männer*). What implications this all has in view of the invocation of the name Bellarmine from *Hyperion* cannot be considered here.

108. See also R. B. Harrison, *Hölderlin and Greek Literature* (Oxford, 1975), pp. 271–72.

109. Cf. note 145 below.

110. The way in which, in one place and in the depiction of the structure of its significance, all places can be present in terms of their descent from a single origin and in terms of the significance they have for one another in virtue of that origin—but in such a way that the insight secured by this presence at once transcends all places—can in the end only be understood as a "speculative" relation in Hegel's sense. Cf. note 136 below.

111. Hölderlin makes use of a repetition of the word *dort* in a variety of ways in the poems written after 1800 but prior to "Remembrance." The reiteration of the word serves primarily to evoke a rapid succession of different places that nonetheless belong in a single relational whole (*StA* II, pp. 91, 98, 105, 106), so that one's gaze is led from place to place as if by an agitation within the whole. This already indicates that the two occurrences of *dort* in "Remembrance" point to two entirely different places within a single context. There seems to be no counterpart, however, to the structural form of "Remembrance," in which the

two evocations introduced with the word *dort* intertwine over the course of the entire poem. From this it follows, moreover, that the repetition, unlike that in the previous poems, does not occur with the same agitation and in the same mood in the evocation. And this is simply because the perspective of the evocation itself has changed—irrespective of the fact that the second *dort* indeed takes up and so also contains the first. It is also in virtue of this important detail that the artistic form of "Remembrance" can be understood as the late consummation of a mode of representation cultivated earlier.

Yet another detail in the composition of the poem having to do with the reiteration of the word *dort* must be included in the interpretation of the double evocation and of the double use of the word. Namely, the expression *aber nun* precedes the first *dort*, which introduces the depiction of the sphere of the city:

> Geh aber nun und grüße
> Die schöne Garonne,
>
> But go now, go and greet
> The sweet Garonne

The second *dort* is also introduced by *Nun aber* in the opening line of the final strophe:

> Nun aber sind zu Indiern
> Die Männer gegangen
>
> But now to the Indians
> The men have gone.

Each must be seen in relation to the other, corresponding to the relation between the two occurrences of *dort*.

The word *aber* indicates a shift and a reversal in the point of view of the contemplation; the word *nun* emphasizes by its presence the introduction of something significant, as well as a distinction from something prior. Since the presence indicated by *nun* is the presence of representation, *nun* and *dort* are related.

The shift indicated by *aber* occurs in the opening strophe in the transition from the consciousness of the wind and the spirit of the mariners to the greetings to their city, toward which the wind is blowing. In the final strophe, again, the *aber* corresponds to the transition from a consciousness of the lives and voyage of the mariners to the sphere of their disembarkation in the countryside along the Garonne and the presence of this departure (cf. p. 200 above).

Both transitions are anticipated in the respective contents of the consciousness. The northeaster "promises" (*verheißet*) safe passage to mariners, which is why it is reminiscent of their departure and of the city from which they are setting out. In the fourth stanza the consciousness opens onto the voyage of the mariners through the thought of their forgoing the city's celebrations and of their own memory of those celebrations, so that the course of remembrance itself takes up a new relation to its own entry into the city's celebrations (cf. p. 199 above).

Thus both occurrences of *dort* are bound up with thoughts of the paths of the mariners by the words *aber nun* and *Nun aber*, respectively. At the same time, both are determined by thoughts of the mariners' departure from the city. And yet the first, still indefinite thought of their journey and their departure leads into the depiction of the city on the river and the entry into it. The second thought, which is an all-encompassing consciousness and which is drawn from the city of the mariners itself, on the other hand, leads over into the depiction of the sphere of their departure, the second sphere in the countryside along the river of Bordeaux.

In this way it also becomes clear that the composition of the poem rests on the coordination and conjunction of two spheres in the river region and on the shifting perspective within it. Only by linking the two occurrences of *dort*, and the *nun aber* associated with them, across this conjunction and discontinuity does the poem manage to have the scope that it does internal to its very structure. And only by means of both perspectives does it become possible to fit the triad in the closing lines into its overall form—the lines in which the consciousness of the paths of the mariners is taken up in a thought that holds of all paths in life.

112. Cf. p. 162 above and note 35 above.

113. If one is inclined to the opinion that the "zephyrous peak" has to be the Bec d'Ambès, one would have to reformulate this sentence accordingly (cf. p. 168 above).

114. Hence the poet's first thought when he feels the northeaster, namely, its being dear to him as the wind favorable to mariners. It is thus not just the direction the nor'easter blows that elicits the poet's thoughts and the greetings he sends to Bordeaux; it is above all the thought of the mariners, and with it the thought of the familiar countryside of their port city toward which the wind is blowing. The poet says the northeaster is the dearest "to me" *because* of the fiery spirit and safe passage it promises mariners. This signals the poet's turn toward the separate life of the mariners as the dominant theme of the poem. Cf. note 111 above and D. Lüders, in *F. Hölderlin, sämtliche Gedichte* (Bad Homburg, 1970), vol. 2, p. 345.

115. This is the sense in which "the ocean . . . gives memory."

116. Cf. p. 148 above.

117. This is not the love in which according to the First Epistle of John (4:18) there is no room for fear.

118. According to the first draft of the final strophe (*StA* II, p. 801).

119. Hölderlin had already contemplated the conjunction of three modes of consciousness in "judgment" in his outline of a "theory of modalities" in the text "Judgment and Being." See H. Bachmaier, in Bachmaier, Horst, and Reisinger, *Hölderlin, transzendentale Reflexion der Poesie* (Stuttgart, 1979), pp. 120 ff. This basic conception provides the theoretical foundation for the doctrine of the conflict of vital tendencies that underlies *Hyperion*. See my "Hölderlin on Judgment and Being," in this volume. This is then associated with the poetological theory of the "modulation of tones" which also elaborates the doctrine of the conflict of autonomous vital tendencies.

120. Cf. *Trübners Deutsches Wörterbuch*, A. Götze, ed., vol. 1, s.v. "Andenken"; also the entry in the *Deutsches Wörterbuch* of the Brothers Grimm, vol. 1.

121. Cf. *StA* II, p. 819.

122. Cf. p. 245 below.

123. *StA* I, p. 309; II, pp. 39, 41, 83, 114, and cf. 127–28.

124. *StA* I, p. 307; II, pp. 103, 111, 119, 145, 197, 256. Cf. G. Kurz, *Mittelbarkeit und Vereinigung* (Stuttgart, 1975), pp. 170 ff., and H. Bachmaier, "Hölderlins Erinnerungsbegriff in der Homburger Zeit," in *Homburg v. d. Höhe in der deutschen Geistesgeschichte*, ed. Ch. Jamme and Otto Pöggeler (Stuttgart, 1981), pp. 131 ff.; also this volume pp. 220 ff. below. Even in the "very late poems,"

"recollection" (*Erinnerung*) and its coordination with "thanks" (*Dank*) is still the theme of a reflection now come to a standstill (*StA* II, pp. 281, 289).

125. *StA* II, pp. 43, 53, 91, 148, 168–69.

126. The fragment "On Religion" ("Über Religion") defines the relation between recollection (*Erinnerung*), which involves the notion of awareness (*Innesein*), and thanks in terms of a proximity of the two, which is very nearly an identity. In their unity they form the basis of religion, which is as such essentially mythic and thereby in essence poetic (*StA* IV, pp. 275, 280–81).

127. Cf. my *Fluchtlinien* (Frankfurt, 1982), pp. 126 ff.

128. These elements have been assembled from the philosophical and poetological drafts and from the letters to Niethammer and Schiller, but have not yet been corroborated by diverse sources. I have dealt with Hölderlin's philosophy in "Hegel and Hölderlin," in this volume; "Historische Voraussetzungen von Hegels System," in *Hegel im Kontext* (Frankfurt, 1971); "Hölderlin on Judgment and Being," in this volume; "The Path of Speculative Idealism," in this volume; and "Hölderlin's Philosophical Beginnings," in this volume.

129. If the reasoning of the Frankfurter Ausgabe of Hölderlin's work (vol. 14, p. 379) is sound, then the fragment "The Meaning of Tragedy" ("Die Bedeutung der Tragödien"), too, is later and should be set alongside the notes on Sophocles. The continuity of the fundamental ideas in Hölderlin's philosophical thought would then be very impressively documented. Cf. H. Bachmaier, "Theoretische Aspekte und tragische Negativität," in Bachmaier, Horst, and Reisinger, *Hölderlin, transzendentale Reflexion der Poesie*, pp. 132 ff.

130. So Heidegger in *GA* LII, pp. 119–20.

131. One might refer here to J. Zwilling's remark in the letter of April 1796 to a Jena professor: "Whenever I look at the *Wissenschaftslehre* I am delighted by the exalted thoughts of the imagination." L. Strauß, "Jacob Zwilling und sein Nachlaß," *Euphorion* 29 (1928), p. 388, cf. p. 390.

132. In § 4, II, of the *Wissenschaftslehre*, Fichte's analysis of the synthesis occurring in the third principle defines the imagination as a modulation (*Wechsel*) of the infinitude and the finitude of the I, which reproduces itself and which is thus driven forward (in Fichte, *Sämtliche Werke*, vol. 1, pp. 160–61, 215). These analyses, which were later only rarely attended to, were especially important and familiar to Hölderlin and his friends. For instance, consider the connection between Hölderlin's text "Becoming in Dissolution" ("Das Werden im Vergehen") and Fichte (*Sämtliche Werke*, vol. 1, p. 179), or between Hölderlin's theory of the transcendental dimension of recollection in the construction of the poetic work and Fichte later in the same chapter (vol. 1, pp. 204–5).

133. Fichte, *Sämtliche Werke*, vol. 1, pp. 196, 216.

134. "Vom Abgrund nemlich" (*StA* II, p. 250; cf. Sattler, *Friedrich Hölderlin: 144 Fliegende Blätter*. The draft is conceived entirely in terms of the interweaving, and hence juxtaposition, of experiences from the South of France with images of the German landscape. If one assumes, as Beißner suggests (*StA* II, p. 888), that lines 9 and 10 of the draft are continued by line 11, then in virtue of the observations of the topography of the gardens of Bordeaux there is reason to suppose that, with the "gardens' alleys" on which his voice would "wander like a dog in heat," Hölderlin linked the recollection of the esplanade around the Château Trompette, with its huts and alleyways, to that of the gardens' alleys, which cut themselves off to the south and southwest at the new city and the harbor district of Bordeaux (cf. pp. 179–80 above).

135. It should be noted that the entire eighth paragraph of the second letter

to Böhlendorff, which begins with remarks on the "architectonic of heaven" (*StA* VI, p. 433), is constructed as a series of observations and reflections on "synthetic" relations, which then culminates in the talk of "philosophical light."

136. The way in which Hegel's mature system unites, in a single conceptual framework, the idea of the absolute with that of the singularity of finite things to this day poses Hegel interpretation with one of its most daunting and most crucial tasks. I have tried to elaborate this conceptual framework in "Die Formationsbedingungen der Dialektik," *Revue internationale de philosophie*, nos. 139–40 (1982), pp. 139–62. It also offers a clue to understanding the complex form in which Hölderlin's experience of the presence of all places in one place in terms of a placeless insight would need to be developed, a form that, unlike Hegel, maintains close affinities with "transcendental" analysis. Of the many texts of Hölderlin's that work out such an analysis in advance, I mention here only the final passage of the letter to Sinclair of Christmas Eve, 1798 (*StA* VI, p. 301).

137. One could show that this overview is made possible by what is contained in the linguistic form of remembrance, which is taken up and made precise by the linguistic structure of the poem (cf. *StA* IV, pp. 260, 282). This would yield an understanding of the linguistic achievement proper to Hölderlin's work, and indeed of the relation between natural and poetic language. In another respect it would at once make clear how consciousness is transported and transformed in the poem, though in a way that at once preserves the path of transformation and with it the course of remembrance in the overview crucial to the understanding, without that transformation being somehow suspended. Language, then, is a condition for the dawning of a transforming recollection of a whole, at once an awareness and a preserving.

138. Cf. my "Identität,—Begriffe, Probleme, Grenzen," *Poetik und Hermeneutik* 8 (1979), pp. 133 ff., and on the identity of "person" and "subject," the concluding text in *Fluchtlinien*. It should still be pointed out explicitly that the overview of the main text seeks only to provide a provisional orientation necessary to dispel hidden reservations against the thesis that the course of remembrance is a transporting and transforming one. This is why I have made use of the expression "identity conditions" (*Identitätsbedingungen*) in a way that is not consistent with what is stipulated in the "Identität" essay, which for its part had to accommodate more technical claims concerning the theory of identity.

139. At his most vehement, Adorno has asserted against Heidegger, generally with good reason, that Hölderlin's work must be conceived in terms of its form, not the ideas we can attribute to him. "Parataxis," in *Noten zur Literatur III* (Frankfurt, 1965), pp. 156 ff. He also sees, rightly, that its mode of construction balks at the classicism of a synthesis readily tending toward a first-order harmony. More generally, however, Adorno uses Hölderlin as no more than an occasion for the pure employment of aesthetic categories, which, unlike the elements in Heidegger's thought, are forged directly from Hegelian material. Adorno's application of those categories is carried off well and strengthened by his informed critical judgment concerning the way in which Hölderlin's language prefigures some of the formal aspects of modern music. The arguments that are meant to reveal those aspects of Hölderlin's work, however, are even more tendentious than Heidegger's interpretation, which after all grew out of a long acquaintance with the work. Adorno's notes on Hölderlin's texts are

based on nothing more than scattered observations. Adorno never seriously considers the structural form of a single one of the poems—a fact that certainly fails to lend any credence to polemics against Heidegger. The paratactic linguistic form of the late poems is grounded in the integration of incongruous vital horizons and in the depiction of the unrepresentable emergence of meaning, not simply in an antagonism to the synthetic establishment of the idealist-bourgeois subject. And what Adorno does have to say about the gnomic lines of the hymns misses even further Hölderlin's poetic intention and achievement, for Adorno takes them to be contrapositive artistic means that "obtrude" (*herausstechen*) from the texture of the poems (ibid., p. 165). One could only understand them in this way by paying attention to the style of speech rather than to its structural form. For as I have shown, even purely philosophical lines fit flush into the structure of the poem in virtue of their composition. Thus the line "For all is well" (*Denn alles ist gut*) in "Patmos" strikes Adorno as the "hopeless quintessence of idealism" (p. 203), whereas the proposition must be understood in terms of the conversion of all that is common to Leibniz, Pope, Rousseau, and Kant into the eschatological experience of history and meaning contained in words as it is unfolded and preserved in the poem. One must indeed acknowledge the contrariness in the disposal of Hölderlin's work that Adorno associates with Heidegger, and at the same time oppose both in order to understand and preserve that work even in the philosophical domain into which it ventures.

140. The truly decisive piece of evidence for this is that in the concluding paragraph of the letter Hölderlin calls the work of the poet the holy "image that we shape" (*Bild, das wir bilden; StA* VI, p. 433), and so speaks of it as the work of the "fine" (*bildend*) artist *par excellence*, hence of the sculptor (*Bildhauer*).

141. Cf. J. Schmidt, *Hölderlins später Widerruf* (Tübingen, 1978), pp. 6 ff., and B. Böschenstein, "Winckelmann, Goethe und Hölderlin als Deuter antiker Plastic," *Hölderlin-Jahrbuch* 15 (1967–68), pp. 175 ff.

142. Cf. pp. 169, 200 above.

143. These considerations of Hölderlin's poem also entirely forgo any description of the division of strophes in "Remembrance" as a modulation of tones. It is easy to see that the first two strophes correspond to the naive tone, the two middle strophes to the heroic, and the last strophe to the idealistic (cf. Schmidt, *Hölderlins letzte Hymnen*, pp. 24–25). The real movement in the course of remembrance, and with it the pattern of development in the strophes, can be viewed in terms of this classification, but only in a purely provisional way (cf. note 6 above).

144. The philosophical reasons speaking in its favor stem from considerations indicated in my *Fluchtlinien*: the fundamental experiences of conscious life, like the drives toward the conflicting self-interpretations they foster, are not to be conceived in terms of a prior unity of primordial being-in-the-world. The unity can only be gained in an extension and a transcendence toward ultimate understanding, and hence as a conclusion. Although Hölderlin understands his own basic metaphysical ideas as constituting a fundamental philosophical doctrine, he takes account of the actual relation of experience to the knowledge of its foundation by not deducing the distinction between the vital tendencies from that putative ground.

145. The point of entry into the second sphere of the Garonne is distinguished from the point of entry into the first as much by the significance of the

first sphere in being the site of the departure (of the mariners) as by the fact that, as the point of transition, it is also the point of transition toward the insight whose substance transcends place. One could distinguish the two entries as between the one immanent in the world and the one entering into the transcendence of remembrance. The second occurrence of the word *dort* in the poem is such that a third could never follow it. Cf. pp. 201 ff. above.

146. Hölderlin's later use of the word *stiften* is directly associated with something holding "fast" (*ein "vestes" Bleiben*) in a "structure" (*Bau*): what is provided or established (*gestiftet*) are "empires" (*Reiche*) and "cities" (*Städte*) (*StA* V, p. 45, also Beißner, in the same volume, p. 402). See also W. Binder, "Sprache und Wirklichkeit in Hölderlins Dichtung," in *Hölderlin-Aufsätze* (Frankfurt, 1970), pp. 35–36.

147. Cf. note 7 above.

148. Cf. p. 144 ff. above.

Library of Congress Cataloging-in-Publication Data

Henrich, Dieter.
    [Essays. English. Selections]
    The course of remembrance and other essays on
Hölderlin / Dieter Henrich; edited, with a foreword, by
Eckart Förster.
        p.   cm. — (Studies in Kant and German
idealism)
    ISBN 0-8047-2739-2
    1. Hölderlin, Friedrich, 1770–1843. Andenken.
    2. Hölderlin, Friedrich, 1770–1843—Philosophy.
    I. Förster, Eckart. II. Title. III. Series.
    PT2359.H2A6183413   1997
831'.6—dc20   96-23401
                                                        CIP
                                                        Rev.

⊗ This book is printed on acid-free, recycled paper.

Original printing 1997
Last figure below indicates year of this printing:
06 05 04 03 02 01 00 99 98 97